SOCIOLINGUISTICS

The Study of Speakers' Choices

Second edition

Why do we speak the way we do? What are the social factors that influence our choices of expression? This best-selling introduction to the study of language and society encourages students to think about these fundamental questions, asking how and why we select from the vast range of different words, accents, varieties and languages available to us.

In this new and updated edition, students are taken step-by-step through the analysis of linguistic expressions, speech varieties and languages in complex settings. Enriched with recent findings from different languages and speech communities around the world, this comprehensive textbook equips students with knowledge of the main concepts and gives them a coherent view of the complex interaction of language and society.

- 'Questions for discussion' help students understand how speakers' choices are conditioned by the society in which they live.
- New to this edition are lists of further reading and a repertoire of online resources, including 100 flashcards, enabling students to investigate more deeply and advance their learning.
- Includes a topical new chapter on research ethics, guiding students on the ethical questions involved in sociolinguistic research.

FLORIAN COULMAS is Director of the German Institute for Japanese Studies, Tokyo. His previous books include *Literacy and Linguistic Minorities* (1984), *Language Adaptation* (Cambridge University Press, 1989), *Language and Economy* (1992), *The Handbook of Sociolinguistics* (1997), *Writing Systems* (Cambridge University Press, 2003) and Writing and Society (Cambridge University Press 2013).

Sociolinguistics

The Study of Speakers' Choices

SECOND EDITION

FLORIAN COULMAS

 CAMBRIDGE
UNIVERSITY PRESS

CAMBRIDGE
UNIVERSITY PRESS

University Printing House, Cambridge CB2 8BS, United Kingdom

Cambridge University Press is part of the University of Cambridge.

It furthers the University's mission by disseminating knowledge in the pursuit of
education, learning and research at the highest international levels of excellence.

www.cambridge.org
Information on this title: www.cambridge.org/9781107675568

First published 2013
Reprinted 2014

Printed in the United Kingdom by the Bell and Bain Ltd, Glasgow

A catalogue record for this publication is available from the British Library

Library of Congress Cataloguing in Publication data
Coulmas, Florian.
Sociolinguistics: the study of speakers' choices / by Florian Coulmas. – Second edition.
    pages   cm
Includes bibliographical references and index.
ISBN 978-1-107-67556-8 [Paperback]
1. Sociolinguistics.   I. Title.
P40.C63   2013
306.44–dc23   2012047374

ISBN 978-1-107-03764-9 Hardback
ISBN 978-1-107-67556-8 Paperback

Contents

Figures

Tables

Preface to the second edition

Preparing the second edition of a textbook is a great pleasure. While making new mistakes is perhaps more exciting than correcting past ones, being given the chance to revise, augment, update and, hopefully, improve a text written several years ago is a great privilege. Not only does it imply that the original edition has found its readers, which is, of course, a matter of satisfaction; it also shows that the field continues to thrive and evolve. I have been intrigued by the multifarious interconnections between language and society for many years. Knowing that they are subject to coordinated and ever more sophisticated research that has a place in university curricula makes it a rewarding task to introduce new generations of students to sociolinguistics.

Revisiting one's own writing is an interesting experience that makes you reflect not just on the book at hand, but on the accumulation of knowledge, the many factors that have an influence on how an academic field develops and on progress of scholarship in general. A critical view that takes nothing for granted and tries to look beyond the confines of our own preconceptions is essential for the scientific enterprise. Every research paper and every book could always be better, but many never will be. We all have erudite friends who took the notion that further improvement is still possible too seriously – and thus never finished their PhD theses. Lest excessive perfectionism forever stops us in our tracks, we publish despite some uncertainties and shortcomings and, therefore, happily seize upon the opportunity to make up for some of the inadequacies.

Working on the second edition of *Sociolinguistics* was pleasant enough. It allowed me to take stock and assess new research that has been undertaken since I first planned this textbook. I reworked it cover to cover and in the process weeded out some misprints and other minor mistakes; not many though, thanks to Jo Breeze who was the Production Editor for the original edition. There were no big blunders that called for correction, and in the meantime no major discovery or theoretical breakthrough has fundamentally changed the way research about language and society is done. Hence, the substance of the book is unchanged; but I brought it up to date by incorporating many references to recent research, adding examples and reinforcing arguments by supplying latest data. Sociolinguistics is an empirical science, and data are accordingly very important. Data collection, processing and storage is, perhaps, what has changed most in sociolinguistic research these past couple of decades. This is largely due to advances in technology. Recording devices have been miniaturized, and specialized computer software has been developed to create digital transcriptions from digital audio or video recordings. Large corpora of print, speech data and transcriptions can be shared easily and subjected to statistical analyses on a scale that was hard to imagine just a few years ago. The exponential growth of the Internet has also changed our reading behaviour and the way we come by the information we need for our research. This edition does justice to these developments by including a new list of useful online resources at the end of each chapter.

Rather than objectifying languages, dialects and other varieties by treating them as closed and in that sense invariant systems, sociolinguistics should take a speaker-centred approach focusing on communities and their linguistic resources. The pivotal question uniting the chapters of this book, in this edition as in the original one, is what it is that speakers do with their language(s); how they pass them on to following generations; how they allow them to be influenced by other languages; how they adjust their speech to that of their interlocutors; and how they interact with speakers of other idioms. Empirical research adopting such an approach necessarily has to do with people and, like other research involving human subjects, must conform to certain widely accepted principles. Although sociolinguistic investigations are usually of low risk to informants and research partners, more attention has been paid in recent years to problems of research ethics. I have therefore added a chapter at the end of the book discussing the conditions that must be met for planning and executing ethically sound research that does not exploit informants or in other ways violate their rights. This new chapter not only takes into account evolving sensitivities in the social sciences, but is also a logical consequence of the central position assigned to speakers in sociolinguistics.

Questions and suggestions by students of Chuo University and Tokyo University where I occasionally taught this book as well as critical comments by colleagues helped me to improve it for its present edition. Andrew Winnard of Cambridge University Press suggested the revision and encouraged me to see it through. My gratitude is due to him, Jo Breeze and other members of the editorial department.

1 Introduction: notions of language

> Reality does not speak to us objectively, and no scientist can be free from constraints of psyche and society.
>
> Stephen Jay Gould (2000)

Outline of the chapter

After considering the twofold nature of language as a natural and a social object of study, this introductory chapter explains the position of sociolinguistics in the language sciences. It then discusses some general implications of the fact that languages are the collaborative products of their speech communities, how they spread and affect each other, and that every utterance and every language could be different from what they actually are. Languages are constantly recreated by being used and handed down from one generation to the next. In order to do this, speakers have to make choices from the structural possibilities of language in general and the expressive potential that their linguistic environment offers in particular. The notion of choice is introduced as the most basic concept of sociolinguistics which studies how social factors affect these choices.

Key terms: natural language, language as a social fact, language change, choice, collaboration

Natural language and social language

As human beings we are able to change our behaviour. The idea that we act as free agents is fundamental to our self-conception. Every word we say reinforces this conviction, for whenever we speak we make choices. The ability to consider alternatives and opt for one is basic to intelligent life. It is restricted by our physical nature, the many things we cannot choose, such as the colour of our eyes, our IQ, or whether we are beautiful or ugly. All this may change soon, as the human species gets ready to do with itself what it has done with other species for a long time: interfere with nature's course, select, breed, grow and artificially manipulate their genetic makeup. The life sciences have made spectacular progress over the past several decades, constantly expanding the realm of culture – that which we control – at the expense of nature – that which controls us. No longer confined to science fiction novels, anthropotechnology has crossed the threshold into the real world and become a vital concern of legislation, the paradigm of deliberate regulation of behaviour. The prospects are tempting. Before long, we are told, we will be able to safeguard our offspring against congenital diseases, if not secure immortality for ourselves. At the same time, we are confronted with new challenges, which will be a lot more serious than how to retrain all those undertakers. We will have to decide whether to go down every pathway science opens up or to erect occasional warning signs, STOP HERE, at critical junctures. In short, at the present time, we are forced to rethink our place in the universe, the confines of nature and our own nature.

Language, the inborn

Language plays a peculiar role in this regard. People are born to speak, though they are not born speaking. It is no coincidence that the scientific study of language has been thoroughly impressed by, and, some would claim, has contributed to, the revolutionary changes in the life sciences. For language is seen as an evolutionary adaptation to communicate information. It is what most distinguishes us from other beasts, chatty chimps and brainy dolphins notwithstanding. The exploration of language, therefore, is indispensable if we want to understand our own nature. For language, as cognitive scientist Steven Pinker put it, 'is a distinct piece of the biological makeup of our brains'. 'It is not something that parents teach their children or something that must be elaborated in school' (Pinker 1994: 18f.). Yet, parents around the globe do teach their children language, and only a few would willingly dispense with grammar school because they think their children's language is in no need of elaboration, and not just because they have misgivings about the school's effectiveness in this regard.

Pinker could of course be right. He would not be the first scientist who gets the better of popular ideas. Language has been known for a long time to have a physical base in our brain, and of late the race is on among biologists to track down the language gene. Given the overwhelming importance of language to the survival of our species, it is more than a remote possibility that it is genetically determined. Assuming that it is, we are or aren't equipped with it, and in the latter case no amount of schooling will make up for the deficit. All babies acquire language quickly because they have the ability to do so and because all societies use language. The ability to acquire language is universal and unrelated to intelligence. With the exception of some pathological cases, humans grow up to speak, the dumbest and the brightest. Evidence for that is all around us. What this suggests is that language is innate and common to the species. Those who are chasing the language gene may be on the right track, then. Language helps us survive. But does Italian, or Dutch, or Bengali? Such a proposition would be hard to defend, and no one – except for the authors of 'Survival Italian', etc. – really does.

It would be jumping to conclusions if we were to instruct would-be parents that they must not waste their time teaching their children language, and teachers that they need not bother to elaborate it because the kids are born with it anyway. Thanks to the astonishing nature of language, both sides are right, the researchers who tell us that teaching children language is unnecessary and the parents and teachers who spend so much time and effort doing just that. The disagreement between them is only apparent. This is so because to acquire language both are indispensable, our brain's physical equipment and our society – represented perhaps by a single caregiver – talking to us. Brain damage or genetic deformation *and* social deprivation will both make language acquisition impossible. Thus, language has two sides, the biological and the social, each of which must be studied in its own right.

Geneticists and other life scientists interested in language are concerned with language in the singular, invariant in space and time. Like-minded linguists and cognitive scientists are devoted to the quest for the ground plan of language that is hard-wired in the brain. They speak of 'natural language' that is governed by universal grammar (UG), and some of them, therefore, call their field 'biolinguistics'. Its main task is to elucidate the 'faculty of language' which Noam Chomsky, the most influential linguist of this school of thought, has defined as follows:

> The faculty of language can reasonably be regarded as a 'language organ' in the sense in which scientists speak of the visual system, or immune system, or circulatory systems, as organs of the body.   (2000: 4)

But compare the visual systems of the French and the Fulbe and the Fukienese, and you will find that they are virtually identical. If, however, we compare the French, Fulfulde and Fukienese languages the differences are striking. Even French French and Quebec French differ in many ways. Biolinguists take notice of this diversity only in so far as it may help to clarify aspects of the abstract system of rules and principles underlying all languages. Their focus is on UG, the general immutable properties of language. Disregarding the still remote chances of genetic engineering to design a better language, no choice is possible here. Linguistic diversity must be dealt with, but cannot be explained on biological grounds. If the faculty of language is part of our genetic heritage and an organ of the body, why does it come in so many vastly different guises? Why are languages so much more diverse than lungs and adrenal glands? The fact that linguistic change is much more rapid than genetic change has implications for how we should interpret the notion of a language organ. Assuming that language is a biological system, we have to work out how 'language', UG, in the singular relates to 'languages' and their particular grammars in the plural.[1] From the observable linguistic diversity, we have to conclude two things; one, that genetic hard-wiring determines a range of structural possibilities rather than a fixed set of arrangements, and two, that language change continues, while we do not yet know whether this change is confined to the UG-defined range or potentially transcends it. In the latter case language change would be an aspect of the on-going evolution of the species. However this may be, there is no convincing answer to the question why languages differ unless we open our eyes to the uses of language in society.

Language, the historical

Language has been defined by Ferdinand de Saussure, another great linguist of the twentieth century, as a 'social fact' (Saussure 1959: 6). This definition has many implications. For one, language comes into focus here as a means of communication, for social facts are those that can be studied only if we look at how people associate to form groups, how they communicate and how they act collectively. Investigating a single individual or the species at large cannot reveal the social disposition of humanity. Language is a social fact in that every language is a collective product, an artefact created by its speakers which, at the same time, enables higher forms of social planning and cooperation to evolve. Society is built on language. There is no human society that does not speak and use language as its central instrument of organization.

Social behaviour has instinctive components, too, but those that are learnt predominate. Being socialized means learning the ways of one's society, including its language. No one will ever learn Swahili just by following his or her instinct. Every language must be learnt, and it is the society that teaches its new members how to use it properly, how to conform with established conventions. Language, from a social point of view, is conventional, which is another way of saying that it could be different. Every language could be different from what it actually is. We know this because we know that today's languages were different in the past, that they have changed and will continue to change. For the conception of language as a social as opposed to a natural fact, this is of utmost importance. Social facts are historical facts. They have many contingent features. Biolinguistics ignores the historicity of language because it is interested in invariance, but to sociolinguistics the historical dimension of language is central. William Labov, one of the leading figures in this field, has identified as his primary goal 'to determine what happened in the history of language or language family' because 'the fact of language change is difficult to reconcile with the notion of a system adapted to communication' (Labov 1994: 9). We experience language as a stable system that works and tend to think of different languages as distinct systems. Adaptation and change happen largely unnoticed. Yet, the fact of language change forces us to look at instability, deviation and loss of comprehension across generations (see Chapter 4) and dialects (see Chapter 2). The existence of different languages is a historical fact, a result of language change.

The historical character of language and the fact that it must be learnt are closely related. It is true that all people learn to speak, as pointed out above; but it is also true that the general ability to learn does not imply that we all learn the same, and equally well. There are good learners and not so good learners, and what they learn is never an exact replica of the model. For instance, the Germans learnt from the French the word *baguette*, 'French bread'. They spell it like the French, and the pronunciation is very close, too. But they changed the gender. The French model is feminine, the German copy neuter. Why? Ignorance, perhaps. The Germans may have been unaware that a French *baguette* was feminine and simply given the new word the same gender as their own word for bread, *das Brot, n*. Perhaps more interesting structural reasons were involved, such as the asymmetry between the dual French gender system and the tripartite German one. Perhaps morphophonological rules make themselves felt here. There are many neuter nouns in German ending, like *baguette*, in [-et], such as *Bett*, *Fett*, *Brett*, *Kabinett*, *Skelett* and *Sonett*, but I couldn't find a single feminine one. However this may be, the gender change of *baguette* didn't happen naturally. Somebody performed the operation. What the example illustrates is that learning often implies change.

Since French and German are different languages, it is not surprising that elements of one adapted to the other will undergo modification. But the same also happens within what presumably is one language. In England, *sauce* and *source* are usually homonyms, but in some parts of the United States they are distinct, *source*, true to the French original, but not *sauce*, having an audible [r]. Differences of this sort may or may not be indicative of on-going change. The point here is the same as above, an explanation can be found. If both pronunciations coexist and continue to coexist for a long time, it is hard to argue that one is systematically more essential or sound than the other. It is also hard to argue that these differences are superficial and unimportant, because it is sets of variations of this kind that, if they pile up, can lead to linguistic divergence, mutual unintelligibility, and hence the emergence of a new language. This is so because the distribution of *source* with and without [r] is not random. It distinguishes not individuals but groups of speakers.

Every language is transmitted from one generation to the next by learning and has its unique history. These two facts go a long way to explaining linguistic diversity. Diversity means two things: the multiplicity of human languages – 6,000 is a conventional count – and the enormous variety of coexisting forms in every language. This diversity is the result of many contingent factors working on human speech behaviour. Being open to contingencies, language is neither deterministic nor random. Without such openness, not allowing for adaptation and innovation, it would be rapidly outdated. Luckily, in the process of learning, we do not just repeat what our elders said but recreate our languages anew, adapting them to our purposes, and hence bring about change that is, as pointed out above, much faster than genetic change. If it were possible to delimit clearly one generation of speakers from the next, linguistic change could be observed in every generation. By contrast, DNA changes of humans are thought to occur at the rate of one mutation every 25 to 40 generations. This difference in adaptation rate suggests that genetic change and language change proceed independently of one another; yet, the possibility that culture affects human evolution and that some linguistic change may match genetic change cannot be excluded.

Migration and diversity

If we want to appreciate the great diversity of human languages we need to consider another factor, migration. According to a famous dictum attributed to George Bernard Shaw, England and America are 'two countries separated by the same language'. Most speakers of English are aware of the hiatus between British and American speech, but find it quite unremarkable because the cause is so obvious: the Atlantic Ocean. English, French, Spanish, Portuguese and Dutch in the New World aren't quite what they are in the old. We take it for granted that over long periods of time geographic isolation brings about linguistic divergence. People living in different environments speak about different things; in the process they mispronounce words, create new ones, reinterpret morphological forms, borrow lexical items from others and put them together to form sentences in novel ways. This must have been so from the beginning (assuming that the beginning of humanity can ever be lifted out of the realm of speculation[2]). Where a substantial body of population moves out of one territory and into another, driven by demographic pressure, commerce or the incursion of invaders, it will take its language with it, but after some time this language ceases to be the same as that spoken in its original territory. From a theoretical point of view, this is remarkable because it means that social factors are involved in language change. If language change were deterministic, thrust towards a goal and governed entirely by quasi-natural laws inherent in the language system, as in the past historical linguists have claimed,[3] we should expect it to be unaffected by migration. In the event, English should continue to change along the same lines on both sides of the Atlantic. But as it turns out, once a group splits into two, language change is no longer synchronized. Since the two groups are stripped of the opportunity to adjust their speech to each other, the transmission and recreation of their language is propelled onto different trajectories.

Desires and norms

Migration usually induces language change, but a speech community's spatial contiguity and temporal continuity are no guarantee for maintaining linguistic homogeneity nor a sufficient condition for bringing uniformity about. The obvious function of language as a marker of distinction dividing one speech community from another comes to bear within a single speech community as well. The argument that linguistic variation will decrease with intensity of communication has often been made, but there are good reasons to doubt a causal relationship in this connection. For variation serves important social functions.

> In highly stratified societies such as the caste societies of India, it is quite possible for people to be in constant and regular communication over long periods of time without adopting each other's speech patterns. It would seem that communication leads to uniformity only when there is both the possibility and the desire for social assimilation. Where social norms put a premium on social distinctness, linguistic symbols of such distinctness tend to be maintained.   (Gumperz 1967: 228)

As we will see in the course of this book, it is not at all rare that linguistic distinctions withstand ostensible forces of homogenization. Why linguistic distinctions are maintained in the face of both homogenization pressure and the opportunities offered by uniformity is one of the key questions that brought the discipline of sociolinguistics into existence. Efficiency of communication, considered an important evolutionary advantage of the human species, would seem to call for a reduction, if not elimination, of potentially disruptive distinctions in the speech of individuals and groups. Yet, such distinctions persist.

Two important notions in the passage quoted above are 'the desire for social assimilation' and 'social norms [that] put a premium on social distinctness'. Both are invoked as causal factors in the process of language change. Whose desire he refers to Gumperz does not tell us, but it is clear that speech communities, social groups and their members are at issue. In what sense an assemblage of individual desires can be understood as a collective desire is a difficult question to which we will return later. For the present purposes the important thing to note is that mental dispositions such as the desire for assimilation (or division) influence language change. Desires and the willingness to adhere to, or breach, social norms make a difference, since it is by virtue of its members having desires and preferences that the speech community creates and perpetuates its language.

This is testimony to the intrinsically mental character of language. Speakers, rather than just being the bearers of abstract structures removed from conscious reflection which constrains their speech behaviour, are active, knowledgeable, purposeful agents who make choices whenever they use language. The ability to do so is at the heart of the nexus between language and society, and it is the vantage point of this book. *Speakers make choices*. The subsequent chapters will show that this holds for every level of language, structural and stylistic (Chapter 6), and beyond that for the registers and languages used by different groups and in different domains of society (Chapter 11). Every language represents a choice of the potential held by universal grammar, and every individual's language represents a choice of his or her collectivity's language. Social norms are restrictions on individual choices, making deviations that imperil communication unacceptable, if not impossible.

Speakers cannot avoid making choices, for things can always be formulated differently, and often should be. People high and low have strong feelings about the intentionality of their speech, and they articulate what they believe they should, although they sometimes seem to belie their own words. 'I know what I believe. I will continue to articulate what I believe and what I believe – I believe what I believe is right.' So much for beliefs and articulation. Former US President George W. Bush articulated these words on a visit to Italy[4] near the Forum Romanum where orators used to speak. Surely, they could have been chosen more adroitly, but chosen they were.

Choice is the pivotal notion of sociolinguistics, and I will have to discuss this notion in some detail to see what it means with regard to human action, in general, and to speech behaviour and language, in particular. Before doing so, let me summarize the main points discussed so far concerning the different conceptions of language as a natural fact and a social fact.

Language as a natural fact	*Language as a social fact*
inborn	learnt
genetically fixed	culturally varied
universal	variable
species-specific	group-specific
timeless	historical
governed by natural law	governed by convention

Complementary approaches

In the language sciences it is sometimes thought that the two approaches dedicated, respectively, to the natural and the social side of language are irreconcilable. I prefer to think that they are complementary because neither of them can by itself fathom out the whole complexity of language. In language, the universal is indissolubly interwoven with the particular. More than any other trait, it thus exemplifies humanity's position in the universe as a species that cultivates its own nature. The language sciences all have their own notions of language allowing them to direct their attention to certain phenomena rather than to others, and there is no reason to believe in the superiority of one over another. It is necessary to emphasize this point because the sciences of historical complexity often occupy a lowly position in comparison with 'pure' and 'experimental' disciplines. A hierarchy that ranks biolinguistics or formal linguistics, as it used to be called, with the 'hard' sciences at the top and sociolinguistics with the 'soft' sciences at the bottom is useless and unjustified for two reasons. The late

Stephen Gould, a professor of palaeontology, has formulated them clearly and elegantly. One is quoted at the beginning of this chapter: 'Reality does not speak to us objectively, and no scientist can be freed from constraints of psyche and society' (Gould 2000: 276). The other is that 'historical events do not violate general principles of matter and motion, but their occurrence lies in the realm of contingent detail' (2000: 278). Gould's conclusion is this:

> Historical science is not worse, more restricted, or less capable of achieving firm conclusions because experiment, prediction, and subsumption under invariant laws of nature do not represent its usual working methods. The sciences of history use a different mode of explanation, rooted in the comparative and observational richness of our data.   (2000: 279)

Choice

Since human bodies consist of physical components – molecules, atoms and subatomic particles – their behaviour should be explained in terms of physical components and the laws governing their movements. There is no room for a mind with a free will. At the same time, our everyday experience is that our reasonings and choices govern our behaviour, to a significant extent at least. This is the mind–body problem, also called 'mind–brain problem' – in a nutshell. No attempt will be made here to solve it, but we cannot altogether sidestep it, for, as we have seen, language has both a physical and a mental side, and these are not always easily kept apart.[5] Sociolinguistics is the linguistics of choice, and, if only for that reason, we have to come to grips with the relationship of freedom of the will,[6] human action and language, for choice is a notion which presupposes an agent rather than an automaton. The intricacy of the problem has been pinpointed by two scholars representing, as it were, the two sides – the neurologist John Eccles and the philosopher Karl Popper. Interestingly, they see the very origin of language as being indissolubly linked with choice. Here is what they say:

> We could say that in choosing to speak, and to take interest in speech, man has chosen to evolve his brain and his mind; that language, once created, exerted the selection pressure under which emerged the human brain and the consciousness of self.   (Popper and Eccles 1977: 13)

Choosing to speak before you know what to say, let alone know what language is, seems quite a feat, but, on reflection, it may be quite common. The important point is that making choices is a central part of the human condition. Interestingly, Eccles and Popper's notion of choice does not require full control and foresight. This is important, for, while I don't want to take a position here as to whether or not ontogeny repeats phylogeny, I want to argue that babies make choices, because every line we draw to show where intentionality begins is arbitrary. Our choices are subject to restrictions of various kinds from birth. The division of labour in the language sciences can be understood in terms of the restrictions on possible linguistic choices. Physical and cognitive restrictions are the field of biolinguistics and cognitive science; social and cultural restrictions on linguistic choices are for sociolinguists to investigate.

For instance, our lifespan, or, less dramatically, the need to sleep, puts natural restrictions on the length of our sentences. The range of speech sounds is restricted by our auditory system which is designed to perceive and process sounds in a range between 12 and 20,000 cycles per second, which means that we cannot hear the better part of what bats hear. They have a hearing range of 20 to 120,000 cycles per second. Structural restrictions are the subject matter of grammar studies. Some are very general, forming the theme of universal grammar, whereas others are applicable to some languages or a single language only. Gender agreement between article, noun and adjective is a good example. French *bon* [bɔ̃] and *bonne* [bɔn] are, respectively, the masculine and feminine forms of 'good'. It is *bon mot*, literally a 'good word', that is, a witty remark, but *bonne action* 'a good deed', because *mot* 'word' is masculine, whereas *action* 'deed' is feminine. Choice between [bɔ̃] and [bɔn] is not up to the speaker's taste, but determined by agreement rules. Agreement rules are restrictions on choices. What they mean is that, if a language has a gender system, speakers are not free in their choices of gender forms of nouns and adjectives and articles. The requirement to match adjective and noun in terms of gender could be a peculiarity of French. Comparative studies reveal that it is much more common and typical of all languages that have a gender system.

The central theme of sociolinguistics is variety. To the observer, language presents itself as a seemingly infinite variety of forms, but this variety is patterned. That is, there are restrictions on choices between coexisting varieties. For instance, English words like *fast* have, in standard British pronunciation, a long vowel [a:]. If you want to sound a bit archaic, or Australian, you can pronounce it with a short [a], and in some American varieties it borders on [æ]. Australians living in London tend to lengthen their [a] along with other adjustments they make to blend in with their environment. Such fine-tuning has to do with preferences and social norms rather than structural rules, which is not to say that it is random. Quite the contrary, in the absence of patterning we would be unable to recognize speakers for what they are. Speech varieties are powerful markers of group membership. Outsiders, particularly children, can be observed making great efforts to use the right words and give their pronunciation the right tinge to conform with the group they are trying to join. It can be done. But as George Bernard Shaw's Eliza Doolittle under the able and loving guidance of Professor Higgins found out, discovering, in the great variety of available choices, the socially acceptable one is essential.

Professor Higgins, on a whim, bet his friend that Eliza, the flower girl with that ear-piercing drawl, could be transformed into a lady. The language was the key. With determination and linguistic genius, she made him win his bet, substituting her native Cockney by the unmistakable accent of the upper class. Hers was one speaker's choice, remarkable and, though fictitious, of deep significance to the relationship of language, social class, gender and upward mobility, topics that will be dealt with in Chapters 2 and 3 below. Eliza Doolittle is so noteworthy because her choice is readily recognizable as such, implying as it does a change in group affiliation. It is also remarkable because the nuances of pronunciation were raised to the level of conscious manipulation. More commonly we leave these to the automatic pilot and stay with our group, because we see no reason or opportunity to do otherwise. Strictly speaking, this is also a choice which corresponds to the above remark that everything can always be formulated differently. It implies that every speaker has the ability to change the way he or she speaks. The choices speakers make in this regard are not made in a vacuum but are constrained in many ways. The principal task of sociolinguistics is to uncover, describe and interpret the socially motivated restrictions on linguistic choices. Demonstrating where and how these restrictions interact with grammatical restrictions is one approach to explaining stability and change in language, a topic to be further explored in Chapter 5. For, while every speaker's every speech act is the manifestation of choice, the individual act of choice does not reveal the social nature of language. That only becomes apparent if we can show how individual choices add up to form collective choices.

Cooperation and choice

Choice is based on judgment, but it is not fully controlled. Eliza Doolittle's case is extraordinary because, for all practical purposes and thanks to Professor Higgins and the omniscient playwright, judgment (on the right accent, how to emulate it and what to accomplish with the emulation) was fully controlled. More typically, judgment results from the interpretation of available, that is, incomplete, information and an individual's beliefs and preferences. 'It is seldom possible for an individual to accurately describe his or her judgment process' (Dhir and Savage 2002: 11). What the economists Krishna Dhir and Theresa Savage say about judgment in general is particularly true of judgments about one's own speech. Human judgment is often inaccurately reported and inconsistent, and self-assessment is clearly not one of the greatest strengths of most people. These limitations must caution us not to rely too much on self-reports if we want to find out why people speak the way they do. This does not invalidate the attempt to understand linguistic choices, but we need some analytic tools that are independent of speakers' self-assessments.

We can benefit here from certain concepts developed by psychologists and political scientists interested in cooperation. For language is a means of cooperation on two levels. (1) It enables its speakers to exchange information in order to request, announce and promise certain actions. And (2), it works as long as its speakers use it in such a way that they understand each other. In normal speech behaviour this is taken for granted. That is, *speech behaviour is fundamentally cooperative*. What, then, is cooperation?

The theory of cooperation developed by Axelrod (1984) and others aims at a maximally wide range of applicability. Citing the example of patterns of behaviour found in various biological systems, it shows that foresight is not necessary for cooperation to evolve. This makes Axelrod's approach more suitable to language than other decision theories that assume rationality. For example, the behavioural decision theory (Edwards 1992) is based on the concept of expected subjective utility and attempts to prescribe rational decisions. By contrast, Axelrod's theory does not assume that interactants are always rational. 'Their strategies may simply reflect standard operating procedures, rules of thumb, instincts, habits, or imitation' (Axelrod 1984: 18). Moreover, it does not assume that the actions taken by the interactants are necessarily conscious choices. Notice that even in economics where rational and fully informed decision makers used to be assumed for the sake of modelling, this conception of humanity is giving way to one of agents who have emotions and lack complete information.[7] For language choices, the idea of cooperation being achieved even in the absence of fully informed rationality is highly relevant; because whenever communication proceeds smoothly stable mutual cooperation has been established. In most cases this is better described as standard operating procedure than the result of conscious choice on the part of the interactants.

Another word for standard operating procedure much used by psychologists and economists is 'path dependence'. It captures well the nature of choice restricted by habit and inertia. You can leave the trodden path, but doing so takes an effort and bears a risk. We can think of a language as a path. New members of a speech community get set onto this path which, under normal circumstances, they will never try to deviate from. Staying on the path appears natural, not a matter of choice. Usually, it is tantamount to cooperative behaviour. But it is the result of choice, all the same. This is apparent from instances of uncooperative behaviour. For example, francophone Swiss often complain about being addressed, by their compatriots in German-speaking Switzerland, in Swiss German. The francophones learn standard German at school but have difficulties understanding Swiss German. Since the Swiss Germans control both varieties, their choice of Swiss German is perceived as not being cooperative. Another example can be found in teenage slang. Words like *sick* and *seen*, as used by teenagers, meaning 'cool' or 'good', are not immediately understood by members of the older generations. While confusing their interlocutors may not be the speakers' primary intent, it is well known that teenagers do not necessarily go out of their way to cooperate with older people from whom, moreover, they rather set themselves apart in their lifestyle, dress and language.

Yet, cooperation is the unmarked case in speech behaviour and vital for preserving the functionality of the language. It can be explained in terms of the (perceived) probability that the speakers concerned may interact again. In a generalized way this is what keeps a speech community together and its language intact. As the theory of public choice emphasizes, reciprocity is essential for maintaining cooperation. Linguistic communication is a cooperative game, not a zero-sum game. Both players – assuming there are just two – benefit if they cooperate. They should not regard the other player as someone who is out to defeat them. The payoffs are for doing what everyone else does. The classic example is traffic: it does not matter which side of the road we drive on, but it is extremely important that we all drive on the same side. Having to drive on the same side of the road is a restriction of our choice that we hardly notice, given the obvious alternative.

The cooperative nature of linguistic communication is most dramatically evidenced under very unpromising conditions where the speakers involved have no common language at their disposal. Betokening the intimate connection between choice and cooperation in language, a new language is then brought into existence, a pidgin. This remarkable accomplishment will be dealt with more extensively in Chapter 8 below. It is of great interest to sociolinguistics because the basic condition of normal communication, a common language, is suspended. This only happens when interactants venture outside their territory and reference group and meet others, like them, willing to cooperate. Pidginization demonstrates how cooperative verbal behaviour develops in the face of extremely adverse circumstances.

A common language is usually taken for granted, since locations, institutions and situations are associated with a certain language or variety as *the unmarked choice* required by a cooperative game. Unmarked choice is a psychological notion which Myers-Scotton (1993a) has successfully applied to the analysis of multilingualism, a subfield of sociolinguistics to be discussed at length in Chapter 7 below. By the population concerned, an unmarked choice is not usually perceived as a choice at all. But it is a choice in the sense that alternative courses of action are possible, however unlikely. Many actions are carried out routinely, such as walking or shifting into gear when driving a car. A great deal in language behaviour, too, remains on a subconscious level. When we employ routines and enact unmarked choices without thinking, we allow our movements to follow trodden paths, as a matter of convenience. We say hello to our neighbour in the morning without deliberating the question what language to use, but there are other situations where it is obvious that the first step in every communication is to negotiate a common language, for example when you sit on an aeroplane and want to talk with the person seated next to you. Whenever there is an unmarked choice, it functions as a shortcut that allows us to skip this step. Thus, unmarked choices are choices, although they go largely unnoticed.

As we will see, societies and social groups differ as to what choices are marked or unmarked. For example, in largely monolingual environments, multilingual conversations tend to be perceived as uncooperative, while people in multilingual environments are more familiar with situations where speakers expect each other to understand several languages but use the one they speak best. In the event, for speakers to use a language that is not the same as that in which they have been spoken to may be readily tolerated, not being perceived as uncooperative. Uncooperative behaviour is not accepted, the most effective sanction being the refusal to understand a speaker. Linguistic socialization means learning to avoid sanctions by discovering the restrictions that define unmarked choices. A basic assumption of this book is that this is what speakers usually do. They are active creative agents, able to choose their verbal means and, in so doing, prone to cooperate. Sociolinguistics strives to explain why they speak the way they do.

Conclusion

Let us now sum up the main points of this chapter. Sociolinguistics distinguishes itself from other language sciences, notably from biolinguistics and theoretical grammar, by focusing on those traits of language that are noticeably variable and hence subject to choice. Variability in language means that speakers are able to adjust their speech to selected aspects of their environment. This has a number of implications.

- Speakers make choices from the variety of the expressive means offered in their environment.
- Their choices are subject to restrictions.
- Speech communities and smaller social groups are recognizable by virtue of the restrictions they place on the linguistic choices of their members.
- Membership is accomplished and maintained through cooperation.
- Speech behaviour is cooperative.
- Every language and language variety is the result of collective choice, that is, cooperative creation.
- Where a common language exists it restricts its speakers' choices.
- Where no such language exists one is created by virtue of interactants' choice.

Questions for discussion

(1) You choose every word you say. Nobody else does. Does this imply that choice is always based on free will?

(2) Think of some expressions you use when talking with your friends that you would not use in the presence of your parents. To what extent does your choice of words depend on who it is you are talking to? What other factors influence your choice?

(3) 'Be it in public or in private, we must have the temerity to rail at ghetto grammar. Otherwise, soon we won't be able to understand a word our young people are saying, and we'll only have ourselves to blame. You get me, blood?' This is the conclusion of journalist Lindsay Johns' (2009) appeal to speak 'proper English' in London. Do you agree with him? What are the choices, and whose choices are at issue?

Notes

1. Christiansen, Chater and Reali (2009) discuss evidence from computer simulations pointing to strong cultural restrictions on the biological evolution of language and advance an argument for cultural evolution as the primary factor underlying linguistic diversity.
2. Renfrew (1987) is a highly readable account of how archaeology and linguistics can be brought together to study the spread and dispersion of language in prehistoric times.
3. The idea that sound change is regular and that, accordingly, its investigation must reveal general laws (Lautgesetze) was first defended in the latter half of the nineteenth century by a group of linguists who called themselves 'Neogrammarians'. Their ideas gave rise to extensive debates accompanying the development of linguistic thought throughout the twentieth century. And although empirical methods and techniques have changed, their principles still inform research into the mechanism of sound change. Cf. Philological Society (1978).
4. Reuters, 23 July 2001. This is an example of what has been called 'Bushlexia'. See www.bushwatch.com/english.htm
5. In the history of Western philosophy, the most prominent approaches to the mind–body problem are, briefly, three: (1) Materialism: the universe consists of physical objects only (some of which we don't know). (2) Idealism: matter is a manifestation of mind which is all we can know. (3) Dualism: mind and matter both exist, though as entities of different kinds. Chalmers (1996) offers a good review of the problem.
6. If you want to get serious about the problem of freedom of the will, Wegner (2002) is an excellent account by a psychologist and Searle (1984), by a philosopher.
7. In 2002, economists Daniel Kahneman and Vernon L. Smith were awarded the Nobel Prize for this departure from the paradigm of 'rational choice theory'. See, for example, Kahneman, Slovic and Tversky (1982).

Part I

Micro-choices

2 Standard and dialect: social stratification as a factor of linguistic choice

> The Standard language was the possession only of the well-born and the well-educated.
>
> J. E. Dobson (1956)

Outline of the chapter

This chapter describes the social dimensions of dialects, demonstrating that choice of words, pronunciation and other linguistic features has been observed to reflect speakers' social position in various speech communities. It then goes on to explain how dialectal and standard speech should be conceptualized for purposes of sociolinguistic investigation. These notions are always interrelated, but do not mean the same thing in all speech communities. The same holds true for the concept of social structure. Social stratification changes over time, and the factors determining class are not the same in all places. Only empirical research can show how social structure is reflected in linguistic variation. At the outset of every sociolinguistic study, it is accordingly necessary to determine the relevant parameters of social stratification and how standard and dialect relate to each other. Network analysis and accommodation theory are briefly introduced as analytic tools, which are particularly useful at a time of rapid social change and technology driven change in communications.

Key terms: dialect, standard language, social stratification

A samurai speaks his mind

Dialect differences have been recognized for as long as observations about language have been recorded. A central concern of sociolinguistics is to account for the functions dialects fulfil and how speakers choose their dialects. For, in addition to the horizontal distribution across geographical regions, dialects correlate with social stratification. Consider the following travel report.

> After a while I began to feel the lack of someone to talk with, so I stopped a man who looked like a farmer and asked him the way. Probably there was

something of the samurai manner in my speech and, without realizing it, I may have sounded commanding. The farmer replied very politely and left me with a respectful bow.

'Well, this is interesting,' I thought. I looked at myself and saw that I was carrying but an umbrella; I was plainly dressed too. I thought I would try again, and when another wayfarer came up, I stopped him with an awful, commanding voice:

'I say, there! What is the name of that hamlet I see yonder? How many houses are there? Whose is the large residence with the tiled roof? Is the owner a farmer or a merchant? And what is his name?'

Thus with the undisguised manner of the samurai, I put all sorts of nonsensical questions on the stranger. The poor fellow shivered at the roadside and haltingly answered, 'In great awe I shall endeavour to speak to your honour . . .'

It was so amusing, I tried again when another passer-by came along, this time taking the opposite attitude.

'*Moshi, moshi,*' I began. 'But may I ask you something, please? . . .'

I used the style of an Ōsaka merchant, and began the same nonsensical questions. I knew all the dialects of Ōsaka, having been born there and lived there as a student. Probably the man thought I was a merchant on the way to collect money; he eyed me haughtily and walked on his way without giving me much of an answer.

So I proceeded, accosting everyone who came along. Without any allowance for their appearance, I spoke alternately, now in samurai fashion, now merchantlike. In every instance, for about seven miles on my way, I saw that people would respond according to the manner in which they were addressed – with awe or with indifference.

Finally I became disgusted. I would not have cared if they were polite or arrogant so long as they behaved consistently. But here it showed that they were merely following the lead of the person speaking to them. It was quite natural that the petty officials of the provinces should grow domineering. The government had been called oppressive and despotic, but it was not the fault of the government. People themselves invited oppression. What should I do about it? I certainly could not leave them as they were. Could I teach them? That could not be done easily or quickly.   (Fukuzawa 1966: 245)

Several lessons can be drawn from this story.

- Dialects show a speaker's regional origin.
- There may be more than one dialect in one place.
- Dialects show a speaker's social position.
- Speakers adjust their speech behaviour to how they are spoken to.
- Dialects can be chosen.
- Speakers adjust their speech behaviour to a particular social circumstance.

Let us examine these points one by one and consider what we can learn about the choice of dialects.

The episode was recounted by Yukichi Fukuzawa, Japan's most enlightened thinker of the nineteenth century. It took place in 1872, at a time when

Japanese society was in the throes of modernization. A keen observer, Fukuzawa noticed not just that dialects were specific to a region, but that samurai and merchant spoke differently. The expressions he used – 'something of the samurai manner in my speech', 'style of an Ōsaka merchant' – are not rigorously defined technical terms, but they capture well the main point of what he found so remarkable, the relation between language and the speaker's social position. In order fully to appreciate his observations, one must know that in premodern Japan samurai and merchant were at opposite ends of the social scale. The feudal system of social ranks was hereditary, involving four groups, from top to bottom: samurai, farmers, artisans and merchants. This system was coming under pressure at the time, and Fukuzawa, though himself a samurai, enthusiastically welcomed the advent of a new, more egalitarian social order. He was very sensitive, therefore, to what was an overt marker of social inequality, speech. His remark that he knew 'all the dialects of Ōsaka' shows that he was aware of the function of dialects to signal not only the speakers' local identity but also their social identity. Almost one hundred years later, the recognition of this very relationship became the point of departure of the sociolinguistic project, and, although this was not in Japan, it is no coincidence that in the event the issue of language and inequality was on people's minds.

A Western science

In the 1960s, the British sociologist Basil Bernstein (1971) constructed a model which linked class, power and other aspects of social structure to varying patterns of phonological and syntactic differentiation. His main concern was that what he called different 'codes' not only identified different social classes but were instrumental in class reproduction in Great Britain. A pedagogical concept that grew out of the studies by Bernstein and his associates called for compensatory education to enable working-class children to cope better with the demands of school, an institution dominated by middle-class speech. Similar concerns were taken up in the United States (Gordon and Wilkerson 1966) where correlations between speech varieties and scholastic achievement were observed. The normative idea that in a democratic society language should not contribute to perpetuating social inequality provided a strong incentive to research into the linkages between social stratification and linguistic variation. William Labov's 1966 monograph, *The Social Stratification of English in New York City*, pointed the way ahead.

Sociolinguistics has since expanded into many other fields, but the societal dimension of dialects remains one of its main themes. The study of the social significance of dialect variation is now known as 'variationist sociolinguistics'.[1] It rests on the assumption that 'whenever a choice exists among two (or more) alternatives in the course of linguistic performance, . . . then it is appropriate to invoke statistical techniques' (Tagliamonte 2002: 730). This marks a substantial departure from traditional linguistics, as the notion of a grammar as a set of fixed rules is replaced by one where rules come with a probability index, and where the probability of a certain rule or feature occurring is assumed not only to be socially meaningful but to affect the language system. This research paradigm was formulated in Western Europe and North America, largely without other traditions being noticed.

This is not because in other parts of the world the social dimensions of dialects were never considered. The fact that sociolinguistics, like other social sciences, is grounded in the Western tradition is not because it is original, but because it is original in the West, and because theories and methods developed in the West are more likely to be noticed in other parts of the world than vice versa. Both India and Japan, to mention but two examples, have rich traditions of linguistic scholarship which sought the link with society long before sociolinguistics as we know it today came into existence.

In 1933, the Japanese dialectologist Kyōsuke Kindaichi proposed that sociology and linguistics should join forces to analyse the social nature of language.[2] Only a few years later another Japanese linguist, Juri Tanabe,[3] published a book entitled *Gengo shakaigaku* [Sociology of Language]. Language standardization had been an issue for some time in Japan,[4] and there was a general awareness among dialectologists that the investigation of dialects could benefit from, and contribute to, social analysis. In the course of the following decades a great deal of empirical research was carried out which was largely ignored in the West. Quite apart from the fact that this research was articulated in Japanese and, therefore, not easily accessible outside Japan, it was ignored because, from a Western point of view, Japan fell outside the range of countries from which scientific innovations were expected to emerge.

A similar story can be told about the history of linguistics in India where the social dimension of the relationship between standard language (Sanskrit) and dialects (Prakrits) has been known for centuries and where socially indicative speech varieties have long been investigated. T. C. Hodson's paper 'Sociolinguistics in India'[5] was published in 1939. Deshpande (1979) deals with the complex interplay of social stratification, religion and language in Vedic India some two and a half thousand years ago when Indian scholars were well aware of the prestige of various languages and dialects, but again this was not a tradition that could be built on in the West.

Sociolinguistics, then, dealing as it does with modern industrial societies, is in this sense a Western science. This may be stating the obvious because it is true of all social sciences, but if we take seriously Gould's remark that 'no scientist can be freed from constraints of psyche and society' (quoted above, p. 1), it is an important point. For sociolinguistics, though concerned on the empirical level with particular communities, must strive to uncover general relationships between language and society. Given that its key concepts and assumptions were formulated in the context of Western societies, it is possible, if not likely, that they are more germane to these societies than to others. This is not to say that sociolinguistic methods and theories cannot be applied to other societies, but it should be remembered that these methods and theories grew out of a particular tradition and are unlikely to be unaffected by it. Considering the object of investigation, this is a point of some consequence. It should alert us to the necessity of examining the applicability of the concepts and categories of sociolinguistics to a given speech community. To understand what this implies, let us return, for a moment, to Fukuzawa's story, which is instructive in this regard.

The notion that commerce is a lowly pursuit and that those engaging in it stand on the lowest rung of the social ladder does not agree with our present picture of Japan or how the Japanese see themselves. Intuitively, we would not expect expressions such as 'the samurai manner in my speech' to mean anything today, and whether the 'style of an Ōsaka merchant' would be perceived as a despised variety seems doubtful, too. This is because certainly 'samurai' is by now a historical term which cannot be meaningfully applied to the description of present-day Japanese society, and 'merchant' as a feudal status meant something quite different from an occupation in a capitalist society. This brings us to the most general issue discussed in this chapter. *If there is a relation between dialect variation and social stratification, how do we conceptualize the one and the other?* Let us turn first to language and then to society.

Dialect variation

Fukuzawa referred to all the dialects of Osaka. What did this notion mean at the time, and how does it relate to the linguistic situation of Japan's second largest city in the early twenty-first century? Are there as many Osaka dialects as there were in the 1870s? Do they differ as much from the dialects of Tokyo and other parts of Japan today as they did in Fukuzawa's day? More generally, are regional dialects in a feudal society comparable to those of a modern industrial society? What we need is an operational notion of what a dialect is.

This is a thornier problem than might appear at first thought, for there is no universally accepted basis for distinguishing the terms 'dialect' and 'language', but it is possible to give both terms a clear meaning by relating them to each other. For instance, the Osaka vernacular is a dialect of Japanese, and the Yorkshire vernacular is a dialect of English. The relationship expressed here is transitive, not symmetric: English is *not* a dialect of

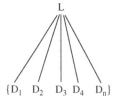

Figure 2.1 *Language and dialect*

the Yorkshire vernacular. A language, L, is conceived as consisting of an assemblage of dialects, D_1–D_n, a relationship that can be schematically summarized as in Figure 2.1. The connecting lines indicate affiliation rather than genetic derivation.

A dialect identifies the regional background of its users. How dialects relate to each other is the subject of dialectology or dialect geography.[6]

In the absence of major physical obstacles such as wide rivers, lakes and insurmountable mountain ranges, adjacent dialects are mutually intelligible forming a dialect continuum or chain. For instance, although there are pronounced differences especially in pronunciation, no point can be found between, say, Devon and York where speakers of adjacent counties cannot understand each other. Similarly, the chain of mutually intelligible dialects of continental Germanic stretches from Vienna to Amsterdam. In Italy local dialects are very distinct, but as you go from north to south there is no unbridgeable gap, no mutual unintelligibility between neighbouring villages. The dialect chain in the northern part of the Indian subcontinent extends over almost 2,000 km from Bengal to the Punjab with no clear-cut dialect boundaries. Yet, speakers may see themselves as using different languages. Within the Germanic dialect chain, three languages are distinguished, *Hochdeutsch* or Standard German, *Algemeen Beschaafd Nederlands* or Standard Dutch and *Lëtzebuergesch* or Luxembourgish. These languages are separated by virtue of political rather than linguistic criteria. Two have a clearly defined standard; one, Luxembourgish, is a national language whose identity is defined negatively: not German, not French, not Dutch. Thus, in dialect chains we may get a situation where the diagram in Figure 2.1 reveals itself as what it is, an idealization. For example, on both sides of the Dutch–German border people speak very similar dialects, which makes it difficult to determine precisely where they stop speaking Dutch dialects and where dialects affiliated with German start (see Figure 2.3). A similar situation is found at the Spanish–Portuguese border, at the Serbian–Croatian border and in many other parts of the world. Such a relationship can be depicted as in Figure 2.2, which indicates that a dialect chain $\{D_1$–$D_n\}$ may incorporate elements whose affiliation to a language is variable.

Even though a speech variety such as Low Franconian, also known as Meuse-Rhenish, spoken at the German–Dutch border (D_3 in Figure 2.2) is

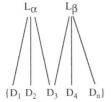

L_α L_β

{D$_1$ D$_2$ D$_3$ D$_4$ D$_n$}

Figure 2.2 *Variable affiliation of dialects*

hard to classify on linguistic grounds as a dialect of German or Dutch without drawing an arbitrary line, German and Dutch are distinct languages with all the necessary paraphernalia, such as codified grammars and standard dictionaries. The resulting general picture is a two-tiered order with continuous variation of dialects on one tier and clear discontinuity of languages on the other. This is testimony to the force of two factors in the evolution of language, historical contingency and volition.

The dialect of the Île de France has become the superordinate norm of the French language area, while historical circumstances never allowed southern French or Occitan dialects to gain more than regional recognition. In the Dutch language area, *Algemeen Beschaafd Nederlands* is recognized both in the Low Countries and in the Flemish part of Belgium. In the English-speaking world things are very complex, partly on account of the enormous expansion of English around the globe (see Chapter 13). Because of the great multiformity in which English manifests itself, on the one hand, and the recognition by most native speakers of the language that there is a common core, on the other, Standard English is considered a dialect with no local base that is accepted throughout the English-using world. It is certainly not what is spoken by the majority of English-speakers or a compromise variety thereof (Strevens 1985). More important for making it 'standard' is a different factor, its written form. Though often discounted as an extralinguistic artefact, writing does play a crucial role in establishing a standard.[7] More to the point than the oft-quoted adage that a language is a dialect with an army and a navy, it can be said that a (standard) language is a dialect with a written norm. Let us look at another important example for illustration.

The tacit assumption underlying the designation of a set {D$_1$–D$_n$} of dialects affiliated with a language is that its elements are mutually intelligible, but this is not always the case. Take the linguistic situation of China, for example (see Figure 2.4). In English the major varieties of spoken Chinese are usually called 'dialects', Mandarin, Wu, Min, Hakka and Yue being the major ones. These five 'dialects' are not mutually intelligible, being as distinct as Italian, French, Spanish and other Romance languages. The comparison with Romance languages is justified on numerical grounds, too. Used by a population of at least 80 million, Wu Chinese alone has more speakers than Italian. Yet, the said Sinic languages are traditionally, in

Figure 2.3 *Low Franconian dialect spoken in the German-Dutch border region*

scholarship, and by their speakers today considered dialects of Chinese. Actually, each of the five names, Mandarin, Wu, Min, Hakka and Yue, designates groups of more closely related varieties. In Chinese it is common to make a distinction between *fāngyán* ('regional speech') or major forms of

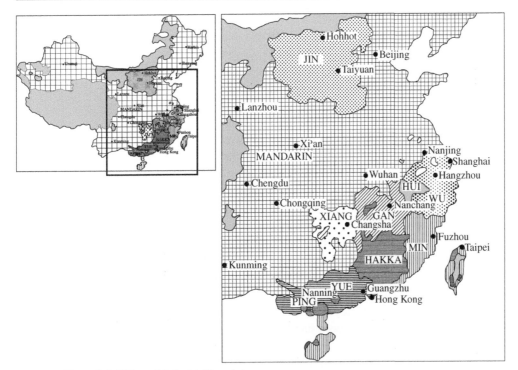

Figure 2.4 *Chinese 'dialects' (fāngyán)*

speech such as Wu, the dialect of the greater Shanghai region, and Yue, that of Canton, and *dìfang-huà* ('local speech') or lesser local varieties. *Fāngyán* are not easily interintelligible, whereas variation between *dìfang-huà* does not reach a level to impede communication (DeFrancis 1984: 57f.). On linguistic grounds alone Chinese might well be called a family of languages such as the Romance and Slavonic families, but this would ignore the importance of extralinguistic factors. No political boundaries exacerbate linguistic separation, as in the Romance language area where people want to speak French, Italian, Catalan, etc. In China people want to speak Chinese, at least in the sense that they acknowledge the northern Chinese variety as the standard form of Chinese. A common written norm has played a decisive role in maintaining the unity of the Chinese language. No attempts were ever made to elevate Wu, or Min, or Hakka to independent language status by settling on a separate written norm. As a result, the configuration of standard and dialects in the Chinese language area differs significantly from that in other parts of the world.

Fāngyán and *dìfang-huà* are emic terms, that is, terms that are not universally applicable but dependent in their interpretation on a particular linguistic (or cultural) system.[8] French *patois* and German *Mundart*, both often rendered as 'dialect' in English, are similar terms, for what the French mean by *patois* and the Germans by *Mundart* is not quite the same as 'dialect', or *fāngyán* for that matter. What is true of 'dialect' also holds for 'standard', a notion that likewise means different things to different people and that, in a sense, is even more difficult to grasp, for 'the standard language is not typical of a well-defined social or regional community, which would enable us to find and describe speakers' (Smakman 2012: 27). On the basis of an international survey in which 974 non-linguists from seven countries (England, Flanders, Japan, the Netherlands, New Zealand, Poland and the United States) were asked to give their definition of a standard language, Smakman (2012) comes to the conclusion that two different notions are current. The more widely held concept of the standard language sees it as being a socially distinctive variety based on strict rules and admitting for little variation. The other concept emphasizes the socially cohesive function of the standard language that, admitting for heterogeneity, takes a large population of speakers and its role as lingua franca as defining criteria. In everyday conversation there may be a tacit understanding of what 'standard language' means, but in a sociolinguistic context it is important to clearly state one's own definition.

The apparent need to employ emic terms to identify language varieties shows that the relationship between standard language and dialects can take on various forms which defy universal definition because both linguistic and extralinguistic factors are involved. Factors such as the demographics and political organization of the speech community, the availability of a written norm(s),[9] and the desire to maintain unity or, on the contrary, to emphasize distinction all have a bearing on how the various speech forms relate to each other and to an overarching standard. In subsequent chapters, especially Chapter 8, we will get to know some other configurations which will lend further support to the view presented here that terms such as 'language', 'dialect', 'variety', among others, require for a useful definition a view of language as a social fact. Models of standard-and-dialects configurations known from certain Western speech communities cannot be assumed to do justice to other language areas. The same holds true of models of social stratification to which, therefore, we now turn.

Social stratification

If we want to explain how language and social stratification interact, we need a model that shows how society is stratified. Fukuzawa's story quoted at the beginning of this chapter refers to a society in transition. The feudal system, with a small ruling class of warrior-administrators at the top supported by a landed class of farmers and the emerging bourgeoisie of townspeople, no longer reflected actual power relations, as the latter, comprising artisans and merchants, became ever wealthier and more powerful. There was a strong tendency towards status inconsistency: the samurai had only their inherited rank, but no wealth to back it up, while merchants were looked down upon, but economically potent. Pressure for radical change mounted because the system of feudal ranks included no mechanism of regular social mobility.

Similarly, in the passage quoted above (p. 7), Gumperz (1967) refers to India as a highly stratified caste society. Like feudal ranks, castes are closed and hereditary, allowing for little social mobility. A caste is a social group based on occupation and kinship, and the relationship between castes is that of rigid horizontal stratification. Each caste is either superior or inferior to its neighbours. At the top of the caste system are Brahmin (priests) followed by Kashatria (warriors), Vaisya (scribes), Sudra (workers) and Harijan or Untouchables (cleaners and beggars), each caste being divided into many local and occupational subcastes. They are distinguished from one another by detailed rules regarding marriage, food and occupation. In accordance with its democratic constitution of 1950, modern India officially abolished the caste system. However, old habits do not fade away overnight. Caste is an integral part of the cosmic order of traditional Hinduism. Caste consciousness is still strong, as may be inferred from marriage ads which routinely refer to caste, such as this one: 'Match for Brahmin SP girl 27/165/30000 fair b'ful employed Multinational. Bangalore employed boys from Lucknow preferred. Contact Phone: 0522-000000 Email: xxxxxxx@yahoo.com.'[10] Language may well contribute to the continuing significance of caste in India. As Bright (1990: 3) put it: 'India offers exceptionally clear cases of dialects which are spoken in a single spot, but which may be arranged in a vertical scale correlated with social class. These are the caste dialects.'

In the course of the twentieth century, both Japan and India have experienced enormous changes, and the societies of Western industrialized democracies have undergone massive economic and social restructuring as well. At the end of World War II, almost half of all Japanese were in agriculture, but by the end of the century this share had been reduced to some 5 per cent. At the same time, social mobility increased, differences among social strata were equalized and the number of Japanese who consider themselves 'middle class' rose to a staggering 90 per cent. In the course of one century, a rigidly stratified and class-conscious society has given way to a meritocratic society with relatively little hierarchical structuring and weak class consciousness. Some scholars describe Japan as a highly egalitarian society in which basic cleavages are between corporations and organizations rather than social classes and have begun to look at it as a possible model of postmodern society.[11] Yet, 'the Japanese have a clear conception of stratification in their society even if their notions may not be conceptually identical to their Western counterparts' (Sugimoto 2010: 59). Borrowing a notion which originated in linguistics and is widely used in cultural anthropology, sociologist Sugimoto (2010), therefore, speaks of 'Japanese emic concepts of class'.

Now, if it makes any sense to talk about *Japanese* emic concepts of class, this must be so for any society. Democracy is predicated on the normative concept of equality, but it is well known that this means different things in different countries. In most Western democracies aristocracy as a class no longer represents a meaningful division which, however, does not mean that members of the erstwhile aristocracy do not continue to see themselves as such or that mechanisms of class reproduction no longer exist. At different levels of development, as measured against the usually accepted standard of the West in general and the United States in particular, different patterns of social stratification prevail, and even relatively similar societies in terms of collective wealth and its distribution, such as the Western European countries, may differ with regard to social structure, economic relations and power asymmetries between classes. And if we look at societies outside the Western world, differences are much more profound.

For example, when Rickford did fieldwork in a village in Guyana he discovered that the instruments provided by Western sociology for class analysis were inapplicable in a West Indian, sugar-estate community. The Marxist perspective on class which uses ownership of the means of production as the defining criterion and focuses on an individual's position in a system of production, distribution and exchange[12] was no more meaningful than Max Weber's notion of social classes as aggregates of people with common life chances distributed by the market according to the resources that individuals bring to it.[13] A class analysis based on multi-index scales in which informants' scores on scales like occupation, income and education are combined (e.g. DoE 1995) was also of little help since these scales were designed for areas of urban deprivation in Western countries. Rickford (1986: 217) found that the local stratification system involved only two primary groups, which he labelled '*building on local usage*, Estate and Non-Estate Class' (emphasis added). For present purposes it is irrelevant how exactly these two classes were composed, for Rickford's concern was with what is at issue here, the problem that class analysis poses for sociolinguistics. Lack of a better alternative made him build 'on local usage', granting the terms 'Estate and Non-Estate Class' technical status.

Class, however defined, caste and other divisions such as the twofold order of an Estate and a Non-Estate Class constitute different types of social stratification. The ambitious project common to Marxist and Weberian social analysis was to develop universally applicable concepts which would reveal common principles. This is the main reason, and a good reason, why these two approaches continue to dominate the debate on social class. Yet, it is safe to say that they have lived up to their claims to universality only at the most general level at best. There are certain general characteristics such as the unequal distribution of wealth, but students of particular societies – late nineteenth-century Japan; late twentieth-century South American plantation community; a downtown neighbourhood in contemporary Tokyo – often fall

Table 2.1 *A simple class division model for Western societies (after Chambers 1995: 37)*

Middle class (MC)	Upper (UMC)	Owners, directors, people with inherited wealth
	Middle (MMC)	Professionals, executive managers
	Lower (LMC)	Semi-professionals, lower managers
Working class (WC)	Upper (UWC)	Clerks, skilled manual workers
	Middle (MWC)	Semi-skilled manual workers
	Lower (LWC)	Unskilled labourers, seasonal workers

back on concepts that are locally more meaningful than 'social class', that is, on emic terms.

Even in Western societies it is doubtful that such class divisions as are shown in Table 2.1 capture the socially relevant divisions. Several other ascribed characteristics such as gender, ethnicity and race, as well as acquired features such as education, professional accomplishment, age and immigrant status cut across traditional class boundaries and may be better predictors of an individual's social position and life chances. Contemporary society is characterized by new divisions such as that between the employed and the unemployed. And what is more, to a larger extent than in earlier times, social divisions take on cross-national features, as low-productivity jobs are relocated from the most advanced countries to those that are catching up. Some sociologists, therefore, would rather do away with class altogether, suggesting that this notion should be replaced by those of *social deprivation* and *social mobility*.

In the sociological literature class has been a hotly debated topic for some time.[14] 'Class theory: still the axis of critical social scientific analysis?' asks Becker (1989); 'Class counts', affirms Wright (1989). In the second decade of the twenty-first century, this debate is still indicative of the changing nature and increasing fuzziness of class boundaries as well as of the growing awareness that both mobility patterns and class consciousness are subject to significant variation between countries and historical epochs. Furthermore, class is being superseded by other distinctions such as gender, age, ethnicity and race which influence stratification in modern societies. The 'racialization' of social class is an important topic of social analysis in industrial societies where, especially in the big cities, a new multiracial underclass is forming in the wake of a mass influx of poor migrants. What remains is one thing above all: inequality. The principal aim of any analysis of social stratification is to examine the relationship between the unequal positions occupied by individuals in society and their variable life chances. The key term is intergenerational social mobility, that is, the penchant and ability of individuals to rise above their parents' position in society. A highly mobile society is thought to be more egalitarian than one with low social mobility. This is not the place to resolve the question of whether a Marxist or a Weberian theory of stratification is a better explanatory tool to deal with social mobility, or even whether the one or the other is more suitable for the purposes of sociolinguistics. But we draw attention to the need for every sociolinguistic study to decide on a stratification model, because the socio-linguistic project strives to explain how stratification and movements up and down the social scale are reflected in language behaviour. This is so regard-less of whether class consciousness plays an important role in public discourse, for a modern society without a measure of inequality along several scales does not exist. In addition to reflecting objective economic differences that derive from control or lack of control of the means of production, modern societies are differentiated in terms of skills and educa-tion and immigrant status that find expression in different lifestyles and speech behaviour.

A simplest model and its limitations

As the discussion in the previous two sections has revealed, the sociolinguistic project brings together two historically contingent phenom-ena, language and society. 'Dialect' and 'social class' are equally fuzzy concepts and hard to define in the abstract. This must be kept in mind when the distribution of standard and dialectal forms of speech is set into a relationship with social stratification. Sociolinguistic research in many different environments has provided evidence that this linkage can be explained in terms of correlations between *independent* social variables and *dependent* linguistic variables (Chambers 1995: xvii). That, in this correlation, the social variables are the independent ones means that choice of variant speech forms depends on social (and other non-linguistic) factors such as class, sex, age, ethnicity/race and the formality of the situation. Since these factors always occur in combination with each other, every model that correlates dialect and class is an abstraction. The most widely quoted model of this sort is 'Trudgill's triangle' (see Figure 2.5).

This triangle relates two continua. At the horizontal base is an unbroken chain of regional dialects. The vertical axis represents social stratification with the highest class on top and the lowest at the bottom. The triangular shape expresses a correlation between dialect variation and social class typical of the linguistic situation of twentieth-century England. As you move up the social hierarchy, dialect differences diminish. The speech of the disadvantaged or underclass is more pronouncedly regional than that of middle-class speakers. At the apex, a speech form closest to Standard English spoken with RP is used by the numerically small upper class. This model is attractive for its simplicity, its generality and its intuitive cogency, but it should not be taken for granted that it can be transferred without modification to other societies or that its validity for England is still beyond question.

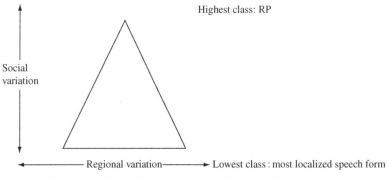

Figure 2.5 *'Trudgill's triangle' (after Trudgill 1984: 42)*

The real challenge of sociolinguistics today is to examine the validity of the message expressed by this triangle, namely that dialects are strongly indicative of class. An obvious weakness of the model is that it is static. From its inception sociolinguistics has been interested in social mobility because empirical evidence suggests that speakers' socially upward orientation finds expression in their speech. In his survey of New York City speech, Labov (1966) found that speakers classified as upwardly mobile used significantly fewer non-standard variants than speakers classified as stable in the social class of their origin. These findings suggest that speakers adjust their speech to the perceived ideals of a norm which they intuitively understand as a means of social advancement. However, some of the premises on which the triangle is based may be outdated. These are as follows.

(a) Intergenerational mobility compares parents' levels to that of their children. Mobility is either up or down.
(b) Language is a decisive marker of social standing: the closer your speech to the standard, the higher your class.
(c) Thanks to general education and mass media, standard speech is accessible to all members of society.

Taken together and in conjunction with speakers' ability to make choices, (a)–(c) seem to lead to the inevitable conclusion that the standard is bound to be embraced by all speakers and to spread throughout society. Indeed, modernization in many European countries brought in its wake a levelling of regional dialects, a tendency the mass media were thought to accelerate. Language standards were invariably associated with urban centres and often with political power.[15] Modernization consists in the spread of innovations affecting economy, society and culture. The encroachment of a standard on dialects is one of the processes associated with it. Innovations tend to spread from a centre towards the periphery in a wave-like fashion. This takes time. New words and pronunciations, just like any other fad, arrive in outlying areas with some delay. In the course of modernization, regional differences in speech, therefore, were reinterpreted in temporal terms. Dialects, in as much as they differed from the speech of the metropolitan centre, came to be regarded as outmoded habits lagging behind modern life. And speakers of rural dialects became stigmatized when they left their circumscribed rural dialect area to move to the city. Since urbanization has been one of the most salient features of modernization, and since big cities are places where people hailing from different parts mingle, one should expect that the reduction of dialects is a necessary concomitant. The overall result should be a shift in the direction of the standard, convergence and linguistic homogenization. The 1950–1961 survey of English dialects was carried out with the expectation in mind that access to standard speech through the mass media would inevitably lead to the marginalization of dialects (Orton, Halliday and Barry 1962–71).

Yet, dialects continue to exist. People do not give up their local accents, grammatical idiosyncrasies or vocabulary. On the contrary, new dialects keep emerging. For instance, research by F. Inoue (1994) has revealed that, unlike standardization which occurs as change from above, non-standard forms disseminate through the Japanese speech community from below as an informal style. Such forms, moreover, often originate outside of Tokyo in the dialects of outlying regions. Subsequently, they move to Tokyo where they are integrated into the capital's prestigious informal non-standard dialect, and then spread back out. A new variety called 'Tokyo New Dialect' thus emerges. Inoue sees in the dissemination of new dialect forms, as illustrated in Figure 2.6, a counter-force to the social pressure that promotes standardization.

Big urban agglomerations are an everyday laboratory of the generation of new speech varieties. London is one of the most cosmopolitan cities in the world, having attracted vast numbers of immigrants from many countries during the second half of the twentieth century. Notwithstanding the metropolitan image of the city that sets rather than follows trends, this development has deeply affected the language of London where sociolinguists Jenny Cheshire, Paul Kerswill and their associates have diagnosed the emergence of a new dialect that rapidly supplants old-fashioned Cockney: MLE or Multicultural London English (Cheshire et al. 2011), so called

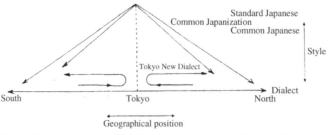

Figure 2.6 *Inoue's triangle: Common Japanese and Tokyo 'New Dialect'*

because this variety is widely used by inner-city London youths and not indicative of ethnicity. It is also known as *Jafaican* or fake Jamaican because it is heavily influenced by Jamaican English, but not limited to Jamaican immigrants. The discussion about how MLE and Jafaican are related continues, indicating a situation that is as fluid as the demographics of London.

***What endz you from?* Multicultural London English (MLE) – some examples of a new dialect in the making**

Word	*Meaning*
air	rubbish
bait	stupid, obvious
blud	friend
choong	attractive
draw	marijuana
endz	neighbourhood
grinding	working hard
innit?	sentence tag
jacked	being robbed
nuff	emphatic: very
sick	good
wack	not so good
wasteman	a worthless person

Grammatical features

Indefinite pronoun *man*

2nd person plural pronoun *youse*

was, wasn't with plural subject

conjoined verbs without *and*: 'They sit chat.'

Sociolinguistic theory endeavours to explain linguistic variation as an outcome of social conditions. The persistence of dialects and the surfacing of new ones, therefore, are important to explain. Social factors that vary with linguistic variation should be specific, but if the premise is valid, general statements should be defensible, too. For example, 'Feudal societies are more linguistically fragmented than industrial societies, because in feudalism the population is largely rural with little need of cross-regional horizontal communication and little opportunity for social mobility.' Or, 'Modern industrialized nation states foster language standardization because the population is drawn to urban centres and needs a common language.' Presumably, postmodern society is also characterized by specific communication needs and conditions that influence language behaviour. Postmodern societies are more mobile, have fewer class markers and are more tolerant of heterogeneity. Achievement is more important than class. Imada (1991) has suggested that class is losing its importance as a

determinant of behaviour. People are less concerned about class as differentiated by income, property and school education. Social mobility is along
both the vertical and the horizontal dimensions. Thanks to the mass media
and the Internet revolution, the spread of information is instantaneous rather
than gradual, which reduces the importance of the centre. Urban dialects and
new dialects originating outside the metropolitan areas can be explained as a
component of postmodern social reality. Variation is acceptable and identities are multidimensional. Dialects in postmodern society are not distributed
in the same way as in modern industrial societies where patterns of covariation of class and non-standard speech forms are relatively clear-cut.
Nowadays, observes leading dialectologist Jack Chambers (1995: 7), 'the
effect of occupational mobility blurs the class lines not only socially but also
linguistically'. Isolated dialects are an endangered species and, therefore, no
longer attract much attention in sociolinguistic dialect studies which instead
focus on mobile populations and dialects in contact (Trudgill 1986) and the
emergence of new varieties such as MLE in complex contact situations.

Contact is always between speakers, and since speakers (as Fukuzawa
observed) tend to accommodate and adjust their speech to each other, the
nature of the contacts that speakers maintain has become an object of
sociolinguistic interest which is being studied as a supplement to investigating correlations of dialect and class. This approach is known as social
network analysis. To explain why people continue to use their local dialects
in spite of the fact that these are often negatively evaluated is one of its main
objectives. In this approach, which is closely associated with the work of
Lesley and James Milroy (1992), rather than an abstract ascription of class,
the density and diversity of speakers' communication networks is regarded
as the crucial variable that determines their dialect loyalty. 'The closer an
individual's network ties are with his local community, the closer his
language approximates to localized vernacular norms' (Milroy 1980: 175).
Network analysis focuses on the nature and dynamics of communication
networks and on their function for the enforcement of norms and group
conformity. The advantage of using a micro-sociological notion such as
community network is that it can explain the persistence of dialects without
referring to the unwieldy concept of social class. On the negative side, it has
nothing to say about the covariation of social stratification and variable
language use. Network analysis is no substitute for social class analysis in
sociolinguistics because all societies, big and small, postmodern, modern
and developing, are stratified and because social dialect research in many
different speech communities has revealed relationships between social
divisions and linguistic variation. It is best, therefore, to consider communication networks as another important social variable that influences speakers' choices.

When the link was made between linguistic variation studies and social
network analysis, attention was focused on face-to-face communication.

Mediated social interaction – through letters, radio and television broadcast – was largely disregarded. Thanks to the internet revolution this is no longer prudent, because new technologies not just extend, but also change the ways people speak and interact. These technologies allow us to be constantly connected, in writing and in speech, with people in unspecified places, inhabit virtual worlds, participate in online discussion groups, and engage in forms of communication that were unimaginable just a few decades ago. Among other things, the space of large-scale and often anonymous inter-actions opened up by internet technology allows linguistic fads and inno-vations to spread – go viral – much more rapidly than language change progresses in face-to-face conversation. Research on the effects of online social networks on language change and the emergence of new varieties is still in its infancy, but clearly a sociolinguistic domain of great potential (Androutsopoulos 2006).

Accommodation

Returning to Fukuzawa, in the final passage of his story, he remarks that he became disgusted because people 'were merely following the lead of the person speaking to them'. In his view, speakers should be consistent, true to themselves. However, it is the rule rather than the exception that in the course of a conversation people converge, and this has nothing to do with subservient attitudes in feudal society, as Fukuzawa apparently believed. What he observed is a very general phenomenon and therefore of considerable interest. In the ways people speak they adjust to their interlocutors, and this adjustment has a social dimension. Adjustment can be upwards – as when a dialect speaker adopts his interlocutor's standard pronunciation in a job inter-view – or downwards – when an adult uses simple vocabulary in explaining a technical matter to a child. Power comes to bear here, but rather than absolute power it is a power differential that prompts speakers to converge in one direction or the other. People also accommodate in order to display solidarity with or common membership of a particular group. Using the same accent, for example, is a way of signalling communion. The research concept which has been developed to investigate these processes is known as accommodation theory. It explores 'the motivations underlying certain shifts in people's speech styles during social encounters' (Beebe and Giles 1984: 7).

Since Fukuzawa understood speech accommodation as a behavioural characteristic of feudal society, he thought that he ought to teach people not to adjust so willingly. In this regard, too, he anticipated a leitmotif of sociolinguistics, social commitment. He realized that it wasn't easy to change people's ways because 'this situation was the result of hundreds of years in our history'. Yet, he was convinced that something had to be done, giving expression, as it were, to a common sentiment shared by many who concern themselves in our days with how the linkages of social stratification and dialect differentiation are perceived and socially evaluated. Two positions concerning dialect and standard speech in modern industrial societies have been discussed and pursued.

(1) Since dialect differences are defined on a vertical social axis enjoying variable prestige and recognition, it is best to change the way people speak, that is, rid them of their low-esteem dialects and help them converge on the standard. This is the Henry Higgins and Eliza Doolittle approach: howling with the wolves. The concept of compensatory education has its roots in this approach.

(2) Rather than the way people speak, the way people think about accents and ways of speaking should be changed. This is the counter-culture or 'aesthetics of the oppressed' approach which embraces the postmodern principle of acceptance of heterogeneity. Its rationale is 'that the failure to recognize the legitimacy of dialect differences may lead to a kind of discrimination that is as onerous as other types based upon race, ethnicity, or class' (Wolfram 1997: 124).

The variable prestige dialects enjoy, the fact that some are praised and considered elegant while others are belittled and denied recognition, has been a matter of concern in sociolinguistics from its inception. Dialect differentiation is known in virtually all speech communities of any size, and the general insight that such differentiation is patterned rather than arbitrary has been borne out time and again. In industrialized urban societies horizontal geographical dialect differentiation has been reinterpreted as being ordered along a vertical axis of social stratification. People's social position influences the way they speak, whether they choose to use their local dialect or a speech form closer to the standard. In this chapter we have seen that, accordingly, language varies along a social dimension. However, the diversity of social stratification throughout the world makes it difficult to design a model that captures the social dimension of variation in speech in a way that is comparable across speech communities. The general point to remember is that regional variation in language lends itself to social differentiation. How such differentiation is effectuated is contingent upon the social system of the community in question.

Conclusion

Dialect and standard are two concepts commonly used to characterize a language's internal heterogeneity. The questions of how linguistic variation comes about and how standard and dialects relate to each other are of considerable theoretical interest. Dialects are traditionally understood as regional or local speech forms; however, different varieties can also be discerned in the same location. Recognition of the fact that social parameters, especially social class, function as the locus of linguistic difference is at the origin of the sociolinguistic enterprise. As illustrated in this chapter with the keen observations of a nineteenth-century Japanese intellectual, the insight that social differences find expression in speech is not new or of Western origin. But it was in Western industrialized countries that researchers started looking at society and language in order to better understand, and perhaps correct, social discrimination on the basis of language.

To this end it is necessary to define the notions that are correlated with each other. This is not easy on either the social or the linguistic side, as social stratification and language variation are subject to historical contingencies, meaning different things in different countries. The lesson to be learnt is that, although it is safe to say, very generally, that social structure and language variation are interrelated, care must be taken in sociolinguistic research not to commit the one-size-fits-all fallacy by unquestioningly applying to every study the same model of social stratification and the same model of linguistic differentiation. It is necessary to take locally meaningful notions of language and social structure into consideration.

While correlating dialectal features with social class and/or social mobility is the predominant method of sociolinguistic analysis, network analysis has been introduced in this chapter as an alternative approach. Growing migration flows, progressing urbanization, super-diversity in metropolitan areas of advanced countries and the expansion of worldwide internet communication are changing societies and their languages, as we watch. Network analysis may turn out to be a more flexible and suitable analytic tool for investigating the resultant sociolinguistic volatility characteristic of the present time than models of (relatively) rigid class and dialect divisions.

Questions for discussion

(1) In what sense is sociolinguistics a Western science, and why does it matter?

(2) What is the difference between a language and a dialect?

(3) Why was Yukichi Fukuzawa disgusted? What did and what didn't he understand about the variable ways in which his interlocutors reacted to him?

(4) Some researchers find it necessary to conceptualize both 'dialect' and 'social class' as emic notions. What are the implications for sociolinguistic research?

(5) Accents closer to standard pronunciation tend to be more highly regarded than localized accents. In industrial societies, universal education and mass media make the standard accessible to all strata of society. Yet dialects persist. Why?

Notes

1. The most comprehensive account in one volume is Chambers, Trudgill and Schilling-Estes (2002).
2. Kindaichi coined the term 'language life' (*gengo seikatsu*), providing the label for an entire research paradigm, Japanese sociolinguistics, which, however, was never much noticed outside Japan. See Heinrich (2002).
3. Tanabe Juri (1936). *Gengo shakaigaku* [Sociology of Language]. Tokyo.
4. Sanada (1987) describes the process of language standardization in Japan in great detail.
5. *Man in India*, XIX, 94.
6. For a good introduction see Breton (1991).
7. For a discussion of the role of writing and literacy for language standardization, see Coulmas (2003), especially Chapter 12.
8. *Emic* is originally derived from 'phonemic' as opposed to 'phonetic', the idea being that, much like the sound system of language, a cultural system can be studied on two levels, that of universal properties, etics, and that of system-specific properties, emics.
9. The plural is relevant in the case of languages with multiple norms such as English and German as well as many other smaller languages. Cf. Clyne (1992).
10. Classifieds samples for 'Wanted Groom' advertisement in newspapers, 2012. www.advertisementindia.com/Matrimonial-Sample-Advertisements.aspx. In the variety of Indian marriage ads 'boy' means unmarried male.
11. This view is, however, not universally accepted. Marxist sociologists diagnose increasing inequality and robust class reproduction in Japanese society. Cf., for example, Hashimoto (2003).
12. Contemporary Marxist class analysis is represented by the work of Wright (e.g. 1989).
13. For contemporary work on the Weberian approach to class, see Goldthorpe and Marshall (1992).
14. See, for example, Navarro (1990); Clark and Lipset (1993); Edgell (1993); Devine (1996).
15. Cf. Grillo (1989) for an in-depth account of how political power was involved in the establishment of dominant standards in Britain and France.

Useful online resources

British Library website on accents and dialects of the UK: www.bl.uk/learning/langlit/sounds/index.html

Website on Multicultural London English: www.lancs.ac.uk/fss/projects/linguistics/multicultural

Linguistic Atlases of the USA: http://us.english.uga.edu

The American Speech-Language-Hearing Association on social dialects: www.asha.org/docs/html/PS1983-00115.html#AP1

For entertainment, try comedian Ali G interviewing (unperturbed) Noam Chomsky on language, easily found on YouTube.

Further reading

Chambers, Jack K. 1995. *Sociolinguistic Theory*. Oxford: Blackwell.
Kerswill, Paul. 2007. Socio-economic class. In C. Llamas and P. Stockwell (eds.), *The Routledge Companion to Sociolinguistics*. London: Routledge, 51–61. Offers a comprehensive overview of how social class has been conceptualized in sociolinguistics.
Labov, William. 1966. *The Social Stratification of English in New York City*. Washington, DC: Center for Applied Linguistics.

Milroy, Lesley and James Milroy. 1992. Social networks and social class: toward an integrated sociolinguistic model. *Language in Society* **21**: 1–26.

Trudgill, Peter. 2001. *Sociolinguistic Variation and Change*. Edinburgh University Press.

Wolfram, Walt. 1997. Dialect in society. In F. Coulmas (ed.), *The Handbook of Sociolinguistics*. Oxford: Blackwell, 107–26.

3 Gendered speech: sex as a factor of linguistic choice

In the eighteenth century, when logic and science were the fashion, women tried to talk like the men. The twentieth century has reversed the process.

Aldous Huxley, *Two or Three Graces*

You can't really know a person until you have heard them speak.

Anne Karpf, *The Human Voice*

Outline of the chapter

Inequalities between women and men pertain to biology and culture. This chapter starts out from physical differences between male and female vocal tracts and the resulting differences in pitch. It then goes on to consider the question of how biological distinctions are culturally modulated to produce female and male ways of speaking. Two theoretical approaches to the analysis of observed linguistic differences between men and women, labelled respectively 'difference' and 'dominance', are reviewed. Recent developments in the field of language and gender that, taking notice of sexual minorities, question the utility of fixed binary categories *f* vs. *m* are also introduced. The connection between the feminist movement and linguistic gender studies is discussed with a view on deliberate changes in gender-related speech practices.

Key terms: gender, sexuality, discrimination, variation, difference, dominance

(In)equality, difference, domination

Women and men choose their words differently. Why? An obvious answer is because they are different. What is more common sense than that the sexes are dissimilar, distinct and contrasting?! It's nature, a fundamental of the settled terms of existence. Intersexuality is an anomaly in any society. The overwhelming majority of all people know what sex they are (and want to be). That women and men speak differently is only natural. Just look at our speech apparatus. Men's vocal tracts are longer, their larynx is bigger and, accordingly, their voices are deeper because their vocal cords vibrate at a lower frequency than women's. Between 80 and 200 cycles per second (hertz) is the average range of male voices, while female voices range between 120 and 400 hertz. Frequencies are determined by physical conditions, the shape and length of the vocal tract. Does the resulting difference in the perceived pitch of female and male voices have anything to do with the fact that men and women talk differently? Isn't it just a natural given? It certainly is. However, the vocal tract is like a trumpet. You cannot make it sound like a double bass or a piano, but there are still many different ways of playing it. And this is exactly what people do with their voices, which is why we can speak of choice in this connection, too, choice within a scope of possible options.

Consider vocal music. Great singers can do wonderful things with their voices, spanning an enormous range of frequencies. Their performance is the result of instruction and practice. In different cultures, musical recitals differ in characteristic ways. The head voices of the Peking Opera, for example, sound distinctly strange to the untrained ear, and so do the outbursts of high-pitched wailing by professional mourners in Greece. Distinctions of this sort can be attributed to cultural traditions. Speaking, too, is part of cultural traditions and, accordingly, variable. For example, there is a register of female speech in Korean which is marked, among other things, by deliberately high pitch. In Japan, evidence was found that in the course of the three decades between the 1950s and 1980s the average pitch of Japanese male voices rose significantly.[1] During the same period, the incidence of men and women mingling in the same workplace increased, accompanied by other incremental changes in the division of labour between the sexes. No incontrovertible proof that this social change caused the change in the male voices exists, but it is a possible explanation and an interesting hypothesis to pursue. The change suggests, once again, that in matters of language nature is subject to cultural modulation. In this particular case it seems that men changed to talk more like women.

There is, furthermore, experimental evidence to suggest that there are sociolinguistically analysable reasons for differences in voice pitch between men and women. Ohara (1997) recorded natural conversations and reading of sentences in Japanese and English by the same speakers. She found that women speak with a higher pitch in Japanese than in English, while men's pitch was the same for both languages. How deep a male voice is and how high a female one thus is to some extent subject to variation and choice. Japanese culture favours a clear distinction between maleness and femaleness which finds expression, among other things, in the tendency to emphasize the differences between female and male speakers by pitching their voices higher and lower, respectively. As a result, Japanese speakers are more gender-polarized in their pitch range than speakers of other languages. When Japanese women want to sound polite, their voice can be pitched above 400 Hz, a peak heard only as a shriek in European languages. Vocal differences are a way of articulating social differences, which are expressed differently in different countries. The low pitch of Dutch women is a case in point, the Netherlands being one of the most egalitarian societies in Europe (van Bezooijen 1995). The more gender-equal a society, the smaller the differences between female and male voices. When we speak, we not only activate our own individual voice, we also accommodate to our social environment and its default expectations. From the observation that the same speakers' pitch varies with the language they speak, it can be concluded that social norms extend to pitch. Individual speakers can choose to deviate from the norm, but since language is essentially a cooperative game most speakers adhere to it. This explains why the female speakers in Ohara's data speak with a higher pitch in Japanese than in English.

Karpf's (2006) stimulating book about the human voice describes in great detail how the complex physical system of our larynxes and sound tracks enables us to modulate our voices from high to low and with an incredibly wide range of prosodic qualities. Interestingly, it includes a discussion of how the differences between male and female voices have changed in the course of the past half century. Women's voices in English-speaking societies have become significantly deeper. Examining various voice recordings of female English speakers aged 18–25, Karpf found that between 1945 and 1993 the average pitch was lowered by 23 Hz (Karpf 2006: 175). Thus, physical differences between the sexes notwithstanding, everything cannot be reduced to nature. Rather, much of what in the relationship between the sexes used to be considered natural or god-given has been exposed as a cultural construct of nature. Pitch is so interesting in this regard because it seems to be closer to the natural and physical than, for example, the words men and women use, the ways they address each other and other features of linguistic etiquette[2] of which social variation would be expected. If the pitch of male and female voices is affected by social and cultural factors, then other features of speech behaviour should vary across and within the sexes too. As it turns out, there are very many such features. The linguistic forms used by women and men differ in all speech communities that have been studied.[3] As a by-product first, and then an important topic on the agenda of the feminist movement in Western societies, these differences have attracted a great deal of attention since the mid 1970s. Instead of asking what is feminine and masculine, many scholars and activists questioned the notions of femaleness and maleness prevalent in Western societies and began to ask how feminine or masculine they wanted to be. Sex change is possible, though rare. But there are other means of altering sex roles. In the Chinese opera, as well as in Japan's Kabuki theatre, female characters are enacted by men. This was also common practice on Shakespeare's stage in Elizabethan England. Sex roles are staged in everyday life too. Every society and every culture write their own scripts. In the previous chapter we learnt about social class that, as soon as we leave the confines of our own society, the emic nature of all notions of stratification becomes apparent. This is also true of sexual differentiation. The emic term for sex is 'gender'. Sex is nature, gender is culture.[4] (Sex is a compulsory exercise, reproduction; gender is the fun of it, an art, a cultural achievement. You may thus want to say, 'Let's have gender', or, 'Do you like gender?' However, language use, as in so many cases, lags behind scientific insight. This is not really a problem, although it is sometimes seen as one, especially by linguistic relativists, a point to which we will return below.)

Difference

From the inception of sociolinguistic gender studies,[5] it has been a contentious question whether sex-specific speech behaviour ought to be understood in terms of difference or domination (Cameron 1992). Both approaches seek explanations for why a society may accentuate or de-emphasize distinctions between the sexes and how language is used to mark such distinctions, but their explanations are different. By virtue of certain linguistic forms and types of speech behaviour, men are recognizable as men and women as women. There are many functional explanations for that. For example, in New York City women were found to use fewer non-standard forms than men. The difference approach assumes that this is due to the role of women as principal caregivers in childrearing, which makes them more status-conscious. This finds expression, among other things, in their desire to teach their children the standard variety in order to enhance their future chances of social advance (Labov 1990; Gordon 1997). Similar tendencies have been observed in several other speech communities, such as Norwich (Trudgill 1984) and Amsterdam (Brouwer and van Hout 1992). According to the difference approach, the speech behaviour of men and women is different for a variety of reasons which cannot all be reduced to a one-dimensional scale of power and domination. Men and women have different conversational norms as a result of interacting in single-sex peer groups as children. Different socialization patterns cause boys to be concerned with status and self-assertion, while girls are more geared to involvement and understanding. The resulting conversational styles have been described as competitive and cooperative, respectively (Eckert 1989; Tannen 1991). Additional evidence for gender-specific speech patterns comes from observed preferences for different genres. For instance, in patient interviews, female speakers' preferences for narratives contrast with the tendency of male speakers to report their problems in non-personalized ways (Wodak 2006).

Dominance

The dominance approach focuses on power and inequality. Sex-specific variation in language behaviour is seen as expressing and reinforcing power differentials. For example, naming conventions such as the wife's adoption of the husband's surname upon marriage and the use of patronymic surnames for the offspring are interpreted not as a neutral practice, but as a manifestation of male dominance (Gibbon 1999: 61). While the dominance approach stresses the instrumental function of language as it is being used in various ways to shore up male domination, it also credits language itself with the power to influence or determine thought. For example, Spender's book *Man Made Language* is based on the deterministic notion that language, rather than serving the expression of thought, shapes our conceptual categories and the way we think: 'It is language which determines the limits of our world, which constructs our reality' (Spender 1985: 139). The standard counterargument is that translation is possible, for if our thoughts were determined by a specific language, how would we be able to judge a translation into another language correct or mistaken? The position taken in this book is that although people do not necessarily think before they speak – for which there is a lot of evidence all around you – they are able to do so in principle. Language is not an inescapable prison house of thought. From the fact that we say the sun rises, it cannot be concluded that we are committed to a pre-Copernican world-view. Language is an open system which allows us to make choices, including those concerning the avoidance of sexist or otherwise offensive language. It is worth noting in this connection that sociolinguistic gender studies has contributed significantly to the promotion and adoption of non-sexist language by media and public institutions, which would have been quite impossible if language 'determined the limits of our world'. Terminologies that, for one reason or another, are found wanting can be changed or replaced, making people think and, sometimes, change their attitudes.

Linguistic determinism and relativism are controversial theories.[6] Although they have been the object of a great deal of empirical research for decades, and although most linguists and psychologists believe that evidence offered in their support is flawed or unconfirmable, the general idea is still liked by many. It has proven persistently difficult to discuss in a disinterested way 'because linguistic and cultural relativity is often felt to imply moral relativity' (Stubbs 1997: 359).

This is also true of other issues relating to sex-specific language use. It is therefore not surprising that no other field in the social sciences and humanities has been as intensely politicized as gender studies. Gender in the 1980s and 1990s was what race was in the 1960s and 1970s, especially in the United States and some other Western countries. Both gender and race are less abstract than social class and more likely to affect the research agenda on these social parameters. Researchers can pretend to be classless or in a class by themselves, but they cannot pretend to be sexless. The difference approach and the dominance approach reflect different ideologies. The position adopted here is eclectic, not unlike Uchida's (1992) which seeks a compromise between both. She considers gender as a holistic and dynamic concept that influences language use as one of several factors constituting the social context. Some aspects of sex-specific speech behaviour can be explained in terms of power, but not all.

Observations of diminishing differences between female and male pitch and extensive research about other aspects of the speech behaviour of the sexes have led some sociolinguists to rethink the male–female opposition (see, e.g., Livia and Hall 1997, Motschenbacher 2011). Following the lead of other social sciences, they question the validity of 'normative gender binarism' calling for the deconstruction of heteronormativity, that is, the assumption that male vs. female and heterosexual vs. homosexual are clearly distinct categories. Much as research about the characteristics of female and male speech first entered sociolinguistics in the wake of the second wave of the Women's Movement, the critique of heteronormativity, which came to be known as 'Queer Linguistics', is an offshoot of the Gay and Lesbian Movement that fights discrimination against homosexuals and the cultural preference for opposite-sex relationships (of a sexual nature) that characterizes society's most important institutions, notably family, school and state. Hence, more obviously than other branches of linguistics, the Queer Linguistic approach is politically motivated. It advocates reconsideration of established identity categories, and by bringing bisexuality, intersexuality, transsexuality and androgynity into the discussion seeks to promote a different approach to the study of language, gender and sexuality which allows for blurred and shifting categories[7] that are constructed socially rather than being immutable givens. There is an obvious parallel with race in that social conventions force people of mixed ancestry into simplified racial categories. This approach presents a challenge to earlier feminist perspectives on sociolinguistic research by undermining generalizations about binary gender differences in speech, advocating a more diverse range of gendered speech that is shaped by local communities of practice instead.

Categories are always abstractions; the categories referring to human sexuality and gender are no exceptions. In the present context of investigating linguistic gender display as socially conditioned, it is worth noting that in some Western societies gender identity is treated as a matter of choice. For instance, you can find online ads for speech therapy on how to change your voice from that of a male to that of a female. While mainstream society pays little attention to transgenderism, the phenomenon is a cogent reminder of the porosity of even the seemingly most basic differences. From time to time, it is prudent to examine established categories in the light of new knowledge, but categories are usually hard to dispense with entirely, especially in quantitative research which needs to collect and classify data.

Gender and phonetic variation

Turning to some specific examples, let us now consider gender as a factor of linguistic variation. Mainstream research has concentrated on segmental phonological variables. A variable in this sense is a phonological segment that is regularly realized in different variants. Regional as well as social dialects are often differentiated not by the presence or absence of features, but by the relative frequency with which these features occur. This is one of the lasting lessons of sociophonology. For example, the participle suffix in words like *walking, running*, and *jogging* is variably pronounced as *-in'* [ɪn] and *-ing* [ɪŋ]. All speakers of all social groups control and use both forms, but the frequencies of their choices differ. The fact that these frequencies are not random is what makes them interesting, because their distribution exhibits systematic preferences by various groups of speakers, which are thus imbued with social meaning.

Many surveys have revealed a clear correlation with social stratification. The general pattern is that the proportion of the reduced form *-in'* is highest in the lowest social group and lowest in the highest social group. Because of this, the *-ing* variant, which is preferred by the highest social group, is considered standard and more prestigious, while the *-in* variant is the vernacular form. The direction of the distribution is the same for both sexes in that male and female speakers of the lowest social group choose *-in* more frequently than their counterparts of the highest social group. However, when the data are broken down along gender lines an interesting difference appears. Summarizing more than three decades of research, Labov (1990: 210) confirms what has been observed over and over again: women tend to choose the standard variants more frequently than men. This holds across all social strata, although the differential between men and women is more conspicuous in some than in others. Figure 3.1 shows the increasing frequency of *-in* from the highest social group (1) to the lowest social group (5) and the consistent higher frequency of use by males than females.

The variable differential of male and female choices has been interpreted as indicating that at the extremes of the social scale social group overrides gender, whereas the penchant of women in the middle range to choose the standard form significantly more often than men of the same group indicates upward social mobility. These women are oriented in their speech behaviour towards the prestige norm in order to improve their social position. This explanation is focused on a single factor of what is a complex process involving a variety of motives and conditions that likely affect speakers' choices. One stressed by Fasold (1990) is that using standard rather than vernacular forms allows women to sound less local and thus have a voice more suitable for rejecting social expectations that place women in an inferior position to men. Gordon has argued and presented some evidence

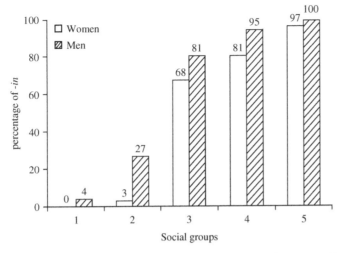

Figure 3.1 *Distribution of -in pronunciation across social groups and broken down for speaker-sex (after Trudgill 1984)*

that lower-class speech by young women carries the implication of sexual availability. This can be a strong incentive in some situations for a woman 'to modify her speech in order to indicate her respectability' (Gordon 1997: 61). It is also important to remember that the preferred use of the standard or prestige variants by women is a tendency typical of groups of speakers, not individuals. Women and men do not speak as women and men only, but as teachers and students, friends and strangers, clerks and customers, employers and employees, as members of an ethnic group, religious community and so on, and in many other more individualized capacities. As Nichols (1983: 54) points out, women 'make choices in the context of particular social networks rather than as some generalized response to the universal conditions of women'.

The critique of normative gender binarism mentioned in the previous section comes to bear here. Rather than registering women's and men's speech as indexing gender identity only, the analysis has to cut deeper recognizing gender, sexuality as well as situational and contextual factors that impinge on a speaker's performance to variable degrees.

Social networks

As we saw in the previous chapter (p. 36), looking at social networks is another way of investigating linguistic variation. Research along these lines has shed light on the relationship between gender and linguistic variation from a different perspective. In a large survey of the Belfast vernacular, James and Lesley Milroy (1997) concentrated on variation according to gender and age differences. They found that the different roles men and women play in social networks are reflected in their speech behaviour. For example, words that in Standard English have the low front vowel [æ] as in *that* have a local variant with the back vowel [a]. At the same time, in words like *flat*, *trap* and *rather* [æ] is replaced with a raised [ɛ]: [flɛt, trɛp, rɛə]. However, these two features of the local vernacular are not distributed evenly across the sexes. Vowel backing is characteristic of the Belfast vernacular generally, while vowel raising, [æ] > [ɛ], is associated with prestige and, therefore, more frequently used by females. By contrast, the variant [a] shows a converse pattern of social distribution. It is indicative of a casual style and associated with male speakers. Both [æ] and [a] were identified by the Milroys as relatively new features of Belfast speech. They have acquired social meanings coinciding with speaker-sex. These examples show that gender often makes itself felt in minute, inconspicuous ways rather than by virtue of readily noticeable contrasts. Variation on the phonetic level in particular can be very subtle. Yet, these subtle distinctions contribute to the overall differences between male and female speech.

The interpretation of the findings of the Belfast survey is rather complicated, pointing to a complex interaction of gender, social status and network integration. Women tend to interact more than men in dense and multiplex networks, and they 'appear to correlate their choice of variant more closely with their personal network structure than do men ... Although women are much less likely than men to select the back variants of /a/, this generally lower level of use does not prevent individual women from varying their realization of /a/, within the female norms, according to their social network structure' (Milroy 1992: 119). Notice that the significance of gender-differentiation in speech is considered important enough to justify the stipulation of two distinct norms, a male one and a female one. Similar choices, Milroy suggests, must be interpreted in terms of social class for male speakers, but in terms of personal network structure for female speakers.

The relationship between gender, social network and preferred speech forms is a very complex one. Network analysis helps to explain sex-preferential differences in the occurrence of phonetic variables and to show that linguistic variables may function as gender markers. However, speaker-sex is a very broad category, too broad perhaps as a primary independent variable. It has been argued, for example by Brouwer and van Hout (1992), that additional variables must be introduced in order to assess the impact of sex on speech behaviour. If childrearing comes to bear on the nature of a speaker's social network as a major factor determining women's role in the network and by consequence their speech behaviour, then it is plausible to expect differences between women who act as mothers and those who do not. Furthermore, the different roles men and women play in social networks have been explained on the grounds that women are more focused on the family, whereas men have more opportunities to interact in work-related environments. In their sociolinguistic survey of Amsterdam,

Table 3.1 *Seven phonetic variables in Amsterdam speech; (1) is the standard variant, (5) the most localized variant (Brouwer and van Hout 1992)*

	aa	ee	oo	au	ei height	ei monophthongization	z
(1)	a.	e.	o.	ɔu	ɛi/ɛ.$^{(ɔ)}$	ɛi/æi/ai	z
(2)	ɑ	e.^{i}	o.^{u}	ɑu	æi/æ.$^{(ɔ)}$	ɛ.$^{(ɔ)}$/æ.$^{(ɔ)}$/a.$^{(ɔ)}$	z̧
(3)	ɑ.^{ɔ}	ei	ou	au	ai/a.$^{(ɔ)}$	–	s
(4)	ɔ.	ɛi	ɑu	ɑ:	–	–	š
(5)	–	æi	–	–	–	–	–

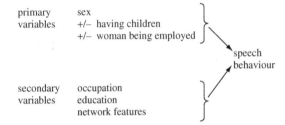

Figure 3.2 *Independent social variables and speech behaviour (after Brouwer and van Hout 1992)*

Brouwer and van Hout, therefore, introduced as additional variables the presence or absence of children and employment status (Figure 3.2).

Brouwer and van Hout investigated seven phonetic variables along a scale of five variants ranging from (1) Standard Dutch to (5) Amsterdam vernacular, as given in Table 3.1.

These variants were correlated with the independent social variables of the survey in order to determine the influence of sex on speech behaviour and to find out whether there is covariation to the effect that the seven variables belong to identifiable registers. Yet another dimension of complexity and sophistication of this survey is that data for three styles were recorded from all informants, *casual speech*, *reading style* and *word list*. This is a standard method in sociophonological surveys which controls speakers' attention and monitoring. In casual speech the speakers are assumed to pay least attention to their own phonetic performance, in word lists most. The Amsterdam survey corroborated previous observations of women's speech being closer to the standard in essence, but it also revealed that the variable sex is subject to other significant effects by secondary variables. Figure 3.3 shows the interaction of speaker-sex, employment and the presence of children. The lower the score, the more standard forms are used. Men use more non-standard forms than women consistently, but the two other variables, children and employment, bring about significant effects. Interestingly, the most standard-speaking group of this sample are females with employment and without children.

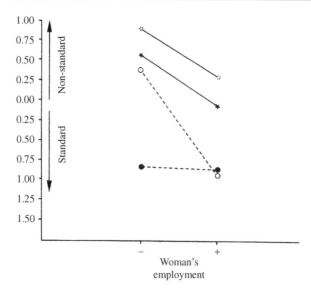

Figure 3.3 *The interaction of speaker-sex, employment and the presence of children in the Amsterdam survey (Brouwer and van Hout 1992)*

In statistical surveys of this sort, it is equally important and difficult to control all variables. In the case under consideration here, education, occupational level and network density are potentially relevant variables that Brouwer and van Hout (1992) consider along with speaker-sex. They found that having children and employment promotes the use of the standard language and that, as might be expected, use of Amsterdam vernacular forms decreases the higher the informants' educational level. In the end they conclude that gender is the strongest predictor of language use. While this appears to be a clear result, the Amsterdam survey also reveals that gender-specific speech variation is not a one-dimensional distinction, but one that is part of a complex set of interacting variables including social stratification, education and cultural definitions of gender. Simple correlations between a single independent social variable, such as gender, and dependent linguistic variables, such as a set of phonetic variants, are always problematic. The assumption of separate gender styles as a general notion has therefore proven hard to defend.[8] More promising is a comparative approach which can demonstrate that the effect of gender on speech behaviour is more striking in some speech communities than in others.

In their speech behaviour people are influenced by various factors including their interlocutors, a point we dwelt on briefly in Chapter 2 above. Face-to-face communication is characterized, among other things, by the salience of visual and auditory cues of a speaker's gender. Since these cues are absent from computer-mediated communications, it is of considerable interest to explore whatever differences between women and men exist in electronic discourse. Internet practices are as yet a little researched subfield of gender sociolinguistics to which network analysis might be fruitfully applied. Some researchers have observed that women and men use social network sites and other forms of computer-mediated communication differently (Herring 2003; Crowston and Kammerer 2010). However, more research is needed to find out how gender-related differences in computer-mediated communication correspond to or deviate from those in face-to-face interaction.

Gender across cultures

In recent years, the investigation of correlations between isolated variables in search of 'women's' and 'men's' language has given way to more context-oriented research that views the linkage between gender and language use as being mediated by social practice. Differing gender identities and accompanying speech styles are a component of the different practices women and men engage in (Cameron 1992). Clearly, the relative segregation and integration of the sexes and their (in)equality vary across cultures (Günthner 1996). For instance, the hypothesis mentioned above that 'the different roles men and women play in social networks have been explained on the grounds that women are more focused on the family, whereas men have more opportunities to interact in work-related environments' is grounded in a Western industrial society. The social division of labour by sex is subject to cultural difference. That gender-specific speech forms are more pronounced in some cultures than in others is therefore not surprising. The question is how such differences can be explained and how they ought to be interpreted.

Once again, a difference approach and a dominance approach can be distinguished. The former considers the division of labour between the sexes, including variable linguistic practices, part of the totality of any cultural system and is content to note that humanity has produced a multiplicity of cultural systems just as it has produced a multiplicity of languages. The latter, on the other hand, is based on quasi-social Darwinist ideas according to which the degree of equality of the sexes is a measure of progress. Traditional societies (formerly called 'primitive') practised exogamy, that is, the exchange of women for marriage between clans or tribes.[9] That men and women spoke differently would be an expected outcome of such a situation. At the opposite end of the evolutionary scale are the most advanced Western societies in which the highest degree of equality between the sexes has been accomplished and, accordingly, linguistic differences between the sexes have been levelled. All societies and cultures can be ordered along this scale where each has its place according to how much the languages or speech styles of men and women differ.

The underlying assumption of this view is that gender-specific differences between speech styles are indicative of how far a given society has progressed in the direction of the common goal of non-discrimination. Conforming to the general penchant of differences to be valued, it equates difference with inequality and discrimination. There are two obvious problems with this view. One is the asynchrony of social developments and cognitive and linguistic ones. The other is that it is highly doubtful that sex can be reduced to gender, that is, that the sociocultural construction of maleness and female-ness is everything and the biological constitution of men and women nothing. The difference approach, on the other hand, recognizes that gender-specific speech forms can be, but are not necessarily, part of a cultural system and an ideology which 'contribute to sustaining unequal power relations' (Fairclough 1989: 107; cf also Cravens and Giannelli, 1995).

The literature on language and gender includes many specific case studies of linguistic features of various languages which differentiate men's and women's language use by virtue of differing preferences for lexical items, syntactic constructions, discourse strategies and performance features such as sending out backchannel signals and interrupting each other. For instance, in a corpus of Swedish speeches and interview texts men were found to have a higher proportion of unique words than women. There were also gender-preferential lexical choices as well as a difference in the average number of words per sentence. That women's sentences were longer was unexpected because previous studies had shown a correlation between high sentence length and high status (Swan 1992).

A number of empirical studies on discourse strategies in Greek revealed gender preferences. Women tend to adopt indirect strategies for expressing disagreement, followed by accounts and explanations, while men express disagreement more directly and with fewer mitigating remarks (Kakavá 1997). In another study using culture-specific scales of 'Individualism vs. Collectivism' and 'Masculinity vs. Femininity', Greek is described as 'moderately masculine' (Bayraktaroğlu and Sifianou 2001: 6). This inves-tigation, which compares Greek and Turkish, is focused on politeness, a topic which has been linked to speaker-sex in many studies (Zimin 1981; Burstein 1989; Harris 1992). We will come to the sociolinguistics of polite-ness in Chapter 6. In the present context it is useful to note the principal reason why gender research and politeness research overlap: a higher level of politeness is generally expected of women than of men. Languages differ with respect to the lexical and grammatical devices they have for the linguistic realization of politeness (Mills 2003). Some East Asian languages, Javanese, Korean and Japanese among them, are often quoted as examples of languages in which levels of politeness are encoded in the grammatical system rather than being expressed by means of lexical and phonetic choices alone. These same languages are said to include styles that are gender-specific, to the extent that these styles are referred to as 'women's language' (not usually 'men's language'). Japanese is the most intensely researched of these languages (Okamoto and Shibamoto Smith 2004).

For example, modal particles in sentence-final position are a feature of Japanese grammar. Ide and Yoshida (1999) present evidence for gender-specific frequency of use of these particles (Figure 3.4). Some are used

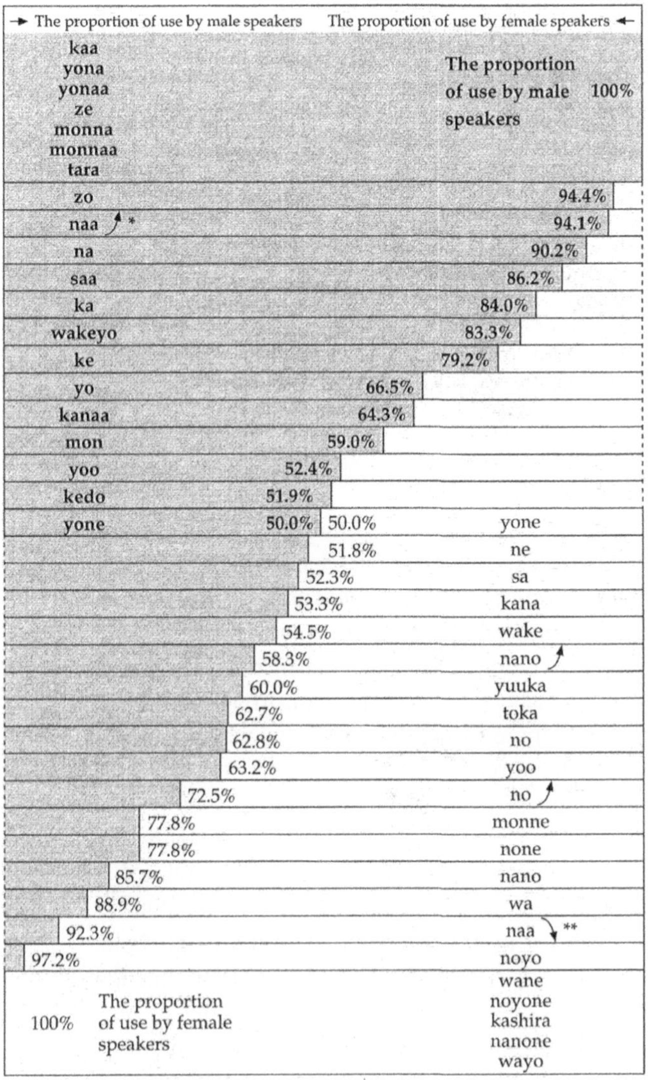

→ The proportion of use by male speakers	The proportion of use by female speakers ←
kaa yona yonaa ze monna monnaa tara	The proportion of use by male 100% speakers
zo	94.4%
naa ⤴ *	94.1%
na	90.2%
saa	86.2%
ka	84.0%
wakeyo	83.3%
ke	79.2%
yo	66.5%
kanaa	64.3%
mon	59.0%
yoo	52.4%
kedo	51.9%
yone	50.0%	50.0% yone
	51.8% ne
	52.3% sa
	53.3% kana
	54.5% wake
	58.3% nano ⤴
	60.0% yuuka
	62.7% toka
	62.8% no
	63.2% yoo
	72.5% no ⤴
	77.8% monne
	77.8% none
	85.7% nano
	88.9% wa
	92.3% naa ⤵ **
	97.2% noyo
	wane noyone kashira nanone wayo
100% The proportion of use by female speakers	

Key: *⤴ indicates rising tone   **⤵ indicates falling tone

Figure 3.4 *Gender-specific frequencies of Japanese sentence-final particles (Ide and Yoshida 1999: 464)*

evenly by males and females or show only minor differences in rate of recurrence, while others are used by males or females exclusively.

Sentence-final particles are just one of several devices Japanese provides for expressing politeness which, as the expressions listed in Figure 3.4 suggest, also differentiate the sexes. Although the distribution of some sentence-final particles as well as other expressions is sex-specific rather than just sex-preferential, each one of them is chosen in accordance with the speaker's assessment of the situation. 'The choice of one linguistic form over another reflects a perception of the structure of cultural understandings and represents the speaker's identity as a member of the society ... The appropriate linguistic choice has the effect of avoiding conflict or misunderstandings in the interaction' (Ide and Yoshida 1999: 477). The point to stress is that, while the avoidance of conflict and misunderstanding is undoubtedly a general principle of cooperative conversation, there may be situations where speakers have reasons to breach this principle in the interest of pursuing other goals such as indicating non-acceptance of sex-differentiating conventions. For example, Japanese female high-school students have been observed to use the first-person pronouns *boku* and *ore* which in standard usage are reserved for male speakers (Backhaus 2002). Their choice of pronoun was widely regarded as deliberately deviant behaviour and a challenge to existing social norms.

Linguistic ideology

There is in Japanese, as in Korean, a multiplicity of pronouns of self-reference and addressee-reference which are gender-specific. However, as the high-school students' use of *boku* and *ore* illustrates, speakers can make unconventional choices without violating the rules of grammar, in contradistinction, for example, to morphological gender-marking languages such as French and German. Whether sex-exclusive and strongly preferential expressions in Japanese add up to form a 'women's language' or just a set of conventions of use which are relatively easily altered is, therefore, a contentious issue. The stereotype of Japanese 'women's language' is often presented as an inherent part of Japanese culture or a remnant of the subservient position of Japanese women in feudal society. But notice that Hibiya (1988), in what is still one of the most comprehensive quantitative studies of sociophonetic variation in Tokyo speech, found no significant gender correlations for any of the variables she studied. Gender distinction in Japanese may be less than is commonly accepted as a matter of fact. Notions of Japanese 'women's language' reflect observations and common-sense ideas. An important lesson of sociolinguistics is that both must be carefully distinguished if we want to understand language behaviour. M. Inoue (1994: 322) argues that to this end 'we must consider the extent to which sociolinguistics is focusing not on speech but on the natives' linguistic ideology of women's language'. The question she asks about Japanese, 'How and why did the relationship between femaleness and speech come to be objectified as "women's language"?' marks a general concern of sociolinguistic gender studies. As for Japanese 'women's language', M. Inoue (1994) makes the case that it is not a vestige from feudal Japan, but rather a product of Japan's modernization in the nineteenth century reproduced in contemporary common-sense notions of 'femaleness' and 'Japaneseness'.

The general point to note is that, in every particular case, the complex relationship between sex and speech behaviour involves a language that has been formed by many generations of speakers, as well as the ideological formation of that community's ethnolinguistic tradition. On both levels speakers make choices that reproduce or alter existing conventions, unwittingly or, in some cases, deliberately. Linguistic practices and concepts that constitute a crucial element of a speech community's self-image tend to become quite path-dependent, leading people to think that they are 'essential' to their culture and cannot be changed; but usually they can.

Language reform

Language behaviour, as we have noted repeatedly, is a cooperative game which means that conventions are usually upheld and changes brought about in a piecemeal fashion below the threshold of conscious recognition. In some cases, however, deliberate changes are undertaken with a purpose in mind. The study of social dialects was associated from the very beginning with the insight that certain linguistic distinctions between what Bernstein (1971) called 'restricted and elaborated codes' were to the disadvantage of lower-class children and should, therefore, be changed and that, moreover, the way people think about these distinctions should be changed. The study of language and gender has been accompanied by similar ideas.

Various proposals have been made for the avoidance of sexist expressions on the syntactic, lexical and morphological levels, and in English and other Western languages significant changes have been brought about (Cameron 2006). Generic *he* in pronominal function – 'A good reporter must protect *his* sources' – has all but disappeared from English publications, and the number of other androcentric generics, once brought to public attention, declined rapidly (Cooper 1984). Androcentric generics are masculine forms that refer to both sexes. If it were written today, Alexander Pope's 1734 *Essay on Man* would probably be entitled *Essay on Humanity*. *Chairman* has been replaced by *chairperson* or *chair*, and for several names of occupations ending in *man* alternatives have been found. Many examples have been collected and dictionaries analysed to show that the language about women reflects discriminatory attitudes towards women. Semantic derogation has been uncovered in certain asymmetries such as can be seen in pairs like gentleman/lady, master/mistress, sir/madam where the words for women are more likely to refer to women in a sexual capacity or with a low-status meaning than the corresponding words for men.

The feminist critique of prevalent usage has been directed against accepting the attitudes underlying these and many other expressions. The changes that were enacted in academic circles first and then in public were very conspicuous, and the speakers who first tried them out, who said *he or she* or used *they* as a pronoun with an antecedent in the singular as in the quote at the head of the chapter, came across as uncooperative because they intentionally violated existing conventions. But eventually, and within a relatively short time, the campaign to reduce sexism in language in the English-speaking world was very successful. Other speech communities such as the Dutch and German have experienced similar changes, but it is by no means clear that this campaign can be transferred to other languages. It must be seen as what it is, a social movement that appeared on the scene during the final decades of the twentieth century in some highly industrialized Western societies using their particular languages which encode sex in particular ways. All of these factors are contingent and cannot be assumed to enter the complex relationship of gender and speech behaviour in like fashion everywhere. For instance, gender-neutral, inclusive phrasing is more difficult to realize in languages with grammatical gender agreement systems, such as French, Italian, German and Russian, among many others, than in morphologically simple languages like English and Chinese. But even complex morphologies are not necessarily insurmountable hurdles to change. An important general point demonstrated by the changes brought about by the feminist language reform is this: languages can be profoundly affected by deliberate choices of their speakers.

Conclusion

The interplay of natural sex and culturally constructed gender roles is highly complex. This chapter has shown that gender is a major determinant of language choice and that, therefore, sociolinguistic research, by analysing gender-related differences in language use, has much to contribute to a better understanding of the social division of labour of the sexes. We have also seen that the linguistic encoding of gender roles is subject to cultural variation. From this it follows that such encoding, while responding to natural differences between the sexes, is not immutable. The politically motivated promotion of anti-sexist, inclusive language in the English-speaking world is impressive proof of the fact that deliberate change of ingrained linguistic practices is possible, demonstrating that, although given in the sense that every individual and every generation receives it from their predecessors, language is also made, as its speech community adjusts it to its current needs.

Questions for discussion

(1)   'English does more than hinder and hurt women: it proscribes the boundaries of the lives we might imagine and will ourselves to live' (Julia Penelope 1990. *Speaking Freely: Unlearning the Lies of the Fathers' Tongues*. New York: Pergamon). Discuss this statement and its implications. Can languages lie, hurt, proscribe?

(2)   Why is the pitch of female speakers higher when they speak Japanese than when they speak English? Discuss pitch as a natural and as a sociocultural phenomenon.

(3)   In what sense are pairs of words such as *gentleman/lady, master/ mistress, sir/madam* asymmetric? Try to think of reasons why such asymmetry evolved.

(4)   Every society has common-sense notions about the relationship between femaleness and speech behaviour that reflect a linguistic ideology. What are the noteworthy features of gender-related linguistic ideology in your society?

Notes

1. Nakano (1993). Changes in the pitch of male voices were also reported in the Japanese press where they were discussed in terms of changes of traditional gender roles (*Mainichi Shinbun*, 12 May 1995).
2. See Chapter 6 below.
3. The most comprehensive and up-to-date account of sex-specific speech differences across languages is Hellinger and Bußmann (2001/2).
4. For a compelling and wonderful account of the culture of sex and some of its linguistic aspects, see Siegel (1999).
5. See, for example, Lakoff (1975), Thorne and Henley (1975).
6. The notion that language is an active force working on our thought processes goes back to nineteenth-century linguist and philosopher Wilhelm von Humboldt. It is often referred to under the label 'Sapir/Whorf hypothesis' after Edward Sapir (1889–1939) and Benjamin Lee Whorf (1897–1941).
7. Smyth, Jacobs and Rogers (2003) present an illustrative example. They have developed a data bank of twenty-five male speakers' speech spanning the range from 'very gay-sounding' to 'very straight-sounding', according to listener ratings. The data enable research about phonetic variables and contextual and/or socially conditioned categorizations.
8. Togeby (1992) has demonstrated that the question of 'a separate women's language' suffers from an imprecise use of the term 'language'.
9. Cf. Lévi-Strauss (1949). The view of marriage as an economic transaction in which women rather than men were exchanged between clans is controversial and has been much criticized, especially in feminist circles. It has the advantage, however, of identifying a common structural principle underlying various different marriage systems.

Useful online resources

International Language and Gender Association homepage: www.lancs.ac.uk/fass/organisations/igala/Index.html offers information on relevant conferences, publications and links to language and gender-related syllabi and other online materials.

'Introducing Phonetic Science', by Michael Ashby and John Maidment (2005): www.cambridge.org/uk/linguistics/cill/resources/ipswebhome.htm introduces the basics of phonetics with examples from a variety of English accents and other languages.

The Language and Gender Page of Mary Bucholtz, one of the leading scholars in the field: www.linguistics.ucsb.edu/faculty/bucholtz/lng

Tips for using gender-neutral language: www.marquette.edu/wac/neutral/NeutralInclusiveLanguage.shtml

Guidelines on Gender-Neutral Language. United Nations Educational, Scientific and Cultural Organization (UNESCO), 1999: http://unesdoc.unesco.org/images/0011/001149/114950mo.pdf

Further reading

Cameron, Deborah (ed.) 1990. *The Feminist Critique of Language: A Reader.* London and New York: Routledge.

Cooper, Robert L. 1984. The avoidance of androcentric generics. *International Journal of the Sociology of Language* **50**: 5–20.

Eckert, Penelope and Sally McConnell-Ginet. 2002. *Language and Gender.* Cambridge University Press. Second Edition

Hellinger, Marlies and Hadumond Bußmann (eds.) 2001/2. *Gender Across Languages*, vols. I–III. Amsterdam and Philadelphia: John Benjamins.

Holmes, Janet and Miriam Meyerhoff (eds.) 2003. *Handbook of Language and Gender.* Oxford: Blackwell.

Stokoe, Elizabeth. H. 2005. Analysing gender and language. *Journal of Sociolinguistics* **9**: 118–33.

4 Communicating across generations: age as a factor of linguistic choice

You've had your time, I'll have mine.

T. S. Eliot, *The Waste Land*

... a fashionable old man is almost a contradiction in terms.

Dwight Bolinger, *Language – The Loaded Weapon*

Outline of the chapter

This chapter presents age as one of the principal factors of socio-linguistic variation. Life stages from early socialization to adolescence, adulthood and old age are reviewed, as are theoretical and methodological issues of relating linguistic performance to speaker age and discovering age-specific language patterns. The sociolinguistic significance of age is then discussed in regards to the demographic imbalance of declining languages and language attitudes separating the younger and older age cohorts.

Key terms: age, age grading, age specific language use, ageing, inter-generational communication

Time depth

People come and go; words come and go; and languages come and go. How are these processes connected? Connected they are, for how could words be coined, passed on and discarded if there were no speakers to do the coining, passing on and the discarding? Language is a tradition; otherwise we would not understand one another. It must be handed down from one generation to the next in a way that allows members of coexisting generations to communicate. But it is not handed down unaltered. For each generation recreates the language of its predecessors. Cases of language demise – the discontinuation of a tradition – provide compelling evidence of the intergenerational gap. In the event, speakers of generation G_{n+1} fail to use language L_α in the same way generation G_n did. When this happens there is often a continuum of decreasing use and proficiency in that language that correlates with succeeding generations of speakers. Eventually, L_α ceases to exist as a spoken language because no one chooses to speak it and no one can speak it anymore.[1] This is the outcome of intergenerational progression only in extreme cases; the general point to note is that there are differences in the speech of G_n and G_{n+1}. Generations, or age cohorts, each have their own language world. Two functional explanations for this are as follows. (1) In the course of time communication needs change, forcing each new generation to adjust the language to suit the changing world of their experience. (2) At a set time the communication abilities and needs of contemporaneous generations differ, hence the young and the old speak differently. These are not conflicting but complementary and interlocked explanations, both of which account for age-specific variation within a language.

Old words

Once upon a time	*Meaning*
agliff	frightened
beldam(e)	old woman, witch
calash	a folding bonnet
corrade	to scrape together
cupidity	greed
dashr	a showy person
freck	to move swiftly
iwis	certainly
izzard	the letter 'Z'
malagrugrous	dismal
obambulate	to walk about
prentice	apprentice
running board	a board to step on alongside a car
sirrah	fellow
tripudant	dancing
welkin	the sky

Every living language has time depth, which is not the same as historical language change. For the purpose of the present chapter, it just means that words wither; that teenagers don't speak like octogenarians; that every language comprises expressions, constructions and pronunciations that have been there for a long time and others of more recent origin; and that these expressions, constructions and pronunciations are chosen by speakers of different generations at different frequencies. What is more, there are parts of the language, more so on the lexical and syntactic level than in pronunciation, that are felt by its speakers to be fashionable or outdated. Both may be used with a purpose in mind – to make fun of the 'olde worlde', to make a claim for dignity, to show that we are up to date or loathe the trendy. Whatever the reason for using archaisms and modernisms, both remind us of the fact that a language is not a monolithic formation clearly differentiated from what was and what is coming, but a system in permanent flux which includes elements of variable durability. At any given time, archaisms are not reserved for use by the older generation or modernisms for the young, but there are tendencies in these directions, if only because older speakers are more likely to know archaic expressions, while the modern is by definition associated with the young. Some modernisms gradually lose the taste of newness and gain a more permanent place in the language, others are ephemeral; and conversely, some archaisms are on their way out of the language, while others may stay there as archaisms indefinitely. What is in and out is a matter of degree and, to some extent, a matter of intergenerational variation.

On the level of linguistic expression, time depth means that words and other expressions are introduced into the language at one point and continue to be used for variable lengths of time. On the level of speakers, it means that at any time several generations coexist who share a common language but whose share of that language is not identical. Figure 4.1 schematically depicts a set of expressions first used by speakers of the young generation who continue using them as they grow older. Figure 4.2 indicates that the linguistic systems of three successive generations, $G_n - G_{n+2}$ overlap, but also include generation-specific parts. We will put the question of what the linguistic differences between the generations have to do with language change aside until the next chapter. In this one we will concentrate on the variable linguistic choices of coexisting generations of speakers.

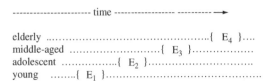

Figure 4.1 *Dynamic model of age-grading of speakers and temporal dimension of language. {E₁} is a set of expressions first used by members of the young generation who continue using it as they grow old*

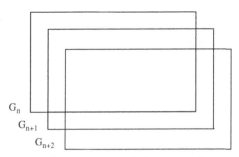

Figure 4.2 *The language of three successive generations, $G_n - G_{n+2}$*

Age cohorts

Like sex, age is a biological fact that is basic to human experience. At the same time, its effects on human behaviour are mitigated by social and cultural notions of the lifespan and its stages. Childhood, youth, middle age and later life are not objective, immutable stages of human existence, but affected by sociodemographic changes and culturally shaped classifications. In some cultures, age cohorts are marked by very pronounced divisions concerning social roles, rights, obligations and behavioural patterns that are considered appropriate. In traditional societies the transition from one stage to the next is marked by rites of passage. Modern industrial societies generally rely less on community rites for social control, but there are still many ceremonies that accentuate stages in a member's lifespan, such as first communion, bar mitzvah, graduation, coming of age and retirement. Chronological age is an important principle of social organization with numerous legal implications, such as school age, military service, driving licence, active and passive voting rights, juvenile courts, majority, X-rated movies, senior citizens' privileges, etc. Not surprisingly, therefore, notions of proper comportment, physical appearance and dress relative to a person's age remain strong.

Young words	
Of recent origin	*Meaning*
affluenza	stress resulting from excessive materialism and consumerism
brain candy	intellectually undemanding entertainment
cyberchondriac	a person suffering from imaginary symptoms he or she read about on the Internet
defriend	to break off an online relation
E-Lancer	a professional who works with the Internet from his or her home
E-Quaintance	someone you know only through online contact
felx-cuff	an adhesive bandage to stabilize wrists or ankles
hoody	someone wearing a hooded top
hotspot	1 a lively place 2 a location where internet access is available 3 an area contaminated by radiation
netiquette	behavioural rules for the Internet
nonlinear	someone who doesn't use the Internet much
prebuttal	pre-empting a contrary argument
shonen	manga targeting boys
shojo	manga targeting girls
upskill	to teach an employee new skills
weblish	English as used for texting, etc.

Speech, too, is one of the characteristics which reveals age-grading and is expected to differentiate one age cohort from another. Keeping in mind that these are relative rather than absolute divisions exhibiting cultural and historical modulation, we can divide the lifespan into four age cohorts – infancy, adolescence, adulthood and old age. They differ from each other in various ways, not least with regard to language use.

Infancy

Age differentiation of speech begins at the very beginning. Naturally, babies don't speak like grown-ups because they don't have the capacity to do so. Language socialization takes time. At the outset, the communication between those involved, the infant and the caregiver, is characterized by extreme inequality in the range of possible choices. The latter has full control of the target language, the former none. Language socialization is the process that eliminates this disparity. It is based on social interaction rather than deliberate instruction, although both sides devote considerable effort to the task. Children acquire language by using it, but to use it they depend on those who provide the input, the talk they hear both around them and directed at them. In monolingual environments what children will hear people say and say to them is the same language, yet there are stylistic differences between these two sources of input. Language acquisition research has found lots of evidence that parents and other adults who interact with babies and young children systematically modify their speech while talking to them.[2] This addressee-specific register has been observed and analysed in many countries around the world, and it has been found that there are many common features across languages and cultures (Ferguson 1964; DePaulo and Coleman 1981).

Speech directed to children by adults tends to consist of short and simple grammatical constructions delivered slowly with careful articulation and clear pauses at the end of utterances. Subordinate clauses are avoided, the vocabulary is restricted and intonation is emphatic. The semantic content is limited to the here and now. The stylistic register that adults use in talking with young children has been given the felicitous name 'parentese', née 'motherese'. It is also referred to as 'child-directed speech'. 'Baby-talk' is an exaggerated form of parentese, but as Menn and Gleason (1986) have noted, this term lacks a clear definition. They distinguish four different meanings of *baby-talk*: (1) the social stereotype of how babies talk; (2) the stereotype of how adults talk to babies; (3) the baby-talk register, that is, the actual language adults use when talking to babies; and (4) the way infants actually speak. The difference between stereotypes on one side and registers on the other is a point of general significance. People entertain ideas about their own speech, but these ideas do not always reflect actual usage but are distorted by stereotypical notions of what ought to be, or is assumed to be, the case. Adults are aware that babies do not speak like adults, and they are aware that they adjust their own speech when they talk with children, but they are not typically aware of the fact that the way they speak to children is a product of their own individual stylistic choice and of the stereotypes current in their society.

From a sociolinguistic point of view, parentese is interesting as a stylistic register which is chosen by its speakers to manage a particular kind of social interaction, that between adult and child. It exhibits features of child speech, such as reduplication, *choo-choo*, onomatopoeia, *bow-wow* and simplified grammar, but it must be noted that this register is learnt by its speakers from other adults, not from children. Parents evidently believe that by giving feedback in the form of features characteristic of the early speech of children, they help the child to build up communicative competence. On the basis of an empirical study of language acquisition in a Tamil-speaking family, Narasimhan (1998: 83) suggests that the features that characterize parentese are 'precisely the ones that are needed to enable the child to segment and schematize the utterances and relate them to the behavioural aspects'. There is wide agreement among child language researchers that in this sense parentese facilitates language learning, at least in the earliest phase.

Another sense in which a simplified input fosters the development of the child's communicative competence is less frequently noted and not intended by the speakers of parentese. It teaches children to adjust their own speech to their interlocutors, and that for this adjustment age is a critical variable. This can be concluded from the fact that not just adults but children, too, use simplified speech when talking to younger children. For instance, 4-year-old children were observed to use simplified speech when talking to 2-year-olds but not when talking to adults (Steinberg, Nagata and Aline 2001: 38). Once their language learning has progressed beyond the stage where simplified speech is effective in communicating with them, children retain the ability to use this variety when needed, that is, when socially expected. In the course of language learning, children replace simplified speech when talking to adults and converge towards the adult norm. Some cultures actively promote this transitional step. For instance, the Comanche of the North American Plains have been observed to teach their children a rich vocabulary of special baby-language words. But only a short while after they had mastered these words, the children were told not to use them and encouraged to switch to normal language (Casagrande 1948). If they failed to make the transition at the expected age, they were ridiculed. In other societies where the shift away from child-like speech is not so explicitly prompted by adults, more indirect mechanisms are at work. Children are taught by casual remarks to avoid the risk of being regarded as babies by older children and adults. The important point is that children learn to take both their own age and the addressee's into account in selecting appropriate speech forms. The ability to do so is an integral part of language socialization acquired at an early age. Language learning means, among other things, expanding the range of stylistic choices and shifting from one style to another.

In a longitudinal study of preschool children's linguistic choices in Trinidad, Youssef (1993) found that all children exhibited stylistic variation. She used a scheme called 'audience design' first developed by Allen Bell in order to account for the factors that are operative in style shift. The name reflects the underlying assumption that speakers design their utterances with an audience in mind. Trinidad is a sociolinguistically complex environment where Trinidad Creole (TC) and Standard English (SE) are used side by side with differential social functions. TC is the language of emotion, kinship and solidarity, while SE is associated with formality, education and officialdom. At the same time, there are social and individual preferences for TC and SE. Some families use more SE at home than others. However, the children Youssef studied were confronted with both varieties from an early age and were found to differentiate between them in their own production.

Audience design proved to be a useful concept to explain the children's style shifting according to addressee. In a multilingual environment such as Trinidad, language choice is rooted in both society and the individual, and the extent to which individual and social factors are effective is itself variable. Youssef's study presents evidence that small children learn to adjust their speech to their audience early on, and that social norms determine individual expectations and choices. Children are sensitive to role relationships expressed through language, and the social system underlying these relationships influences children's speech from their earliest childhood.[3]

In another study of a group of children between ages 4 and 6, Andersen (1992) investigated children's ability to use speech appropriate to certain roles. She collected data by means of a methodology she calls 'controlled improvisation' that engages the children in role play. The children were given puppets designated as father, mother, child, doctor, patient and foreigner (the controlled part) and were then encouraged to play these roles impromptu. The results of the study show the developing ability of children to make lexical and paralinguistic choices to fit different roles. For example, she found that the children never used *well* as a discourse marker, except when playing roles associated with authority. Detailed lexical choices of this sort testify to great sensitivity on the part of the children for role-specific and, in the event, by implication, age-graded language use.

To sum up this section, parentese reflects certain features of child language. It is conducive to the development of communicative competence in two ways: (1) in the earliest phase it facilitates language learning, and (2) it shows the youngest generation that members of the community are differentiated by age and that speech forms are to be chosen accordingly.

Adolescence

The language of adolescents is perhaps the most thoroughly investigated of all age-specific varieties. Characteristic features of adolescents' speech have often been described. The question is how such features can be accounted for. Some researchers hold that a *distinct youth register* differentiates the language of adolescents from that of children, on one hand, and adults, on the other (Widdicombe and Wooffitt 1995). Publications such as the German *Lexikon der Jugendsprache* [Dictionary of Youth Language] (Müller-Thurau 1985) suggest that such a register is an identifiable entity, but because of the short half-life of many of the entries listed, this notion is not uncontested.[4] Other researchers prefer the distinction between age-exclusive and age-preferential features of the language of all age groups. Age-exclusive features are used only during a certain stage of life. An example will be discussed below. Age-preferential features exhibit noticeable differences in frequency of use across age cohorts. In many cultures, age-preferential features in the language of adolescents are very conspicuous, a phenomenon that demands explanation.

For, unlike young children, adolescents are competent speakers of their language, unrestricted in their linguistic choices by incomplete acquisition. While they continue to appropriate the language by expanding their vocabulary and their stylistic range, they have full control of it. Yet they often choose their words in ways that deviate from adult usage. By so doing the young demonstrate that the language they received from their seniors is theirs, and that they use it as they see fit. For example, in English-speaking communities adolescents use double and multiple negatives more than adult speakers of the same social class (Holmes 1992: 184). In a study of Edinburgh schoolchildren Romaine (1984) found that during adolescent years the use of substandard forms was at its maximum. Rampton (1995) observed that in multicultural settings in Britain, adolescents, in marked contrast to their elders, use words of a language not usually associated with their ethnic group, a phenomenon he calls 'lexical crossing'. Danish youths have been observed to make use of quotations as a dramatizing feature of speech in ways distinctly different from adult usage (Møller and Quist 2003).

In recent years the language of Japanese adolescents has attracted some attention. It is documented on many private homepages, discussed in letters to the editor and investigated by sociolinguists. The expressions in question are summarily referred to as *kogyaru kotoba* 'high-school-girl language'. As suggested by this name, this variety is characterized by both age-exclusive and sex-specific features. It is girls rather than boys who have created it and use it along with other non-linguistic features, especially dress, hairstyle and makeup, to set themselves off as a group from the rest of society. With their choice of words, Japanese teenage girls exemplify the general function of the language of adolescents to signal membership of a closed social group.

Many *kogyaru kotoba* expressions are unknown to adult members of society and, if they hear them, incomprehensible. Acronyms and other abbreviations abound. Slang expressions and fanciful neologisms proliferate, many of them extremely short-lived. The term *kogyaru* itself is an example. It is composed of *ko* < *kōtōgakkō* 'high school' and *gyaru*, the Japanized rendition of English 'girl'. Exemplifying a general feature that distinguishes adolescent speech, *kogyaru kotoba* is much more prone to rapid change than adult speech. The fast turnover of these expressions makes it difficult to keep track of how the variety evolves. Dictionaries bank on time, but records of the language of adolescents are likely to be outdated upon publication. However, the transitory nature of the expressions that function as code words of adolescent trendsetters and followers doesn't make the variety less real. In the Japanese speech community around the turn of the century, *kogyaru kotoba* was recognized, and disliked, as a genuine variety of the language. It was disliked because it manifested not just creative unconventional language use but contempt of traditional notions of propriety. Some conspicuous features of *kogyaru* speech are monotonous pronunciation without stress accent; word truncation (*kimoi* < *kimochi warui* 'disgusting'); formation of hybrid Japanese–English compounds (*chō SBS* < *chō* 'ultra' + super beautiful sexy); avoidance of honorifics, especially the use of last names for address without any of the obligatory suffixes *-san*, neutral, *-kun*, for boys, *-chan*, for girls, and *-sensei* 'teacher'.

Since they were first observed in the late 1990s, none of the expressions listed in Table 4.1 have made it into standard Japanese, and it seems unlikely that they will ever leave the taste of slang behind them. Not only that, most of them won't be passed on to the next generation of adolescents. *Kogyaru kotoba* is a recent phenomenon. *Wakamono kotoba*, 'the language of the

Table 4.1 Kogyaru kotoba, *the language of Japanese high-school girls*

Kogyaru kotoba	composition	translation
choberiba	**chō** 'ultra', **beri** 'very', **bad**do 'bad'	worst
chō BM	**chō** 'ultra', **baka** 'fool', **marudashi** 'bare'	obvious fool
deniru	**Deni**(su), **-ru** 'finite verb ending'	go to Denny's (fast-food restaurant)
makuru	**maku** (donarudo), **-ru** 'finite verb ending'	go to McDonald's (fast-food restaurant)
kirapaku	**kari**ta mono 'borrowed item', **paku**paku 'grasp'	not return a borrowed item
kinpa	**kinpa**tsu 'blond'	someone with blond hair
keronpa	kaminoke 'hair', **ron**gu 'long' kinpasu 'blond'	a boy with long (dyed) blond hair
kimai	**ki** 'feeling', **ma**zui 'unsavoury'	bad feeling
kiwai	**kiwa**doi, 'dangerous'	precarious

young', of which it can be considered a subvariety has long been recognized as a variety of Japanese characterized by many age-preferential expressions, substandard pronunciation and the absence of honorifics.[5] But *kogyaru kotoba* made its appearance only in the mid 1990s. The term is first attested in 1994[6] and has since captured the attention of Japanese sociolinguists and sociopsychologists. Their task is to explain why female youth language emerged as a distinct variety in Japan when it did.

In Japanese society, the seniority principle fulfils important functions of social organization. Even slight differences in chronological or institutional age (the length of time one belongs to an institution) determine the nature of social relationships. Age is a defining criterion of social groups. Members of the same school interact as seniors and juniors. Companies recruit new employees once a year who are initiated together, proceed together through a series of responsibilities and for a long time follow parallel career paths. Higher rank often goes with higher age. Respect for the elderly is valued, and the young are expected 'to wait for their turn'. Another feature of traditional Japanese society is the subservient role of women. Although female participation in the labour market is on a par if not higher than in other industrialized societies, notions of distinct gender roles are strong. Taken together, these two features, seniority and gender inequality, put female teenagers in a socially special position at the forefront of societal change. *Kogyaru kotoba* can be understood as a concomitant of social developments which challenge traditional assumptions of Japanese society. The mannerisms that characterize it must furthermore be understood as an expression of a lifestyle and a means young people use to define themselves and construct their identity.

Let us now summarize the features and functions that characterize adolescent speech. Use of substandard, dialectal and vernacular forms, slang and innovative, often very short-lived expressions serves three main functions: (1) to appropriate the language for the speakers' own purposes; (2) to manifest group membership and construct a distinct identity; and (3) to indicate the speakers' willingness to resist the pressure to conform to societal norms.

Adulthood

The language of children and adolescents has been investigated extensively, but studies of age-cohort-specific language do not usually include a chapter about adults. This is so because, in terms of social strength, young and middle-aged adults form the dominant age cohort in most societies, investing their behaviour, including speech, with norm-setting potential. Adult language is the norm, as it were the unmarked choice for all age groups. Young children who speak of their 'chronometer' will be precocious, but 'watch' will be inconspicuous, while an adult who says 'tick-tock', not to a

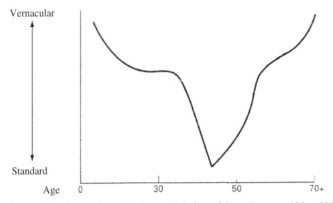

Figure 4.3 *Age and standard speech (adapted from Downes 1984: 191)*

child, will be decidedly infantile. And when middle-aged and elderly adults speak like adults, it will go unnoticed. Adolescents will likewise attract little attention outside their own group when they follow adult usage. On the other hand, it will be noticed when adults garnish their speech with up-to-the-minute expressions which recognizably belong to an adolescent subculture. That is a marked case. Two things follow from this. (1) adolescent speech is more restricted, and (2) adults are seen as the norm guarantors. They command maximum societal strength and at the same time experience maximum societal pressure to conform to existing norms.

As people grow older, their speech becomes less dialectal and converges towards the standard. A decrease with age in the use of socially stigmatized features can be observed in most industrial societies. Between the ages of 25 and 60, people choose standard as opposed to dialectal forms most frequently. Figure 4.3 displays this tendency. It also shows that, with advancing age, the pressure of societal norms, or the willingness to conform, decreases. In this sense young and middle-aged adults form an age cohort between adolescents and the elderly, but since their speech is the yardstick of what is socially acceptable, they are not perceived as a distinct group.

Yet, young and middle-aged adults are set off from the other age groups in various ways, some of which are linguistically encoded. For example, in languages with complex personal pronoun systems, such as Russian, French and German,[7] the transition from adolescence to adulthood is often marked by a change of pronominal address. Differences of one or more generations call for different pronouns, that is, second-person plural, French and Russian, or third-person plural, German, rather than the more intimate second-person singular. However, as will become clear in Chapter 6, more is involved than age in the appropriate choice of pronouns. In the present context it is sufficient to note that pronominal address systems are used, among other things, to give expression to the social meaning of difference in generation.

Old age

The last phase of the lifespan brings with it a weakening of the pressure to conform to societal norms. For example, a return to more dialectal speech forms after retirement has occasionally been observed; however, the social reasons that might underlie changing preferences of elderly speakers have been much less investigated than actual and presumed age-related changes in language ability. To the extent that the language of the elderly has been investigated at all, it has come into focus mainly from a clinical perspective where various sorts of deficiencies ranging from hearing loss and reduced speech-recognition ability to word-finding difficulties, aphasia, Alzheimer's disease and other geriatric communication disorders are dealt with. Outside these areas of physical and mental health, detailed analyses of the speech of elderly people are sporadic. Characteristics of elderly speech forms are not seen as a matter of choice, but as a natural concomitant of ageing which implies progressive decline of competence.

This perspective, which has dominated research on language behaviour in later life, has been criticized by Coupland, Coupland and Giles (1991: 13) for its 'ageist ideological slant'. They emphasize the importance of considering the possibility that 'the deficit tradition in language research [of the elderly] is just another branch of cultural prejudice against the elderly, with its selective design and pervasive concern with linguistic decrement' (1991: 13).

Speech forms and communication disorders that result from age-induced deterioration of communication are of little sociolinguistic interest, because the underlying restrictions on elderly speakers' choices are biological rather than social. Nevertheless there are important issues for sociolinguists to investigate in cross-generational talk with older people. An important question is that of how to improve asymmetric communication between healthy people and people suffering from language impairment. While psycholinguistic research and psychological speech pathology has dominated this field, a sociolinguistic perspective on patients' communicative behaviour and the reactive anticipatory behaviour of their healthy interlocutors is equally important (Hamilton 1994), as in today's ageing society degenerative diseases are becoming more common. The older age cohorts of the population are increasing, making their communication preferences and needs more prevalent and hence more urgent to understand (Nussbaum and Coupland 2004; Backhaus and Coulmas 2009). Life expectancy gains and population ageing are changing the reality of communication across generations as the temporal distance between the youngest and the oldest members of society expands, making more mutual accommodation necessary. Applying a research paradigm developed by Howard Giles and his associates, Kemper (1994) has described a special speech register, termed 'elderspeak', as an accommodation to communicating with older adults. The gist of accommodation theory is what Yukichi Fukuzawa, in his observations of the dialects of Osaka reported in Chapter 2, so deplored (see pp. 19–21): rather than being immutable and consistent in their stylistic choices, speakers accommodate to their interlocutors. In so doing, they cannot but rely on their own image of their interlocutors which more often than not is shot through with societal stereotypes. Hence, they do not necessarily accommodate to the communication needs of their interlocutors, but to their own ideas of these needs. The characteristics of elderspeak, for example, slow production, simplified syntax, avoidance of difficult words, and exaggerated prosody, testify to this tendency. They are reminiscent of other simplified speech registers such as those directed at babies, foreigners and pets. It has, therefore, been characterized as the result of over-accommodation and aptly labelled 'secondary baby-talk' (Coupland, et al. 1991: 20).[8]

A behavioural feature that elderspeak shares with baby-talk is the patronizing attitude its speakers often display towards elderly people, both those who are cognitively impaired and those who are not. Especially in institutional settings, such as hospitals and nursing homes for the elderly, simplified speech varieties are routinely employed in cross-generational talk regardless of whether or not circumstances require such a stylistic choice. Many elderly people find it distressing to be addressed in this way (Baltes and Wahl 1996), a problem that in 'greying' societies is beginning to be noted by a growing number of people and, therefore, opens up a new field of sociolinguistic research (Pecchioni, Wright and Nussbaum 2005; Shaw, Haxell and Weblemoe 2012).

Elderly speakers and declining languages

At the beginning of this chapter, we mentioned one area of research where elderly speakers have captured the attention of linguists not because they are old, but because there are no others (Dorian 2009). In the event, it is elderly speakers' proficiency rather than their declining competence that is of interest, since they are the last generation of speakers of a waning language. For example, Anvita Abbi has undertaken a study of the languages of India's Andaman and Nicobar Islands (Abbi 2006). One of them, Bo, lost its last speaker in 2010. Having no one to talk to in her native language for decades, she had to learn Hindi to communicate in everyday life. Other varieties of Great Andamanese are awaiting the same fate because they do not 'get transferred from the older to the younger generation. Another important feature of the moribund languages is loss of registers and reduced domains of use' (Abbi, Som and Das 2007: 345). The languages in the Andamans can be traced to Africa from where they came to South Asia perhaps more than 50,000 years ago. For anthropologists they are of particular interest, but whoever wants to study these, as well as many other endangered languages, will have to rely on elderly speakers as informants. This raises the intriguing and methodologically problematic

Figure 4.4 *The competence level of a declining language diminishes from elder to younger age cohorts (Abbi, Som and Das 2007: 335, with permission)*

question of whether or to what extent a parallel must be assumed to hold between the fading competence of elderly speakers and the declining expressive power of a language which is about to fall into oblivion. As Dorian (1989) and others have shown, language obsolescence involves both diminishing numbers of speakers and language contraction. In terms of linguistic choices, this means that as a language is chosen less frequently for communication, the range of expressive choices it affords its speakers shrinks. The work by Abbi and her associates about Great Andamanese leaves no doubt that the contracting social domains in which the language is used make its speakers rely increasingly on other varieties in a process that further reduces its communicative functionality. For 'the loss of various registers also results in the lack of total mutual intelligibility even among the speakers who have retained the language' (Abbi et al. 2007: 345).

The problem of contracting languages is directly related to the theme of this chapter, age differentiation in language. For when only old people speak a language, its survival chances are not good, and the very fact that it is spoken by old people only is one of the reasons. This is not primarily because they are going to die, but because young people are disinclined to speak like old people. Bolinger's remark, quoted at the beginning of this chapter, that '*a fashionable old man* is almost a contradiction in terms' comes to bear here. Once a language has become associated with the elderly, it is an up-hill battle to shed this image. Like a bear market where no one wants to buy because no one wants to buy, a waning language is chosen by no one because no one chooses it. In mono-lingual communities, adolescents deviate from the adult norm, but in many cases their deviant choices are innovative and reinvigorate the language. In multilingual communities, however, adolescent minority-language speakers' deviant choices often amount to a rejection of the language of their elders.

The general lesson to be learnt from this most dramatic instance of intergenerational linguistic gap is that linguistic choices are driven among other things by beliefs and attitudes about age divisions and notions of age-specific suitability.

Beliefs and attitudes

Coexisting generations not only use language differently, but also have beliefs about, and attitudes towards, their different speech varieties. Such beliefs and attitudes reflect social power relations and, being as they are inextricably interwoven with language socialization, perpetuate the age modulation of language. Childhood, adolescence and old age are often singled out as problematic life stages separated from normal social life. Grown-ups constitute the mainstream who are expected to take care of those too little or too frail to manage their own affairs. More generally, those who control the material resources of society determine what is and what isn't deviant. Their pivotal position of social strength finds expression in age differentiation of language behaviour and in social attitudes towards age-specific speech varieties.

The natural process of ageing is thus given a social form which impacts on speech behaviour from birth. Many observations testify to the contingent nature of the resulting differentiations. For example, assumptions about the age at which children are able to understand speech vary across cultures. The Ashanti of Ghana interpret infants' vocalizations as manifesting a special language which is quite different from adult language and used only to communicate with other children. According to this belief, the native language is a second language to everyone (Hymes 1974: 31). In some societies 'children are to be seen, not heard', while their active participation in adult talk is encouraged in others. Just as different cultures take different positions on language socialization (Schieffelin and Ochs 1986), attitudes and ideas about intergenerational linguistic differences are variable.

For example, the clash between the upcoming generation of adolescents and the adult establishment typical of the dynamic societies of the West seems to find expression in the notion that language is always going down the drain. From the point of view of the adults there is no uncertainty about who is to blame. That '*they* can't even say it properly now' is a complaint that reverberates through the ages, and they are invariably the young who are accused of sloppy pronunciation and disregard for grammar and good taste.[9] While people get more respectable with growing age, language seems to be deteriorating all the time, or does anyone remember the language of the young being praised for its beauty and refinement? 'Youngspeak' is liable to be branded as deviant, obscene, unsophisticated, if not an insidious attack on the language itself, while 'oldspeak' need not fear a more serious reproach than being quaint. Certain aspects of youngspeak are designed to distinguish the speakers from their elders. Fed by the past, they don't want to swallow it whole, but appropriate it, make it their own. The young have reasons, other than incompetence, for choosing their words as they do. The perennial generation conflict is played out on the stage of language. Youngspeak is designed to threaten time-tested ways which the older generations, being used to them, want to retain. It has many ephemeral elements, like a fad, but is also an expression of creativity and innovation. There is always a tug of war between progress and decay. Language acquisition, it must be remembered, is not copying, but reconstruction of a system which overlaps with the previous generation's system but never completely duplicates it.

Like the relative brevity of adolescence, the language that characterizes it is transitory. It is often ahead of codified norms; the young leave the old behind, but intergenerational differences are kept in bounds by the individual need to communicate with one's parents and children. This necessity can be understood as constraining the range of deviant choices. Age-cohort stereotyping thus contributes to the self-regulation of language as it moves through time, by assigning to the young the role of making adjustments and to the old that of preventing dysfunctionally rapid change. How this complex interplay between coexisting generations can be interpreted as evidence of language change in progress is the question we will discuss in the next chapter.

Conclusion

Age determines the way we speak. As we grow older our voice changes and our vocabulary, our control of grammar and the range of topics we talk about. Biological and social conditions combine to determine the linguistic choices we typically make at a certain age. In any sizeable speech community, age-preferred, age-specific and age-typical ways of speaking can be identified, although speakers in conversations across generations tend to converge. We compare other people's behaviour to our own and strive to resemble them. However, in intergenerational talk convergence is often unbalanced, the young being expected to accommodate to the old more than vice versa. Age-homogeneous conversations bring out age-specific language use more clearly, and adolescents in particular use language as an identity marker to emphasize the differences between themselves and members of other generations. Thus, at any time coexisting varieties are distinguished by age.

Chronological age, social age and subjectively felt age do not necessarily coincide, and the human life course is not subdivided in the same way in every society. In different societies age-related varieties are more or less distinct, but since language changes as it is passed down from one generation to the next, age is a factor of variation everywhere. How a society and a culture imagine age cohorts is very much reflected in language, and a language that displays no age-related variation is doomed, for this means that it has lost its younger age cohorts who not only transfer it to the next generation of children, but also keep it alive through innovation.

Questions for discussion

(1)   What is it that makes an expression archaic or modern? Make your own list of such expressions and discuss their properties.

(2)   What general conclusions can be drawn about speech behaviour from the phenomenon of parentese?

(3)   How is baby-talk different from parentese? Discuss different meanings of the former term.

(4)   Make a list of age-exclusive and age-preferential expressions and discuss the differences.

(5)   Do you have a pet or know someone who does? Do you, or does the pet owner, speak to the pet and if so, how? (Hint: is there anything that babies, foreigners and elderly people in need of care share in common?)

Notes

1. In recent decades an increasing number of publications have dealt with language obsolescence, indicating both growing awareness and the urgency of the problem. See, for example, Dorian (1989), Robins and Uhlenbeck (1991), Krauss (1992), Grenoble and Whaley (1998). The activities of the Foundation of Endangered Languages are documented at www.ogmios.org/home.htm

2. The literature on first language acquisition in psycholinguistics and developmental psychology is vast. See Fletcher and MacWhinney (1995) and Steinberg et al. (2001) for an overview.

3. Menn and Gleason (1986) have studied adult beliefs about the ways in which different age groups talk. They found that children acquire these strongly stereotypic notions current in their society at an early age. Adult communicative competence includes beliefs about age differentiation in speech, which they acquired as infants.

4. For an in-depth discussion on stereotypes about, and the empirical investigation of, speech styles of German youth subculture, see Schlobinski (1995).

5. Honorifics are an important stylistic device for the expression of politeness. See Chapter 6 below for a discussion of linguistic politeness.

6. *Gendai yōgo no kiso chishiki* (Tokyo, 1994: 1093). This is an annual publication that follows social trends and records new terms that receive attention in the media.

7. Cf. Head's (1978) survey of pronominal address in 100 languages. Mühlhäusler and Harré (1990) offer a critical discussion of the sociolinguistic issues involved in personal pronouns, which covers a wide canvas but is not always reliable.

8. The similarity of baby-talk and talk directed to elderly speakers was first pointed out by Ferguson (1977), who characterized both as simplified registers.

9. To borrow the title of Baron's 1982 book.

Useful online resources

CHILDES Child Language Data Exchange System. This site is a component of TalkBank, a system for sharing and studying conversational interactions: http://childes.psy.cmu.edu/

SACODEYL European Youth Language. This website lets you search and browse corpora of structured video interviews with pupils between 13 and 18 years of age in seven European languages: www.um.es/sacodeyl

US National Institute of Aging: www.nih.gov/icd/od/ocpl/resources/wag/documents/checklist.pdf

Documentation of endangered languages: www.volkswagenstiftung.de/index.php?id=172&L=1

VOGA, Vanishing Voices of the Great Andamanese: www.andamanese.net/

Further reading

Coupland, Nikolas, Justine Coupland and Howard Giles. 1991. *Language, Society and the Elderly: Discourse, Identity and Ageing.* Oxford: Blackwell.

Devine, Monica. 1991. *Baby Talk: The Art of Communicating with Infants and Toddlers.* New York: Plenum Press.

Maxim, Jane. 1994. *Language of the Elderly.* London: Whurr Publishers Ltd.

Romaine, Suzanne. 1984. *The Language of Children and Adolescents.* Oxford: Basil Blackwell.

Schieffelin, Bambi B., and Elinor Ochs. 1986. *Language Socialization across Cultures.* Cambridge University Press.

5 Choice and change

They say that time changes things, but you actually have to change them yourself.

Andy Warhol

Certaynly it is harde to playse every man, by cause of dyversité and change of language.

William Caxton (1422–91), *Prologue to Eneydos*

'To travel through Time!' exclaimed the Very Young Man. … 'One might get one's Greek from the very lips of Homer and Plato,' the Very Young Man thought.

H. G. Wells, *The Time Machine*

Outline of the chapter

In this chapter language change through time is introduced as a major dimension of linguistic variation. First, it lays the theoretical and methodological foundations of studying language change from a sociolinguistic point of view, discussing the question of what the transmission of a language from one generation to the next and the incremental change it undergoes in the process imply for our notion of what a language is. Age-grading, the fact that coexisting speakers of different generations use language differently, is explained, and the construct of 'apparent time' is introduced as a technique of investigating language change while compensating for the paucity of recorded speech data from former times. To illustrate phonological adjustments in the course of dialect levelling, standardization and other alterations, surveys of several speech communities are adduced, and the influence on language change of gender and age is examined. The chapter concludes with a brief discussion of demographic change, a so far largely unexplored factor of language change that is of potential interest for future research.

Key terms: language change, age-grading, apparent time, standardization, gender disparity

As time goes by

Languages change through time. This simple statement seems to be equally trivial and easy to verify. Actually, it is a major intellectual challenge. For its appreciation requires two things – a notion of time and an understanding of how languages can be distinguished one from another. Just one of them is sufficient to cause a headache; taken together they pose a serious problem. The general form of the problem is this. The statement

(1) x changes in time.

presupposes an existential statement such as

(2) x exists.

But if x changes it is no longer x but x'. To deal with this difficulty, we might just modify our terminology and rephrase (1) as

(3) x is transformed into x' in the course of time.

However, this is no solution to the problem because we have to come to terms with what distinguishes x from x' and how we get from x to x'. Our original statement (1) is intuitively cogent, since experience tells us that yesterday's English and even last year's English has a lot in common with today's English. That is, while x changes it retains its x-ness. What this means is that change is gradual and too slow to disrupt communication. x and x' can be distinguished only if the temporal interval between them is sufficiently large. Consider a clear case.

(4) *þeossum wordum geĺicum ōðre aldormen ond ðæs cyninges geeahteras sprǣcon.*

(4) is not how speakers of English speak today (as far as the pronunciation is reflected in the spelling), although some of the words look familiar. *Wordum* minus the ending *-um* looks like 'word', *ōðre aldormen* is recognizably 'other aldermen', and with some imagination we can relate *sprǣcon* to 'spoke'. Speakers of Dutch or German will notice the similarity of *spreken* and *sprechen*, respectively. Historical linguists tell us that (4) is a variety of English they call 'Old English' that was current in the ninth century CE. In present-day English, (4) would be rendered as

(5) The other aldermen and the king's councillors spoke in words like these.

Clearly, (4) and (5) are quite different, and we may want to equate (4) with x and (5) with x' in (3). Yet, what exactly it means to say that x was transformed into x' remains a conceptual problem that has no easy solution. If x' is the present-day form of x, it must be possible to retrace the steps that led from x to x'.

The observations that, on one hand, (4) and (5) exemplify rather different languages and, on the other, we cannot find a point, or a finite number of points, between the ninth century and the present time, at which (4) was transformed into (5) result in a contradiction which cannot be resolved as long as we hold on to the notion that a language is a *thing* that exists and changes its form in time, for example, like a cloud and the water droplets and the molecules and atoms it consists of which change the place they occupy constantly. We must be clear about the abstract nature of a term such as 'language' and its designatum. What we are dealing with is not a thing but an *event* which can be broken down into subevents. Consider as an example a race in track and field games. A race can be said to consist of a number of steps which can be counted although it is impossible to say where step s_1 ends and step s_2 begins. In one sense the term 'race' is less problematic than 'language', because a race has a beginning and an end. What is more, the steps that make up a race are all of the same kind. Progressing from one step to another involves no change in quality. Still, 'race' is an abstraction and so is 'language'. A race, most speakers of English would agree, is not a *thing* that can be described as changing its form in the course of time, but an *event*. In order to understand language change we should likewise look at languages not as things, but as events.

That events are treated as things is, however, not uncommon. For example, geologists detect and describe eras in the evolution of the Earth, and within the context of their field they are fully justified in looking at the Earth as a thing. But when you investigate terrestrial evolution on the level of molecules and atoms, it becomes necessary to look at it as an event. Much depends on our point of view and on the level of our analysis. When we try to analyse an event in terms of parts, we will run into difficulties. This is very obvious when we consider as x and x' not two stages of a given language – the whole planet in different geologic eras – but smaller elements that move through time – the atoms and molecules.

When we narrow our focus, x and x' will be individual speech sounds classified as phonemes. The implicit assumption is that the phonological system of language is autonomous and that the fundamental unit of sound change is the phoneme, unaffected by meaning. In Bloomfield's (1933: 364) classical formulation, 'the effect of sound-change … will be a set of regular phonemic correspondences'. For instance, modern English *church* can be traced back to Greek *kyriakón*, 'of the Lord', pronounced with initial /k/. Greek *thygatēr*, with initial /θ/, yielded *daughter*, and *fish* comes from Latin *piscis*. We then get correspondences such as

(6) /k/ – /tš /
/θ/ – /d/
/p/ – /f/

Conventional explanations thus treat sound segments as things, that is, objects that change their form in the course of time. /k/ becomes /tš /, /θ/ becomes /d/, and /p/ becomes /f/. But what is it supposed to mean that /k/ becomes /tš /, etc.? To say that a voiceless velar stop becomes a voiceless palato-alveolar affricate just doesn't make sense; for we know that both speakers of English and speakers of many other languages continue to pronounce the voiceless velar stop. However, they may not pronounce it in the same phonetic environments as did speakers of previous generations.

This, then, is what we should say adopting a speaker-based perspective instead of a language-based perspective. It is not the sound segments that change, but the speakers who change their pronunciation. Little by little, they shift their preferences from one variant to another. More specifically, what relates, for example, the Old English long vowel [aː] as in [staːn, baːn, raːd] with the modern English diphthong [ow], as in [stown, bown, rowd], *stone, bone, road*, is a growing number of speakers who gradually increased the frequency at which they pronounced these words with a diphthong and decreased the pronunciation with a long vowel, [aː]. This does not mean that a long vowel 'became' a diphthong. From a speaker-based perspective, as advocated by Milroy (1992), what actually happens in sound change is more realistically described as piecemeal substitution rather than change.

Notice that phonological theory, too, is moving away from segments as operational units. In modern phonology, the phoneme is much less important than it used to be. Just as nuclear physics has replaced the atom by lesser particles, phonology has shifted its attention from phonemes to phonetic features. For the study of change in progress, this is highly relevant, for if the end result of a sound change can be described in terms of phonemic correspondences, as Bloomfield and many others suggested, such correspondences can only be explained if shifts in the articulation of individual features, such as gradual raising or backing, in the case of vowels, or palatalization, devoicing, etc., in the case of consonants, can be shown to lead from one member of a contrasting pair to the other.

We are now in a position to reconsider the initial sentence of this chapter. In the light of our discussion so far, the statement that languages change in time must be seen as a metaphorical way of saying that speakers change their choices, in the event, their choices of phonetic features in the pronunciation of speech sounds. A major tenet of sociolinguistics is that language change, thought by historical linguists to be investigable only by comparing texts from different points in history, can be observed as it happens if we direct our attention at how speakers alter their pronunciation. Shifts in pronunciation have been known since antiquity. In the dialogue *Cratylos* (418 BCE), Plato noted that

> Our ancestors made good use of the sounds of iota and delta, and that is especially true of the women, who are most addicted to preserving old forms of speech. But nowadays people change iota to eta or epsilon, and delta to zeta, thinking they have a grander sound … For instance, in the earliest times they called day *himéra*, others said *heméra*, and now they say *hēméra*.

It is very hard to tell what Plato meant by 'earliest times' and how he knew that the first vowel of the word in question which was pronounced [eː] in his days was formerly pronounced as [i]. Evidently he attributed changes of this sort to speakers' shifting preferences. Unfortunately, we cannot get our Greek 'from the very lips of Plato', as H. G. Wells' Very Young Man quoted at the beginning of this chapter imagined. At the present state of technological development, it is impossible to revisit Plato to ask him. Instead, what we can do is examine present-day speech communities for facts that can support his observations. Sociolinguists have been doing this for some time in order to find out how shifting preferences can be observed and how language change in progress can be studied. An important concept that has been developed as a means to make up for (1) lack of recorded speech data of 'the earliest times' and (2) imperfect time travelling equipment is that of 'apparent time'.[1]

Apparent time and real time

As we have seen in the previous chapter, teenagers and elderly people speak differently. We have interpreted this observation as evidence of social norms favouring the linguistic differentiation of generations at any one time: *Sunt pueri pueri puerilia tractant*, 'children are children, and they do childish things'. And so it should be. However, this need not be the only interpretation of linguistic differences between young and old speakers. These observations may also be indicative of on-going change. This is what is called 'apparent time'. It is *apparent* as opposed to *real* time, since the observed variants were recorded at the same time rather than years or decades apart. Instead, the age difference between the speakers of a sample spread out over three generations is construed as a timespan. For instance, if at the time of data collection one group of speakers were, say, between 15 and 20 and another between 65 and 70, differences between them would be taken to represent linguistic evolution over a half a century. For example, in a study of Spanish in Panama City, Cedergren (1973) found that 60 per cent of subjects aged 20–29, but only 20 per cent of the 60–69 age group, used *ch*-lenition, replacing [č] with [š] in the pronunciation of words like *muchos, muchacha*, etc. All of the data were recorded at the same time, in 1969 (see Figure 5.1). Yet, Cedergren interpreted the difference between the younger and the older group as a trend in the evolution of the Panama vernacular.

Thus, apparent time makes it possible to see temporal variation in data recorded at one time and, in this sense, to bridge the gap between synchronic and diachronic linguistics and get a grip on how language change actually happens. Its theoretical significance lies in establishing a link between language as a mental construct subject to individual choices, and language as a collective product that at all times represents an aggregate of individual choices.

To avoid any misunderstanding, notice that 'on-going change' and 'norms favouring the linguistic differentiation of generations' are not mutually exclusive explanations of the observable differences between younger and older speakers. On the contrary, both are characteristic of what societies

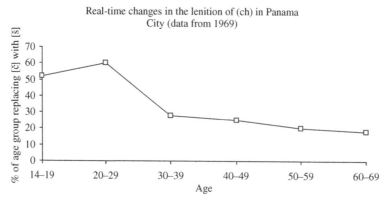

Figure 5.1 Ch-*lenition in Panama, from [č] to [š] (adapted from Cedergren 1973)*

do with their languages. The age differentiation of the community into linguistically recognizable groups which are reproduced generation after generation accounts for 'age-grading', as discussed in the previous chapter. At the same time, individual speakers change the frequencies of choice of variants in a way that can be inferred from 'apparent-time' studies.

The apparent-time concept is predicated on the hypothesis that individuals retain, by and large, the characteristic features of their speech after language acquisition, from childhood through old age. Put differently, speakers are not assumed to change the frequency of their choices of variant forms significantly as they grow older. If, on the basis of this assumption, a certain feature is examined and shows an even distribution of frequency of occurrence across all age groups, this is taken to indicate stability. The conditions of using or not using this feature are stable. French *oui* 'yes' is pronounced by most speakers of French at different frequencies variably as [wi], [wɛj] or [ʰwi], but the coexistence of these forms, though not dialectal, does not indicate on-going change. In the same sense, there are age-stratified variables that do not represent an intermediate state between one and the other, or change in progress. If, on the other hand, an increase or decrease of the frequency of occurrence of a variant is observed among young as compared to old speakers, this is interpreted as indicating change in progress.

The big question, then, is whether the underlying hypothesis of speakers' conservatism can be substantiated. It is rooted in the theory that there is a critical period for language acquisition before adolescence. Over the past several decades, a great deal of psycholinguistic evidence has been accumulated to support the 'critical age' or 'critical period' hypothesis.[2] It claims, among other things, that, due to the physical maturation of the brain, full proficiency will not be accomplished if, for some extraordinary reason, language acquisition is begun after puberty. Yet, it is not so clear what critical age implies for linguistic alterations later in life by speakers with a normal language acquisition history. Certain linguistic subsystems are undoubtedly open to alteration and development throughout most of people's lives – the lexicon, for instance. Post-adolescent adjustments in other subsystems, especially phonology, may be more restricted.

The investigation of age differences at the time of data collection is not suitable to substantiate or refute the hypothesis on which the apparent-time concept rests. Other means must therefore be sought. Since we cannot see past events directly, we must go forward. The crucial test of the hypothesis can only be provided by longitudinal studies conducted in the same community years and decades apart. Not many such studies exist, and the reason why is obvious. In large surveys it is very difficult to avoid data contamination and guarantee undiluted comparability across temporal intervals. For example, the demographic composition of the investigated community may change as a result of migration, war or natural disaster. Ideally, therefore, a follow-up survey must target not just the same community but the same individuals. Their limited lifespan, as that of the researcher, poses another obvious problem, not to mention the legal and ethical aspects of data anonymization that will be discussed in Chapter 14 below. Real-time surveys on a big scale can, therefore, only be carried out by institutions rather than individual researchers.

Standardization

An early example of such a study is a survey on language standardization in Tsuruoka, a town in northern Japan. At intervals of about twenty years, the National Institute for Japanese Language and Linguistics[3] of Japan collected data in 1950, 1971 and 1991.[4] The objective of these surveys was to determine how the Japanese standard language, based on the speech of educated Tokyo residents, spread to rural areas outside the metropolitan centre. The linguistic items investigated included phonetics, syntax and lexicon. We will here review some phonetic changes only. Notice in passing that language change is here conceptualized in terms of an interaction between regional, temporal and social variation, the last being indexed on educational level. As speakers in rural areas follow (educated) speakers in the metropolis, standard forms spread from the centre to the periphery.

In the Tsuruoka study, language standardization was measured on the basis of variant speech sounds. For example, if the word *eki* 'station' was articulated in standard pronunciation with [e-] at the onset, one point was counted, but if it was pronounced in dialectal form with initial [i] or [ɪ] no point was counted. Thus, a higher score indicates a higher degree of

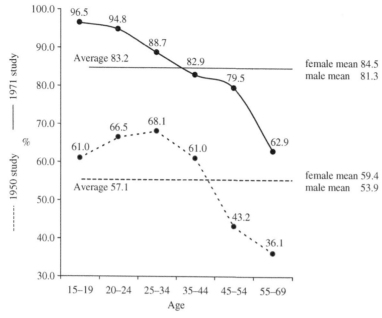

Figure 5.2 *The Tsuruoka study of language standardization in Japan: percentage of standard speech responses with respect to phonetic quality for different age groups (adapted from Nomoto 1975)*

standardization. Scores on some 35 features were taken for all subjects individually, 497 in the 1950 survey, 402 in 1971.

Mean scores were then calculated for both samples and compared. Figure 5.2 shows (1) higher scores in 1971 than in 1950, a clear indication that standardization progressed in the two-decade interval; and (2) age-grading in both samples: younger speakers achieve higher scores than older speakers. Again, this can be interpreted as progressive standardization. However, the curves of the two surveys display one noticeable difference. In 1950, the 25–34 age group had the highest standardization score, while in 1971 the score continues to go up in the younger age groups. Nomoto (1975: 52) offers an explanation in terms of social networks. In 1950, it was this age group whose members were most in contact through business and personal interaction with speakers of the standard speech.

Another interesting feature of the study is that 107 subjects of the 1950 sample were again interviewed in 1971, allowing for some conclusions about modifications by individual speakers over time. Later sociolinguistic studies designed for real-time verification of change in progress had much smaller samples than the Tsuruoka study. For example, Paunonen (1996) revisited a study carried out in Helsinki in the early 1970s investigating morphological change in possessive constructions in colloquial Finnish. Twenty-nine of the original speakers were reinterviewed. In a study of French in Montreal, conducted by Henrietta Cedergren, David Sankoff and Gillian Sankoff, 120 speakers were recorded in 1971. Sixty of the original speakers were recontacted in a follow-up study in 1984 (Thibault and Vincent 1990; Sankoff 2004). Trudgill (1988) partially replicated his 1968 study of Norwich after a fifteen-year interval, contacting some of the original speakers but also adding speakers of the new generation not interviewed in 1968. This study, too, comprehensive and methodologically sound as it is, uses a much smaller sample than the longitudinal study of Tsuruoka. Bailey et al. (1991) compared data from the *Linguistic Atlas of the Gulf States* (Pederson et al. 1986), gathered in the mid 1970s, with data from a survey of Texas, gathered in the late 1980s. But since there were no common informants and the geographical areas covered were not quite the same, this study cannot be considered a restudy of a community. Similarly, some other studies do not represent community patterns, such as Hermann's (1929) pioneering investigation, which tracked individual vernaculars in real time, for several decades in the case of one Yiddish speaker (Prince 1987), some ten years in the case of four speakers of African American Vernacular English (Cukor-Avila 1995). Other studies of change in progress, such as Hansen's (2001) investigation of change in French nasal vowels over fifteen years between 1974 and 1989, are based entirely on cross-sectional data, not including any recontacts.

These and many other studies indicate some shift over speaker lifetimes, while intergenerational change is going on at the same time (Tillery and Bailey 2003). Not surprisingly, the propensity to adopt innovations decreases with speaker age. Difficult questions remain, however. One is whether advancing individual speaker age is an independent variable, or whether it is susceptible to social influence. In other words, are old speakers always equally stable or are there periods when changes progress more rapidly than at other times throughout the whole speech community? Another question has to do with differences in lifestyle. How do social changes – another job, another spouse, retirement, etc. – influence individual speaker choices? Traditional dialectology sidestepped these questions by using as informants only NORM speakers, that is, non-mobile old rural males. Since this is not an option for sociolinguistics, attempts must be made to cope with the multiplicity of factors that are involved in how individuals take part in the social process of language evolution.

The results of the Tsuruoka study suggest that individuals continue modifying their speech well beyond the 'critical age' of puberty until the age of 35 or even older. Findings of this sort do not invalidate the concept of apparent time, but they alert us to the necessity of examining for every variable feature whether it is susceptible to change over individual lifetimes. Labov (1994) has presented a lot of evidence that suggests that individual speakers continue changing their lexicon and discourse-level features more readily and for a longer period of time than phonological features. He argues that, throughout the course of an adult lifetime, 'the phonological categories that underlie the surface variation remain stable' (Labov 1994: 112). At the same time, he concedes that older speakers are 'influenced slightly by the changes taking place around them' (1994: 105). In a study about Montreal English, Boberg (2004) found evidence of post-acquisition adoption of new forms, that is, continuing language change over speakers' lifetimes. It remains an open question whether or to what extent the propensity of older speakers to be influenced by changes in their linguistic environment is itself variable. The Tsuruoka study indicates that phonological features are not immune to change after the crystallization of language in puberty. Let us consider some specific examples in Figures 5.3 to 5.5.

In the dialect of Tsuruoka, the initial palatal fricative [ç] of standard Japanese as in [çiŋɛ] 'beard' has as a variant, the bilabial fricative [ɸ], a very close variant in terms of articulation. Figure 5.3 shows that increasing standardization of this feature correlates with decreasing age. In the youngest age group of the 1971 survey, 100 per cent of the speakers chose the standard pronunciation as compared to 64.3 per cent of the oldest age group. That was an increase of 50 per cent for the oldest group and almost 40 per cent of the youngest group over the 1950 survey. Even a comparison between the youngest age group of the 1950 data and the oldest age group of the 1971 data reveals an increase of standard forms.

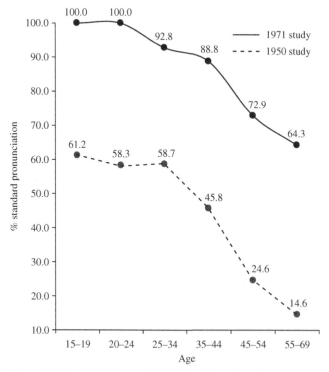

Figure 5.3 *Non-labialization of the dialect form: from [ɸiŋɛ] to [çiŋɛ] 'beard' (adapted from Nomoto 1975)*

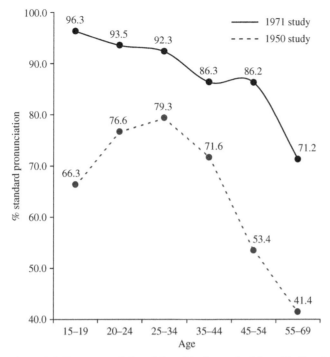

Figure 5.4 *Devoicing: dialectal form [d, ţ], standard form [t], [hatɔ] 'pigeon'*
(adapted from Nomoto 1975)

A similar tendency, though not always the same extent of increase in the standard form, was observed for most other dialectal variants, for instance the voiced or semi-voiced pronunciation of dental and alveolar plosives, as in *hato* 'pigeon', Figure 5.4. That the 25–34 age group is at the forefront of standardization is particularly obvious here.

In the dialect, there is prenasalization of the voiced consonants [b,d,z] in postvocalic position, as in *obi* 'sash' which is [ɔbi] in standard pronunciation, but [ɔ̃bi] in the dialect. With regard to this feature, too, speakers changed their choices very noticeably over the two decades between the first and the second survey (Figure 5.5). Another twenty years later, standard pronunciation had advanced further across all age groups, although pitch accent was still markedly different from the standard. The measurable statistical difference between standard and dialectal accent was as wide in 1991 as that between standard and dialectal phonetics in 1950 (F. Inoue 1997). This suggests a hierarchy of structural levels in terms of adaptability: lexical and morphological changes are more accessible to speakers' choice than phonetic segments and features, and the latter are in turn easier to change than pitch accent and other suprasegmental features of speech. The standardization of accent, F. Inoue (1997: 89) predicts, will trail segmental phonetic standardization with a delay of forty years or more.

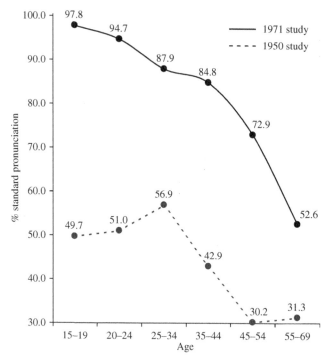

Figure 5.5 *Non-nasalization: dialectal form [~b], standard form [b], [ɔbi]*
'sash' (adapted from Nomoto 1975)

The Tsuruoka study documents language standardization, a process which involves the readjustment of speakers' choices over time. It is an excellent example of socially motivated change in language behaviour, the language system of individual speakers and, by consequence, that of the speech community. Age-grading and lifetime changes combine in the process. The phonetic changes effectuated in the course of standardization can be explained, in large measure, in terms of minute adjustments of the articulation movements. Why and under what circumstances they are brought about, only an examination of the social forces favouring standardization can reveal.

In the European context, language standardization has been associated with industrialization, compulsory education, and mass media. The retreat of traditional dialects and dialect levelling has long been observed in many speech communities (Ammon 1979; Auer and Hinskens 1996). However, it has become increasingly obvious that complete homogenization is not the inevitable outcome. While regional variation is lost, new dialects evolve in large urban centres. For English, Trudgill (2001) describes a complex interaction between convergence and divergence.[5] The mass media seem to push lexical convergence, but accents continue to function as regional markers of speaker identity, showing little sign of weakening. On the international plane, they are becoming less similar rather than more similar. Another factor that prevents diminishing regional diversity from leading to total phonological convergence is the changing impact of class differentiation on the prestige norm. Pedersen's (2003) observations about Danish capture a trend observed in other European languages as well.

> What happens nowadays is not only, or not so much, standardization as an urbanization or metropolization. There was a close relationship between Copenhagen speech and the spoken standard, but it used to be High Copenhagen, that is, the speech of the educated middle class ... Now Low Copenhagen speech, or at least certain features of Low Copenhagen speech, have been included in young people's perception of what standard Danish is.   (Pedersen 2003: 25)

Similar developments have been observed since the early 1980s in England where a large new dialect region centred on London has been formed, superseding smaller traditional dialects. This new variety which has become known as 'Estuary English' combines features of RP with features of Cockney, such as prevocalic *t*-glottalling, [ðæʔˮɪz], *that is*. *T*-glottalling once was a stigmatized London working-class variant, but has spread both geographically and socially, becoming more acceptable in middle-class speech. As Fabricius (2000) has demonstrated, *t*-glottalling is still avoided in formal speech. However, along with other features such as vocalization of postconsonantal *l*, as in [ˮdženʔli], *gently*, it has become a characteristic of Estuary English which, because it is less indexed to social class than RP, has been hailed as 'the new Standard English' (Coggle 1993). The socially upward diffusion of *t*-glottalling exemplifies Labov's generalization that 'changes from above are introduced by the dominant social class, often with full public awareness [whereas] changes from below are systematic changes that appear first in the vernacular' (1994: 78). Language change, then, is not propelled evenly in all its facets, and equally by all members of the speech community. And it doesn't stop. In more recent developments of the Inner City of London, some observers see Estuary English being superseded by Multicultural London English (Kerswill and Trudgill 2005).

Who drives change?

Standardization is brought about by speakers adjusting their speech to a perceived prestige norm. It is one of several forces effective in language change. The actual choices leading to convergence on a standard are made by individuals. These choices are not random but lean in a particular direction, thus adding up to form what amount to collective choices. This is what the tenet that language is a social fact means in specific terms. Just like variation along dimensions of social class and spatial extension, variation along the temporal dimension reveals its patterns only in representative samples. The crucial question, as one pioneer in the study of linguistic choice put it, is this:

> A student of social factors in the choice of linguistic variants would wish to know for a fairly large stratified sample of a speech community how often members of a given sub-group used a sizable sample of series of socially significant variants, and for at least some of the sub-groups one would want to know how these frequencies of choice of variants changed under different situations and in the presence of conversants of different social status and personal relationship.   (Fischer 1958: 53)

Many speakers' awareness of their own shifting choices has been shown by numerous sociolinguistic studies to be unreliable, especially concerning pronunciation. More often than not they are not aware that they do not act alone but in accord with others. Incremental adaptation is an instance of cooperative behaviour and mutual adjustment. However, as the notion of standardization suggests, shifting choices do not necessarily happen simultaneously in all sections of society. Who then leads the way?

The idea that language change is not driven evenly by both sexes has been around since antiquity. Plato's above-quoted remark that 'women are most addicted to preserving old forms of speech' testifies to his belief that speaker-sex played a role in language change. In modern times, this idea has inspired a great deal of research, and Plato's observation of a sex-factor in language change has been corroborated dozens of times, though not necessarily in the sense that women stick to old forms. In the Tsuruoka study discussed above, gender consistently turned out to be a significant determinant of variant choice. Women led men in standardization in 1950, 1971 and again in 1991, although men had caught up a bit in the second survey. These findings contradict Plato's observation of female speakers being more conservative than their male counterparts. They are in agreement, however, with many sociolinguistic studies in Western countries that have shown women to lead change. Changes led by men are few and geographically isolated (Labov 1990). But, once again, linguistic choices defy simple explanations, for women not only are more innovative, but, much as Plato observed, also tend to uphold established prestige forms more than men. (See p. 48, above.) Various explanations have been offered for these seemingly contradictory findings. Most influentially, Labov (1966) suggested that women, striving for social advance, use hypercorrect forms going beyond the norms expected of their class. And Trudgill (1984) saw the preference for prestige forms by women as a linguistic expression of insecurity.

Chambers (1995) has reviewed these explanations and proposed an alternative. Rejecting earlier accounts that see women's standard adherence as a strategy they adopt to compensate for lack of power and social recognition, he proposes to resolve the apparent contradiction – innovative and conservative – by emphasizing female verbal superiority. Women, he argues, control a wider range of linguistic variants and are thus superior in terms of their sociolinguistic competence. They have also been shown to surpass men in fluency, listening comprehension, speaking, vocabulary, sentence complexity and spelling. Males are more likely to have reading disabilities and other dyslexic problems. Even aphasic disorders disfavour men. Female superior sociolinguistic skills, Chambers (1995: 132) argues, are part of a wider picture. Against this background, the fact that women prefer prestige forms must be reevaluated. Rather than following the norm, women play a leading role in establishing, maintaining and recreating it. Females tend to have more diverse social networks and are hence exposed to a greater variety of dialects.

In this connection, another known aspect of female speech behaviour has been noted by Woods (1997). Thanks to their cooperative and listener-oriented discourse style, women tend to accommodate to their interlocutors and are open to adopting phonological features from other variants which they then introduce to their primary reference group. A wider network and an accommodating style thus make them leading actors of change.

Like social class and age, speaker-sex is one of the basic social variables that research about variation and change takes into account. As pointed out repeatedly here and as others have argued (e.g. Croft 2000), actual utterances are where language change happens. Thus, linguistic differences between people belonging to higher and lower strata of society, between the young and the old, and between men and women can be observed directly on the individual level and substantiated by statistical sampling. Much sociolinguistic work has shown that these three variables affect language behaviour and hence change. However, so far sociolinguistic research has ignored population dynamics that affect the population structure, assuming stable age cohorts and sex ratios within and across speech communities. On the basis of this assumption, potentially interesting questions concerning language change have to remain unasked. For example, if youths' speech behaviour has a stronger influence on language change than that of their elders, does this imply that a speech community's age composition is a factor, for example to the effect that language change in societies with a high proportion of young people, as is typical of developing countries such as Uganda (Figure 5.6), is faster than in advanced industrial societies characterized by a high proportion of old people, such as Italy (Figure 5.7)? Population ageing is one of the mega-trends of the present age. Given that social variables impinge upon language change, it would be counterintuitive that it should have no effect on language change. Italy's median age – 44.3 years – is three times that of Uganda's – 15.0 years.[6] As the two graphs reveal, many fewer Ugandans than Italians live to exercise an influence on their language in old age. What is more, population ageing brings about a shift in the sex ratio, as women survive men and the disparity increases with overall life expectancy gains. Figure 5.7 shows that in Italy, in the oldest age

Uganda's population composition

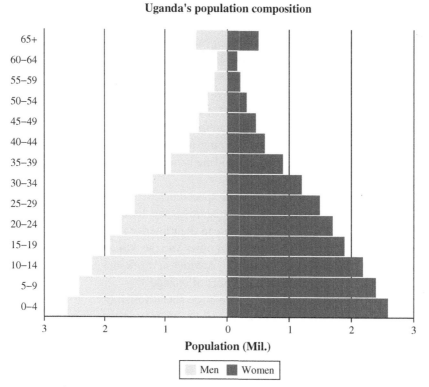

Population (Mil.)

Figure 5.6 *Uganda's population composition 2010 (Data: UN Population Division)*

cohort women outnumber men by a wide margin, whereas in the younger cohorts the sex ratio is balanced.

Another demographic variable to note is life expectancy. In the course of the twentieth century, the industrialized world experienced unprecedented lifespan expansions. Looking just at our two examples, Italy's life expectancy at birth is 82 years (in 2012), compared with Uganda's of 52 years. Among other things this means that the age span for communicating across generations is more than one third longer in Italy than in Uganda. It is also much longer in Italy today than it was in the nineteenth century when it was on a par with Uganda's life expectancy today. What are the implications of these population developments for language change? Once again it seems unlikely that there shouldn't be any. However, all we can say is that they are worth studying as an important supplement to age and gender, the variables that have been in the foreground of sociolinguistic research about language change. Any investigation of the influence of population dynamics, for instance whether the proportion of old speakers in a community has an effect on the rate of change, would require very large samples allowing for long-term comparisons spanning several generations. Clearly, the apparent time method is inapplicable, since it is

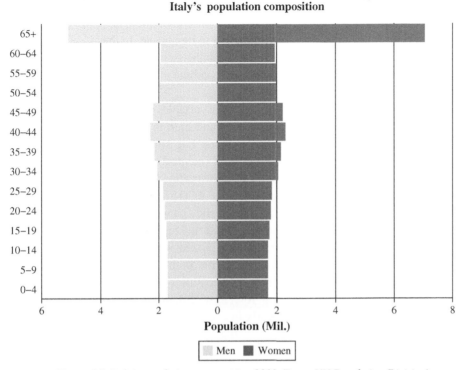

Figure 5.7 *Italy's population composition 2010 (Data: UN Population Division)*

insensitive to population structure. The rate of linguistic change depends on many factors, such as the structure and density of social networks, language contact, migration, bilingualism, schooling, language ideology and community size. The community's age structure is yet another variable that comes into play and must be studied if we want to arrive at generalizations about linguistic change that are valid beyond the confines of a particular community. How changes in the population structure influence linguistic change is too early to tell, but it is good to know that there are still fields to be ploughed.

There are some intriguing parallels between language evolution and population dynamics deserving to be investigated. Demographic change, like language change, is brought about by individual behaviour, although a single utterance does not noticeably change a language and a single birth or death does not alter the population structure. Few people would concede that they have as many children as they do because they behave as is expected or follow a trend. Having a child is a very personal decision in every single case. Yet, within less than half a century, the number of children per family in the UK dropped by more than 10 per cent, from 2.0 in the 1970s to 1.7 in 2010. Entirely a matter of individual choice though nowadays it is, people's reproductive behaviour is influenced by the social conditions in which they live. Similarly, people's individual language behaviour is subject to various external influences, for example when they move to a different region, and to social developments, new technologies, responding to trends, etc. In the case of both demographic and linguistic change, the challenge is to explain how individual choices are socially conditioned and combine to form non-random collective alterations in turn.

Two things remain to be said about the demographic variables discussed above. One is that the differences between women and men in terms of language skills and linguistic change are noticeable but slight. They should not be overrated, although they seem to hold the most promising answer to the question 'Who drives change?' In industrialized countries they should be studied in the context of population ageing. The other point is that, although the propensity to bring about linguistic change has been demonstrated to be yet another difference between male and female speech behaviour, generalizations that go beyond industrialized societies are unwarrantable because too little is known about earlier points in history and about the division of linguistic labour in other cultures. In Western societies, however, women play a leading role in safeguarding social norms, including linguistic ones. This is clearly in evidence in yet another area of linguistic choice to which we turn in the next chapter, verbal politeness.

Conclusion

Language change is a complex process. Why it happens, how it happens, who propels it and at what rate it proceeds are the important questions that sociolinguistics strives to answer in order to understand how societies keep their language(s) functional as they transmit them from one generation to the next. The research reviewed in this chapter makes it clear that language should be conceptualized as an event rather than an object or natural organism governed entirely by its own inherent structural properties and regularities that, if properly recognized, suffice to explain the changes it undergoes in the course of time. An important lesson of sociolinguistics is that these structural properties and regularities are not shielded off from the influence of external forces, notably various social developments, as well as speakers' age, sex, social class, education and media exposure. The extent to which a community's age structure, life expectancy and sex ratio affect language change is yet to be established. In the case of declining languages that are spoken by elderly speakers only, the influence of demographic variables is obvious. By contrast, in investigations of language change in speech communities unthreatened by extinction these demographic variables have not generally been accorded much attention. In the age of population ageing this is a gap to be filled.

Questions for discussion

(1)   Can you think of characteristics in the pronunciation of your grandparents or other elderly people you know that you consider out of date and would not expect to use yourself? What makes them out of date?

(2)   Discuss the notion of 'apparent time' and its significance for the study of on-going linguistic change.

(3)   In a study of Spanish in Panama City, Cedergren (1973) found that 60 per cent of subjects aged 20–29, but only 20 per cent of the 60–69 age group, used *ch*-lenition, replacing [č] with [š] in the pronunciation of words like *muchos*. How do you interpret this observation?

(4)   Can you think of reasons why accentual features change more slowly than phonetic ones?

(5)   Women are more innovative than men in their speech and, at the same time, more conservative in the sense that they choose prestige forms more often than men. Is this inconsistent?

Notes

1. The apparent-time construct is of central significance to variationist sociolinguistics. It was first introduced by William Labov (1963) as a methodological tool to track the progress of linguistic changes. Its theoretical implications have been widely discussed in the literature since. See, for example, Labov (1981), Bailey et al. (1991), Bailey (2002), Sankoff (2004).

2. The critical age hypothesis for language acquisition was first proposed by Lenneberg (1967), for a good overview and discussion see Hurford (1991).

3. Formerly called National Language Research Institute: www.ninjal.ac.jp/english/

4. The documentation of this research is mostly in Japanese. In the English language, results of the first two surveys are reported in Nomoto (1975) and compared with those of the third survey in F. Inoue (1997).

5. The emergence of an American standard is described at length in Bonfiglio (2002).

6. The median age divides the population evenly into two halves, one comprising all people older than it, the other younger.

Useful online resources

The British Library site Sounds Familiar? offers audio samples of how pronunciation varied across the UK in the 1950s, as well as samples of lexical and grammatical change: www.bl.uk/learning/langlit/sounds/changing-voices/phonological-change/

A site by the Center for History and New Media at George Mason University maintains The Speech Accent Archive with many samples of English accents as well as other languages: http://accent.gmu.edu/

The Telsur Project at the Linguistics Laboratory, University of Pennsylvania, documents linguistic changes in progress in North American English: www.ling.upenn.edu/phono_atlas/home.html

The International Corpus of English is a joint project by twenty-four research teams devoted to the documentation of varieties of English around the world: http://ice-corpora.net/ice/soundaus.htm

Further reading

Bailey, Guy. 2002. Real and apparent time. In J.K. Chambers, Peter Trudgill and Natalie Schilling-Estes (eds.), *The Handbook of Language Variation and Change.* Oxford: Blackwell, 312–32.

Gregory, Gerry. 2011. Teaching and learning about language Change (Part one). *Changing English: Studies in Culture & Education* **18**(1): 3–15.

Inoue, Fumio. 1997. S-shaped curves of language standardization. *Issues and Methods in Dialectology* **8**: 79–93.

Labov, William. 1994. *Principles of Linguistic Change,* vol. I: *Internal Factors.* Oxford: Blackwell, chapters 3, 4.

Thibault, Pierette. 2004. Cross-sectional and longitudinal studies in sociolinguistics. In Ulrich Ammon, Norbert Dittmar and Klaus Mattheier (eds.), *Sociolinguistics, Soziolinguistik: An International Handbook of the Science of Language and Society,* 2nd edn. Berlin and New York: Walter de Gruyter.

6 Politeness: cultural dimensions of linguistic choice

Politeness is but a strategy for avoiding that others feel despised.

John Locke

Learn politeness from the impolite.

Ali ibn Abu Talib (600–661 CE)

Outline of the chapter

Social interaction relies on language not just as a means of communicating information, but also for establishing rapport between speakers. To this end societies have developed various conventions for the linguistic expression of politeness. This chapter first explains the difference between every-day and technical notions of politeness and then introduces theoretical concepts for its analysis. It shows that the necessity to differentiate speech behaviour in terms of politeness arises from the need to cooperate under conditions of inequality. The Cooperative Principle of conversation serves as a point of departure, and the concept of 'face' is adduced as an analytic tool for distinguishing two kinds of politeness strategies, positive face and negative face. Further, it is demonstrated how the markedness theory can explain speakers' choices of more or less polite expressions. The question of whether politeness is a feature that characterizes language or speech behaviour is discussed, and it is argued that, while languages differ in regards to how strongly they encode politeness distinctions, the politeness level of every speech act depends on speakers' choices from the grammatical, lexical and stylistic means afforded by the language. Examples from many different languages illustrate the complexity and variety of linguistic politeness.

Key terms: cooperation, face, inequality, distinction, indirectness, markedness, honorifics

Basic concepts

Verbal communication is not limited to the exchange of information but includes, as one of its major functions, the shaping of interpersonal relationships. In making their linguistic choices, speakers take this function into account. In order to adjust their speech behaviour to the communicative purposes at hand, they monitor their speech. Among the many choices they make in conversation, the politeness level of their utterances is one of the more conspicuous, and it is one where social constraints are most keenly felt. Socially adequate behaviour depends on the observance of general principles and specific norms which, in the broadest sense, are subsumed under the concept of politeness. Various definitions of the notion of politeness have been proposed, and over the past several decades a large body of literature on politeness has been produced.[1] Because of its ubiquity in language use, it is difficult to delimit the phenomena that should be dealt with in the empirical investigation of politeness. Suffice it for present purposes to describe politeness as the practice of organizing linguistic action so that it is seen as inoffensive and conforming to current social expectations regarding the trouble-free management of communication. From this point of view, politeness appears not as decorum added to what really matters (the propositional content of an utterance), but rather as fundamental to social life.

Common sense and theory

A distinction to be made at the outset is between (1) a common-sense notion of politeness and (2) a theoretical one. (1) refers to the assessment of behaviour in everyday life by members of the speech community in question on the basis of that community's social values. It is thus an emic and normative notion which derives its meaning from a particular socio-cultural system. Grasping this notion, however implicitly, is a prerequisite for competent behaviour in that community. By contrast, (2) is concerned with the general conditions and the behavioural and linguistic means of realizing politeness. A theoretical notion of politeness must strive to be culturally neutral and suitable to uncover universal mechanisms of linguistic politeness differentiation. It is a non-normative theoretical construct designed to compare various standards used in different societies for the assessment of speech behaviour; and it is etic in that it seeks abstractions that make theoretically well-founded comparisons possible. Sociolinguistic politeness research depends on a clear differentiation of (1) and (2) on the part of the researcher who, at the same time, must be careful not to cut off theory (2) from empiricity (1) or conduct empirical investigation without theoretical motivation.

Cooperation and face

Notice, however, that any theoretical notion of politeness has to come to terms with the fact that every society operates a normative notion of politeness. Leech (1983) offers a general approach to the analysis of politeness, building on the Cooperative Principle which, according to philosopher of language Paul Grice (1975), is the foundation of all conversation. It assumes that people engaging in natural conversation are cooperative and assume each other to be cooperative. The Politeness Principle proposed by Leech is likewise a basic operating principle of all verbal interaction. Leech suggests a number of maxims such as the Tact Maxim, the Generosity Maxim and the Modesty Maxim, which are applied in accordance with the Politeness Principle. These maxims govern speech behaviour serving the ultimate goal of 'establishing and maintaining comity' (Leech 1983: 104).

Much like Leech, Brown and Levinson (1987) take the Cooperative Principle as their point of departure. Their influential model of politeness is centred upon two primitives, rationality and face. Speakers are endowed with reason to make informed decisions in pursuit of their best interest, and with a social persona. Face, in Brown and Levinson's terminology, has a negative aspect and a positive one. Negative face is the desire to be unconstrained by others in one's actions, and positive face is the desire to be appreciated and accepted by others. Negative face has been said to be characteristic of Western cultures, whereas Asian cultures are more inclined towards positive face. However, other distinctions, such as 'personal' vs. 'interpersonal' face and 'connection' vs. 'separation' face have been suggested in order to emphasize that self-centred and other-centred notions of politeness are not mutually exclusive, but tendencies that different cultures accentuate to a greater or lesser extent. Terkourafi (2012) presents a detailed overview of the theoretical discussion surrounding these concepts (see also Ogierman (2009). However framed, balancing the desire to be unconstrained but also respected by others while taking into account in one's social actions that every interactant has negative and positive face needs is the art of politeness, that is, the art of not committing face-threatening acts and of protecting oneself against such acts. It is an intricate art because every society is built on inequality. *Do unto all men as you would they should do unto you* is a pious maxim, perhaps, but it is one that assumes paradise and no social differentiation along the common dimensions of sex, age, class, power and wealth which find expression not least in polite behaviour. As a matter of fact, the biblical directive is the very opposite of a politeness maxim. There is no politeness in paradise, because no face-threatening acts are committed there; no mitigation strategies and repairs are needed to reaffirm the social order that for a moment may have seemed to be put at risk by an ill-considered, disrespectful or otherwise offensive remark. In paradise no distinctions are made. Human society, however, is built on difference, and politeness is the modus operandi to make it sufferable. Picard (1998: 79), therefore, identifies distinction as one of the basic principles guiding polite behaviour.[2] Politeness is the evolutionary response to inequality. Gestures of submission and compliance, status assertion and recognition are effective means of social organization and conflict avoidance in the animal kingdom and must be considered as old a part of our heritage as language.

Politeness is socially contingent. Hence the linguistic expression of politeness is an area where the social functions of language are clearly in evidence. Politeness is inextricably linked with social differentiation, with making the appropriate choices which are not the same for all interlocutors and all situations. This raises the question of whether politeness belongs to language or to language use.

Speakers and expressions

Another important distinction thus concerns the politeness of speakers and that of expressions. In every language that has been studied, expressions vary along a politeness scale, and speakers can be more or less polite. How do these two aspects of politeness interrelate? Some expressions seem to be inherently more polite than others. For example,

(3) Do I hear the phone ringing?

is more polite than

(4) Answer the phone!

But it is not difficult to think of situations where the actual utterance of (3) is not considered polite or (4) as impolite. Fraser (1990), therefore, argues that being polite is attributable not to language on the basis of inherent properties of expressions, but only to speakers in specific speech situations. Clearly, politeness is always a dimension of dialogic contextualized speech, if only because speakers cannot avoid addressing each other. To this end they have to choose terms that are indicative of, and define, a social relationship. What counts as impolite said in a formal setting to a superior may pass unnoticed in relaxed conversations among friends. For instance, permissive *may* as in (5) is polite when offering something to a child, but inappropriate when used to someone who is in a position of authority over the speaker.

(5) You may go outside now.

It is with respect to specific conditions that speakers and their utterances are perceived and assessed as polite, vulgar, disrespectful, ill-mannered, unseemly or rude. Yet, there are expressions that, at a given point in history, are regarded as impolite under all circumstances, such as cuss words, and others that belong to a polite register. Expressions are graded for politeness in all speech communities, but the normative criteria for their employment are not the same. It has also been argued that language systems are differentially polite, depending on the richness and fine grading of the means specialized for politeness marking (Coulmas 1992a).

As we shall see below, the interrelationship between speaker politeness and expression politeness is not the same for all languages and speech communities. It is hard to be polite if you lack the polite register of speech, but in some languages this is harder than in others, because some languages provide richer lexical and grammatical encoding of politeness than others. This makes verbal politeness an important concern of sociolinguistics, because in order to make adequate choices speakers must bring together the linguistic means and the social norms of appropriate conduct.

Politeness and social structure

Politeness conventions are often said to reflect social structure. However, plausible as this argument would seem in the abstract, it is hard to substantiate concretely. The tenets of linguistic relativism and determinism discussed in Chapter 3 are usually evoked in this connection, but little empirical corroboration has been produced. There are two principal reasons for this. One is that social change and linguistic change do not happen in synchrony. The other has to do with the all-pervading nature of politeness phenomena in language. Individual politeness markers such as personal pronouns can be investigated, but they form just a small subset of the linguistic means employed for the expression of politeness.

For example, what does the fact that in present-day English there is just one pronominal form of address say about the structure of English-speaking societies? For one thing, there are enough significant differences in terms of distribution of wealth and power between English-speaking societies to foil any generalizations. And it would be hard to argue that, say, British society is more egalitarian than the Dutch, French, German, Italian and Greek societies because Dutch, French, German, Italian and Greek force their speakers to make a choice between two pronominal forms of address, one intimate and informal, and one respectful and formal (Table 6.1).

What choice of pronouns in one language can accomplish for the construction of social relationships can be done by other means in other languages. In contradistinction to most European languages, English is not socially indexical in the second-person pronoun of address (disregarding the quaint *thou* and *thee* of Quaker Plain Speech (Birch 1995)). Does that mean that respect, intimacy, social distance and power differential cannot be expressed in English? Clearly not. But social relations are usually expressed in English by other, less overtly and systematically encoded devices. This brings us back to the question of whether politeness is part of language or language use.

Table 6.1 *Pronominal address*

English	Dutch	French	German	Italian	Greek
	je	tu	du	tu	εσύ [esi]
you	u	vous	Sie	lei	εσεῖς [esis]

Table 6.2 *Vietnamese terms of self-reference and address*

	1st person	2nd person
child to father	con	bố', ba
child to mother	con	mẹ, má
father to child	bố', ba	con
mother to child	mẹ, má	con
younger sibling to elder brother	em	anh
younger sibling to elder sister	em	chi
elder brother to younger sibling	anh	em
elder sister to younger sibling	chị	em

History and metaphor

The historicity of language implies among other things that many words have multiple meanings, their use having been extended and transferred in various ways.[3] It is not rare that entire sets of terms have both a literal and a metaphorical meaning. Kinship terms are a good example. In Vietnamese, kinship terminology provides the main source of address and reference terms inside and outside the family. Where English uses first-, second- and third-person pronouns, Vietnamese uses kin terms. Such a classificatory use of kinship terms takes family relations as the paradigm of social relations, interpreting relative age and generational differences as social distance and hierarchy. Self-reference and address, in addition to identifying speaker and addressee, thus also include social deixis defining the relationship between the two. This implies that there are several terms both for first person and second person, some of which are given in Table 6.2.

In this system, choice of terms of address and self-reference is determined by the family relationship and, by extension, the social relationship between speaker and addressee. Accordingly, several other terms in addition to those included in Table 6.2 are used, such as *ông* 'grandfather' and *bà* 'grandmother'. Outside the family they are used irrespective of speaker's and addressee's actual age and age difference. A young female speaker can call a man in his twenties *ông* which implies social distance, not kinship or generational distance. As both of them become acquainted, she may switch to *anh*, literally 'elder brother'. In this way person deixis is inextricably linked with social deixis. It is impossible to say *I* and *you* in Vietnamese without at the same time saying that 'I relate to you' as a younger sibling to an older brother, as a mother to a child, as a daughter-in-law to a father-in-law or in any other way deemed socially relevant. In the system ascending and descending generations are equated with status and respect. Calling one's addressee *cuông* 'great-grandfather' is thus more respectful than simply *ông* 'grandfather'. To interpret this usage as an outgrowth of the seniority principle would not seem farfetched; whether it is indicative of the actual importance of seniority in present-day Vietnamese society is, however, a different question.

In many ways Vietnamese kin terms have functions similar to those of personal pronouns in European languages, but they are not usually called pronouns because unlike pronouns they have a lexical meaning that is not just etymological but, thanks to the intra-family usage of these terms, present in the speaker's mind.[4] How and when these terms began to be used in a figurative sense is a question for historical linguists to answer.[5] The generalized use of kinship terms for reference and address suggests an important role of the family for social organization, but it would be rash to draw any conclusions from present-day usage about the structure of Vietnamese society. Family structures change. Nuclearization, that is, the reduction of the extended family including non-kin to the nuclear family, is a common concomitant of modernization. It is not clear that linguistic usage will follow suit, for the use of kin terms for non-kin does not represent a creative figure of speech but a conventionalized metaphor which is essentially idiomatic and without obvious alternative.[6]

Tôi originally meant 'subject of the king'. The word is still used although Vietnam has had no king for many decades. It is a term for 'I, me' suitable for expressing modesty. Its choice, like that of other forms of self-reference and address, is determined by the relative status of the speaker vis-á-vis the addressee. Once again, it is not the term itself that is polite or less so, but its selection in a given situation. Its appropriate, socially sanctioned choice is no more marked than *I* and *you* in English.

Marked and unmarked

In each society there is a normal linguistic usage which allows social actors the expression of modesty, respect, deference, solidarity, authority and formality in an uncomplicated way. To follow this usage makes for unmarked utterances. Marked utterances are conspicuous, out of the ordinary with respect to a certain point of reference or prototype. 'Marked' and 'unmarked' are technical terms defined within the framework of markedness theory. This theory assumes a general human capacity to perceive people, objects, actions and events as conforming with, or deviating from, a paradigmatic measure. If we describe a person as intelligent, short or rude, a category of intelligence, height and politeness is implied. This is not necessarily an average, because not all qualities can reasonably be measured on a numerical scale. Rather, it is what counts as typical and representative of a kind.

Markedness was first recognized as an important property of language early in the twentieth century by Roman Jakobson. Following in his footsteps, Joseph Greenberg (1963) noted that categories describable in terms of pairs of polar adjectives – *long and short* – or nouns – *sheep* and *ram* – include an 'unmarked' member which refers to the whole category as well as to a subcategory of that phenomenon, and a 'marked' member which refers to a subcategory only. Thus an oblong object is long, rather than short, and has a length, rather than a shortness, because *long* is the unmarked term which covers both the entire dimension and one of the extremes, whereas *short* refers to 'shorter than normal' only. Similarly, *sheep* refers to animals of either sex and is thus more inclusive than *ram* which is reserved for male members of the species. *Ram* is the marked term, *sheep* the unmarked one. The contrast 'marked/unmarked' pervades all formal, grammatical and lexical systems and is highly relevant to human behaviour. It thus provides an important link between language and its use. Being a competent member of a speech community means to have a sense of what kind of language behaviour is marked and unmarked relative to everyday situations.

'Marked' does not mean ill-formed, ungrammatical, deviant, wrong, immoral, illegal or impossible; and it does not mean excellent, striking or grand. Marked can be positive or negative. In certain realms of human action, the marked is intended. The fine arts, fashion, dramatic performance, even lecturing are good examples of activities where departure from the unmarked, and hence unremarkable, case is appreciated. On the other hand, marked behaviour patterns that are deemed pathological, illicit or otherwise scandalous are not desirable. The marked/unmarked contrast is relative rather than absolute, indexed to epoch, culture and situation.

In the late fifteenth century, *thou* and *you* were both available for addressing a single person. When used to address children, close friends and servants, *thou* was unmarked, but in the subsequent centuries it was chosen ever less frequently and thus became increasingly marked except in certain dialects, in religious contexts and in the speech of Quakers.

> The early Friends were not using a new dialect of English; rather, they were deliberately ignoring or breaking the linguistic conventions of the time. They addressed social equals and superiors in urban public places with the intimate or contemptuous lower-class rural *thou*, which must have been the linguistic equivalent of spitting in their addressee's face.   (Birch 1995: 41)

A marked choice, indeed. Today, *thou* would be marked under any circumstances, though not in the same way, since few speakers have a sense of its one-time condescending and insulting potential. It would be marked as cranky and weird.

Markedness theory is a valuable analytic tool for understanding the workings of politeness devices in linguistic interaction. Every unmarked choice functions as an affirmation of the existing social order, and every marked choice is a potential threat to it. The very fact that linguistic choices are perceived as either marked or unmarked protects the integrity of both linguistic and social structures and hence their functionality. Society favours unmarked behaviour which in the present context means polite to the extent deemed appropriate. One can, of course, make marked choices, but at a risk. Depending on the kind and degree of digression, marked choices face sanctions ranging from a raised eyebrow to prosecution.

On occasion, marked choices can cost dearly. The case was reported of a German market vendor who addressed everybody 'as she addressed her Lord', with the intimate *du*, the familiar form of 'you', rather than *Sie*, the unmarked term for unacquainted adults. A policeman took offence and, since she was non-compliant with his request to be addressed with *Sie*, he filed a complaint of misdemeanour. The policeman prevailed; the vendor had to pay a fine. The justice was very specific in his verdict: an uninvited *du* was an infringement of personal rights (Wunderlich 1980: 280).

An even more dramatic event occurred in Japan where a company employee was so enraged at his younger colleague's calling him 'X-*kun*' instead of using the more respectful form 'X-*san*' that (under the influence of alcohol) he smashed his colleague's head against a wall, with lethal consequences (Coulmas 1992a: 299). These incidents are exceptional, to be sure. But precisely because of this, they underscore the effectiveness of the marked/unmarked contrast in calibrating politeness levels in speech. Thus, the general question to ask with respect to terms of address is: which is the unmarked form?

What is marked and unmarked varies from one society to another. 'Politeness' itself is a term which betrays its sociohistorical origin, as do cognate terms such as 'courtesy', 'chivalry' and 'civility'.[7] However, the modulation of language behaviour in terms of social appropriateness and the assessment of every speech act on its markedness relative to the speech situation are universal aspects of the social nature of language. The extent to which politeness devices are overtly encoded in the language is variable, however.

Encoding

English has been called 'the most weakly socially encoded European language' (Mühlhäusler and Harré 1990: 134) because its simple tripartite personal pronoun system represents no social distinctions, and other grammatical means for this purpose are also poorly developed. French is a bit more refined. The systematic employment of the second-person-singular pronoun *tu* and the second-person-plural pronoun *vous* for singular address has served as a model for other European languages. The differentiation of two pronominal forms of address looks like a small detail, but it has many consequences. The pronouns, though forming a self-contained subsystem, have a bearing on the grammar because European languages have number and gender agreement. Accordingly, an action predicated on *tu* requires a singular verb ending, *vous* a plural one. Coupled with the convention that associates the plural pronoun with higher status, the grammar of pronouns thus encodes social distinctions.

When we look at languages further afield, the differences between English and other European languages seem insignificant. As compared to several Asian languages in particular, no European language encodes much social distinction. Chinese, Javanese, Japanese, Korean, Madurese, Thai and Vietnamese, among others, incorporate social information on a quite different level.[8] The linguistic means provided to this end are known as 'honorifics'. Like the *tu/vous* distinction, honorifics index social relations of speaker, addressee and referent, but in a much more elaborate way.

In languages that have honorifics, the unmarked choice of words is dependent on relative status, rank, office, generation, sex and gender, formality and a network of relationships which ideally should be known to speaker and addressee and, in the event that it is not, must be explored at the beginning of a conversation and concluded from other cues, such as dress and demeanour. For instance, Thai has at least eight terms for self-reference which speakers select variably according to sex, relative status level and formality of situation. The social hierarchy as schematically displayed in Figure 6.1 is a strong determinant of choice of expression.

In the event, social hierarchy bears on language use not just in terms of stylistic adjustments but by forcing speakers to choose between the options

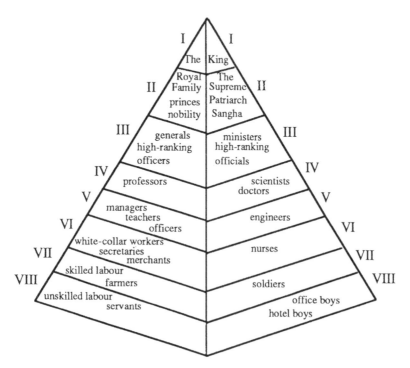

Figure 6.1 *The hierarchy of Thai society (Kummer 1992: 330)*

encoded in the language. Honorifics are not frills that can be dispensed with at will, because there are no encounters that take place in a social vacuum. Accordingly, there is no default mode that is neutral with regard to honorifics. Speaking without honorifics is incompetent or childish at best, and otherwise an affront to convention and social order.

Consideration must also be given to the pragmatic as distinct from the social functions of honorifics. For instance, Japanese grammar does not mark person at the verb and allows the subject position in the sentence to remain empty. How, then, can the agent of a sentence predicate be understood? The answer is that the Japanese lexicon has a set of directional verbs of giving and receiving which distinguish between 'giving down' (*kureru*) and 'giving up' ((*sashi*) *ageru*). 'Giving up' cannot have a second-person subject, while 'giving down' cannot have a first-person subject. More generally put, there is a systematic pairing of lexical and morphological means reserved for predicating actions of the lowered self and the elevated other. In this way figurative relational asymmetries are grammaticalized. Whether or not such encoding reflects social asymmetry, in the conversation at hand or in the society at large, is a different question. The point to note is that a common politeness strategy, exalting the other and lowering oneself, is encoded in the Japanese grammar.

Much like Japanese, Korean encodes social relations by means of speech levels which mark the different degrees of formality, distance and deference the speaker shows to the addressee. Various morphological and lexical means are employed to mark speech levels, the most salient being sentence-final particles. Every utterance must be situated on one level or another. It is virtually impossible to avoid choosing one of the levels. Hence, speech level must be considered an integral part of the grammatical system of Korean. The systematic nature of speech levels is evident from what Hwang (1990) calls *cooccurrence restrictions*. These are not strict grammatical agreement rules, but restrictions on stylistic choices of address terms, first- and second-person pronouns, lexical items and sentence-concluding endings. In European languages cooccurrence restrictions regulate the selection of terms of address. For example, the cooccurrence of French *tu* with first name is unmarked, whereas *tu* plus last name and title would be highly marked. In strongly socially encoded languages, cooccurrence restrictions of this sort extend to a wider range of stylistic choices. Pairing, for instance, a lexical item marked as honorific with a plain finite verb form usually makes for a marked utterance.

In the Korean system of honorifics, as in the Japanese, politeness is marked along two dimensions, by addressee-controlled forms and referent-controlled forms. First, lexical and morphological means are employed to distinguish plain and honorific reference to objects and actions. For example, plain verbs can be made honorific by adding the infix *-si-*, as in *o-ta* vs. *o-si-ta* 'to come'. A parallel distinction is made in the lexicon which

Table 6.3 *Plain and honorific Korean words (adapted from Hwang 1990: 46)*

	Plain	Honorific	Meaning
Nouns	pap	cinci	meal
	nai	yensey	age
	ilum	sengham	name
Verbs	mekta	capswusita	to eat
	cata	cwumwusita	to sleep
	cwukta	tolakasita	to die

Table 6.4 *Korean speech levels classified by sentence-concluding endings (adapted from Wang 1990: 28)*

Levels	Declarative	Imperative
Most formal	-pnita	-sipsio
.	-eyo	-eyo
.	-(s)o	-(s)o
.	-ney	-key
.	-e	-e
Least formal	-ta	-ela

provides two terms for many objects and actions, the choice of which depends on whether respect and/or deference must be shown to the referent, as in Table 6.3.

Referring to someone worthy of respect calls for choice of the honorific variant. This can be the addressee or a third person. At the same time, sentence-concluding endings must be chosen, irrespective of the referent, to differentiate levels of formality. Various models for the description of Korean speech levels have been proposed, distinguishing between two (+ formal vs. – formal) and six levels (from most deferential to most lowering) (Wang 1990); see Table 6.4. While this discrepancy shows that there is some variation in the conceptualization of speech levels and in their differentiation in practice, it is nevertheless clear that Korean is a strongly socially encoded language which requires its speakers in their stylistic and grammatical choices to always reckon with their own position in society and in relation to addressee and referent.

The system allows for very subtle differentiations in terms of expressing respect, deference, formality and interpersonal distance/intimacy. Yet, since most choices of politeness expressions are socially conditioned, they can be formally modelled as decision-making flowcharts, that is, alternative sequences of reasoned choices. As an example, consider the factors that have a bearing on the unmarked choice of Korean address terms displayed in Figure 6.2.

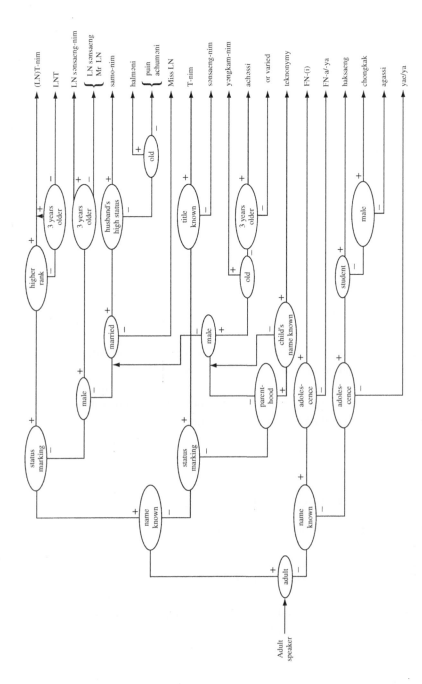

Figure 6.2 *Choice of Korean address terms (Hwang 1990: 45)*

Strategies

In the previous section we have seen that languages differ with respect to the social information they encode. Strongly socially encoded languages include a subsystem of lexical and morphological honorifics. The extent to which honorifics are present in a language must not be confused with the ability of its speakers to modulate their speech for politeness. Just as time reference does not depend on the presence of a morphological tense system but can be accomplished by other means, such as nouns, adverbs and prepositions, so verbal politeness does not depend on honorifics. In both strongly socially encoded languages and weakly encoded ones, a number of strategies for the expression of politeness are employed. The difference is that strongly socially encoded languages promote the speakers' awareness of the social indexicality of their utterances since unmarked choices depend on the appreciation of social relationships and one's own position within a hierarchy. Speakers of weakly socially encoded languages have to rely more on less formalized strategies which, however, are also commonly employed in strongly socially encoded languages.

Indirectness

Observations in many languages have established a correlation between indirectness and politeness. Expressing one's communicative purpose in a roundabout way is perceived as more polite than saying directly what one wants. For example, a request in the form of an interrogative sentence (6) is more polite than declarative (7) or imperative (8).

(6) Could you have this done by three o'clock this afternoon?

(7) I need this by three o'clock this afternoon.

(8) Have it ready by three o'clock this afternoon!

As a technique of maintaining face and conflict avoidance, the identification of indirectness with politeness is rooted in the cooperative nature of language behaviour. A request puts the speaker's face at risk, since it can be turned down, and is a potential threat to the addressee's face, since it is hard or impossible to turn down. The effect of indirectness is to reduce the risk and soften the threat by lowering obligations and providing the opportunity to continue the conversation without leading it to a point where conflicting preferences become explicit. Indirectness reduces responsibility and leaves the addressee with more options to continue the conversation. The speaker's intent must be concluded rather than being spelt out explicitly. Many indirectness strategies are completely conventionalized. For instance, *Could you please* … said by a superior to a subordinate is not a question and allows for no denial. Yet, the interrogative form is a conventional concession to the addressee's face wants.

Syntactic devices

Syntactic strategies of indirectness include causative and passive mood. In Hindi, Bengali and other Indian languages, causative constructions are used to employ positive politeness, as in (9) and (10) (Subbarao, Agnihotri and Mukerjee 1991: 42).

(9) Hindi: a:p khila:yẽ ge to zaru:r kha:yẽge
         you make eat then surely (I) will eat
         'If you insist, I will definitely eat.'

(10) Bengali: a:pni khaowale khabo
         you cause to eat will eat (1st person)

The rationale of using the causative, *you make me eat*, is to express positive politeness by indicating the speaker's willingness to submit to the addressee's wish.

Passive is widely used in very different languages to avoid responsibility ascription. Thus (11) is seen as more polite than (12).

(11) I asked for the file cabinet to be cleaned out, but it wasn't done.

(12) I asked for the file cabinet to be cleaned out, but you didn't do it.

It should be pointed out, however, that the same syntactic devices, for example causative and passive, are assigned different politeness functions in different languages. In Dravidian languages, the active voice is generally considered more polite than the passive which is avoided except in prohibitive statements (Subbarao et al. 1991: 50). In Japanese, on the other hand, passive is systematically used as an honorific voice. An action predicated of the addressee or a third person worthy of respect is put in the passive voice. For instance, depending on context, the passive form *warawareru* of *warau* 'to laugh' means 'be laughed at' or 'laugh'.

(13) Minna ni warawareru.
     everybody by be laughed
     'I'm laughed at by everybody.'

(14) Sensei ga warawareru.
     teacher Subj. be laughed
     'The teacher laughs.'

The honorific use of the passive voice corresponds to the functional distribution of the verbs *suru* 'to do' and *naru* 'to become', the latter being used for referring to an action in a polite way. Saying that a certain state of affairs has come about rather than attributing it to an actor's intervention is indirect and hence more polite, since overt responsibility ascription is avoided.

Address and reference

Another indirectness device is speaking *about* a person instead of addressing that person. Direct address implies direct involvement, while reference, even where it fulfils an appellative function, creates greater distance and hence reduces the potential threat to the addressee's face. Not to address another person too directly seems to be a very general politeness strategy that relates to territoriality, that is, the recognition of other persons' spatial and symbolic territories. As Ide and Yoshida (1999: 449) argue, this could explain the scarcity of second-person honorifics in socially strongly encoded languages where direct address (15a) of a superior is dispreferred, titles and other descriptive terms of address being used instead (15b).

(15) a. You wrote this book?
     b. The teacher wrote this book?

Idiomatic circumlocutions for address are also used in weakly socially encoded languages such as English. Expressions such as *Your lordship, Your royal highness*, etc. require *is* rather than *are* for a predicate, thus creating a greater distance between speaker and addressee than second-person forms of address. The distance created by third-person address, as in (16) can, however, also be indicative of condescension rather than respect.

(16) If he thought he wouldn't be found out ...

Other strategies

Other verbal politeness strategies include speaker choices that are not so easily formalized, such as length, 'elaborate' words and reduction of dialect. Adorning an utterance with hedges and embellishments raises its politeness level. More generally, the relative length of an utterance seems to be directly related to its degree of politeness. In some measure, this holds for expressions, too. No prize awarded for guessing which of the three Japanese finite copulas (17a–c) is the most polite.

(17) a. da
     b. desu   } is/are
     c. degozaimasu

Lexical distinctions of this kind are, of course, not necessary when varying the length of an utterance or text for other than referentially informative purposes, as the following example of Indian English, cited by Mehrotra (1995: 107), illustrates.

(18) Most Respected Sir,
With due reverence and humble submission I, Beef hawker beg most humbly and respectfully to send your Honour's kind request to inform you and pray as follow, which I hope that you will kindly take into your favourable consideration ...

Clearly a cultural factor makes itself felt here, but that politeness favours elaboration rather than concision is a general tendency.

Lexical choices, too, affect the politeness level of speech. A stylistic division of labour between a high and a low register is common in many languages, often with a genetic background. Thus, the Greco-Latinate stratum in English and other European languages, Sanskrit words in Indo-Aryan and Dravidian languages, and Sinicisms in Korean, Japanese and Vietnamese belong to cultured speech historically associated with such domains as cult, court life and learning. Using Latin/French *beef, pork, mutton* and *veal* in polite conversation at the dinner table, while relegating their Anglo-Saxon counterparts *bull, pig, sheep* and *calf* to the less elegant domains of livestock breeding and food preparation, is an example of such choices that have become conventionalized.

Culture and power

In Chapter 2 we discussed the relation of dialect and class. Historically politeness, too, has a class aspect. These two interrelations combine to form a stylistic preference hierarchy that disfavours dialectal speech in contexts that require politeness. Thus, the standard-and-dialect continuum is yet another dimension of politeness gradation. Typically, the geographical centre of standard speech is also the centre of power. This being so, indexing a power differential between speaker and addressee is one of the many facets and functions of politeness. To see in linguistic politeness conventions nothing but a means to keep everyone in their place and maintain asymmetric power relations hardly does justice to the complexity of the phenomenon, but this aspect must not be overlooked either.

One area where this is particularly obvious is gender. Women in many societies are commonly expected to, and actually do choose more polite strategies than men, a tendency which has often been linked to their sub-servient position in society (Holmes 1995). However, more is involved here than power. In one study of a weakly socially encoded language, English, the general politeness level in conversations of members of both sexes was found to be higher than in same-sex conversations of either sex (Rintell 1981). And another study of a strongly socially encoded language, Japanese, found that differences between male and female speech patterns diminish and eventually disappear with the increasing formality of the setting (Takahara 1991). Thus, speaker-sex interacts with other variables such as social setting to determine politeness levels. In Java, politeness, rather than indicating deference, is associated with authority and control. In public settings, men tend to be more polite than women, while the reverse is true in private contexts (Smith-Hefner 1988). The hypothesis that women are, or are expected to be, more polite than men is too simplistic.

Also, observations of this sort argue against the assumption that strongly socially encoded languages reflect, more or less directly, very hierarchical social structures. In the light of what has been said in previous chapters about the effects of social variables, especially relative status, age and sex, on language choices, we are not surprised to find that the same variables affect politeness behaviour. These variables interact in complex ways, and there are other factors that come into play. The formality of the situation is one, the personal relationship between speaker and addressee is another. And all of these factors together interact in different ways in different cultures.

In polite language, especially in encoded honorifics, we can hear an echo of history, but any conclusions from current linguistic usage about contemporary social structure, relative power and the rights and duties of speakers should be drawn with great care. Many politeness strategies have a ritualistic character and are employed as conversational routines.[9] Politeness strategies are bound not to languages but to speech communities and cultures. The best evidence for this comes from national varieties of English which differ from each other because of their speakers' differing politeness strategies that have congealed into different conventions. Forms of address, greetings, apologies, compliments, requests, thanks and complaints are some of the speech acts that are carried out in conventionally different ways in different English-speaking countries. The same linguistic resources are available, but the choices considered unmarked are not the same in all speech communities. Customers can be called *yes, dear* or *yes, love* in Britain, but not in India. As an honorific address form, *sir* is used more frequently in Indian English than in British or American English. Combining the title *Mister* with a person's first name is strongly marked in Britain and North America, as is the reference to one's own wife as *Mrs X*, but in India such usage is quite common.

The acculturation of English on the Indian subcontinent shows that, at any given time, the politeness conventions current in a speech community represent the collective choices from the resources provided by the language to suit the requirements of culture. Societies differ with regard to how much leeway speakers have in making their choices, and languages differ with regard to how strongly social distinctions and relations are encoded in lexicon and grammar. Determining the specific nature of the relation between linguistic politeness and social structure for a given speech community is, therefore, an important task. The overall goal of politeness research must be to reveal the specific conditions of making unmarked choices of socially indexical expressions and thus to establish how expressions of politeness are employed to construct social relationships.

Conclusion

The linguistic expression of politeness is a universal of human behaviour, but it is not executed in the same manner in all languages. Rather, languages vary as to how they encode politeness differentiations in the grammar and the lexicon. Social distinctions are strongly encoded in some languages and much less so in others. Notably, languages of East Asian countries have highly developed grammatical and morphological subsystems for indicating and thus defining social distinctions. Politeness encoding in language reflects power differentials and social class distinctions; however, because language change tends to lag behind social change, the observable linguistic distinctions are not necessarily indicative of the actual social stratification at the time of observation. In any event, speakers have to attune their utterances to a politeness level that befits normative requirements taking into consideration interpersonal relations, situation and the communicative purpose at hand. While in all societies individual variation is balanced by the pressure to conform, more specific generalizations are difficult to substantiate. Selecting appropriate verbal strategies for keeping social interaction free of friction is part of every normal speaker's competence and an important component of language's proper functioning in society.

Questions for discussion

(1)   Is politeness attributable to speakers or to expressions?
(2)   How does verbal politeness give expression to social distinction and inequality? Discuss examples of your own experience.
(3)   Why does the relative length of an utterance correlate with its politeness?
(4)   How does your father refer to your mother/his wife
            – in the presence of his children;
            – in the presence of non-family members;
        and what does it have to do with politeness?
(5)   In Shakespeare's comedy *As You Like It* (Act 3, Scene 2) we read that 'those that are good manners at the court, are as ridiculous in the country as the behaviour of the country is most mockable at the court'. How can you relate this statement to present-day politeness conventions? Discuss this question using the notions of 'marked' and 'unmarked'.

Further reading

Brown, Penelope and Steven Levinson. 1987. *Politeness: Some Universals in Language Usage*. Cambridge University Press.
Jaszczolt, Katarzyna and Keith Allan (eds.) 2012. *The Cambridge Handbook of Pragmatics*. Cambridge University Press.
Mills, Sara. 2003. *Gender and Politeness*. London: Cambridge University Press.
Pan, Yuling. 2000. *Politeness in Chinese Face-to-Face Interaction*. Stamford: Ablex.
Watts, Richard J. 2003. *Politeness*. New York: Cambridge University Press.

Notes

1. For critical reviews: Kasper (1996), Eelen (2001), Bargiela-Chiappini and Kádár (2010); see also the *Journal of Politeness Research* (www.degruyter.com/search?q=Journal+of+Politeness+Research&searchBtn=Search).
2. The others are attention, accommodation, equilibrium, harmony, respect and discretion (Picard 1998: 75–9).
3. Work by semanticists has shown that metaphorical extension is one of the essential processes at work in language and of great importance for the cognitive organization of experience (e.g. Givón 1986; Lakoff and Johnson 1985).
4. In Vietnamese, these terms are called 'substitutes' (*đại-từ*), a word class which lies at the boundary between content words and function words.
5. Kinship terminology is a big topic in cultural anthropology and hence ethnolinguistics. For a good overview of the literature, see Trautmann (2001).
6. It is even less clear whether and if so how linguistic conventions influence social changes. For instance, it is an intriguing question as to whether a highly differentiated address system is conducive or detrimental to the evolution of a more egalitarian society or has no influence at all. But the obstacles that stand in the way of investigating such a question empirically seem insurmountable.
7. For a discussion of how 'courtesy', the elitist manner of the court, was replaced by 'civility', the more egalitarian manner of civil society, see Ehlich (1992).
8. In recent years, politeness research about status conscious Asian societies has flourished. See, for example, Ji (2000), Pizziconi (2003), Haugh (2005), Kádár and Mills (2011), Pan and Kádár (2011).
9. Conversational routines represent collectively sanctioned devices of control and regulation of behaviour in recurrent everyday situations (Coulmas 1981a). The notion of ritual is present in most analyses of politeness, cf., for example, Brown and Levinson (1987: 43f.), Held (1992: 148f.).

Useful online resources

LPRG, the site of the Linguistic Politeness Research Group, provides information about conferences and publications on the subjects of politeness and impoliteness and invites readers to join a mailing list: http://research.shu.ac.uk/politeness/index.html

The site of the *Journal of Politeness Research*: www.degruyter.com/view/j/jplr?rskey=WSbnj5&result=5&q=politeness

Part II

Macro-choices

7 Code-switching: linguistic choices across language boundaries

> In order to resume. Resume the – what is the word? What the wrong word?
> Samuel Beckett, *Ill Seen, Ill Said*

> The speech which had started off one hundred percent in Ibo was now fifty-fifty. But his audience still seemed highly impressed. They liked good Ibo, but they also admired English.
> Chinua Achebe, *No Longer at Ease*

Outline of the chapter

Code-switching is a topic that comes into focus where two or more languages coexist in a community, forming the linguistic resources from which bilingual speakers can choose. In their conversations, these individuals do not necessarily choose one language or another, but often go back and forth. This chapter deals with the social and linguistic aspects of such speech behaviour. After introducing the concept of code-switching and distinguishing it from other language contact-related phenomena, it explains why the key term of this field of research is *code*-switching rather than, for example, *language*-switching and then goes on to discuss the questions, 'Who switches?', 'How?' and 'Why?' At the end of the chapter, brief mention is made of diachronic aspects of code-switching as a force of language change.

Key terms: language contact, code-switching, mixed discourse, constraints, markedness

Whereas in the first part of the book we focused on linguistic choices concerning features of expressions and lower-level units of a language system, this part deals with higher-level choices in language-contact situations. In previous chapters it has become apparent how variation and choice render the notion that a language is a homogeneous, clearly delimited system untenable – be it as a naïve idea or a theoretical abstraction. Taking the notion of language as a social fact seriously forces us to reckon with variation in space and time, across social strata and determined by the speakers' sex and age, and to see in it not deviation or imperfection, but an essential prerequisite of using language to construct society.

So far, however, it was understood that we were dealing with choices among the varieties of one language. Only occasionally have we touched on

Table 7.1 *Lexical correspondences in English:*
verbs of Anglo-Saxon and French origin

Anglo-Saxon	French
to begin	to commence
to bother	to annoy
to clothe	to dress
to end	to finish
to fight	to combat
to gain	to profit
to give up	to abandon
to hinder	to prevent
to shape	to forge
to shun	to avoid
to take	to apprehend

linguistic choices that traverse the boundaries of a language. In Chapter 6 we saw that stylistic diversity can be accomplished by incorporating elements of one language into another, and that politeness, a social variable, can determine the choice of a register or style. In the event, French-origin words had become integrated into the English lexicon, as displayed in Table 7.1. This is how, in retrospect, linguistic borrowing can be described. The process itself, however, poses difficult questions because the moment of borrowing is not usually observable. One thing is clear, however, there must be speakers proficient in the two languages. There would not be a Latin–French stratum in the English lexicon had there been no speakers in England with some knowledge of French who, under certain circumstances, chose French rather than English words.

Where speakers competent in more than one language are present, language contact takes place. The results of such contacts are various, and some of them, such as, for instance, borrowing, seem to pose few theoretical problems. The lexicon of one language has been enriched by tapping the resources of another. However, just as language change is clear after the fact but difficult to observe as it happens, it is easy to determine that a word has been borrowed only in retrospect. This is so because when we observe a word of one language being used within the context of another, we may be witnessing one of several different occurrences resulting from language contact, such as nonce-borrowing (Haspelmath and Tadmor 2009), quotation (Coulmas 1986), interference (Tóth 2007), mixed discourse (Olson 2004), pidginization (Siegel 2008), or code-switching (Jacobson 1998a, 1998b, 2001b). Whenever we are able to say that an item of one language has been incorporated into another, two basic assumptions about language and linguistic communication are intact; the assumptions, that is, that languages are distinct, and that one language is used at a time. A number of language-contact phenomena make it hard to hold on to these assumptions without qualification. Code-switching is among the most intriguing of them.

In both descriptive and normative grammars and in dictionaries, languages are treated as discrete systems, but societies are less orderly than bookshelves, allowing speakers of different languages to live side by side and to mingle, and allowing individual speakers to make use of whatever language resources they can access. As we will see in the chapters that follow, communication practices in multilingual societies are characterized by various patterns of functional distribution of the available languages and varieties. Some of them pose a challenge to the analytically neat separation of languages, as speakers cross linguistic boundaries on a regular basis. Yet, their individual choices are not arbitrary. Multilingualism research has revealed that the languages coexisting in one society are hardly ever equal, if only because they are associated with demographic strength, power and prestige. Choosing one language or another, or choosing elements of one language or another, therefore, invariably carries social meaning. Every choice has a motivation and hence can be explained.

A distinction is sometimes made between micro-sociolinguistics, or variation sociolinguistics, and macro-sociolinguistics, or sociology of language. The former is concerned with lower-level choices of phonetic, morphological and syntactic variants, whereas the latter deals with the choice of styles and languages and their functional allocation in society. This distinction is useful for analytic purposes, but it does not always correspond to a clear-cut division in reality. Rather than forming two distinct sets, micro- and macro-choices overlap to some degree. There is a grey zone where speakers are not necessarily aware in every situation whether, for the communicative purposes at hand, they are choosing an element of a language or the language itself. This is most in evidence in a range of linguistic phenomena subsumed under the umbrella term 'code-switching'.

Why 'code'?

Bilingual individuals living in bilingual communities are regularly faced with the question of which language to use. In many cases, the answer is not that they choose either one language or the other, but rather that they select now portions of one language and then of the other, alternating back and forth. To outside observers not familiar with this language practice, it is hard to recognize any pattern, to the extent that the language being spoken cannot be identified. The resulting admixture has, therefore, often been considered a deficient and bastardized blend, certainly not a language worthy of that name. It has also been assumed that speakers engaging in such communication practices are forced to do so because their command of the languages involved is limited. A great deal of research into the relationship of linguistic diversity and societal complexity carried out during the past four decades has falsified both of these assumptions. It is not necessarily for lack of competency that speakers switch from one language to another, and the choices they make are not fortuitous. Rather, just like socially motivated choices of varieties of one language, choices across language boundaries are imbued with social meaning. Uncovering the social motivations of language-boundary-crossing choices therefore is a sociolinguistic task on a par with investigating the social motivations of dialect choice, gender-specific speech forms, or age-grading.

The systems that are utilized concurrently in linguistically complex situations are not always languages in the common sense of the word. Pioneering research in this area of sociolinguistics has been done in Norway where speakers were observed to use both Bokmål and Ranmål, two distinct varieties of Norwegian. Blom and Gumperz (1972) were able to show that choice of one over the other variety could be explained in terms of differing values, Bokmål being associated with pan-Norwegian concerns, while Ranmål symbolizes local values. In other parts of the world similar connections between linguistic varieties and values, as social meanings which determine the individual's choice, have been noticed. For instance, a functional distribution of Indian English and Standard English is quite common on the South Asian subcontinent; German and Romance are concurrently used in the Romance-speaking areas of Switzerland (Solèr 1991), each carrying different social meanings; as are Arabic and French in Morocco and other countries of the Maghreb (Youssi 1995), German and French in Alsace (Gardner-Chloros 1991), Swahili and English in Kenya (Myers-Scotton 1993a), Appalachian and Standard American English (Wolfram 1991) among many others. Whereas German and Romance, French and Arabic, Swahili and English are clear cases of distinct languages, Bokmål and Ranmål and Indian English and Standard English, though quite dissimilar, are usually considered varieties of one language. Yet, the social meanings that are linked with the members of these pairs and the mechanisms underlying individual choices are sufficiently akin to create the need to cover concurrent choices from both kinds of pairs with a single term. This is one of the reasons for using the term '*code*-switching', rather than 'language-switching'. As can be inferred from the title of Myers-Scotton's seminal book, *Codes and Consequences: Choosing Linguistic Varieties* (1998), a code in this sense can be a language or a variety of a language.

Code-switching occurs where speakers are aware of the two varieties being distinct and are able to keep them apart, although they may not do so habitually and may not be conscious of every switch they make. Code-switching is regarded as a controllable strategy, differing from both ordinary borrowing of individual lexical items and unavoidable interference. Theoretically these distinctions are clear. When a borrowing has occurred, the borrowed word belongs unmistakably to the language into which it has been borrowed following the constraints of that language on all grammatical levels. Thus, all the items in Table 7.1 are English although those in the right-hand column once were French. There must have been a time, however, when this wasn't so clear because the frequency of occurrence of the items in the right-hand column was very low. The difference between borrowed and switched items is one of frequency, clear only at the extremes of a continuum that relates both phenomena.

Interference, on the other hand, results from the default use of the first language of a person as a reference system for other languages. Such interference is manifest as a 'foreign accent' on the phonological level (Major 2010), but affects other linguistic levels, such as vocabulary, grammar and style as well. In practice, it is not always easy to decide whether an incidence of concurrent choices of multiple languages constitutes code-switching because patterns of code-switching are varied and border on other language-contact phenomena. A common thread that binds these phenomena together is that they compromise the conceptual integrity of a language as a homogeneous system and force us, once again, to recognize the fuzzy nature of sociolinguistic reality.[1] Notwithstanding that, some abstractions and generalizations are inevitable in order to make these phenomena manageable and investigable. What this means specifically will become clear as we proceed to discuss step-by-step the following question: *Who code-switches how and why?*

Who switches?

Who, then, practises code-switching? This question has two dimensions. On the empirical level, it is the question of where to find speakers who regularly engage in code-switching; whether they can be found in all bilingual communities; whether there are in bilingual communities speakers who code-switch and others who do not and, if so, what it is that distinguishes them from each other. It has long been known that tolerance for transfer of material from one language into another is variable, some communities being very receptive while others tend to reject elements of other languages. Comparative studies show that the lexicons of some languages, such as, for example, English and Japanese, are hybrid in nature including many words of different origin, while others, such as Chinese and Greek, are much more homogeneous.[2] Does this have anything to do with code-switching and, more specifically, with who practises code-switching? Since borrowing and code-switching are related phenomena, it does. Many loans are a historical sediment of code-switching.[3] The question is whether the members of some speech communities have a greater propensity to insert in their speech elements from other languages than those of another. The answer to this question is a clear yes. Both bilingual speakers and speech communities differ as to the extent they practise code-switching in everyday life; speakers, because some find themselves in situations where switching is possible or called for more often than others; communities, because norms for allocating languages to functional domains, keeping them apart or allowing for a mixed code, are variable. For example, in multilingual environments of South Africa studied by Finlayson and Slabbert (1997), code-switching is very common, while in Switzerland widespread bilingualism, notwithstanding language separation, is preferred.

On the theoretical level, the question of who switches is the question of how to characterize the ideal code-switcher in such a way that his or her performance constitutes an object of investigation that is reasonably well defined and conducive to our understanding of the social underpinnings of language choice and the working of language itself. It is not the question of where to find bilinguals who practise code-switching, but rather the question of how code-switching can be distinguished in a theoretically reasoned way from other kinds of bilingual speech behaviour. Consider some examples.

(1) A flight attendant en route from London to Hong Kong makes an announcement in English first and then in Chinese.

(2) A wine connoisseur remarks in mock consternation, 'He drank this wine from a beer glass, quelle horreur!'

(3) A foreign language teacher uses the foreign language, L2, in class, but occasionally provides some explanations in the students' native language, L1.

(4) A man in a pub in Dublin inserts some Irish formulaic expressions into a conversation with his friends otherwise held in English.

(5) A clerk at a Singapore post office serves one customer in Chinese and another in Malay.

(6) A Moroccan immigrant living in Amsterdam speaks Moroccan Arabic with her mother and Dutch with her children.

(7) Italian immigrant children in Germany fluctuate from dialectal Italian to dialectal German producing many deviant forms in both varieties.

(8) Speakers of Marathi, an Indo-Aryan language spoken in central India, insert many Sanskrit words into their speech in formal settings, but not in the market-place.

(9) A Sicilian fishmonger addresses a customer in the local dialect. He switches to Italian in answering the customer's question, but then switches back to the dialect, while the customer continues speaking Italian.

(10) A Kikuyu speaker in a middle-class Nairobi home speaks Swahili to her children most of the time, but Kikuyu to tell them off. The children, too, speak mostly Swahili garnished with a lot of English insertions.

All of the above have been described as code-switching, but there is much controversy over whether language choices of such diversity should be subsumed under the same label. Some are easier to exclude from code-switching research than others. Code-switching happens spontaneously, not in a rehearsed fashion as (1). A fairly fluent command of L1 and L2 is generally considered a defining characteristic of speakers who engage in code-switching. This criterion excludes (2), (3) and (4), although cases such as (2) and (4) are sometimes referred to as 'affective switching' or 'switching for rhetorical effect'. If the addressee is the only factor determining code choice and L1 and L2 are used exclusively with no overlap, as (5) and (6) suggest, many code-switching specialists would eliminate these cases. (7) is problematic because limited proficiency in L1 and L2 seems to be a major characteristic of this language-choice pattern which has been called 'code fluctuation'. Although Sanskrit and Marathi are two distinct languages and Sanskrit items in Marathi speech are identifiable as such, (8) constitutes style shifting rather than code-switching because the Sanskrit lexicon functions as an adjunct resource for educated Marathi speakers. That leaves (9) and (10) as incontrovertible cases of code-switching, although (9) would be described as a bilingual conversation with diverging preferences by some researchers. Lüdi (2010), for example, who has done extensive work on language choice in Switzerland and Alsace uses the term 'multilingual speech behaviour' that includes code-switching in the narrow sense (also Lüdi and Py 2009).

In language-contact situations speakers of various linguistic backgrounds make diverse code choices not all of which should be regarded as code-switching. The ideal code-switcher is a phantom appearing in almost as many guises as there are scholars interested in his or her performance. However, some common features stick out. Ideal code-switchers speak at least two languages which are habitually spoken in their community. They are fluent in both languages, although they may not be completely balanced bilinguals. As Oksaar (1997: 289) points out, their linguistic repertoire encompasses not just two main systems, L1 and L2, but at least three, L1, L2 and LX, which is directly connected with code-switching. Switching, then, is a linguistic skill in its own right rather than a makeshift solution to an anomalous communication problem. Code-switchers accommodate to each other. They possess a wider repertoire of adaptive strategies and modification devices than monolingual speakers (Grosjean 1985), but they do not feel the need to settle on a lingua franca in the sense of 'one conversation, one language'. Rather, the conversation is the frame in which they code-switch. In sum, bilingual speakers who regularly and competently engage in the practice of concurrently choosing portions of L1 and L2 in the same conversation fit the bill in answer to this section's question.

How?

How do they do it? Assuming that code-switching constitutes a skill, what does it consist of? Many observations have shown that in terms of cooperation, transmitting information and building rapport, bilingual conversations involving code-switching function much like monolingual conversations, smoothly and without disruption. This is what makes code-switching such an intriguing phenomenon, undermining as it does the fundamental assumption that in trouble-free linguistic communication interlocutors follow the rules of one shared language. Language, as we have seen on several occasions, is a cooperative game, each player following the same rules and making his or her choices with the interlocutor in mind. How can this be done in the absence of an agreed-upon common language that constitutes the framework of the rules and elements to be selected? If there are no rules, utterances cannot be interpreted. The obvious conclusion is that code-switching itself must be rule-governed and, accordingly, that it must be possible to determine the rules that speakers apply in code-switching.

The general question is how, when L1 and L2 are used concurrently, the grammars of L1 and L2 are coordinated. Is one grammar given precedence over the other, are both grammars suspended, or is there a third grammar of code-switching? In one form or another, the latter assumption has guided early research into code-switching and continues to do so for some scholars. It implies that switches are possible only under specifiable structural conditions which can be formulated as restrictions on choices. L1 and L2, being human languages, include many common structural ground plans and grammatical rules. It can be predicted, therefore, that intrasentential switches are more likely to occur where the grammars of L1 and L2 harmonize. Working largely on English/Spanish data, Sankoff and Poplack (1981) have sharpened this general principle to postulate specific formal constraints. What has come to be known in the literature as 'the bound morpheme constraint' stipulates that 'a switch [is prohibited] from occurring between a bound morpheme and lexical forms unless the latter has been phonologically integrated into the language of the former' (Poplack 1982: 12).

For example, this constraint should bar an L1 suffix from being combined with an L2 noun unless the noun has been phonologically integrated into L1. Consider (11) where the English word *now* is combined with the Japanese suffix *-NA* which attaches to adjectival nouns.

(11) *now-NA hito*
      modern person

That this expression violates the bound morpheme constraint could mean two things: one, that expressions of this sort should not occur; and, two, that such expressions should not be considered 'true' code-switching. One can be discounted because, in the 1980s, *nowNA hito* became a common if somewhat faddish expression in Japanese which is still in use in the 2010s. The condition of phonological integration does not clarify the issue because the sounds occurring in English [naʊ] and their combinations are available in Japanese. Clearly, *nowNA hito* results from Japanese–English language contact. Like many other similar expressions, it violates the bound morpheme constraint and should, therefore, not be included among the expressions to be analysed as code-switching but classified as something else, for example as borrowing. Such a classification is supported by the fact that most speakers of Japanese would flatly deny that they code-switch when choosing elements from English and Japanese to form an expression such as *nowNA hito*. Thus (11) does not need to be considered as a counterexample of the bound morpheme constraint.

However, as in other areas of sociolinguistic research, speakers' self-assessments do not constitute reliable criteria for classifying data. How to deal with (11) is a theoretical question concerning a reasonable definition of what constitutes code-switching. The lesson to be learnt from (11) is a fundamental one. The issue is to distinguish constraints extracted from the data which can be shown to govern language behaviour from constraints projected onto the data which govern model-building. Because of the diversity of the phenomena involved, this is not an easy issue to resolve. Carol Myers-Scotton's (1997: 220) remark that 'there is still no agreement among CS researchers themselves as to what constitutes CS' highlights the difficulty.

Ever since the bound morpheme constraint was proposed, numerous counterexamples have been put forth. For example, studying Spanish–English bilinguals in the United States, Silva-Corvalán (1983) demonstrated that violations of this structural constraint were motivated rather than prevented by the speakers' relative fluency in both languages. The bound morpheme constraint was intended as a universal constraint on code-switching. A question of some importance is, therefore, whether it is affected by the genetic relationship between L1 and L2. Pandharipande (1998) demonstrated that Marathi–Sanskrit code-switching and Marathi–English code-switching do not follow the same structural constraints, a finding she attributes to the fact that the genetic connection between the members of the two pairs is very different, Marathi and Sanskrit being genetically close, while Marathi and English are genetically distant languages. Annamalai (1989) similarly points out differences between code-switching involving Indian languages only and an Indian language and English. Indian languages are non-configurational languages in the sense that the word order is not fixed and may hence lend themselves to code-switching relatively easily. He therefore emphasizes the importance of genetic affinity and language type as variables affecting the ease and relative frequency of switching.

Other counterexamples to the bound morpheme constraint emerged from data of Spanish–Hebrew (Berk-Seligson 1986), Lingala–English (Bokamba 1988) and Moroccan Arabic–French (Bentahila and Davies 1998). As a result, this constraint increasingly looks like a model-driven constraint rather than a data-driven constraint. More generally, this is the fate shared by all attempts at formulating syntactic and morphological constraints of a general nature which are valid for code-switching in any L1/L2 pairs. Yet, the theoretical challenge to identify universal principles or even specific rules that govern the coordination of two grammars at the sentence level has attracted a great deal of research. One line of thought, pursued by Pieter Muysken (2000) among others, has it that the study of code-switching, far from constituting a niche of marginal phenomena, can help to resolve one of the most hotly debated issues in linguistics, the question of how the grammar and the lexicon of a language interact. Typological differences are possibly relevant, too; for bound morphemes may not behave in the same way in inflected languages, such as Spanish, and in agglutinative languages, such as Japanese.

Constraints such as the bound morpheme constraint should throw new light on the connection between language and language use by individual speakers. For, if morphosyntactic constraints on intrasentential code-switching can be found, the expectation is that they will contribute to a better understanding of where in a sentence a speaker can change languages, and where grammatical processes and lexical processes are put to work. Another constraint that was proposed predicts that a head will project its language index on the constituents it governs. For example, a direct object is governed by its verb and should therefore follow the grammatical restrictions of the language to which the verb belongs. Accordingly, a switch such as *he saw DOS OFICIALES* should not occur because the determiner *DOS* should be in English. In fact, switches like this one are quite common. Thus, the uncomfortable alternative is to exclude these switches from the data or to abandon the restriction. To conclude, up to now the search for universal structural constraints on intrasentential code-switching which holds on to the simultaneous effectiveness of two grammars has been fruitless.

An alternative approach to tackle the issue of processing and combining elements of two languages is Myers-Scotton's (1993b) influential Matrix Language Frame (MLF) model. As opposed to the morphosyntactic constraints model advanced by Poplack and others, the MLF model does not require a categorical distinction between borrowing and code-switching; on the contrary, it suggests that code-switching is something much like borrowing, the difference being one of frequency. The model assumes that language processing consists in the construction of a frame into which matrix language elements and embedded language elements are incorporated. Working largely on data from genetically and typologically distinct language pairs, especially English/Swahili and English/Kikuyu, Myers-Scotton proceeds from the assumption that in all instances of code-switching a matrix language can always be identified. A distinction of crucial importance for this model is that between system morphemes and content morphemes. The matrix language supplies the system morphemes for the frame, whereas content morphemes can be inserted from both the matrix language and the embedded language. Example (12) illustrates this functional division. In the mixed Verb Phrase constituent *zinafunction right now*, the grammatical elements, especially the verbal prefixes *zi-na-* come from Swahili, the matrix language, whereas content morphemes such as the verb stem *-function* are English.

(12)   It's only essential *services amba-zo zi-na*-function right now

        Comp-Cl. 10 Cl. 10-Pres-

    'It's only essential services that function right now.' (Myers-Scotton 1993a: 130).[4]

Code-switching that conforms to this pattern has been called 'classic' code-switching, because in many cases matrix language and embedded language are more difficult to distinguish since system morphemes and content morphemes are supplied by both L1 and L2. In the event, it is not easy unequivocally to identify the matrix language. Structural criteria such as the supposition that the finite verb in a sentence comes from the matrix language, have proven inadequate, and it seems unlikely that it will ever be possible to define the division of labour of matrix language and embedded language on structural grounds alone. Myers-Scotton (1993a: 66f.) suggests that a combination of psycholinguistic, sociolinguistic and statistical criteria can best achieve empirical verification. The relative frequency of system morphemes of the languages involved will thus identify the matrix language, which is almost always the speaker's first language and the more salient language in the community in terms of the number of types of interaction for which it is the preferred choice.

As we have noticed repeatedly, sociolinguistic reality is almost never as tidy as our theoretical concepts and categories indicate. There are speakers who find it difficult to say which is their first language, and there are entire communities for which this is true. In code-switching research, there is general convergence on the notion that completely balanced proficiency is rare and that, therefore, even fluent code-switching, as opposed, for example, to mixed language use resulting from attrition or incomplete acquisition, usually involves an unequal pair of languages, a dominant L1 and a subordinate L2. However, cases in which no dominant language can be established must not be ignored and must not be excluded from the realm of code-switching research. The following example (13) of Arabic–French code-switching by Moroccans illustrates at some length that this bilingual speaker has not settled on a language that supplies the frame.

(13)   *wahed nnuba kunt ana w thami.* ON S'EST ARRÊTÉ
     one the time was I and Thami. We stopped

     JUSTE AU FEU ROUGE, ON PARLAIT. *kunna bγina*
     exactly at the fire red, one talked. we were we want

nmšiw l merakš ma nmšiw l merakš w kunt
we go to Marrakesh not we go to Marrakesh and I was

qrit. IL M'A VU ENSEIGNER *w dakši w*
I taught. He me has seen teaching and that thing and

žajin ħna, ON HABITAIT ICI. *waqef,* IL FAUT
coming here, one lived here. Standing, it is necessary

VOIR, *ħda* LE DIX-SEPTIÈME ÉTAGE *f dak* LE FEU
to see near the seventeenth floor in that the fire

ROUGE *faš zawlu žžerda lwstanija. Ɛad*
red where they removed the garden the central just

sawbulha lgas ET J'ÉTAIS DEVANT, IL Y,
they put for it the concrete and I was before, there

AVAIT UNE CENTAINE DE VOITURES DERRIÈRE MOI, *w ana*
was a hundred of cars behind me and I

waqef. J'ATTENDS LE FEU POUR CHANGER. *wahed saƐa,*
standing I wait the fire to change one time

COMME ÇA JE DEMARRE *JaƐ ni, w kant dak* LA
like that I take off. I mean, and was that the

SEMAINE *djal tajzawlu* LES PERMIS. JE DÉMARRE *hakda*
week of they remove the permits. I take off thus

w nnas kulhum waq fin muraj.
and the people all standing behind-me.

Translation
'Once there were Thami and I, we stopped right at the red light, we were talking. We were wondering whether to go to Marrakesh or not, and I had been teaching. He watched me teaching and so on, and we were coming here, we lived here. I was waiting you should have seen, near the seventeen-story building, at that traffic light where they have taken away the garden in the middle, they have just put concrete there and I was in the front, there were about a hundred cars behind me and I was waiting. I was waiting for the traffic lights to change. After a while, I moved off, I mean, and it was the week where they take driving licenses away, just like that, I moved off. I moved off like that and all the people were waiting behind me.'

(Bentahila and Davies 1998: 45f.)

Bentahila and Davies (1998: 46) point out that (13) is almost perfectly balanced, consisting of 57 Arabic words and 59 French ones. Also, on the clause level there is a near-even division. Of the 26 clauses, 11 are entirely in Arabic and 9 entirely in French. The remaining 6 clauses are mixed, 3 each being predominantly French and Arabic, respectively. They call this kind of switching 'language alternation'. Since it exhibits no obvious dominance of any language, it does not lend itself to an analysis on the basis of the MLF model unless the monolingual clauses, by far the largest part of the entire passage, are put aside as intersentential code-switching and only the mixed clauses are analysed in terms of embedded language and matrix language. In any event, it is necessary to recognize that there are several different mechanisms of code-switching for some of which the MLF model is more suitable than for others.

Various classifications have been proposed. Myers-Scotton (1997: 222) is content with a basic distinction between intersentential switching, which is of lesser interest for structure-focused code-switching research, and intra-sentential switching which treats the complement phrase (rather than the complete sentence) with mixed constituents as the relevant unit for analysis. Bentahila and Davies (1998: 49) propose a tripartite division: alternation, as described above;[5] insertion, corresponding roughly to Myers-Scotton's intersentential code-switching; and 'leaks' where insignificant items from a speaker's L1 infiltrate the language of the discourse, L2. On the basis of a corpus consisting of various combinations of Mandinka, Wolof and English speech, Haust puts forward a categorization differentiating twelve kinds of code-switching (Figure 7.1) which begins with a general division between insertion (IL) and matrix-language change (ML change) and then branches out into finer distinctions.

Other classifications reflecting other distinctions are conceivable. At the present state of knowledge, all classifications are motivated by the desire to establish a coherent framework for the analysis of code-switching. A comprehensive theory that can deal with all documented kinds of switching and explain the underlying mechanisms is yet to be developed. Theoretical stringency is still achieved at the expense of trimming down the empirical

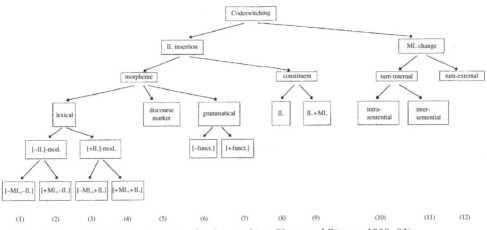

Figure 7.1 *Twelve categories of code-switching (Haust and Dittmar 1998: 83)*

base, that is, by excluding or reclassifying data that do not fit the model. The most successful model to date is Myers-Scotton's MLF model. It offers a reasoned account of how code-switching is done under very specific circumstances, that is, whenever speakers are guided in their choices by a matrix language supplying the frame into which material of both L1 and L2 are incorporated.

Why?

The *how* and *why* of code-switching correspond, respectively, to the linguistic and social dimensions of bilingual speech. As we have seen in the previous section, the structural processes involved are manifold, frustrating any attempt at simple uniform explanation. Does, then, the question of why bilingual speakers choose to compose their utterances of two languages rather than keeping them apart permit a simpler answer? Certainly not in the sense that the motivations for code-switching are few and clear-cut. Notice, first, that different speakers may have not just different motives, but also different capabilities. Jacobson (1996: 85), for example, on the basis of comparing Mexican-Americans and Malaysians, considers this variable so important that he proposes the following classification of bilingual individuals which will predict what kind of switching they are likely to perform and why.

A: Those with largely balanced use of two languages;
B: Those with slightly predominant use of L1;
C: Those with markedly predominant use of L1;
D: Those with slightly predominant use of L2;
E: Those with markedly predominant use of L2.

Speakers belonging to these categories manifest differing allegiances and identity configurations. This is a variable of particular importance in immigrant communities which, however, may interact with fluency in such a way that both identity and fluency cannot be considered independent, as identifying with a community is usually conducive to becoming more proficient in its language, and a higher degree of proficiency in a language tends to reinforce identification with the community of its speakers. In immigrant communities, for example, Turkish–German bilinguals living in Germany (Pfaff 1990), Ghanaian-Italian bilinguals in Italy (Guerini 2006), Arabic–Dutch bilinguals in the Netherlands (Nortier 1989) and Spanish–English bilinguals living in the United States (Jacobson 1977, 1998b), alternating between two languages was described as being a way of creating a unique language variety suitable to express the dual identity of these groups. On the basis of their research on code-switching among Zairians in Belgium, Meeuwis and Blommaert (1998: 80) point out that 'Code-switched speech can be, for all practical purposes, *one variety of its own*, unconnected to and unconditioned by the full knowledge of two separate languages.' In the event, the why of code-switching is self-evident: the speakers have no other choice. Clearly, this is true of some groups only.

Distinguishing groups of bilingual individuals may thus facilitate the question of why they switch but is unlikely to lead to a comprehensive social theory of code-switching. There is agreement about one important point: proficiency limitations and other properties of individual speakers cannot account for the normality of concurrently choosing from the resources of two or more languages in certain communities. Code-switching both has and creates social meaning, which calls for explanation, and it is here that the answer to the question of why speakers switch must be sought. The social environments in which code-switching occurs are varied and, accordingly, many social variables which potentially influence speakers' choice of language in conversation need to be considered. Each one of them is quite complex by itself. These variables include community norms and values, ethnicity, speakers' level of education and fluency, immigrant status, social relations, relative prestige of the languages involved and setting, among others. Such a multifaceted cluster of language-external factors is not easy to handle within a common theoretical framework.

However, Myers-Scotton's (1993b) 'markedness' theory of code-switching is designed to do just that. In Chapter 6 above, we discussed the notion of markedness in connection with verbal politeness, and it is the same concept that comes to bear here. The markedness theory of code-switching assumes that language use in a community is characterized by sets of rights and obligations (RO sets) which are part of the speakers' social knowledge. Code choices, according to Myers-Scotton, are indexical of the RO sets that participants recognize in a given situation. Up to this point, this account builds on the idea of symbolic code-switching first developed in Gumperz's (1982) pioneering work, but Myers-Scotton goes beyond that. The important step ahead is not just that any of the available languages are recognized as being charged with social meaning and as constituting the preferred, more probable and thus the unmarked choice in a given situation, but also that in bilingual communities code-switching, too, must be recognized as what it often is, the unmarked choice.

The great advantage of this theory is that it makes elaborate additional explanations of why speakers code-switch unnecessary for the great majority of instances. Speakers code-switch because, under certain circumstances, code-switching is the unmarked choice. That is enough of an explanation, since language behaviour generally is characterized by unmarked choices. In certain domains, then, for example in the classroom at school, code-switching may be dispreferred, threatened with sanctions and accordingly marked, while it may be an unmarked choice in the school yard or on the way to school. In this way, indexicality appears as 'a property of linguistic varieties', which 'derives from the fact that the different linguistic varieties in a community's repertoire are linked with particular types of relationships, because they are regularly used in conversations involving such types' (Myers-Scotton 1993b: 85).

However, such a neat correlation of varieties and types of relationships is not always discernible. The markedness theory of code-switching has therefore been criticized as too rigid and too static, presupposing as it does more or less fixed social meanings which are predictable and as such determine speakers' choices (Auer 1998). The weakness of the theory, its critics argue, is that it cannot deal with the fact that everyday life does not consist of well-defined recurrent situations and relationships with similar precedents. Communicative interaction should not be seen as unfolding in a space of pre-existing social meaning but rather as a dynamic process whose participants create social meaning as they go along, accommodating each other in a continuous give and take.[6]

Unmarked choices derive their significance from the possibility of making marked choices which are by definition rare but do occur. The markedness model of code-switching recognizes marked choices as the speaker's strategic use of a new code, but it does not provide a universally applicable answer to the question of why a speaker may choose not to conform to societal norms and, by consequence, cannot show how code-switching is employed to organize verbal interaction as a linguistic resource similar to other resources such as prosody or style. For instance, Li Wei (1998) describes how, in the interaction of Cantonese–English bilinguals of three successive immigrant generations in Newcastle upon Tyne, code-switching fulfils such organizing functions. Cantonese and English play different roles and are associated with different values for the members of the three generations who, however, interact. Li Wei demonstrates how speakers switch for various locally contingent reasons, for example to draw the interlocutor's attention; to comply with the interlocutor's choice of language; to help the conversation along. On the basis of his observations, he concludes that it seems far-fetched to suggest that by making their choices 'speakers are trying to index some predetermined, extra-linguistic RO sets' (Li Wei 1998: 161). Instead, an answer to the question of why they code-switch must be sought locally, conversation by conversation, speaker by speaker, turn by turn (Guerini 2006).

Finlayson and Slabbert (1997) discuss what is likely the most complex case of code-switching described in the literature so far. Linguistic and ethnic diversity is a well-known feature of South Africa's urban centres (Herbert 2001). Most speakers control, at various levels of proficiency, several languages and varieties and are able to calibrate the extent to which they want to emphasize ethnic differentiation by means of code choices. Finlayson and Slabbert analyse the code-switching behaviour by a group of six male friends who use as many as seven languages in the course of a single conversation:

Zulu, Xhosa, Southern Sotho, Tswana, Afrikaans, Tsotsitaal and English. They are able to show how social meanings are created by an intricate interplay among the speakers who all code-switch more than would be required by functional needs, the desire to make themselves understood or to manifest their ethnolinguistic identity. Finlayson and Slabbert (1997: 397) demonstrate that, in the event, a major motivation of code-switching is to 'maintain a delicate balance in the proportion allocated to each of the participating languages'. This could be interpreted as being a part of a relevant RO set; however, the proportion is not fixed but dependent upon setting and context of situation. In every conversation, 'the speaker may foreground any of the salient features according to what he/she wishes to index, either by code-switching or by tipping the balance'. Again, the analysis proceeds from one utterance to the next. The general rationale of a local analysis that imposes as little theory as possible on the data is stated succinctly by Auer. He stresses

> the sequential implicativeness of language choice in conversation, i.e. the fact that whatever language a participant chooses for the organisation of his or her turn, or for an utterance which is part of the turn, the choice exerts an influence on subsequent language choices by the same or other speakers.   (Auer 1984: 5)

According to this approach, every conversational move holds the potential to change not just the context but the assumptions, including assumptions about the relative markedness of possible code choices that are associated with it. Reasons for making marked code choices are many. Comparison of different communities in which code-switching is practised suggests that there is considerable variation with respect to how code-switching is used as one linguistic resource among others. This is so because the association between code and social meaning is variable, being relatively stable in some communities and very volatile in others. Accordingly, the most promising analytic approach to answering the question of why speakers code-switch may not be the same for all communities and all settings. Where the indexicality of a code is clear and stable, markedness theory is relevant; where this is not so or only to a lesser degree, as in the cases discussed by Li Wei (1998) and Finlayson and Slabbert (1997), the reasons for code-switching are better explained in terms of bringing about social meanings contextually.

Another important topic that has emerged in the discussion of social and linguistic constraints of code-switching is contact-induced grammaticalization as described and theoretically substantiated by Bernd Heine (Heine and Kuteva 2008). Rather than considering code-switching as a process of alternating between languages, grammaticalization theory introduces a diachronic dimension of the phenomenon. The speech behaviour of individuals is where language change happens, and this is also true of bilingual individuals who engage in code-switching.

Recognition of this fact makes code-switching appear in a new light as an external force of language change. So far the relationship between individual acts of code-switching and changing group norms that affect the language system is poorly understood, but this is clearly a promising field of sociolinguistic research about language contact (Matthews and Yip 2011).

Conclusion

In sum, the diversity of code-switching is such that the reasons why speakers switch can be explored fruitfully only if particular conditions are taken into account. Individual speakers who use the resources of two or more languages in the construction of conversations all have their own motivations for choosing now elements of L1 and then elements of L2. These motives are multifaceted, and hence their localization on a markedness scale captures one dimension only. The general lesson to be learnt from the study of code-switching is that the bilingual speaker has at any point in a conversation the capacity by means of code choice to activate social meanings, display preferences and attitudes, as well as his or her compliance with, or unwillingness to conform to, community norms. Code-switching highlights an issue of critical importance in this book: speakers make choices. Because at least two languages are involved, this is perhaps more obvious and more generally recognized than in other kinds of speech, but except for the fact that speakers choose from the resources provided by two different codes the general procedure is the same, choices being subject to linguistic and social restrictions. In code-switching these restrictions allow for the concurrent and alternating utilization of different codes. In other language-contact situations, the social restrictions are different, prompting speakers to make their choices in such a way that switching occurs less frequently or is avoided. To these we turn in the next chapter.

Questions for discussion

(1)   What is the difference between borrowing and code-switching?

(2)   What was the 'bound morpheme constraint' designed to do and why did it fail?

(3)   Discuss the implications of the distinction between intersentential and intrasentential code-switching for a linguistic theory of code-switching.

(4)   Code-switching has been described as a division of labour between a matrix language and an embedded language. What distinguishes them from each other, and how can the matrix language be identified?

Notes

1 The problem of classificatory procedures is spelt out rather categorically by Mühlhäusler (1996: 35) who argues that 'The difficulties of distinguishing between languages, dialects, communalects and such phenomena by present-day linguists do not so much reflect their inability to find these "objects" as their non-existence.'

2 Thomas (1991: 202) suggests that the standard languages of the world may be divided into two groups: '(1) those basically opposed to enrichment from other languages, (2) those which have generally assimilated foreign elements.' This division, he argues, has socio-political rather than structural reasons. Fodor (1983: 466) has proposed a similar distinction between languages ready to adopt loanwords, such as Hausa, Japanese, Vietnamese and Urdu, and those that do not, such as German, Croatian, Persian, Portuguese and Tamil.

3 The sociopsychological and socioeconomic motivations for borrowing have been analysed for various languages. A historically interesting case is that of Dutch loans in Japanese, since for about two hundred years from the mid seventeenth to the mid nineteenth century Dutch was the principal donor of non-Chinese lexical innovation in Japanese (cf. Coulmas 1992b: 264–73). More generally, Dutch, French, English, Spanish and Portuguese loan-words in languages around the world are testimony to Europe's expansion since the fifteenth century. For instance, Ngom (2002) demonstrates how French, Arabic, English and Spanish loans in Wolof reflect the colonial history of Senegal.

4 'Comp-Cl. 10' is a class 10 complementizer; 'Cl. 10-Pres-' is a class 10 present-tense inflection.

5 Jacobson (2001a), too, uses the term 'language alternation', referring to it as the third kind of code-switching where it is impossible to determine a dominant language.

6 The idea that code-switching ought to be analysed as dynamically progressing conversational events which include as a crucial component speaker expectations builds on Conversation Analysis, a sociological approach which stresses the importance of local contextualized production for an understanding of all verbal action. Auer (1998) brings together work on code-switching by researchers committed to this approach.

Useful online resources

A bibliography database on the subject of code-switching maintained by a research group at the University of Pennsylvania: http://ccat.sas.upenn.edu/plc/codeswitching/

Brian MacWhinney's CHAT transcription format, which includes a long list of references of coding and transcription systems: http://childes.psy.cmu.edu/manuals/chat.pdf Chapter 8

The LIPPS project strives to set up a computerized database of code-switching data. Its website also offers an introduction to a transcription system and various links that are relevant for the study of code-switching and other forms of mixed-language: www.ling.lancs.ac.uk/staff/mark/lipps/lipps.htm#What%20is

Journal of Language Contact: www.jlc-journal.org

Further reading

Auer, Peter (ed.) 1998. *Code-Switching in Conversation: Language, Interaction and Identity*. London and New York: Routledge.

Gardner-Chloros, Penelope. 2009. *Code-switching*. Cambridge University Press.

Jacobson, Rodolfo (ed.) 1998a. *Codeswitching Worldwide*. Berlin and New York: Mouton de Gruyter.

2001. Language alternation: the third kind of codeswitching mechanism. In Rodolfo Jacobson (ed.), *Codeswitching Worldwide II*. Berlin and New York: Mouton de Gruyter, 59–72.

Muysken, Pieter. 2000. *Bilingual Speech: A Typology of Code-Mixing*. Cambridge University Press.

Myers-Scotton, Carol. 1993a. *Social Motivations for Codeswitching: Evidence from Africa*. Oxford: Clarendon Press.

  1993b. *Duelling Languages: Grammatical Structure in Codeswitching*. Oxford: Clarendon Press.

Treffers-Daller, Jeanine. 1994. *Mixing Two Languages: French-Dutch Contact in a Comparative Perspective*. Berlin and New York: Mouton de Gruyter.

8 Diglossia and bilingualism: functional restrictions on language choice

– About my school, mum, dit l'enfant en marchant vers l'arrêt d'autobus.
– Oui? Dit la maman.
– It's a great school, isn't it?
– Oui, c'est une école formidable, répond-elle avec sincérité.
– The best school in town?
– La meilleure de la ville, oui.

Pierrette Flatiaux, Allons-nous être heureux?

Linguistic or cultural homogeneity of even one group is in a sense a fiction.

D. P. Pattanayak (1985: 402)

Outline of the chapter

Given that some 6,800 languages are spoken in the world, which nowadays is divided into some 200 polities, there is bound to be a large number of situations where several languages coexist in close proximity: in one country, in one city, in one company, or in one family. These situations form the substance of this chapter. They are of interest to the sociolinguist because the coexistence of languages is patterned rather than random. To discover the social patterns of bilingualism is to understand an important dimension of speakers' linguistic choices. To begin with, we consider a characteristic pattern of functional allocation of different languages or varieties that has attracted a great deal of attention. It is known as diglossia (from Greek δύο 'two' + γλῶσσα 'language'). The role of writing for the emergence of this pattern is discussed, comparing the Greek paradigm case with others in South Asia where it is particularly common. The remainder of the chapter treats other forms of societal bilingualism, considering the most important factors that have a bearing on the use of various languages, speech forms and styles. In language-contact situations, people develop a great variety of strategies to adjust their linguistic repertoires to the communicative purposes at hand, but whatever the situation, they invariably cooperate. This is most impressively in evidence when people of different linguistic backgrounds who do not share a common language interact for any length of time. In the event, they create a new one, a pidgin, that bridges the gap and, to the student of language in society, is testimony to the human desire to cooperate and to the ability to produce the means they need to do that. This process is touched upon, however briefly, at the end of the chapter.

> *Key terms:* diglossia, bilingualism, domain separation, (restricted) literacy, status and function

In communication speakers take into account normative expectations acquired in the course of socialization which allow them to anticipate the consequences of their linguistic choices. So far, we have discussed a number of social variables that affect choices, including the choice of codes which may be different languages or dialects of the same language. The range of choices is variable, but that speakers can and have to choose from more than one code is very common, both in bilingual societies and in monolingual ones whose members think of themselves as making choices between two noticeably diverse varieties of one language. In a number of cases, choice of these varieties does not depend on region, class, gender or age, but primarily on function and context. Such a configuration is known as 'diglossia'. In this chapter we will first examine the specifics of a diglossic situation and then compare it with other forms of societal bilingualism.

Diglossia

Consider the description of code choices in Bengali presented in Table 8.1. Chatterjee (1986: 298) adds this comment to his description: 'Ridiculous or sometimes comical will be the effect if the norms of situational selection between the two are violated.' It is not difficult to recognize in 'ridiculous or sometimes comical' a reaction to what in the previous chapter was called a marked choice. Norms do not determine a speaker's choice, but they give it a markedness measure relative to a particular speech event. The allocation of the two varieties of Bengali to different functional domains is very strict, with no overlapping, theoretically. Following a terminology introduced in a seminal paper on the subject by Charles Ferguson (1959), they are called 'High' (H) and 'Low' (L). 'Diglossia', too, became a fixed part of sociolinguistic terminology as a result of this influential article.[1]

H and L are varieties of the same language, Bengali in the example, but they are not dialects in the usual sense of the word or caste dialects, because the key determinants for choosing one or the other are not region or caste but functions and contexts. L is used by people for vernacular purposes in their homes, in the street and other informal contexts. It is the colloquial style that conveys intimacy and solidarity. H, on the other hand, is a formal style associated with power and formality. It is based in the written language which is used in public speeches, for religious functions and in other formal contexts. Because of its literary tradition it enjoys high esteem and has

Table 8.1 *Complementary functional distribution of varieties in Bengali (adapted from Chatterjee 1986: 298)*

FUNCTION	HIGH	LOW
Public address of all sorts	+	−
Scripted speech	+	−
News broadcast	+	−
News journals	+	−
Creative literature except novels, dramas and short stories	+	−
Narrative description in novels and short stories	+	−
Formal letters	+	−
Class lectures	+	−
Dialogues in novels and dramas	−	+
Informal personal letters	−	+
Conversation with family members	−	+
Instruction to workmen, servants and subordinates	−	+

Table 8.2 *Common characteristics of diglossia*

	L	H
Function	intimacy, solidarity	formality, power
Context of use	informal	formal
Mode	predominantly spoken	predominantly written
Norm/standard	based on modern speech	based on classical texts; archaic
Lexicon	mixed	purist; technical
Acquisition	home transmission	schooling
Prestige	low	high

norm-setting potential. The grammar of the H variety is more conservative and more rigidly standardized than that of L, and the H lexicon, though largely shared with L, tends to be puristic and includes a portion of technical vocabulary. Another difference between H and L concerns acquisition: while L is acquired spontaneously in the home, H must be learnt by instruction. This implies that H is not spoken as a native variety by anyone, a feature which distinguishes diglossia from a standard-and-dialects situation, since the standard variety of a language is often locally based. Thanks to its association with schooling and a classical literature, H enjoys higher prestige than L. These differences can be summarized in Table 8.2.

There are, of course, many local specifics distinguishing diglossic situations from one another, but the general functional compartmentalization of H and L is frequent enough to warrant a special term to distinguish this configuration from other situations of two coexisting varieties, one of which has higher prestige than the other. The prestige gradient is also noticeable in standard-and-dialects situations. However, Trudgill's triangle (see. p. 33 above), which correlates dialect and social class, does not so obviously apply to diglossia. This is because in a diglossic situation the low-prestige variety is to a much lesser degree indexical of the social identity of the speakers than dialectal speech in a common dialect-and-standard situation where some speakers always use the standard or a variety close to the standard, which is also the language of education, of the media and of officialdom, while for others a dialect is the main means of expression most of the time.

Diglossia is very common in South Asia where it goes back many hundreds of years. Chatterjee (1986: 301) remarks that 'all the Indo- Aryan languages of India, except perhaps Hindi-Urdu, are typically more or less analogous to Bengali in this respect'. And Britto (1986) has demonstrated, especially with his detailed study of Tamil diglossia, that this is also true of the Dravidian languages. In India, the H/L distinction does not coincide with caste dialects because in everyday settings everyone speaks L. The basic distribution is functional, not social. Yet, by virtue of the fact that H is acquired through formal schooling, there is still in many societies a social dimension to the choice between H and L. Proficient control of H implies the ability to make choices from the full range from L to H. But individuals with little or no education are limited in their choices, since H is not a part of their linguistic repertoire. For this reason, diglossia has been characterized as a language situation that not only coincides with but causes and helps to maintain high levels of illiteracy, thus reinforcing social inequality.[2]

However, cases of diglossia in other parts of the world where illiteracy has ceased to be a social problem several generations ago while, nonetheless, the wide gap between H and L persists, raise doubts as to whether diglossia can be considered an independent variable in social development. The Swiss German diglossia, identified by Ferguson (1959) as one of the clear cases, is a prominent counterexample. In the event, H is Standard High German, which the Swiss call *Schriftdeutsch* 'written German', and L is Swiss German, or rather any of the regional varieties so labelled. Diglossia has been upheld in German-speaking Switzerland without social asymmetry in the range of available choices by teaching H to everybody (Haas 2002). The Swiss German diglossia shows little sign of weakening because it is supported by the speech community, many of whose members 'try deliberately to cultivate diglossia by making the distinction between standard and dialect as clear as possible'. It gets official backing, too, for 'the political and educational authorities of Switzerland are interested in the preservation of the diglossic situation' (Keller 1982: 77).

Individual speakers' context-specific code choices solidify to form a collective preference for maintaining the distinction between H and L rather than bringing about convergence which, given that the same standard language, German, is part of the common standard-and-dialects configuration across the border, would be a realistic option; it is, however, dispreferred. In the event, manifested preferences are reflected in the official language policy which is designed to protect not one variety or the other but their functional complementarity. The idea that different functions and different contexts require different varieties is characteristic of all diglossic situations. In some it is given official endorsement. For example, it was reported about Greek diglossia, another of Ferguson's original cases, that in 1941, the senate of Athens University called on the Ministry of Education to discharge a professor for publishing two articles in L rather than H. This was considered provocative and the minister, accordingly, complied by suspending the professor for two months from his post because he used 'a linguistic idiom inappropriate for university teaching' which was 'harmful to the Greek language and consequently to the Greek nation' (Frangoudaki 2002: 106).

This incident is reminiscent of the punitive consequences of a marked choice of address terms discussed in Chapter 6 above (see p. 107). In both cases it is clear that collective concerns are affected by individual choices. Regulatory mechanisms to sustain norms do not necessarily involve legal action. The point to note is that choices concerning H and L in a diglossia situation like those of politeness expressions are always subject to social sanctions.

Diglossia is part of a linguistic tradition which in the cases that have been studied has proved to be very stable. Greek diglossia goes back to the Atticist movement around the first century BCE which preached the doctrine that language must not be allowed to change (Browning 1969: 49f.). The Byzantine Middle Ages saw the development of a Christianized Atticism based on the high style of the Scriptures. Its hypotactic syntax and purist lexis stood in sharp contrast to the paratactic syntax and mixed lexis of the low style (Eideneier 2000). A further reinforcement in modern times came when early in the nineteenth century Greece regained independent statehood and fervent nationalism found expression, among other things, in a purist movement harking back to Ancient Greek, as a result of which the 'purified language' *Katharevousa* became the official language of the state, H, contrasting with Demotic Greek, L. In 1976, Katharevousa lost state support and Standard Demotic Greek became the official language of Greece. The expectation that 'the language question', as it is known in Greece, would thus be settled was not borne out, because the debate about what elements of Katharevousa should be admitted to Demotic continues.[3]

Some diagnostic features of the two varieties are given in Table 8.3 for illustration. The actual relationship between Katharevousa and Demotic Greek is much more complex with intermediate varieties (μεικτη *(mikti)*), fusion or hybridization of H and L and gradual retreat of Katharevousa to the benefit of Demotic (Alexiou 1982; Frangoudaki 1997). The point to note in the present context is the long history of the diglossic split in the Greek language.

Table 8.3 *Differences between Katharevousa and Demotic Greek*

	Katharevousa	Demotic
Lexical differences		
water	ídhor	neró
fish	opsárion	psári
bread	psomíon	psomí
cup	kípelon	fidzáni
house	íkos	ikía
hearth	estía	dzáki
door	thíra	pórta
eye	ofthalmós	máti
nose	rís	míti
flower	ánthos	louloúdi
bird	ptinón	poulí
Lexical innovation		
	calques	foreign loanwords
Phonological differences		
	K	D
	final /-n/	no final /-n/
	shifting accent in adjectives	fixed accent in adjectives

Morphological differences:
Different declensions, conjugations and derivations

Syntactic differences:
        'He will come tomorrow.'

Katharevousa: théli afíhthí   ávrion
                        he wants arrive_{aor. Subjunct.} tomorrow

Demotic: tha ftási   ávrio
      fut. particle he comes tomorrow

In India, too, where diglossia is most common, domain separation of H and L is very old (Schiffman 1996), as it is in the Arabic-speaking world (Blau 1977). What caused the split, and what sustained it? This is a difficult question not just because it involves a complex interplay of variables but also because, much like 'code-switching' discussed above (pp. 126f.), 'diglossia' is a notion whose definition has been contested (see below). We shall concentrate here on three factors only, which are widely considered essential in the aetiology of diglossia: writing, standardization and linguistic ideology.

Writing

The social motivations of domain separation are many, but the introduction of writing is incontrovertibly of crucial importance. It has been argued that writing is a necessary, though not in itself a sufficient condition for diglossia to evolve (Coulmas 1987, 2003). In all cases recognized in the literature as diglossia, H is used in writing. It may also be used for some functions in speech, and L may be used in writing, too. However, the historical roots of the phenomenon, as well as contemporary practice, lie in the fact that H has been and continues to be more closely linked to the written medium. After the introduction of writing into a community, restricted literacy creates a hospitable environment for diglossia to evolve, because only a thin elite have access. However, the fact that established diglossia is not necessarily eliminated by mass literacy has already been noted above. Writing interacts with the next factor, standardization.

Standardization

Societies that have developed stable institutions of government and cult, not necessarily distinct, tend also to develop a code of religious and administrative-ceremonial practices recognizably different from the more volatile codes of ordinary everyday life. This is another force behind the functional complementarity of diglossia. Like a dress code that functions as a symbolic expression of power relations, this linguistic code becomes subject to deliberate regulation leading to a canon of good usage. Normative grammars fixing a standard thus evolve. The standard variety which eventually becomes H serves important functions, providing the language with a centre and helping to protect the privileges of the power elite. In diglossic situations, H is generally more highly standardized than L.[4] The main reason is that the basis for standardization is a body of literature; sacred texts, such as the Koran which was instrumental in preserving the standard of Classical Arabic; or literary works, such as the rich body of Tamil epic, bardic and didactic texts which serves as a reference point of Tamil H. Standardization and writing go hand in hand. H is a literate variety, L is oral. The monopoly of H on writing can be undermined, of course, or altogether abolished, as happened when the Romance vernaculars in medieval Europe started to be used in writing. As a result, the vernaculars gained the status of independent languages with standards of their own. The diglossia of Latin-H versus Romance vernaculars L thus broke down (Wright 1991; Adams 2003).[5] The newly established standards were once again based on writing, often on a vernacular translation of the Bible. A similar development took place in East Asia where for centuries Classical Chinese served H functions in ways that have many parallels with Latin in Europe. While no one's native language, it was used for written communication both in China and in adjacent countries, notably Korea, Japan and Vietnam, that adopted the art of writing from China. In these three countries, the incremental expansion of writing in the vernacular eventually led to the abandonment of Classical Chinese and the establishment of all-purpose national standard languages. In China, too, a diglossic domain differentiation between the classical language and the vernacular persisted for a very long time constituting what Ferguson (1959) identified as diglossia on the largest scale ever. Today, as a consequence of modernization with mass literacy and general education, diglossia in the Sino-centric world has given way to a situation of standard and dialects. Only in Hong Kong can distinct diglossic patterns still be identified, 'the H role being played by Standard Chinese (Mandarin) as opposed to the L role played by Cantonese' (Snow 2010: 156). Hong Kong is a very special case where the colonial heritage of English as the language of the governing class looms large. However, diglossia in Hong Kong still rests on the popular perception that Standard Chinese is a more appropriate vehicle for writing than Cantonese which is less rigidly standardized than Mandarin (Snow 2010: 167).

A standard does not come about naturally. In all speech communities of any size, it is based on writing, which lends it a discernible form and hence stability.[6] Wurm (1994: 257) sees in a standard 'the artificial unification of several dialects'. The creation and preservation of a linguistic standard involve deliberate acts of choice which must be justified. Providing such justification is the task of linguistic ideology.

Linguistic ideology

Common themes of linguistic ideology revolve around notions of a language's beauty, authenticity, purity and sacredness. They converge on the doctrine that a certain variety embodies the language in question in its best form, which must be guarded against corruption (Lippi-Green 1997, Kroskrity 2004). This is much easier when a clearly defined written standard is available than in the absence of such. With regard to Greek diglossia, Sotiropoulos (1992: 164) claims that 'graphicentrism', defined as the primacy of the written language, permeates the linguistic ideology of Greek culture. Similar precepts more or less explicitly endorse function-specific H/L separation for all speech communities living with diglossia. The actual contents of cultural belief systems supporting diglossia differ; their common function is to single out a variety of language as H which is subject to norms investing it with the prestige necessary for being accepted as a standard language.

The close calibration between writing, standardization and linguistic ideology, which is at the heart of diglossia, has far-reaching significance for a more general understanding of how society manages its linguistic resources. More clearly than other varieties, every H is an artefact and so is the functional domain allocation of H and L. A theory of how linguistic ideologies affect language remains to be formulated. For present purposes, suffice it to note that an ideologically legitimized standard variety set in writing is clear testimony to deliberate canalization of the 'natural' development of language.

The genetic question

One question remains to be mentioned because it has fuelled the discussion about diglossia for decades. What if the functions associated with H are carried out with a superposed language unrelated to L? What if domain separation is not between German and Swiss German, Standard and vernacular Arabic, and literary and spoken Tamil, but between English and Welsh, Spanish and Guarani, or Hebrew and Yiddish, Chinese and Korean, Chinese and Japanese, etc.? Fishman (1967) made a strong case to extend the notion of diglossia to include such cases of bilingualism, provided that the functional domain allocation sufficiently resembles that of Ferguson's (1959) 'classical' cases of genetic diglossia. The question, then, is whether genetic relatedness of H and L ought to be considered a critical feature that distinguishes diglossia from other configurations of societal bi- or multilingualism. The mainstream position on this issue at present is an affirmative answer to this question, and the ensuing view that a broad definition of diglossia as including domain-specific arrangements of both genetically related and genetically unrelated codes obscures rather than elucidates sociolinguistic theory. Diglossia is one kind of societal bilingualism, not vice versa.

Notice that, as in the case of code-switching, much hinges on the weight assigned to the defining features of diglossia. The proponents of a narrow definition see in the genetic relationship of H and L many common underlying grammatical parameters and a lexicon with many shared and recognizably related elements, while at the same time being so different that intercommunicability is not always given, a situation that is fundamentally different from any other arrangement of linguistic domain separation. Yet, the counterarguments in favour of admitting other kinds of linguistic differences in the overall H/L schema, most forcefully and succinctly advanced by Fishman (1967, 1980), have their own merits and are found compelling by many.

Fishman's argument rests on a twofold distinction he makes with respect to the aetiology of diglossia: genetically related versus unrelated codes, and monocultural versus bicultural environment. His paradigm case is the Hebrew/Yiddish diglossia in pre-nineteenth-century Ashkenaz. Hebrew and Yiddish are unrelated languages, but Hebrew was not a superimposed exogenetic H to the Jews who always considered it 'their' language. Rather, the population changed its L as a result of migration and contact, creating the Yiddish language within their own cultural sphere. The eventual outcome was a monocultural domain separation comparable from a functional point of view with diglossia of the endogenetic type. What is more, if we go further back in history, the complementary distribution of Biblical Hebrew and Mishnaic Hebrew in antiquity fits the description of endogenetic diglossia. In a sense, Yiddish and other Jewish languages assumed the functions colloquial Hebrew once had. The temporal horizon that is needed to see this link is, however, considerable and not open in the inspection of

Table 8.4 *Four types of conventional domain separation*

	monocultural	bicultural
endogenetic	1 Classical Arabic H Vernacular Arabic L	2 French H Haitian Creole L
exogenetic	3 Hebrew H Yiddish L	4 Spanish H Guarani L

most other languages. In the end it is thus for historical reasons that Fishman considers a common cultural aetiology and conventional domain separation essential. If, following this line of thought, the cultural aspect of aetiology is taken into account, a cross-tabulation with the genetic aspect can be construed, yielding four types of conventional H/L domain separation, as illustrated in Table 8.4.

Cells 1 and 2 represent two different types of endogenetic diglossia, although this holds true for 2 only if Haitian Creole is considered a kind of French rather than something else. Cell 1 differs from 2 in that Arabic diglossia developed within the monocultural sphere of the Arabic-speaking Islamic world, while 2 came into being in the wake of colonization which brought together two very different cultures. Cell 3, the Hebrew/Yiddish case, shares with 1 the monocultural aetiology, although the codes are unrelated. Finally, cell 4 is an arrangement where H and L are genetically and culturally unrelated but conventionally allocated to complementary domains in much the same way as in the other three cases.

Even leaving aside for a moment the question whether the four cells of the above matrix should be subsumed under the single rubric of 'diglossia', this is not the end of the issue. As pointed out above, Fishman (2002) adds to it another important dimension: time depth. How long, for how many generations, a consensual arrangement of asymmetric domains has been in place, and whether it evolved gradually over a long period of time or was brought about abruptly are important predictors for the stability or transitory nature of that arrangement and, therefore, also additional characteristics that distinguish sociolinguistic situations. There are, in his view, 'more than four kinds of diglossia' (Fishman 2002: 95). The issue of whether they should all be called 'diglossia' or, on the contrary, endogenetic and exogenetic domain differentiation of codes warrants terminological differentiation; it is an issue not likely to be resolved by further debate or research. The lesson to be remembered about diglossia, no matter how narrowly or broadly defined, is that speakers choose varieties, mainly to suit different contexts and social domains, thereby creating and perpetuating a verbal repertoire of asymmetrical allocation of codes, one of which is closely associated with a written norm and hence perceived to be more of a cultivated artefact than the other. The arrangement itself is cultural rather than natural, and it is social rather than individual. Diglossia is a social norm to which the individual speaker adheres.

Bilingualism

The matrix in Table 8.4 is designed for just two coexisting codes. In many cases, however, H and L are part of a more complex arrangement of varieties and languages. Consider, as an example, Arabic diglossia as it manifests itself in Morocco. The seemingly simple dichotomy of Literary Arabic, H, and Moroccan Arabic, L, is embedded in a situation that involves another variety of Arabic, called 'Middle Moroccan Arabic', as well as two other languages, Berber, called 'Tamazight' in Morocco, and French. All of these codes serve different functions in Moroccan society dependent on demographic strength, historical and socioeconomic dynamics, and power. Figure 8.1 captures some of the relationships between them. Since the percentage numbers given in the boxes add up to 200, it follows that there is a high degree of bilingualism in Morocco. With the exception of some monolingual rural Berbers, virtually the entire population has the ability to choose between several varieties. Most choices are based on conventional

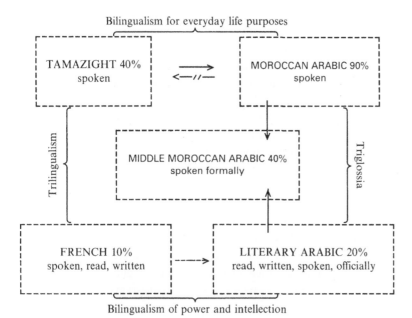

Figure 8.1 *Relationships between the languages and dialects of Morocco (adapted from Youssi 1995: 31). 'Tamazight' is the term used by native speakers of Berber for their language.*

domain allocations, but by no means all; for in Morocco, as in most other parts of the world, speakers negotiate the functional roles of the various codes of their linguistic repertoire.

The codes in Figure 8.1, the functional roles they fulfil, and the conditions under which they are used reflect significant aspects of Moroccan society, both on the level of macro-structure, with regard to social stratification, and on that of micro-structure, with regard to possible forms of social interaction. Generalizing from this example and rephrasing Fishman (1965), the following question encapsulates what a theory of societal bilingualism should explain: *Who chooses to speak what language to whom and when?*

The relevant community

An important preliminary issue that has to be addressed before this question can be dealt with reasonably is to determine the kind of community about which it can be asked. Most countries are multilingual, but a country such as Morocco is not the only relevant unit of research on societal bilingualism and multilingualism.[7] For example, in some restricted areas in the north of Morocco around the two Spanish enclaves of Ceuta and Melilla, Spanish enjoys a certain currency. In the economy and education English is rapidly gaining ground being the 'fastest growing European language in Morocco' (Sadiqi 2003: 50) that together with Literary Arabic and French links Moroccans with speakers in other parts of the world. When bilingualism is being investigated it is crucial to identify the relevant unit: a nation-state, a city, a frontier district, a township, a ghetto, an immigrant neighbourhood, a soccer team or a family.[8] Morocco is a multilingual country in which the above-mentioned languages and some others play different roles in different places. The languages themselves define overlapping communities which, from the point of view of the sociolinguistic situation of Morocco, is not an accidental feature of these languages but one of the factors determining their status and function in that country.

In multilingual societies, language choice takes place on two levels. At a higher level of macro-sociolinguistic investigation, language choice is informed by language planning, language policy and language legislation (see Chapter 11), whereas language choice in a particular interaction is a micro-sociolinguistic process. Both levels are interrelated, since individual choices are subject to social norms and, to some degree, institutionalized restrictions. For the analysis of communication practices in multilingual societies based on the observation of actual language choices, two questions must be asked:

- What are the intentions of an individual when making a particular choice?
- What are the external factors influencing the specific decision?

Status and function

The status of a language has been defined as 'what people can do with a language' as distinct from its functions, that is, 'what they actually do with it' (Mackey 1989: 7). For example, can people use Middle Moroccan Arabic in higher education? The answer to this question is, yes. But do they actually use it in higher education? Here the answer is, only to a very limited extent, the bulk of university courses being taught in French and, increasingly, English (Ennaji 2005). Status has to do with whether a particular language has a written norm, is used in writing, is represented in a body of literature, has a reference grammar, technical terminology, etc., and whether it enjoys recognition on the political level. It is an important variable but does not by itself determine the function that language actually serves in the community. The same language can have a different status and different functions in different countries, for example, being the language of the majority population in one country and of a minority in another. Demographic strength is an important variable in any multilingual situation which, however, interacts with other variable properties of a language. Consider English in India. Nominally, it is a minority language spoken as a first language by a very small section of the population only. But the status and function of English in India do not reflect its demographic strength in that country. Srivastava (1984) has pointed out that the *Quantum* dimension must be related to the *Power* dimension in order satisfactorily to describe the position of a language in a society.

English in India belongs to type C in Table 8.5, combining − *Quantum* and + *Power*. Type B, called 'Janta' meaning the general mass, is the opposite, + *Quantum* and − *Power*. An example would be Cantonese in Hong Kong under British rule and, to some extent, still today. Similar configurations persist in other postcolonial settings.

The *Quantum* and *Power* dimensions interact with each other and they interact with status and function. Japanese is the unassailable national and majority language of Japan, but a small minority language in Brazil. However, thanks to its status as a highly developed written language with a recognized standard, its position in Brazil is relatively strong. The subtle

Table 8.5 *Four categories of languages in multilingual societies (Srivastava 1984: 101)*

		Power	
		+	−
Quantum	+	(A) Majority	(B) Janta
	−	(C) Elite	(D) Minority

covariation of *Quantum/Power*, on the one hand, and status/function, on the other, implies that no two bilingual situations are alike, but it also implies that the languages involved are virtually never on an equal footing. A power differential between language groups is always an aspect of multilingualism.

Domains

Several approaches to differentiate kinds of bilingual situations have been proposed. One is in terms of 'domains', that is by identifying through observation areas of language use which can be classified as requiring a particular language – e.g. the pulpit, the bench – or making its use highly probable – e.g. a neighbourhood pub. 'Domain' is a theoretical concept. It refers to an aggregate of locales of communication – public vs. private; role relationships between participants – family members, official/client; and kinds of interaction – formal vs. informal. The domains which are typically distinguished include home, work, school, church, market, government and leisure. Whether there is need for more fine-grained distinctions – e.g. health services, media, gastronomy – must be decided case by case. If the association between domains and codes is sufficiently stable, as is the case, for instance, in many diglossic situations, a criterial hierarchy for the decision process can be established. As an example, consider Rubin's decision-making chart for language choice in Paraguay (Figure 8.2).

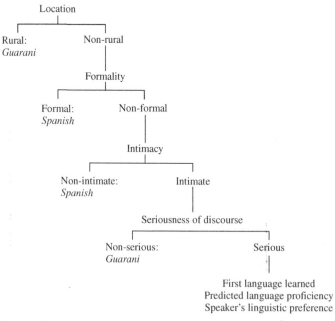

Figure 8.2 *Ordered dimensions in the choice of language: Guarani and Spanish in Paraguay (after Rubin 1985: 119)*

Local context

The chart in Figure 8.2 is an abstraction suggesting a unidirectional process with a definite outcome. It has a certain predictive potential, as it tells us what the most expected choice would be under certain circumstances. However, it does not provide for unexpected choices or a method to evaluate the impact made by such a choice and its consequences for the interaction. And it cannot deal with how, in conversations whose participants are aware of the availability of different codes, social meaning of language choice, for example ethnolinguistic membership, is negotiated on a moment-to-moment basis. An approach that is focused on changing contexts along the lines of the conversation-analytic investigation of code-switching discussed in Chapter 7 above is more suitable for capturing the social meaning of individual language choice and the on-going process of expressing one's social and/or ethnic identity through language. But notice that in some settings language choice is more negotiable than in others. In many European cities that are multilingual to varying degrees, negotiating the language is a regular part of many interactions, whereas in institutional settings where the language is determined by rules of procedure, individual choice is much more limited.[9]

Accommodation

Another contextual approach is speech accommodation theory (SAT), as developed by Giles and his associates, which investigates speakers' strategies of convergence, divergence and maintenance in their speech behaviour, taking into account aspects of style, such as speech rate and pauses, as well as paralinguistic phenomena, such as volume, speech rate and pauses (Giles, Bourhis and Taylor 1977; Coupland 2010). Originally framed as a socio-psychological model of speech behaviour, this theory assumes that people are motivated to fine-tune their speech styles depending on whom they talk to, reducing the distance between them by adopting certain features of their interlocutor's speech, or, conversely, increasing the distance by making their style more dissimilar to their interlocutor's. It is worth noting that the ability to accommodate that finds expression in style shifting is part of normal communicative competence. Style shifting allows speakers to align themselves with a group they want to identify with. The gist of this theory's significance for sociolinguistics is summarized by Trudgill (1986: 39) as follows:

> In face-to-face interaction ... speakers accommodate to each other linguistically by reducing the dissimilarities between their speech patterns and adopting features from each other's speech.

While Trudgill is concerned with how the adoption or copying of dialectal features in face-to-face interaction leads to dialect levelling and language change in the long run, the disposition to accommodate is also effective in conversational encounters involving speakers of different languages. It comes to bear in the initial language choice in an interaction usually leading to a consensual decision on one language for the ensuing conversation and often for future conversations between the interactants. Bilingual conversations such as the one put into Flatiaux's novel quoted at the beginning of this chapter are relatively rare precisely because there seems to be a universal norm to settle on a common code for one conversation. It is, however, possible for speakers to accommodate each other, passively tolerating each other's use of the language in which their respective productive ability is greatest. Such an arrangement is most likely when interactants know each other well (Lüdi 1987). Although millions of people habitually use more than one language in their daily lives, selection of one code for one conversation is generally favoured.

Networks

Individual language choice in multilingual societies often depends on and is predictable on the basis of networks. As discussed in Chapter 2, each individual is involved in a number of social networks. Depending on the density and diversity of a speaker's networks and his or her position therein, language choice takes place. In a study of Hungarian–German bilingualism in Austria, Gal (1979) demonstrated how networks required their members to show solidarity through language choice and how macro-social changes such as industrialization and urbanization brought about changes in the evaluation of the local language, Hungarian, and disrupted the social networks associated with it. Altehenger-Smith (1987) applied the same approach to the more complex situation of multilingual Singapore with four official languages, Mandarin, Malay, Tamil and English, as well as a range of Chinese dialects (see p. 27 above), varieties of Malay, some other Indian languages, and languages for restricted purposes, such as Arabic as the religious language of Singapore's Muslims. In such an environment it is obvious 'that language choice not only in interethnic but also intraethnic interaction is an everyday task in Singapore' (Altehenger-Smith 1987: 82). She demonstrates how the function of networks in language choice is mitigated by other variables such as the demographic strength of the ethnic groups and the linguistic diversity exhibited by these groups. For example, both the Indian and the Chinese ethnic groups use English more frequently for intraethnic communication than the Malay ethnic group, because the latter is more linguistically homogeneous than the former. In interethnic networks, Malays were found to do the least accommodating, an observation Altehenger-Smith explains as an effect of macro-level factors on micro-level choice. The Malays in Singapore do not belong to the dominant culture or to the power elite and, therefore, may feel a stronger need for self-assertion through language. It has also been observed that the close proximity and frequent interaction of Singapore's many language groups have given rise to language mixing and new varieties, notably Singlish (Singapore English) used as an interethnic lingua franca (Rudby 2005; Alsagoff 2010). Li Wei (1994) demonstrated the usefulness of network analysis for predicting the language choice in a Chinese community at Tyneside near Newcastle, UK, and Lanza and Svendsen (2007) applied it to an investigation of language maintenance in the Filipino community in Oslo, Norway.

In these and other studies, network analysis proved a useful tool for modelling language choice and understanding its social significance, but since this approach concentrates on small groups it is often supplemented by other approaches more suitable to fathom the macro-social dimensions of bilingualism.

Measuring bilingualism

Bilingualism in Singapore is different from bilingualism in Morocco, bilingualism in an Austrian border region and bilingualism in Colombo, Sri Lanka. What is more, the bilingualism of one member of a multilingual community differs from that of another. What are the differences, and how can they be integrated into a common descriptive framework? What is needed eventually is a typology of bi-/multilingualism including sufficiently detailed criteria to account for the language choices of speakers living in multilingual environments. Researchers now agree that fully balanced bilingualism at a level of native control of two languages is exceedingly rare for individuals and more so for groups and that, therefore, different types of bilingualism should be recognized. A well-known distinction is that between *simultaneous* and *sequential* bilingualism, which focuses on whether L1 and L2 are learnt at the same time, or whether L2 is built on L1. Another distinction is between *additive* bilingualism, where an individual's repertoire is extended by an additional language, and *subtractive* bilingualism, where the acquisition of an L2 results in the replacement of the speaker's L1. The same distinction is also referred to as elite vs. folk bilingualism, reflecting the different starting points and perspectives of changing a speaker's linguistic repertoire by acquiring another language, for example, learning a foreign language to enhance one's human capital vs. acquiring survival skills in an immigrant environment. It follows from the different kinds of bilingualism that an individual's linguistic repertoire is not necessarily stable over a lifespan (De Bot and Schrauf 2009), that is, one's first language does not always remain one's dominant language. Notice that this observation concurs with the lifetime changes of monolingual speakers discussed in Chapter 5 (pp. 86–90). Measuring the bilingual competence of individuals is a research field in its own right at the crossroads of psycholinguistics, neurolinguistics and language teaching.

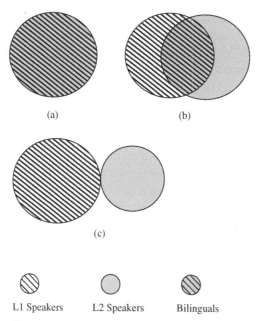

(a)   (b)

(c)

L1 Speakers   L2 Speakers   Bilinguals

Figure 8.3 *Three types of contact between language groups*

Measuring bilingualism and multilingualism at the group level is more complex, because it can refer to very diverse entities, as discussed above. A bilingual community is not necessarily composed of bilingual individuals only; rather, it is the percentage of bilingual speakers with variable degrees of competence in the languages involved that distinguish multilingual communities from one another. In situations of stable grassroots bilingualism, as are common in India, virtually all members are competent in two languages, the ideal case represented graphically in Figure 8.3(a). But like individuals, communities are rarely fully balanced. Intersections of two groups of variable size made up of bilinguals as depicted in 8.3(b) are more common. Arrangements of this sort are more stable in some societies than in others. This issue will be discussed in the next chapter. The imbalanced nature of bilingualism also manifests itself in the fact that L1/L2 bilinguals are usually distributed very unevenly in the groups of L1 and L2 primary speakers, the socially weaker group having a higher incidence of bilingualism.

This is very noticeable in immigrant groups under assimilation pressure. Because of the social inequality commonly associated with it, bilingualism often becomes a political issue, a topic that will be dealt with together with other language policy concerns in Chapter 11.

Cooperation

As we have seen, the phenomenon of societal bilingualism means that speakers of different languages have found ways to communicate with each other and thus regulate their social life. It is the bilingual individuals connecting both groups who create ligatures thus bringing together members of different ethnic and linguistic groups to form a single society. They embody the social nature of language even where language itself seems to get in the way of communication. The extreme case in this respect is a situation where speakers of different languages and no common language are brought together by external circumstances, as modelled in Figure 8.3(c). Conquest, imperial expansion, slave trade, war, colonization and overseas trade have caused such situations in the past, especially in coastal areas of Central and South America, in the Caribbean, in West Africa, in Papua New Guinea, in southern China and in the Pacific. Many of the languages we find in these areas bear witness to these social-historical circumstances: Bislama, Krio, Papiamentu, Sranan, Tok Pisin and Unserdeutsch, among many others. These are called pidgin and creole languages. It is not long ago that they were denigrated as aberrant, corrupted and bastardized, but today linguists agree that these languages not only warrant their attention but are among the most fascinating objects of study, bearing witness as they do to the very humanity of language.

English words derived from pidgin languages

Chinese Pidgin English	*Haitian Creole*
chop-chop	accoma
long time no see	voodoo
Hawaiian Pidgin	*Kriol*
go for broke	walkabout
Jamaican Creole	*Tok Pisin*
baby mama	bus kanaka
punani	titi
	Tok Pisin

In many ways, pidgins and creoles open up a window on the 'roots of language'[10] since as reduced languages they comprise what is essential about the human faculty of language. In recognition of this fact, pidgin and creole linguistics has developed into a huge academic subdiscipline with its own journals and scholarly societies. Research in this field is much too extensive to even attempt a brief review here. However, there is a reason to mention pidgin and creole languages in the present context. It is that these languages manifest not only the structural essence of human language, but also the essence of the function of language in human society. When people by force of circumstances are deprived of a common language, what do they do? The answer we can gather from the existence of numerous pidgin languages around the world is that they set themselves to the task of creating a new one. The important lesson to be learnt from this for socio-linguistics is that language is the result rather than the prerequisite of cooperative action. Language, we have stressed repeatedly, is a collective product and as such a result of innumerable acts of choice by individuals mutually accommodating each other in the interest of achieving comity and understanding. Rather than resigning themselves to the silence imposed upon them by the uncoordinated coexistence of two non-intercommunicable languages, their speakers, when they live in one place, build a bridge enabling them to come together. Out of a situation of abrupt contact of two language groups – societal bilingualism without bilingual individuals, as it were – a new language is thus born.

Conclusion

In this chapter we have distinguished stable and unstable socio-linguistic arrangements. Among the relatively stable ones, diglossia occupies a special position having prompted numerous detailed descriptions and the quest for a general theory. While opinions remain divided as to whether the concept should be reserved to genetically related varieties only or be expanded to include cases of unrelated varieties used by a speech community for complementary functions, this dispute is eventually of a terminological rather than substantive nature. What distinguishes diglossia from other forms of societal bi- and multilingualism is the functional division of labour of the two varieties which gives it stability. More clearly than in other cases of coexisting languages and varieties, this division of labour can be analytically related to linguistic characteristics, perceived and real, of the varieties rather than their speakers; that is, written vs. spoken, standardized vs. variable, etc. Under conditions of diglossia, H, but not L, is deemed suitable for formal and written communication. In other forms of societal multi-lingualism, attributes that can explain how coexisting varieties are used refer to groups of speakers, ethnic, social and power differentials, etc. rather than to structural features of the languages involved. What is more, the instability of sociolinguistic arrangements does not ensue from language-inherent features, but from sociodemographic, economic and political developments which, consequently, must be taken into consideration in order to understand the dynamics. This also holds for contact situations out of which a new language comes into existence. While the linguistic material of which the pidgin is built, that is, two different languages, obviously has a strong influence on the outcome, the manner in which these resources are put together is determined by social rather than linguistic variables.

Questions for discussion

(1)   Is the introduction of writing into a community a necessary or sufficient condition for the emergence of diglossia?

(2)   Is diglossia indicative of, or conducive to, social inequality?

(3)   Is diglossia natural? What does it imply for the notion of 'natural language'?

(4)   How does the status of a language in a community interact with its demographic strength?

(5)   What kinds of bilingualism can you distinguish, and how do individual bilingualism and societal bilingualism relate to each other?

Notes

1. Both the recognition of the phenomenon and the coining of the term predated Ferguson (1959) by more than half a century. Describing spoken and written varieties of Greek, Krumbacher (1902) used the term 'Diglossie', as did Marçais (1930) in his work about Arabic. However, it was Ferguson who saw the commonality of function-specific variety differentiation and made diglossia a crucial concept of sociolinguistics.
2. The issue of diglossia and illiteracy is discussed by Britto (1986: 290f.) who argues that diglossia does not deter the increase of literacy.
3. Holton (2002) sees in 'Standard Modern Greek' a result of intralingual convergence, but also notes that this process has not come to a conclusion.
4. Bi-modal standardization of H and L without mixing has occurred, for example, in Bengali (Chatterjee 1986: 300) and Greek (Frangoudaki 2002: 102), but it is more typical that a single standard evolves.
5. Another case of diglossia was resolved as the result of a new written standard being introduced in Afrikaans which shed its L status vis-á-vis Dutch H early in the twentieth century. Cf. du Plessis (1990).
6. In many environments standardization makes languages, as distinct from dialects, manageable and countable. See, for examples from Ghana and Indonesia, respectively, Amonoo (1994) and Moelino (1994).
7. Although national census data have been exploited for multilingualism research, detailed information about multilingualism requires more focused instruments. Typically, multilingualism is not evenly distributed throughout a country. Significant differences in the degree of multilingualism between urban and rural areas are typical. One of the most extensive projects to date is the Multilingual Cities Project undertaken at Tilburg University (http://babylon.kub.nl).
8. See, for example, Song's (1992) study on multilingual families in China.
9. For a comprehensive comparative study of urban multilingualism in six European cities from north to south, Goteborg, Hamburg, The Hague, Brussels, Lyon, and Madrid, see Extra and Yagmur (2004).
10. The title of Bickerton's (1981) most influential book which, though a bit dated, is an excellent introduction to the subject. Arends, Muysken and Smith (1994) offer a more recent review, and on the basis of a comprehensive review of the literature. Botha (2010) critically appraises the question of whether the study of pidgins can yield insights into language evolution.

Useful online resources

BilingBank is part of the TAlkBank suite of corpora. It provides materials for the study of bilingualism: http://talkbank.org/BilingBank/

Hal Schiffman offers a bibliography on 'Language Standardization, Language Ideology and Standard Language': http://ccat.sas.upenn.edu/~haroldfs/540/cdrom/stdlang.html

Multilingual Matters' quarterly Bilingual Family Newsletter ceased publication, but 27 volumes of back issues are available online for free: www.bilingualfamilynewsletter.com/archives.php

John Myhill (2009) reports on a survey commissioned by the Language and Literacy Committee of the Israel Academy of Sciences and Humanities about the relationship between diglossia and literacy: http://education.academy.ac.il/Uploads/BackgroundMaterials/english/Myhill.pdf

The International Journal of Bilingualism: http://ijb.sagepub.com/

Further reading

On diglossia

Britto, Francis. 1986. *Diglossia: A Study of the Theory with Application to Tamil*. Washington, DC: Georgetown University Press.

Hudson, Alan. 2002. Outline of a theory of diglossia. *International Journal of the Sociology of Language* **157**: 1–48.

Krishnamurti, Bh. (ed.) 1986. *South Asian Languages: Structure, Convergence and Diglossia*. Delhi: Motilal Banarsidass.

Schiffman, Harold. 1996. *Linguistic Culture and Language Policy*. London and New York: Routledge.

On bilingualism

Clyne, Michael. 1991. *Community Languages: The Australian Experience*. Cambridge University Press.

Edwards, John R. 1994. *Multilingualism*. London: Routledge.

Extra, Guus and Durk Gorter (eds.) 2001. *The Other Languages of Europe*. Clevedon: Multilingual Matters.

Grosjean, François. 2010. *Bilingual: Life and Reality*. Cambridge, MA: Harvard University Press.

Li Wei, Jean-Marc Dewaele and Alex Housen (eds.) 2002. *Opportunities and Challenges of Bilingualism*. Berlin and New York: Mouton de Gruyter.

Nelde, Peter H., Miquel Strubell and Glyn Williams. 1996. *The Production and Reproduction of the Minority Language Groups in the European Union*. Luxembourg: Office for Official Publications of the European Communities.

9 Language spread, shift and maintenance: how groups choose their language

Languages, like organic species can be classified into groups and subgroups ... Dominant languages and dialects spread and lead to the gradual extinction of other tongues.

Charles Darwin, *The Descent of Man and Selection in Relation to Sex*

The lure of English has not left us. And until it goes, our own languages will remain paupers.

Mohandas Gandhi (1965)

Outline of the chapter

Some societies are characterized by relatively stable language arrangements; others are more volatile. This chapter addresses the questions of how and why language choices by individuals and groups bring about incremental change of sociolinguistic arrangements in language-contact settings. By way of conceptualizing the inequality of the world's languages, it provides a brief review of their distribution and offers a five-tiered scheme as a general orientation. It then goes on to consider language-demographic statistics, explaining the difficulties of obtaining reliable data. The concepts of language loyalty, ethnolinguistic vitality, territories and domains, and utility are introduced as the most promising theoretical tools for analysing unstable language arrangements. By way of illustration, reference is made to the spread of languages on the Internet and to the ascent of English to the status of global language.

Key terms: migration, language spread, language decline, language shift, language maintenance, language loyalty

Stable and unstable language arrangements

One of the hallmarks of diglossia is its stability over long periods of time, a feature it shares with grassroots bilingualism. In both cases the population is territorially stationary, exhibiting no abrupt changes in residence patterns or language choice. If we think, for example, of German-speaking Switzerland, the Basque country and Jammu, north-west India, the language scenarios of these regions have lasted for many generations. No uncertainties or challenges undermined the alternating language-choice conventions for Swiss German/High German, Basque/Spanish and Pashto/Urdu. Stability is a rather vague notion. If, for present purposes, it is defined to mean that nobody alive remembers different language-choice conventions, it implies that basic patterns have been in place for at least four generations. In this sense the three cases, different though they are in terms of sociogenesis and functional allocation of codes, exemplify stable language arrangements.

However, the stability of multilingual arrangements is by no means the rule. Around the globe speech communities live in close proximity, influencing each other. From a language-centred point of view as suggested by Darwin's above-quoted analogy, languages influence each other, expand, contract or die. The impact of one language on the lexicon, phonology and syntax of another has long been considered as vitally important for the understanding of language change. Contemporary scholarship recognizes that language contact involves speakers and, therefore, has to draw on psychological and sociological as well as linguistic approaches. Historical linguistics asked questions such as 'What happened to language X under the influence of language Y?' and 'Are there any features of X that can be traced to Y?' Contact linguistics,[1] by contrast, is more interested in the communicative aspects and processes of intergroup dynamics, varying communication norms and shifting patterns of language choice. From a speaker-centred point of view, the question to ask is how individuals and groups of speakers react when they get in touch with other groups and their languages. It is very rare that contact is between equals and more or less symmetric. More commonly the relationship between the communities involved is characterized by differences in terms of size, power, wealth, prestige and vitality. Variable combinations of these factors often make for inherently unstable language arrangements where speakers adjust their language-choice patterns during their lifetime and/or from one generation to the next. A major cause of such changes is migration.

Mass migration

Mass migration is not an isolated phenomenon. It involves an area and a community of origin, a destination and, perhaps, transitory stations along the way. On the individual level migration is usually a once-in-a-lifetime event, but seen in a larger historical context it is an extremely long-term process. For example, the Indo-European expansion has been going on for some 6,000 years (Gunaratne 2003), bringing in its wake the dislocation of many languages, the formation of new ones through pidginization and creolization, and the extinction of an indeterminable number of others which have disappeared without a trace. Nowadays, in the age of globalization, this process continues, interacting with others that engender new language-contact situations. At 216 million (in 2010), the global migrant population would equal the fifth most populous country of the world, after China, India, USA and Indonesia.[2] Continuing migration flows of such an order of magnitude have given the questions of what these populations do with their languages and how they communicate with speakers of other languages renewed importance.

Immigrant groups find themselves in a new social and linguistic environment to which they adjust in many ways and which adjusts to them. Sociolinguistic evidence reveals a wide range of patterns of mutual adjustment with host communities insisting on assimilation to various degrees and immigrant communities showing variable inclination to yield to assimilation pressure. The resulting differences in language-choice patterns constitute a major subject of macro-sociolinguistic studies.

Language spread

Dutch enjoys official status and is widely spoken in Suriname, English in New Zealand, French in Madagascar, Portuguese in East Timor, Spanish in Cuba, Chinese in Singapore, Arabic in the Comoros, Turkish in Cyprus and Hindi in Mauritius. These are just some examples of languages that have been carried from their homeland to other parts of the world where they coexist with other languages which had been there before or were brought in later to add another layer to the mix.

The above-mentioned languages have spread, meaning that the populations speaking these languages grew more than the primary speech community in their homeland. For example, the estimated 130 million speakers of French[3] outnumber the population of France by a rate of 2:1. With a demographic strength of some 420 million, Spanish has almost ten times as many speakers as Spain has inhabitants. The ratio of Arabic speakers and Saudi Arabian nationals is more than 10:1, and that of Portuguese speakers and Portuguese nationals exceeds 20:1. Notice that, with the exception of Arabic, all of these languages belong to the Indo-European family of languages, which in a long-term historical perspective has spread more extensively than any other language family, picking up speakers around the globe. And we have not even mentioned the language whose growth over the past 300 years and especially during the twentieth century eclipsed that of any other language, English, which has an estimated 1,000 million speakers in some sixty countries. While the languages of Europe account for just 3 per cent of the world's 6,800 languages, about half of the world population of 7 billion speak European languages.[4] Clearly, a few select European languages have expanded more vigorously than all other languages on this globe.

Table 9.1 *Chinese demographic development*

China's population (estimates)
1751 ± 250 million
1851 ± 400 million
2012 ± 1340 million

Chinese, too, has a huge speech community exceeding 1,300 million speakers if all varieties are included. In a period of two and a half centuries, it has grown by a factor of 5.3 (see Table 9.1). However, the increase of the speech community parallels that of the Chinese population.

To be sure, as a result of Chinese emigration the Chinese language nowadays enjoys some currency in Chinatowns around the world from Amsterdam to New York City and Sydney, but it has not spread outside these settlements. It was never backed up by military might, colonialism and imperialism as was English, promoted by the British Empire first and then the US army, commerce, proselytism and popular culture. The Chinese written language was adopted by literary elites in neighbouring countries,[5] but vernacular Chinese never displaced the indigenous languages. Similarly, Hindi which follows Chinese as the second most populous language in terms of native speakers, has a very compact speech community with few overseas extensions.

Arabic, on the other hand, was disseminated both as a holy written language and a spoken vernacular from the Arabian Peninsula to other lands in the wake of the Islamic conquest. Today it is widely spoken in some twenty-three countries, ranking as one of the world's top ten languages in terms of demographic strength, although no reliable statistics about number of speakers are available (see below).

As these examples show, language spread is not a natural development. Rather, it is a complex process driven by many interacting variables such as the expansion of groups of people, migration, trade, slavery, conquest and the subjugation of others, domination, the establishment of institutions that promote and protect certain languages, such as churches, schools and armed forces, and the undermining of cultures, but also demand for some languages which primary speakers of other languages perceive as more useful or prestigious. Language spread is not just a result of these factors but has an effect on them, too. A language with a wide reach differs from one confined to a small speech community not just in size. The functional range of 'big' languages is wider and more differentiated than that of small ones. For example, the majority of the world's languages are not used for the functions most relevant for modern life. Only a small number of languages have spread to the Internet. In 2007, 17.5 per cent of the world population were connected to the Internet (Pimienta, Prado and Blanco 2009). At the time, about 2 per cent of all languages accounted for close to 100 per cent of online communication, with huge disproportions between them. The only non-European languages of the top-ranking twelve are Chinese, Japanese and Korean. Then follow Arabic, Turkish and Thai. However, the linguistic diversity of the Internet keeps evolving. Various different measures are used to assess the presence of languages in computer-mediated communication and the penetration of the Internet in countries and speech communities. According to a calculation by O'Neill, Lavoie and Bennett (2003), English accounted for 72 per cent of random samples of webpages and Chinese for 2 per cent. In the meantime, Chinese has caught up by leaps and bounds. Internet World Stats (2010) counts 536.6 million English language internet users compared with 444.9 million Chinese users. Spanish has climbed to third rank, Japanese dropped to fourth. According to the same source, English is the language of 26.8 per cent of all internet users, compared to 24.2 per cent who use Chinese. In the first decade of this century, the English language internet population tripled, whereas the Chinese language internet population grew by 1500 per cent, starting from a low baseline. In the eight years since the publication of the first edition of this textbook, the online population has tripled. Figure 9.1 then cited 649 million as of March 2003, compared with 1,966 million in June 2010. This is just one indication of how much the situation is still in flux.

The 27 per cent of the online population who use English are a smaller proportion of the total than English accounted for in the early days of the Internet; however, even this reduced share is indicative of the role of English as the international lingua franca, which at the same time is the language of the hegemonic power of our days. As the only language with truly global reach, it constitutes the topmost layer of the multitiered system of the world's languages today. Supranational languages come next, notably French, Spanish, Portuguese, German, Russian, Arabic and Chinese, followed in turn by a number of languages whose speech communities are still large, but more geographically concentrated and unchallenged in their proper territories, such as Hindi–Urdu, Bengali, Tamil, Malay–Indonesian and Kiswahili. Highly developed but demographically small languages such as Dutch, Danish, Czech and Greek, and all other languages regularly used in writing, form the next two tiers. And finally there are a large number of unwritten languages spoken by small groups of speakers. These five tiers make up the world system of languages which is characterized by an inverse relation between number of languages and number of speakers, as schematically depicted in Figure 9.2. Ten major languages, each spoken by more than 100 million people, account for almost half of the world's population, whereas 52 per cent of all languages are spoken by less than 10,000 people, hundreds of them having fewer than 100 speakers.[6] Approximately 96 per cent of the world's population is being educated in one of the top twenty languages in terms of size. These

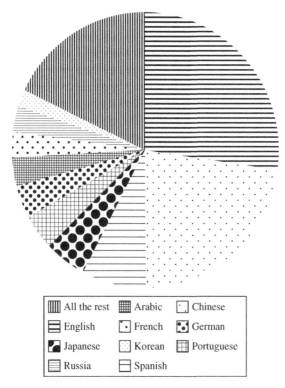

Figure 9.1 *The ten most frequently used languages on the internet. Online language populations, total: 1,966 million (June 2010). Source: Internet World Stats: www.internetworldstats.com/stats7.htm*

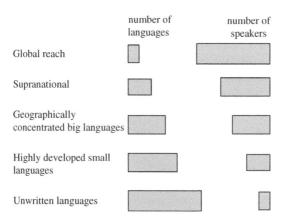

Figure 9.2 *Few languages with many speakers, many languages with few speakers: the linguistic diversity of the world*

are Chinese, Hindi–Urdu, English, Spanish, Arabic, Bengali, Portuguese, Russian, Malay–Indonesian, Japanese, German, French, Bihari,[7] Korean, Vietnamese, Italian, Telugu, Tamil, Turkish and Javanese.

Being equipped with the necessary means to function as the medium of instruction and being formally recognized as such gives these twenty languages an enormous competitive advantage in the endless push and pull and vying for domains and territories between the world's languages.[8] How did this system come into existence, and how does it evolve? As the comparison between Chinese and English shows, demographic strength is just one of several variables involved. It is, however, very important and must be kept in mind because present-day disparities imply that the potential to spread is very uneven for the languages of the world, as are the chances of survival. So great is the imbalance of power between 'big' languages and the 'little' ones, that many scholars predict a dramatic reduction of global linguistic diversity in the near future. The *UNESCO Atlas of the World's Languages in Danger*, available in its 2010 edition in English, Spanish and French, keeps track of some 2,500 languages that are thought to be at risk of extinction.[9]

Language replacement is a process that has been going on for thousands of years, but in the age of globalization it has accelerated dramatically, bringing about a global situation which is quite unstable. The world system of languages is the result of long-term historical processes. How this system changes as we live with it must be investigated on a smaller scale where issues of language shift and maintenance are addressed.

Data

A note of caution is in order here. The above numbers seem neat and precise; in truth they are quite problematic, constituting approximations at best. In addition to the usual hitches with demographic data, a number of problems mentioned earlier, such as language names, the vague and often arbitrary difference between language and dialect, and inconsistencies in self-declared language affiliations[10] make exact assessments difficult. Are Flemish and Dutch one language or two? Maltese used to be considered an Arabic dialect, but in 1990 the government of Malta decided to recognize it as a proper language (Hull 1994: 344). What does diglossia imply for counting languages? Who counts as a speaker of a language: natives only; bilinguals; speakers with reduced proficiency for lack of use? These and similar problems must be dealt with, if only arbitrarily, if data are to be classified and processed.

Language spread can be assessed only on the basis of representative data. The very first step in the study of this process makes it necessary to ascertain who speaks the language under investigation in a given community; what functional roles it fulfils in that community; and whether there is inter-generational change. It should be pointed out that these and other related questions concern not just L1 speakers of that language but L2 speakers, too, for L2 speakers are crucially important for language expansion. Gathering data of this sort is a highly complicated matter.

For illustration, consider what was said about Arabic above. No reliable statistics about number of speakers are available. There are several reasons for this. First, we need a clear-cut definition of 'Arabic'. Suppose we settle on Modern Standard Arabic, which is quite clearly defined, then the question arises as to how to determine the number of speakers of this variety. Only a research instrument that is uniformly designed and applied in all Arabic-speaking countries and in other countries with sizeable Arabic-speaking minorities could yield reasonably accurate results. Now, recall for a moment the relationships between the languages and dialects spoken in Morocco as depicted in Figure 8.1 (p. 151). It is clear from this figure that it contains just approximate percentages, one of the reasons being that Moroccan Arabic, Middle Moroccan Arabic and Literary Arabic are not distinct entities but should be seen, rather, as overlapping sets. Similar sets constitute the language situations in other Arabic-speaking countries which, however, differ from Morocco in various ways. A large part of the Moroccan population are L1 Berber speakers. Many of them are bilingual to various degrees with proficiency in Arabic ranging from totally fluent to severely restricted. How are they to be counted? Whatever the answer, it would be difficult to ensure comparability with data gathered in other Arabic-speaking countries.

Alternatively, both a definition of Arabic and a standard of proficiency could be dispensed with, every variety and every level of aptitude being admitted. The returns of such a survey would be accordingly vague. Since testing every respondent's aptitude level is impracticable in representative surveys, language demographic data are usually based on self-report. Self-report data are notoriously unreliable, but useful information can be extracted from them nevertheless if they are broken down for social variables such as sex, class and generation. In any event, language-demographic data are hard to come by. National census questionnaires rarely include language-related items. Questions about language are sometimes deliberately excluded as potentially troublesome. Where language-related questions are included in a national census, they are often inadequate. For example, respondents may be requested to disclose their mother tongue in such a way that only a single answer is permissible. Language-contact situations call for fine-grained research instruments capable of recording complex patterns of language affiliation, language use, language choice and language preference. As an example of what this involves, consider a selection of some questions about language included in the Ethnic Diversity Survey of the Government of Canada,[11] a country that has a history of immigration and concern with ethnolinguistic diversity.

Language-related questions of the Ethnic Diversity Survey of the Canadian government

(1)   **What was the language that you first learned at home in childhood?**

INTERVIEWER: Specify up to 3 responses. Accept multiple responses only if languages were learned at the same time.

If the respondent answers 'Chinese', ask 'Would that be Cantonese, Mandarin or another Chinese language?'

English
French
Cantonese
Mandarin
Italian
German
Punjabi
Spanish
Polish
Portuguese
Arabic
Tagalog (Pilipino)
Other – Search
Refused
Don't know

(2)   **Can you still <u>understand</u> ^ FirstLang?**

Yes
No
Refused
Don't know

(3)   **Using a scale of 1 to 5, where 1 is not well at all and 5 is very well, how well can you <u>understand</u> ^ FirstLang now?**

(1) – not well at all
(2)
(3)
(4)
(5) – very well

Refused
Don't know

(4)   **Can you still <u>speak</u> ^ FirstLang?**

Yes
No
Refused
Don't know

(5)   **Using a scale of 1 to 5, where 1 is not well at all and 5 is very well, how well can you speak ^ FirstLang now?**
(1) – not well
(2)
(3)
(4)
(5) – very well

Refused
Don't know

(6)   **Besides the language of interview and your first language, are there any other languages that you speak well enough to conduct a conversation?**
INTERVIEWER: Report only those languages in which the respondent can carry on a conversation of some length on various topics.

Yes
No
Refused
Don't know

(7)   **What languages are these?**
INTERVIEWER: Specify up to 6 responses.
Report only those languages in which the respondent can carry on a conversation of some length on various topics. If the respondent answers 'Chinese', ask 'Would that be Cantonese, Mandarin or another Chinese language?'

English
French
Cantonese
Mandarin
Italian
German
Punjabi
Spanish
Polish
Portuguese
Arabic
Tagalog (Pilipino)
Other – Search

(8)   **Using a scale of 1 to 5, where 1 is not well at all and 5 is very well, how well can you speak ^ SpokenLang?**

(1) – not well
(2)
(3)

(4)
(5) – very well

Refused
Don't know

(9)   **What language do you speak most often at home?**
INTERVIEWER: Mark up to 3 responses. Accept multiple responses only if languages are spoken equally often.
For a person who lives alone, report the language in which the respondent feels most comfortable (this can be the language the respondent would use for talking on the telephone, visiting at home with friends, etc.).
Do not include languages used exclusively in a homebased business.

Language of Interview
Language 1 derived
Language 2 derived
Language 3 derived
Language 4 derived
Language 5 derived
Language 6 derived
Language 7 derived
Language 8 derived
Language 9 derived
Refused
Don't know

(10)   **Are there any other languages you speak on a regular basis at home?**

Yes
No
Refused
Don't know

(11)   **What languages are these?**
INTERVIEWER: Mark up to 3 responses.
Do not include languages used exclusively in a homebased business.

Language of Interview
Language 1 derived
Language 2 derived
Language 3 derived
Language 4 derived
Language 5 derived
Language 6 derived
Language 7 derived

Language 8 derived
Language 9 derived

(12)   **What language do you speak <u>most often</u> with your friends?**
<u>INTERVIEWER:</u> Mark up to 3 responses. Accept multiple responses only if languages are spoken equally often.

If the respondent uses different languages with different groups of friends, ask them to answer in a general way (for example, report the language they used most often, thinking of contact with all their friends together).

Language of Interview
Language 1 derived
Language 2 derived
Language 3 derived
Language 4 derived
Language 5 derived
Language 6 derived
Language 7 derived
Language 8 derived
Language 9 derived
Don't have any friends
Refused
Don't know

(13)   **Now, I have two questions about your use of languages when you were growing up.**
Up until you were age 15, what language did you and your parents use <u>most of the time</u> when speaking to each other?
<u>INTERVIEWER:</u> Mark up to 3 responses. Accept multiple responses only if (1) languages were used equally often, or (2) different languages were spoken with each parent, or (3) respondent used one language when speaking to their parents and their parents used another language when speaking to them.

(14)   **Up until you were age 15, what language did you and your brothers, sisters, and any other children <u>in your household</u>, use <u>most of the time</u> when speaking to each other?**
<u>INTERVIEWER:</u> Mark up to 3 responses. Accept multiple responses only if languages were used equally often or if different languages were spoken with different siblings.

If a survey using an instrument of this sort is conducted at regular intervals, it can reveal changes in a community's sociolinguistic arrangement, and even a single survey produces information that is indicative of the status and function of a language and tendencies of change. For example, significant differences in the responses to questions 1 and 9 between generations would suggest intergenerational change, whereas similar results across all age groups are indicative of the stability of a language in a given society. Research along these lines, on the basis of both census data and more specialized research instruments, has been carried out first and foremost in 'classic' immigrant countries, especially the United States (Fishman et al. 1966), Australia (Clyne 1991), but also Western Europe (Verdoodt 1989; European Commission 2006). Various approaches have been developed to explain how languages fare when carried by their speakers to novel environments.

Language shift and maintenance

The key notions here are 'language shift' and 'language maintenance'. Language shift, defined by Weinreich (1953: 68) as the gradual replacement of one language by another, is often the outcome of language contact in an immigration situation. Language maintenance, on the other hand, refers to a situation where a speech community, under circumstances that would seem to favour language shift, holds on to its language. For instance, the transmission of Korean to the next generation of speakers in South Korea is not the result of language maintenance, but in Japan, which has a Korean minority of some 600,000, it is (Maher and Kawanishi 1995). There is no language contact in South Korea which could induce language shift, but in Japan Koreans are in direct contact with Japanese, virtually all of them being bilinguals. Fishman, who laid the groundwork for the scientific investigation of language shift, states the general direction of research:

> The study of language maintenance and language shift is concerned with the relationship between change and stability in habitual language use, on the one hand, and ongoing psychological, social and cultural processes, on the other, when populations differing in language are in contact with each other.   (Fishman 1964: 32)

Language loyalty

It is not easy to ascertain that language shift has occurred or is occurring, some of the reasons for which were given above. Why it occurs is just as difficult to find out. This question can refer to the language choice of an individual, a family or a whole community. Generally, the same variables apply as in language change, that is, sex, age and class (cf. Chapter 5), intercommunity relations – between immigrant and host community or minority and majority – constituting an additional dimension of variation. Focusing on the community-building and culture-sustaining functions of language, Fishman (1972: 123f.) has used the notion of language loyalty, that is, the variable function of language for group maintenance, as an explanatory concept. In immigrant situations, the language loyalties of immigrant and host community meet, producing expectations on both sides as to the immigrants' acquisition of the majority language and maintenance of their language of ancestry. The extent to which a society uses language as an index of acculturation, Fishman maintains, is culturally variable, putting linguistic minorities under more pressure to adapt in some societies than in others. Research has shown that different immigrant communities behave differently in the same host community which would seem to indicate that language attitudes on both sides, the host community and the immigrant community, interact to produce differing language shift and maintenance patterns.

Since both language loyalty and tolerance for linguistic pluralism vary across communities, it is hard to predict the fate of community languages. Migration often leads to language shift within three generations. For the monolingual speakers of the first generation, L1 is the default choice. L2, the dominant language of the target society, will remain a foreign language for most of them. Their children will grow up bilinguals, speaking L1 at home and L2 in most other domains. They have a real L1/L2 choice, but unless they continue to use L1 domestically, the third generation is likely to be L2 dominant if not monolingual. This pattern has been observed in several immigrant communities in the United States, but rather than representing a universal rule it reflects the assimilation pressure at work in the host society. In other environments migration does not necessarily bring language shift in its wake. For instance, Laitin (1993) reports that migrant communities throughout India retain the languages of their areas of origin. Since this is true of various different communities, it is not attributable to greater language loyalty on the part of the migrants, but reflects relatively higher tolerance for linguistic pluralism and cross-linguistic communication practices in India than in the United States.

At the same time, language loyalty is not a constant but a variable part of linguistic culture. In Australia, different ethnolinguistic groups were found to exhibit very different language maintenance and shift patterns (Clyne 1991). For example, after three generations, Danish immigrants had shifted to English almost completely, just 0.6 per cent maintaining active competence and use of Danish. In sharp contrast, after the same length of time Turkish immigrants had a maintenance rate of 83.6 per cent. A comparison reveals a pronounced distinction between, on the one hand, groups with a very high language maintenance rate, such as Turks, Greeks, Lebanese and Vietnamese, and, on the other, groups with low language maintenance rates and rapid language shift, most of them of northern European origin (Table 9.2).

These statistics testify to differing roles of language for individual and group identity in different societies. This is how the fact has been interpreted that the speakers of some immigrant languages living in a host-language-dominant environment abandon their language to replace it with the

Table 9.2 *Immigrant language maintenance in Australia by generation (Clyne 1991: 66f.)*

	1st gen.	2nd gen.	2nd + half gen.	3rd + gen.
French	66.1	39.8	6.5	2.0
French mix	22.6	13.4	4.8	0.8
Mauritian	68.3	31.9	6.5	23.4
German	61.1	27.3	3.7	1.3
German mix	14.5	9.6	2.5	0.4
Austrian	52.4	24.0	3.7	6.2
Dutch	48.9	14.7	2.5	10.3
Dutch mix	13.8	3.3	0.9	0.6
Danish	53.2	19.3	1.9	0.6
Norwegian–Swedish	45.6	21.1	1.2	0.8
Finnish	75.1	59.5	13.3	7.1
Russian	70.0	49.5	14.3	13.4
Russian mix	20.4	11.9	2.4	1.8
Ukrainian	72.1	51.7	43.3	42.1
Polish	73.3	39.3	12.5	13.6
Polish mix	13.6	7.5	1.5	0.8
Czech	64.1	33.4	8.0	18.9
Slovenian	64.4	55.4	9.2	21.1
Hungarian	70.6	49.4	12.8	36.0
Croatian	94.8	92.7	54.2	62.5
Serbian	91.9	91.3	60.0	67.2
Macedonian	96.2	91.2	64.5	61.7
'Yugoslav'	79.5	66.7	26.0	35.8
Greek	92.2	88.3	56.6	48.5
Greek mix	31.4	34.9	11.4	3.6
Maltese	70.5	38.6	12.5	25.3
Italian	88.0	70.0	31.7	27.6
Italian mix	26.4	25.4	6.7	2.4
Spanish	84.2	76.3	6.6	8.1
Spanish mix	41.3	28.3	4.5	0.8
Latin American	89.3	84.2	7.5	42.2
Portuguese	83.0	78.2	15.0	18.2
Turkish	93.6	93.4	67.6	83.6
Lebanese	92.5	82.0	27.8	35.8
Arabic	87.8	87.3	24.3	32.8
Sinhalese	33.8	6.5	2.6	16.2
Vietnamese	94.9	89.4	41.4	79.9
Lao	94.4	93.7	–	76.5
Khmer	91.2	79.1	–	71.6
'Filipino'	75.2	46.0	25.0	50.9
Chinese	81.9	66.4	22.7	16.6
Chinese mix	30.6	13.1	3.5	0.6
Irish	2.2	0.4	0.3	0.2

dominant language faster than speakers of other immigrant languages living in the same environment. How social class interacts with the host country's linguistic culture and with the immigrant group's language loyalty is another dimension of the problem which has to be studied on a case-by-case basis. Social advancement is often contingent on a good command of the dominant language, and the opportunity to acquire the dominant language depends on the employment situation. Immigrants who have to hold down two or three jobs to make ends meet are not in a position to give high priority to language study, which may translate into language maintenance. On the other hand, climbing up the social ladder is often considered more important than language loyalty. How these two tendencies are balanced out depends on culturally transmitted attitudes and educational support. For instance, the maintenance of Turkish in Australia has been on the decline for some time, leading Beykont (2010: 104) to conclude 'that additional policy and program measures are necessary to sustain Turkish bilingualism beyond the second generation'.

Ethnolinguistic vitality

Another concept that has been developed to predict language behaviour in language-contact situations is ethnolinguistic vitality (EV). Giles, Bourhis and Taylor (1977) have defined EV as an aggregate of sociocultural factors that determine a group's ability to function as a distinct collective entity. The major factors involved in a group's EV have already been mentioned in passing. They are *demography, institutional support* and *status*. Demography refers to the absolute size of the group and its relative strength in the total population as well as residence patterns – concentrated or dispersed – birth rate, endogamy and continuing migration. Institutional support concerns the presence of the group's language in the institutions of various social arenas such as education, government, media and religion. And status refers to the group's position in a social prestige hierarchy which is itself a composite factor involving the group's immigration history as well as social, economic, cultural and linguistic aspects.

EV theory has been criticized for methodological shortcomings, especially the difficulty of controlling the many variables involved and the resultant problems of comparing different cases. Yet, it has fostered many studies on language shift and maintenance (Allard and Landry 1992; Landry and Allard 1994).

An important distinction in EV studies is between objective EV and subjective EV, the latter being the *perceived* rather than the actual demographic strength, media presence and prestige of the language. Subjective EV is widely considered a better predictor of changing language-choice and language-use patterns than objective EV because people act on the basis of perceptions, assumptions and assessments rather than facts, most of which, such as the actual size of their ethnic group, are unknown to them. It has been a default assumption that minority languages with low subjective EV are more likely to be replaced by the dominant language than languages with high-perceived EV. Bilingual speakers will be influenced in their language choice, so the argument goes, by their subjective assessment of their own ethnic group's vitality. Speakers with low vitality will tend to increase their choice of the dominant language, leading to linguistic assimilation, that is, language shift. Many case studies corroborate this correlation between subjective EV and language choice. More generally, high- and low-perceived EV predict, respectively, language maintenance and language shift. However, contrasting patterns have also been found (Harwood, Giles and Bourhis 1994), which show the complicated interaction between ethnolinguistic vitality perceptions, intercommunity relations and language-choice patterns in contact situations. Subjective EV is a relative concept which concerns a community not in isolation but in its relation to another, usually dominant, community and, as the case may be, further immigrant/minority communities. Immigrant communities hailing from the same country have different vitality ratings in different immigration contexts and, accordingly, develop different language-choice patterns and preferences.[12]

Territories and domains

Among the factors determining language shift and maintenance two have attracted special attention: (1) the micro-social arena of the family as the agent of spontaneous intergeneration and language transmission; and (2) the macro-social arena of group settlement in a 'territory'. The absolute demographic strength of a group means little if its members are widely dispersed, providing few social settings for using its language outside the family. And if a language ceases to be transmitted domestically the bedrock of its continuing tradition is undermined. Micro- and macro-social factors interact in that families are influenced in their language use by the surrounding community. Family and concentrated minority-residence areas are domains and territories of language. Language-contact situations differ in terms of the separation, upholding and invasion of domains.

Nations, ethnic communities, tribes as well as many animal species are examples of actors which operate mainly within certain territories. These can be understood literally in terms of physical space (Johnstone 2010) or in terms of abstract domain characteristics (Dailey-O'Cain and Liebscher 2011). In this sense, languages and speech varieties are tied to territories and domains. A language can be said to be robust if no other language can invade its territory. What are the conditions for robustness to obtain and, conversely, for a language to invade another's territory? Under normal circumstances a single newcomer is unlikely to make natives convert to his or her language because the natives can communicate more easily among themselves using their native language. Newcomers, therefore, have a strong tendency if not to assimilate at least to adopt the host community's language. However, in social settings characterized by an extreme power differential, such as is characteristic of colonial situations, a small minority may be able to invade a language territory because certain members of the host community – i.e. co-opted colonial elites – defer to the invader by using his language. The time-tested principle *cuius regio, eius lingua* 'whose realm, whose tongue' comes to bear here.

As another example of successful invasion, consider the setting of a scholarly conference in a small country such as Holland. In such a setting a single non-Dutch-speaking participant will in all likelihood function as a carrier of English which thus invades the territory of Dutch. Since Dutch academics all speak English and since, in a context of scholarly exchange, they will give priority to the cooperative principle (see above, pp. 12f.) over other considerations they may entertain, such as attaching importance to the use of Dutch as a language of science, they will accommodate the invader by choosing English rather than Dutch for the discussion.[13] Communication accommodation theory accounts for ways in which individuals modify their speech behaviour in relation to an interlocutor (see above, pp. 37f.). The Dutch conference participants' choice of English can be explained in terms of opting for the lingua franca of the international domain of science by way of accommodation. However, at the same time it is an example of domain invasion if the reference domain is Dutch academia. In this particular case, domain invasion is facilitated by the fact that scientific discourse is one of the domains most susceptible to the forces of globalization.

Eventually domain invasion may lead to colonization, a process that occurs whenever the location/domain of a less successful species is taken over by a more successful neighbour or invader. This is what has happened in Dutch academia over the past two decades or so, though it was not an invasion by brute force. It must be acknowledged that Dutch academics, rather than being passive victims of the process, have an active part in it. Having a choice between Dutch and English, they allowed English into the academic domain, as a supplementary language in exceptional cases at first, whose employment in scientific discourse then gradually expanded. If we want to explain how English penetrated the educational domain in the Netherlands, the role played by those who chose to deliver their lectures, engage in discussions and publish their papers in English must not be overlooked. From a language-centred point of view, English can be said to invade Dutch academia, extending its territory by adding yet another domain of use. A speaker-centred approach focuses on individual acts of choice emphasizing pull- rather than push-factors.

In the maintenance of language, the role of time perspectives is critical. When a sufficient number of speakers anticipate future encounters and care enough about 'their future together', the conditions are good for a linguistic tradition to be continued. Clearly, Dutch academics do not see their future together endangered by the domain invasion of English, because they consider English an addition to, not a replacement of, Dutch. Academia is just one of several communication domains of Dutch society, and in others Dutch is unchallenged. Functional domain allocation and division of labour of languages and language varieties is common in all societies. It should be noted, however, that for a language to be driven out of a domain means a reduction of its functional range which, in turn, will gradually lead to an erosion of the register appropriate to that domain, making a reversal of the process in future ever more unlikely. Partial language shift thus occurs which may spill over into other domains. A rearrangement of functional domain allocations with no consequences for the vitality of the language that forfeits a domain is unlikely. Rather, domain invasion must be considered the most obvious indication of language shift (Fasold 1984: 213; Appel and Muysken 1987: 39f.). Observers have diagnosed the domain invasion of English in the Dutch language area as an indication of on-going functional adjustment:

> Dutch may not be threatened with extinction in the short or medium term, but it is in danger of losing domains. It could eventually become just a colloquial language, a language you use at home ... but not the one you use for the serious things in life: work, money, science, technology.   (Van Hoorde 1998: 6)

In many small speech communities, language shift proceeds domain by domain. The domestic domain, researchers agree, is the last bastion, but a language that is reduced to the domestic domain is increasingly unlikely to be maintained because each domain loss lessens its utility (see below). The general trend is for 'bigger' languages to invade domains of 'smaller' ones. English invades domains of Dutch, Dutch invades domains of Frisian, German invades domains of Rhaeto-Romance, French domains of Breton, etc., and not vice versa. However, in complex multilingual situations it is not necessarily the biggest languages that are the most vigorous invaders. In many African contexts where a three-tiered arrangement of local vernaculars, regional lingua francas and former colonial languages is typical, shift from a local vernacular to a widely spoken African language such as Swahili, Hausa, Manding and Songhai is more common than to English, Portuguese or French. In the event, language shift is not the result of social engineering but happens spontaneously as communities adapt their means of communication to changing communication needs. Matthias Brenzinger, an expert on language shift in Africa, gives the following explanation: 'Assimilation by choice will be the main cause for the worldwide decline of minority languages in the future' (Brenzinger 1996: 282).

As we have seen, the reasons for language shift and the worldwide reduction of linguistic diversity it brings about are many. One sticks out, however, which warrants further discussion. Language shift is always in the direction of the language of greater utility.

Utility

A case of language shift in South Africa well illustrates the complexity of the process, involving as it does an immigrant community's shift to a language that is not native to South Africa but has successfully invaded the South African language territory. In the event, a shift is taking place from Telugu to English. Prabhakaran (1998) describes the adoption of English instead of Telugu as the domestic language in the South African Indian community as a conscious choice that parents made for their children. In their decision they were influenced by several external factors, one of them being the South African government's language policy which assigns no Indian language official status. Yet, they could have chosen to transmit their ancestral language to their offspring, as many immigrants do. No threat of reprisals deterred them from so doing. The principal reason behind the South African Indians' decision not to raise their children as Telugu speakers is that English has greater utility and, therefore, commands higher prestige in South Africa than Telugu.

Utility is an economic notion which has been invoked in the analysis of language shift and other macro-sociolinguistic processes (Coulmas 1992a; Grin 1996). It is assumed that language itself has a utility utility-value which is variable, and that the actual and the perceived utility-value of languages in contact situations are valid predictors of language shift and maintenance.

In the most general sense, economic theory is concerned with the optimization of means–ends relations. Language is a tool, a means designed to carry out certain tasks and to achieve certain ends. If people act rationally, which most theoretical models of economics assume, they will, as a general principle, minimize their expenditure of time and effort to achieve their ends and, therefore, choose the instrument optimally suited for a certain job, that is, the instrument with the highest utility-value. In a number of language-choice situations, it is easy to see the general validity of this principle, especially where the deliberate acquisition of additional languages is concerned. Discussing the reasons why learners find Esperanto unattractive compared to English and why governments fail to add Esperanto to school curricula, Li Wei (2003:44) explains:

> In terms of language choice, with the exception of situations where a predominant language is imposed (as is typical of colonial societies) the choice of one second or foreign language over another hinges essentially on the perception of how useful the target language is.

The foreign language market works much like other markets, foreign languages functioning as marketable goods whose exchange value depends on supply and demand which in turn reflect their utility-value. The vast majority of all languages are not marketed at all or in very specialized niche markets only because they have no utility for non-native speakers, and there is accordingly no demand for them. For the rest, the foreign language market is heavily dominated by a few European languages, English occupying the unrivalled position of greatest demand and greatest supply. As a commodity, English supports a bigger industry, generates a higher turnover and more revenues than any other language (McCallen 1989). And, most importantly, in most contexts the expenditure for its acquisition as a foreign or second language promises higher returns than that of other languages.

The lure of English

Arguably, the dynamics at work in the foreign language market are not the same as those in the world language system at large. When it comes to choosing their mother tongue or their children's mother tongue, people do not submit to market forces as readily as with regard to foreign language acquisition. This is true, because a language has not just instrumental value (utility), but symbolic value, too, the topic of the next chapter. Also, it must be noted that, just as ethnolinguistic vitality has an objective and a subjective dimension, the objective utility-value of a language may differ from its subjective perception. However, in multilingual settings the foreign language market and decisions concerning foreign language learning have implications that are fundamentally different from those in environments operating under monolingual assumptions. Kamwangamalu (2003) discusses the choice of English-medium schools in South Africa's black urban communities as a harbinger of language shift, since it is spreading rapidly from the school to the family domain. The main reason is, as Grin (2001: 73) puts it, that even at low levels of competence English is always associated with higher earnings.

Trivial and, as many who reflect on human nature would think, depressing as it may seem, the promise of higher earnings alone goes a long way towards explaining the phenomenal spread of English[14] which furnishes the goal of language shift in numerous speech communities on all continents. There can be no doubt that relative utility-value differential is the most consistent predictor of language spread and language shift. The utility-value of a language is an aggregate encompassing the following factors:

- the communicative range of a language measured as the demographic strength of the community using it as a first and a second/foreign language;
- the investment made in a language in terms of lexical recording, dictionaries, translations, electronic processibility, etc.;
- demand for a language in the international language market;
- a language's level of development as a societal means of production.

These factors are of a social and economic nature, which should, however, not obscure the fact that linguistic factors, too, feed into the utility-value of languages. In language, as in the case of other instruments, structure is a function of use, which is another way of saying that every language is the product of collective labour, shaped by millions of speech acts to suit the needs of its users. If this is so, it follows that language spread has cumulative effects because it means that a language which spreads is adjusted to ever new functions and domains. In our day, English is the most formidable example. Though looking back on only a relatively short literary history (compared, for example, with Chinese or Greek), it has been acculturated and nativized on all continents and put to use to a greater variety of functions in more diverse cultural contexts than any language in history. Its multiple uses have made it a most powerful and versatile instrument which increases its utility in a snowball-fashion by the day as people of different social and cultural backgrounds around the globe see in it a means of social advance and its acquisition as a profitable investment.

English is unrivalled in terms of the information accessible in it; it is flexible and open to innovation, absorbing elements of other languages uninhibitedly, and as a result commands a breadth and depth of lexical differentiation unmatched by other languages. Some increasingly important domains such as science and technology are dominated by English, which is also the language of choice by those critical of these developments. Hegemony expresses itself in English, and its discontents, too. That is, those who lament the spread of English at the expense of other languages contribute to its growing expressive power. In the passage quoted at the outset of this chapter, Mohandas Gandhi, champion of India's liberation from colonial rule, refers to the 'lure of English' which turns Indian languages into 'paupers'. By choosing English rather than Indian languages for purposes of higher communication – education, science, government, law – the Indian elites failed to develop their languages and adapt them to the requirements of modern life.

What Gandhi observed is quite common. Minor languages are not adapted to modern life which to many of their speakers seems incompatible with the traditions and community values they associate with their language. Such attitudes find expression in the belief that a language itself is a territory that must be protected against invasion by other languages in the form of borrowing, code-switching and other ways of language mixing which are seen as a first step towards impending language shift. Ironically, attempts at protecting the integrity of a language are often counterproductive, accelerating its stylistic deterioration and eventual demise instead of safeguarding it for future generations. As Hill (1993: 84) observes, language shift is driven in some cases by an ideology of linguistic purism promoted by self-styled language masters who denounce the speech of others for use of loanwords and grammatical interference. An unintended side effect of such protectionism is that castigated speakers are discouraged from using the language in public, further pushing it back to the domestic domain. The noble choice of the right and the pure may thus turn out to be the deathblow for a small language under pressure. Purism, and more generally language ideology, is yet another variable that affects language shift.

English is the very opposite of a protected market, functioning as the biggest donor and borrower language at the centre of worldwide linguistic exchange. The resultant lexical and structural properties reflect the multifarious uses to which English has been put and are at the same time conducive to its application to ever new tasks and domains. Manifesting the same self-reinforcing mechanism of mutual dependency in reverse, languages that lose domains undergo lexical and structural impoverishment, continuously weakening the functional incentives of maintaining them.

Although language is not just an instrument, its instrumental functions are vital. A language with limited or no instrumental utility is more likely to be abandoned by its speakers than one that is serviceable in a wide range of domains. The lesson to be learnt from purism and the role it plays in language shift and maintenance is that utility can be ignored only at a cost. At the heart of the study of language shift must be the question to what extent utility as a determinant of collective language choice can be mitigated by cultural and sociopsychological factors. Language shift from smaller to bigger languages locally and the worldwide spread of English testify to the inclination of individuals and communities to act according to the principle of getting the maximum benefits for the minimum of effort. Against this background, the student of language shift and maintenance asks to what extent communities in contact situations rely on cultural and sociopsychological values to withstand the forces of the language market. These forces exert a strong influence on people's choices which, however, does not mean that they have no choice. Language shift occurs as the result of choices made by individuals, most importantly in the domestic domain, in accordance with their own motivations, expectations and goals which they may or may not share with other members of their community. Taken together, individual choices form collective choices that impact on the future of a speech community and its language. It lies in the nature of collective choice that the individuals involved in it do not foresee all consequences of their acts, for example, that by choosing – in the best interest of their children's social advance – the majority language of the larger environment as their domestic language, they may contribute to the recession and demise of their ancestral language. That, by insisting on a native expression rather than a loanword, a purist language guardian may contribute to the same result is likewise a choice with unforeseen consequences. Both in immigrant communities and in small autochthonous communities coming under pressure in their native environment, the continuation of a linguistic tradition depends, ultimately, on individual acts of choice made in a social environment incorporating a vast number of variables whose interaction is hard to predict for social actors as well as for social scientists.

Conclusion

The key insight from the voluminous literature on language spread, language shift and language maintenance is that while speakers have a quasi-natural attachment to their native language, there is great variability in regards to the propensity of individuals and groups to maintain their language under adverse circumstances or, conversely, to abandon it in favour of another. The factors that have a bearing on language maintenance and shift are many and complex. Linguistic diversity/homogeneity, culture, demographics and socioeconomic conditions interact as determinants of individual speech behaviour and language choice. Mass migration and imperial expansion have transplanted many languages from their native lands into disparate environments causing changes in the linguistic ecology. The quest to understand how immigrant languages fare in their new environments and how language arrangements are affected by the penetration of an imperial language or language of wider communication has engendered a number of theoretical notions discussed in this chapter, notably language loyalty, ethnolinguistic vitality, territory, functional domain and utility. They all highlight separate aspects of unstable language arrangements and factors that have a bearing on the language choices that ultimately shape them. For sociolinguists it is important to adopt a speaker-centred perspective: it is not a language that thrives or withers, but speakers who continue or cease to use it. Without speakers no linguistic environment exists. Yet, the extant linguistic environment influences speakers' behaviour and choices, although they do not necessarily realize how. This is at the bottom of the complexity of explaining unstable social language arrangements. It is appropriate, therefore, to conclude this chapter with Georges Lüdi's (1986: 220) pointed remark that 'in language choice, as in other domains of linguistic performance, speakers are not always aware of what they are doing'.

Questions for discussion

(1)   What is the role of demographic strength in language spread?
(2)   Are language shift and language maintenance mirror-image processes or can they be understood each in their own right only?
(3)   What is ethnolinguistic vitality, and how does it bear on language spread and language shift?
(4)   Think of a setting where (the speakers of) one language successfully invaded the territory of another prompting language

shift. Is the concept of domain invasion applicable to all language-shift situations or is it more suitable for some than for others?

(5)   Since language is an instrument, a utility differential in language-contact situations is a predictor of language shift, although utility is not the only determinant of language choice. What other factors modulate its effectiveness?

Notes

1. The range of contact linguistics as an interdisciplinary field relying on methods and theories developed in psychology and sociology, as well as auxiliary disciplines such as demographics and migration studies, is documented in Nelde (1995).
2. UN statistics: http://unstats.un.org/unsd/demographic/sconcerns/migration/
3. Figures in this chapter are taken from *Ethnologue*, 16th edition, released 2009 (www.ethnologue.com/) and the United Nations Population Division (www.un.org/esa/population/).
4. Data from *Ethnologue*, 16th edition, 2009.
5. Cf. Coulmas (1999) for an overview.
6. Figures are again from *Ethnologue* and Internet World Stats (www.internetworldstats.com/). Notice that statistics of this sort are rather short-lived, yet they are indicative of the general situation.
7. Bihari is a cover term for Bhojpuri, Magahi and Maithili.
8. For a system-theoretic analysis of the hierarchical ordering of languages in the world system, see Swaan (2001).
9. UNESCO 2010: www.unesco.org/new/en/culture/themes/endangered-languages/; cf. also Crystal (2000).
10. Khubchadani (1983:103–7) deals at length with the problem of oscillation of census returns regarding mother tongue in India, especially north-central India which he calls a 'fluid zone'. He explains: 'The composite characteristics of communication patterns in the entire Hindi–Urdu–Panjabi region are at variance with the concerns for identity expressed through the claims of mother tongues, which have a marked tendency to shift in every decennial census depending on the prevailing sociocultural climate.' Kamusella (2012) examines extant standards of language classification, demonstrating that many listings by missionary-linguists of the Summer Institute of Linguistics and the *Ethnologue* are arbitrary and ad hoc.
11. Language statistics of Canada's 2006 census can be inspected at www12.statcan.gc.ca/census-recensement/2006/rt-td/lng-eng.cfm.
12. See, for example, Yagmur (2004) who compares Turkish immigrant communities in Australia and Western Europe. While Turkish has generally high vitality scores as compared to other immigrant languages, differences between countries point to complex interrelations between immigrant and host communities and immigrant and dominant language. For instance, in the Netherlands, Turkish has the highest vitality score of all immigrant languages correlating with high language maintenance rates. In France, on the other hand, second-generation Turkish immigrants exhibit a marked tendency to shift to French.
13. The dominant role that in the past half-century English has come to play in science has become a field of sociolinguistic research in its own right with its own scholarly journals and societies and an incalculable number of publications. Cf. Ammon (2002), Sandelin and Sarafoglou (2004).
14. Current explanations for the spread of English fall into two camps. Phillipson (1992) leads the faction of those who explain the spread of English as the result of deliberate language policies by the British and US governments associating it with the evils of global capitalism let loose. By contrast, Crystal ([1997] 2003) takes the view that the

spread of English is a grassroots development largely unconnected to the processes of enrichment and impoverishment accompanying globalization. See also Pennycook (1994), Fishman, Conrad and Rubal-Lopez (1996) and Chapter 13 below.

Useful online resources

The Language Observatory Project (LOP) constitutes a worldwide consortium of partners: www.language-observatory.org/

World Network for Linguistic Diversity: http://maaya.org

Index of Linguistic Diversity: www.terralingua.org/linguisticdiversity/

UNESCO interactive atlas of endangered languages: www.unesco.org/new/en/culture/themes/endangered-languages/news/dynamic-content-single-view-news/news/the_interactive_atlas_of_endangered_languages_updates/

Migration Policy Institute: www.migrationinformation.org/datahub/europe.cfm

Further reading

Brenzinger, Matthias. 1992. Patterns of language shift in East Africa. In Robert Herbert (ed.), *Language and Society in Africa*. Cape Town: Witwatersrand University Press, 287–303.

Coulmas, Florian. 2010. The ethics of language choice in immigration. *Policy Innovations*. www.policyinnovations.org/ideas/commentary/data/000162

Clyne, Michael. 1991. *Community Languages: The Australian Experience*. Cambridge University Press.

Crystal, David. 2000. *Language Death*. Cambridge University Press.

Extra, Guus. 2010. Mapping linguistic diversity in multicultural contexts: demolinguistics perspectives. In J. A. Fishman and O. Garcia (eds.), *Handbook of Language and Ethnic Identity*. 2nd edn. New York: Oxford University Press, 107–22.

Fishman, Joshua A. 1991. *Reversing Language Shift: Theoretical and Empirical Foundations of Assistance to Threatened Languages*. Clevedon: Multilingual Matters.

Hyltenstam, Kenneth and Åke Viberg (eds.) 1993. *Progression and Regression in Language*. Cambridge University Press.

10 Language and identity: individual, social, national

At once, with contemptuous perversity, Mr Vladimir changed the language, and began to speak idiomatic English without the slightest trace of a foreign accent.

Joseph Conrad, *The Secret Agent*

One-dimensional social identities are not what they used to be ... We all make choices about how seriously we take such identities, and many of us make choices about the identities themselves.

Walter Truett Anderson, *Reality Isn't What It Used to Be*

Outline of the chapter

Language serves instrumental and symbolic purposes. Among the latter, the manifestation of identity sticks out as a topic that has inspired a great deal of sociolinguistic research. Departing from the notion of 'native speaker', understood as the speaker of one's proper, inborn language, this chapter investigates the link between language and identity. It discusses various kinds of identity – individual, ethnic, social and national – introducing major theoretical approaches to sociolinguistic identity research. On the basis of the Welsh language and its function for Welsh identity, the chapter argues that ethnolinguistic identity is variably emphasized by different speech communities, often playing a more important role for minority groups existing in the shadow of an overbearing neighbour than for speech communities whose language is not at risk of being replaced. It furthermore demonstrates that the language–identity link, rather than being an inalterable fixture, is historically contingent and can be either foregrounded or downplayed. The problem of shifting and multiple identities is discussed, and it is explained that identity research has moved from a predetermined concept to a more dynamic notion of identity as flexible and negotiable on both the group and individual level.

Key terms: identity, stereotypes, minority, stigma, membership

Beliefs

A basic tenet of sociolinguistics is that language displays its speakers' identity. The stories of Eliza Doolittle and the Osaka samurai discussed in Chapters 1 and 2, respectively, contain the same message: your language gives you away. This theme corresponds to strong popular beliefs about identity and language which on occasion take on rather peculiar forms. For example, when in February 2003, desperate to avert the imminent American attack on Iraq, Saddam Hussein granted CBS reporter Dan Rather an exclusive interview, the English translation of his remarks was aired in an Arabic-accented voice.[1] The voice belonged to Steve Winfield, a professional speaker known for his skills in imitating accents. Upon inquiry, CBS declared the accent was chosen 'to fit the nature of the broadcast'. This looks like an instance of rather bizarre logic, since it was unmistakably clear that Mr Saddam's statements were translated and hence not literally his words let alone his voice. However, CBS's decision testifies to the belief that identity is expressed not just by what is said, but by how it is said; that the language must match the message.

Notwithstanding such unusual choice of accent as in the CBS case, there is, of course, a great deal of inductive evidence for the relationship it was intended to express. If you hear people speak Italian, Japanese or African American English, you assume they are Italian, Japanese and African American; and if you hear English spoken with an Arabic accent, you assume the speaker to be an Arab. A more subtle message, perhaps, conveyed by the accented voice is this: 'once an Arab, always an Arab'. You are what you are. This is the whole point of categories and the logic of identity: p = p. Every individual is identical with itself. In linguistics, an important theoretical concept is grounded in this notion of self-identity. It is called 'native speaker'.[2]

The native speaker is invoked as the arbiter of grammaticality who is needed as a conceptual reference point of grammatical description, although it is generally admitted that it has no real-world referent. In theoretical linguistics this concept is needed to justify the delimitation of the realm of inquiry and in order to be able to identify a language. A language in this sense is what native speakers speak. For the purposes of description and analysis, non-native varieties can be ignored. Like the resultant grammar, the native speaker is a theoretical construct, an idealization, as Noam Chomsky has always emphasized. Yet, this concept has a strong popular appeal among non-linguists, too, who conceive of it not as a construct but as a primitive of what we know about language. Everyone is a native speaker and has a native language, also known as 'mother tongue'. From this point of view, one's mother tongue is often conceptualized in Whorfian terms as an inescapable part of individual identity. A correlate of the belief in the nativity of language is the widely held conviction that we can have only one mother tongue, just as we have only one (biological) mother. People who make us doubt this apparent truism are suspicious, like the above-quoted secret agent described by Joseph Conrad, who, with his non-native but perfect English prose, is a witness of sorts to the case under discussion here. Such suspicion is grounded in an ideological conception of language and identity which conflates individual and collective identity, linking both to loyalty. Only secret agents and other shadowy characters have a divided loyalty.

It should be obvious that the native speaker, the scientific paradigm that employs him and the grammatical descriptions that grow out of his testimony are a product of politics predicated on linguistic nationalism, 'we–they' distinctions and the need for drawing community boundaries. Equally clear is that a unitary notion of native speaker and the linguistic theory based on it will have problems with stylistic variation, code-switching, code mixing, diglossia, bilingualism, semilingualism, language attrition, language shift, nativized varieties of colonial languages, fluid mother-tongue affiliations and other language-contact phenomena that form the mainstay of sociolinguistic interest. They all have in common that they call for a notion of identity more sophisticated than 'p = p, and for ever so', attesting as they do to the great difficulty of distinguishing in a non-arbitrary fashion native from native-like, non-native and other gradations of competence in a language and the consequent difficulty of defining a speech community in objective terms. If, indeed, language expresses identity, individual and collective, then, given the elusiveness of a language and its native speaker, identity, too, must be a rather murky notion.

Destiny or choice?

At the same time, it cannot be denied that language is experienced as a marker of identity, that it is loved and celebrated as a symbol of us-ness, as well as detested and cursed, where the speech forms that are cherished or despised stand in for the people using them. As we speak, we reveal who we are, where we grew up, our gender, our station in life, our age and the group we want to belong to. And we would not be able to do so if others didn't act in like manner. The question is how it is done, more precisely, whether it is done inevitably or deliberately, by destiny or choice. Eliza Doolittle and the Osaka samurai attest the symbolic as distinct from the instrumental function of a language, but their stories have another point in common that is relevant here, and that is that there is nothing native about the sociosymbolic function of identity manifestation. Attracted by the prospects of a better life, Eliza opted for a new linguistic identity that made her acceptable to a group which would admit no Cockney speaker, Cockney being a symbol of the kind of lowly life they distinguished themselves from. And Yukichi Fukuzawa could slip into alternating roles, at one moment that of a samurai and the next that of a merchant, just by altering his speech. Linguistic identity, these examples suggest, is not an inescapable fate imposed upon us but, to some extent at least, a social construct, a matter of choice.

Consider the experience of Alan Davies, a man from South Wales raised in an English-speaking home, who as an adult decided to brush up his school-learnt Welsh as 'a test of his Welshness'. Having acquired a good command of Welsh, the question arose as to what it meant for his future life.

> Proof of Welshness? Perhaps. More important for our present purposes is the appeal to the common human experience of feeling and asserting identity through language. We all want to belong, we all want to be native speakers, we all choose groups which we aspire to even though we may change our minds and leave, as I left, quite promptly, my adult Welsh-speaking group because I found its nationalism and exclusiveness oppressive and proselytising. As a proselyte, I was expected to choose my identity. I had always vaguely assumed that, like masks, identities could be added on ... But among those who were *gryf yn yr achos* (strong in the cause) [dual identity was not acceptable]. You had to be either Welsh or English, either Welsh or British. Not both. Such a choice I found meaningless ... If to be Welsh meant making such a choice, then, I decided, that was a Welsh identity I did not wish to have.   (Davies 1991: viiif.)

Sociolinguistic identity research

Several lessons can be drawn from Davies' reflections for socio-linguistic identity studies, four of which I want to discuss in what follows.

1. *Identity change is possible*. Although Davies was not a native speaker of Welsh, acquiring a certain degree of competence made him eligible, in the eyes of other Welsh speakers, to affiliate himself with the language and use it as proof of his Welshness. Davies decided that he didn't want the kind of Welsh identity that his teachers promoted, but he had the option. Critical age and the general difficulties of learning a new language notwithstanding, millions of immigrants adopt the language of their target country every year, as 'another mask to add on' without discarding the one they were used to wearing, or exclusively as the only language they offer their children. Immigration is an obvious occasion for such a choice to be made, although it does not explain how it is made, that is, whether the new language is acquired principally as a practical instrument or also imbued with symbolic meaning for identity expression. But the circumstances of immigration do not provide the only context for identity change.

Haaland (1969) describes a case of boundary transcendence between the Fur and the Baggara in western Sudan. The former are sedentary cultivators speaking Fur, a Nilo-Saharan language, while the Arabic-speaking Baggara are pastoral nomads. Every year about 1 per cent of the Fur take up nomadic life, joining a group of Baggara, a first step in the process of identity change. Their children will grow up speaking Arabic and will be considered, both by the Baggara and the Fur, as Baggara. The main reason that some Fur choose to become Baggara, according to Haaland, is economic. Although the cattle-herding Baggara and the millet-growing Fur complement each other economically and in lifestyle, many Fur also grow cattle which is more profitable if herds are allowed to migrate to distant pastures than if their owners remain sedentary. More generally speaking, economic incentives provide a principal rationale for crossing group boundaries and identity change.[3]

Another reason for adjusting one's speech behaviour is communicative efficiency. In 2008, English football coach Steve McClaren unintentionally provided an instructive example. After moving to the Netherlands to manage FC Twente, he acquired a Dutch accent becoming the target of ridicule and acerbic comments in Britain's tabloid press. The video clip of a British reporter's interview with 'Shteeve McClaren' went viral on the Internet.[4] Once the hullabaloo over his 'rather strange Dutch accent' had subsided, the press found new fodder when, in 2010, he took over at Wolfsburg where he swiftly picked up a German accent. Clearly, McClaren was as good at adjusting his speech to his players' as he was at instructing them how to kick the ball, but this talent was scorned rather than appreciated by his compatriots. Imitating a foreign accent isn't nearly as laborious as learning a foreign language – but may serve similar functions. Mimicking your interlocutor's accent improves language comprehension. It is unlikely that McClaren changed his accent deliberately, but since he did not speak Dutch or German he reduced the distance between himself and his relevant reference groups, the Twente and Wolfsburg football teams, by moving in their direction. As experimental research found out (Adank, Hagoort and Bekkering 2010), this was a functionally well motivated and effective move, which, however, was evidently perceived as unseemly if not an act of treason by the popular press.

Perhaps you can, but you mustn't change your identity. This is the underlying message of how this episode was played out in the media. Speaking with a foreign accent is as indicative of identity as is speaking a language. Ethnolinguistic identity change is indicative of the kind of association involved. Linguistically defined groups can be joined by outsiders, in principle, although not all groups are equally open or use language as the key entrance ticket. Max Weber (1968: 40f.) remarked that 'ethnic membership ... differs from the kinship group precisely by being a *presumed* identity'. This holds true also of language group membership. It does not mean that a presumed identity is no identity at all, but that it is flexible and dynamic rather than unalterably given.

2. *Identity change requires effort and is not equally easy in all cases.* Asserting Welsh identity by means of learning Welsh as an adult is more difficult than opting out of Welshness in an environment where English is the unmarked choice in most communications. Making a marked choice is always more difficult than making an unmarked choice. This is a structural disadvantage for minority speech communities, because unless they live in

secluded settlements, the minority language will be the marked choice more frequently than the majority language. Displaying one's identity is not equally relevant in all situations, but in a majority/minority context with widespread bilingualism in the minority group, use of the minority language is in many speech situations taken as a manifestation of identity, no matter whether or not such manifestation is intended. For this reason alone and because of the utility differential between majority language and minority language, identity change from minority to majority is always easier than vice versa, provided language is the key identity marker, rather than race, social class or religion.

3. *The emphasis placed on language as an identity marker is variable.* The same language may play differing roles as the vehicle of group identity (Kristiansen and Coupland 2011). For example, Dutch is habitually instrumentalized as an identity marker in Belgium where it competes with French, but much less so in the Netherlands where it is unchallenged. Speaking Dutch in Holland is the default choice. Similarly, in diaspora the symbolic charge of languages generally increases because the question of joining a new group which never arose in the homeland cannot be sidestepped. In a language's homeland few people ever consider the question of whether they should retain it, although very small minorities may be faced with the issue of discontinuing their linguistic tradition.[5]

There is another sense in which the language–identity link is variable. The identity associated with standard varieties of international languages such as English, French, Spanish and German is more diffuse than that of smaller, culturally more homogeneous speech communities. Weak identity expression seems to be an inadvertent by-product of language standardization, but much depends on the linguistic culture. French has been a key symbol of French cultural identity for centuries, the high degree of standardization of the language being a crucial feature of its esteem. It is a common standard that makes French a valuable language, providing the peoples of many countries with a common anchor of identity. The institutional framework of this identity is the International Organization of 'Francophonie', which defines itself as an alliance grounded in French-based culture. As Ager (1996: 57) notes, 'for some, the defence of Francophonie is the same thing as the defence of French culture'. Yet, a certain tension results from the universal appeal and internationalism of Francophonie, on the one hand, and the inalienable conceptual ties between the French language and French culture, on the other. For, in West Africa, in Canada and in the Antilles, French serves the expression of cultures that have notable differences from that of the French. One way of resolving the issue is to consider France as the home of metropolitan cultural identity, which is a critical component of various subidentities expressed by local varieties of French, as in Quebec, and French creoles, as in the Caribbean, whose speakers recognize the metropolitan standard.

Other 'big' standard languages have been enlisted for identity manifestation similarly, internal variability being exploited to that end. Irish English, also 'Hiberno-English', is a good example. In the event, the function of identity has been transferred from one language to another. As a result of steady decline since the early nineteenth century, the Irish language has lost its communicative functions, being reduced almost entirely to a token of identity expression for the vast majority of Irish families. Since this function alone cannot sustain a language, language shift to English as 'a means of gaining access to improved economic conditions both within Ireland and overseas' (Harris 1991: 44) is irreversible. However, notwithstanding the remnants of Irish, English has taken over all functions of Irish in Ireland, including that of identity display, having evolved into a distinct cluster of varieties (Ó Muirithe 1977; Ó Tuathaigh 2005).

A question of great significance for sociolinguistic identity research is what happens when a speaker of Irish English moves to London, and whether it makes a difference if that person is a man or a woman, an adult or a child, a lawyer or a longshoreman. Only some generalizations are possible. Children are more likely and quicker than adults to drop the Irish features of their speech – *I do be here every day.* – and blend in with their new environment – *I'm here every day.* – and the same can be said of professionals and labourers, respectively. But reliable predictions are difficult because individual linguistic identity is a synthesis of given and adopted elements, and, as with deportment and dress, individuals have preferences as to which identity they want to display and whether to display it in a conspicuous or subtle way.

4. *The language-identity link is historically contingent.* Welsh was not always a minority language in the British Isles or in Wales; speaking or not speaking Welsh was not always a political issue. But over time, in the wake of industrialization and much intermarriage (Williams 1987), English made ever more inroads into Wales and Welsh became a language associated with provincialism and backwardness.[6] By the promotion of English, condemned by some as a policy of language eradication and welcomed by others as a way of providing access to the majority culture, Welsh came under pressure, being perceived as a stigma by the English-speaking majority and many of its own speakers. It is only against this background that the radical attitude adopted by the Welsh activists, among whom Alan Davies learnt Welsh, can be understood. A double identity is easy to espouse from the secure position of a dominant language like English, but intolerable from the point of view of the underdog that has been driven out of its proper territory. Welsh activists were intent on reclaiming, and, as they saw it, entitled to reclaim this territory and, therefore, insisted on equating identity claims with undivided loyalty. That was in the 1970s. In the meantime, Welsh has regained institutional support and with it status and function in Wales, which helped Welsh speakers to some extent to come out of the defensive corner fenced

off by the activists (Osmond 2008). Colin Williams (1999: 280), co-author of *The Community Research Project on Regenerating Welsh as a Community Language* (1997), explains: 'Support for Welsh can no longer be interpreted as essentially a symbol of resistance to Anglicization, for the language is deeply imbued in the process of state socialization.' Welsh is extraordinary because its decline, it seems, could be halted, but otherwise similar stories of languages that were charged in their history, at times more and at other times less, with the symbolic manifestation of identity can be found on all continents.

At a certain point in history, Welsh was a stigmatized language, discriminated against by a dominant society and state and despised by many of its own speakers. Such a fate is not uncommon among minority languages. While discrimination and self-hate foster language shift, it has been argued that they also strengthen support for a language. The persistence in the United States of African American Vernacular English[7] in spite of long-standing negative attitudes towards it provides a pertinent example. Why is it that, while 'good' language is widely perceived as a means of social advancement, low-prestige varieties like African American English are not discarded by their speakers and replaced by more highly regarded ones? The most persuasive answer is their role as symbols of identity – local, social, ethnic and national. Black English is a stigmatized variety because it is spoken mainly by those at the bottom of the social hierarchy in the United States. But although its grammatical and pronunciation features are used most by those with least education and smallest earning power, it is also endorsed and enjoyed by blacks who are well educated and hold good jobs. Rather than being a social indicator, it indexes African American ethnicity. 'Black adults of all ages talk the vernacular, and it functions to express their black identity, too' (Rickford and Rickford 2000: 224). Identity assertion by choice of variety, especially by a disadvantaged group, is often an act of defiance which can be understood only against the background of its socio-historical context.

Multiple identities

The picture that results from the above observations is that identity is a multilayered dynamic process rather than an inborn trait that cannot be helped. Social advancement, immigration and identity assertion against the odds of minorization, discrimination and marginalization hold a common lesson. Identities are partly given and partly made. This insight is encapsulated nowhere more pointedly than in the title of Robert Le Page and Andrée Tabourt-Keller's book *Acts of Identity* which foreshadowed a shift in research orientation. In Chapter 1, we noted that, in contradistinction to theoretical linguistics that aims at universal grammar, sociolinguistics focuses on those aspects of language that are learnt, not innate. The variability of language is an immediate consequence of its being learnt, which in turn implies that language can be employed as a marker of identity. However, in the early phase of sociolinguistics, both of the variationist school and the sociology of language, not all consequences of a notion of language that renounces categoricity were appreciated. In particular, the social factors to which linguistic variation was tied – social class, sex, age and ethnicity – were seen as fixed categories that remained stable, if not through a lifetime, at least for the purposes of research. Variation in language was interpreted as being conditioned by these factors, understood as permanent properties of speakers, and varieties were seen as encoding speaker identities based on social category membership. In the sociology of language, ethnolinguistic identities, indexed by languages rather than stylistic varieties, were similarly conceptualized as fixed categories.

It was only in the 1990s that a constructivist approach to identity (Cerulo 1997) took shape in the social sciences and began to inspire sociolinguistic research, too. In the meantime, dozens of books have been published whose titles speak of 'negotiating identities'. Investigating how narrative is used as a means to display the speakers' social identity, Schiffrin (1996: 199) comes to the conclusion 'that identity is neither categorical nor fixed: we may act more or less middle-class, more or less female, and so on, depending on what we are doing and with whom'. In the final analysis, a dynamic, variable conception of linguistically encoded identity is an inevitable consequence of the notion of language on which sociolinguistics is predicated, that is, a multifunctional variable instrument whose identity is perpetually reconstructed by its users rather than being categorically given.

Emblems for identity display

How do you do?
How are you?
How's you?
How're you doing?
What's up?
Howdy?
Hello.
Hi.
Gidday
How na?

The challenge that follows from a dynamic view of the identity of individual speakers, speech communities and their languages/varieties is to show how, and motivated by what, speakers exploit the mechanisms of linguistic identity display strategically. From this point of view, every speech act is an act of identity, and all utterances vary with respect to the relative importance of identity display. To what extent the potential of language as a symbol of identity is actually made use of accordingly varies from one individual to another and from one speech community to another. A great deal of sociolinguistic research has been devoted to various layers and aspects of identity, such as local and regional (Trudgill 1994), ethnic (Fishman 2010), national (Safran 1999; Simpson 2007) and political (Hale 1997; Faas 2010) affiliation as well as social class (Honey 1989), gender (Hall and Bucholtz 1995) and sexual orientation (Jacobs 1996; Motschenbacher 2011), to name but the most widely recognized features to which others could be added, for 'virtually any product of the imagination can be employed for purposes of identification' (Tabouret-Keller 1996: 321). These identities are not mutually exclusive but form a complex fabric of intersecting affiliations, commitments, convictions and emotional bonds such that each individual is a member of various overlapping groups with varying degrees of incorporation. Each individual's memberships and identities are variable, changing in intensity by context and over time.

Sociolinguistic identity research that recognizes this variability is faced with the task of developing models that can explain why languages and language variants are found attractive or unattractive and are utilized as signs of identity in some situations and not in others. The manifold possible relationships between language attitudes and social groups are affected by all the variables mentioned above as well as by the relationship between social groups and the society at large. Strategic identification with a language/variety reflects both intragroup and intergroup dynamics.

To illustrate, consider two instances of language choice involving the variable value of German for identity claims. During World War I, use of German in the United States declined drastically because German Americans who spoke German in public faced open hostility and came under strong assimilation pressure. The intellectual climate in the United States was against multilingualism and multi-ethnicity which found expression in laws against the use of foreign languages (Marshall 1986). As speakers of an 'enemy language', many German Americans felt particularly vulnerable to this kind of officially endorsed antipathy towards minorities and aliens and, therefore, abandoned their ancestral language. The costs of openly manifested German identity exceeded its benefits. In post-Soviet Union Kazakhstan it was the reverse. Ethnic Germans resident there, many of whom had a scant knowledge of German at best, reclaimed German as their mother tongue because this was a requirement for recognition as an ethnic German by the German government and certain immigration privileges that came with it. From the point of view of a resident of Kazakhstan where general living conditions were harsh, unemployment was high and prospects for improvement bleak, professing loyalty to German was attractive. Even if it had to be learnt, the perceived benefits of identifying with

German exceeded the cost involved in acquiring the necessary competence. It is important to realize (1) that in order to identify with a language, competence in it need not be native but can be acquired and (2) that there is no obvious minimal level of competence essential for that purpose. In a survey of North African immigrants in Grenoble, France, reported by Dabène and Billiez, a respondent said: 'Arabic is my language, but I don't speak it' (quoted in Tabouret-Keller 1996: 320). The language–identity nexus expressed here is extreme, to be sure, but it brings into focus an important function, the drawing of boundaries.

Self-fulfilling boundaries

Clearly, some communities attach greater importance to their ancestral language than others, as differing assimilation and language maintenance patterns attest. Communities vary furthermore with regard to how they distinguish 'their' language and by extension themselves from a neighbouring community and its language. Mutual intelligibility of speakers is no objective criterion for identity recognition, as observations in linguistically complex situations have repeatedly shown. For example, speakers of Hindi and Urdu may or may not be willing to understand each other, highlighting or downplaying the relatedness of their speech varieties. The resulting identity features 'extend beyond their linguistic characteristics in the thrust to assert rival claims of solidarity' (Khubchandani 1983: 112). Historically, Hindi and Urdu have been cultivated by borrowing, respectively, from Sanskrit and Perso-Arabic to form two varieties of the same underlying code which, however, are associated with two different literary traditions using two different writing systems and with two different religions, Hinduism and Islam. This example is instructive because it shows that several different features are invoked to create identities and mark off boundaries. Writing systems and scripts represent instruments of identity manifestation which are, perhaps, more obviously subject to deliberate choice and manipulation than other linguistic subsystems. They will be discussed at greater length in Chapter 12. In societies where a standard pronunciation of a standard language is not as clearly defined as, for instance, RP, visible signs of identity differentiation play a particularly important role. However, other social attributes and features of behaviour complement and interfere with the language–identity complex, such as religion, skin colour, gender or culture.

Common to them all is that they can serve as the basis of stereotypes that provide orientation for interaction with others. Experimental research has revealed the self-confirming and reinforcing nature of such stereotypes. Following Axelrod's (1984) theory of cooperation, the underlying mechanism can be explained as follows. Assume that a group of people are divided into two subgroups and everyone is given either a Blue label or a Green label and that each individual is instructed to cooperate with members of his or her group but not with members of the other group. A stable reciprocal behavioural pattern will evolve based on mutual stereotypes, for Greens who think that only Greens will cooperate will find their beliefs confirmed, and so will the Blues. These beliefs need not be grounded in direct personal experience, because they will be borne out by others. Not only that, a Green who decides to break out of the system and cooperate with the Blues will be frustrated because the Green label indicates membership in a group with whose members Blues do not expect to cooperate. Defecting members of each group are thus likely to fall back in line.

If in a language-contact situation, as is usually the case, the two groups are of different size, the minority will suffer more from this arrangement than the majority. For, assuming that the Greens are the majority and the Blues the minority and that everyone interacts with everyone else once a week, then the Greens will interact with their own group, having the satisfying experience of cooperative behaviour more frequently than the Blues. Blues dissatisfied with this situation may try to change it. The obvious behavioural alternative is to join the Greens or, failing that, seek to interact more with Blues. Trying to remain Blue and enjoy cooperative interaction with the Greens is the least likely option. This explains the group-cohesion reinforcing function of stereotypes and why 'minorities often seek defensive isolation' (Axelrod 1984: 148). Language behaviour is a cooperative game which, however, is usually predicated on common group membership of all players. In intergroup relationships cooperation and mutual accommodation are often lacking, especially where boundaries are emphasized by means of stereotypes.

Conclusions

To conclude this chapter, language is a very noticeable indicator of identity that is usually inherited, but can also be adopted. Group affiliation by means of stereotypes and identity manifestation is a matter of relative choice, 'relative' because group membership is a social process involving the individual member and the group. To understand the language-identity complex, both sides must be kept in mind, the self-confirming nature of identity manifestations and stereotypes which transcend the scope of individual action and act as constraints on individual choice, and the volitional aspects of 'acts of identity'. The resulting conception sees language as one of several dimensions which are exploited in the construction of identities, being in variable degrees subject to deliberate modification. Rather than consisting in established social features reflected in a straightforward manner in differing speech forms, identities are constantly made and remade. This tenet is well summarized in the following remark by Le Page (1986: 23):

People create their linguistic system (and we all have more than one) so as to resemble those of the groups with which from time to time they wish to identify. Both the groups, and their linguistic attributes, exist solely in the mind of each individual ... We behave in the way that – unconsciously or consciously – we think appropriate to the group with which at the moment we wish to identify.

Questions for discussion

(1)   Some scholars claim that language and ethnic identity are intimately related, while others deny a necessary link between them, stressing race, social class and national loyalty as more important. Find examples to support both points of view.

(2)   Linguistic identity claims are often linked by their proponents to linguistic relativism of one variety or another. Why should this be so?

(3)   Consider the greeting formulas in the textbox on p. 197 above. What do they reveal about the identity of speakers using them?

(4)   'I believe that my writing in Gĩkũyũ language, a Kenyan language, and African language, is part and parcel of the anti-imperialist struggles of Kenyan and African peoples.'[8] What does this statement by Kenyan writer Ngũgĩ wa Thiong'o say about the problem of language and identity?

(5)   'To experiensh big gamesh, Championsh League ... Arshenal ... The Emiratesh ... will be fantashtic for the playersh, not just for now but for the future ash well. I shay I think we are not just ... what you call? ... underdogsh but mashive underdogsh.'[9] With quotes like this, football coach Steve McClaren was vilified in the British press for 'shpeeking' with a Dutch accent when he managed a Dutch football club. What can be learnt from this episode?

Notes

1. Link to a YouTube video of CBS Dan Rather with Saddam Hussein (Feb. 24 2003): www. youtube.com/watch?v=qC50G8lygBI

2. For discussion of the concept of 'native speaker' and its importance in linguistics and sociolinguistics, see Coulmas (1981b), Davies (1991), Singh (1998).

3. 'Language loyalty persists as long as the economic and social circumstances are conducive to it, but if some other language proves to have greater value, a shift to that other language begins' (Dorian 1982: 47). To the extent that language loyalty depends on the language–identity link, identity itself is subject to fluctuation, which may explain the variable self-esteem of different ethnolinguistic groups.

4. www.youtube.com/watch?v=2ZnoP4sUV90

5. There are, of course, exceptions. For example, in the 1880s, some Japanese intellectuals discussed the idea of substituting English for Japanese as the national language of Japan (Coulmas 1989).

6. It has been argued that industrialization helped Welsh because it began in Welsh-speaking areas. However, Anglicization did come in its wake, as the immigration of 'a predominantly English workforce proved too much for Welsh to assimilate' (Edwards 1985: 69).
7. For a detailed review of the grammatical features of African American English and its sociohistorical context, see Poplack (2000).
8. Ngũgĩ wa Thiong'o (1981: 28).
9. Former England coach Steve McClaren hilariously 'speaksh' the lingo in Dutch TV interview, www.dailymail.co.uk/tvshowbiz/article-1044982/ *Daily Mail*, 15 August 2008.

Useful online resources

'BBC Languages, Your Say – Language and Identity' is a database in the making with people's comments: www.bbc.co.uk/languages/yoursay/language_and_identity.shtml

PSYBLOG 'Why groups and prejudices form so easily: Social Identity Theory': www.spring.org.uk/2007/09/war-peace-and-role-of-power-in-sherifs.php

United States Census Bureau, 'Language Use': www.census.gov/hhes/socdemo/language/data/acs/index.html

Further reading

Appiah, A. K. and H. L. Gates (eds.) 1995. *Identities*. University of Chicago Press.
Fuller, Janet M. 2007. Language choice as a means of shaping identity. *Journal of Linguistic Anthropology* **17**(1): 105–29.
Ige, Busayo. 2010. Identity and language choice: 'We equals I'. *Journal of Pragmatics* **42**(11): 3047–54.
Lauring, Jakob. 2008. Rethinking Social Identity Theory in international encounters: language use as a negotiated object for identity making. *International Journal of Cross Cultural Management* **8**(3): 343–61.
Le Page, R. B. and Andrée Tabouret-Keller. 1985. *Acts of Identity: Creole-Based Approaches to Language and Ethnicity*. Cambridge University Press.
Mendoza-Denton, Norma. 2002. Language and identity. In J. K. Chambers, Peter Trudgill and Natalie Schilling-Estes (eds.), *The Handbook of Language Variation and Change*. Oxford: Blackwell, 475–99.
Ryan, Ellen Bouchard. 1979. Why do low-prestige language varieties persist? In H. Giles and R. N. St Clair (eds.), *Language and Social Psychology*. Oxford: Blackwell, 145–58.

11 Language planning: communication demands, public choice, utility

> ... once His Majesty has subdued people from various nations and languages, and being in need of transmitting the law of the conquerors in this language, I hereby present this Grammar to facilitate its learning ...
>
> Nebrija (1492)[1]

> In order to carry out language planning, one needs a language to plan for.
>
> Peter Mühlhäusler (1994)

> The Carolingian scholars did not merely become conscious that Romance and Latin were different ... they invented the difference.
>
> Roger Wright (1991)

Outline of the chapter

This chapter looks at politically motivated language choices, asking what language policy consists in and how it differs from other sociolinguistic choices. To illustrate the range of political language activities, examples of language policy at different levels of government are presented. A distinction is made between general language *policy* goals and specific language-*planning* activities designed to realize these goals within a set time frame; and the elements of a simple model of language planning are introduced. Language-planning activities are commonly divided into two categories, status planning and corpus planning. These notions are discussed on the basis of specific examples, and it is demonstrated how interventions concerning the status of a language interact with procedures designed to change its makeup. Much as careful preparation of corpus and status planning is necessary, the success of measures of both kinds is not decided at the drawing board. To be successful, a language policy has to be acceptable to the people concerned; for languages do not exist in the absence of a community of speakers. The problem of policies relating to languages whose community is dwindling is addressed, followed at the end of the chapter by a reminder of the conceptual and ideological differences between Western researchers and speakers of reticent languages.

> *Key terms:* language regime, status planning, corpus planning, acceptability, minorities, language decline

Political choices

The world's languages outnumber its independent states by a factor of thirty. They are characterized by internal diversity; and they are marked by gross disparities in terms of number of speakers and functional range. Taken together, these factors make languages an inescapable object of political choices. Political agents taking decisions designed to shape the linguistic behaviour of groups usually act through committees or language academies. The basic assumption underlying the work of some 200 language-planning agencies around the world[2] is that it is possible to change people's behaviour and to adapt the linguistic resources of speech communities to changing communication needs by premeditated planning. Consider some examples.

When, after a protracted and bloody war, East Timor attained independent statehood, the new government of the shattered country lost no time in making provisions concerning its languages. Section 13 ('Official languages and national languages') of the constitution as adopted on 22 March 2002 stipulates that

(1)   Tetum and Portuguese shall be the official languages in the
       Democratic Republic of East Timor.
(2)   Tetum and the other national languages shall be valued and
       developed by the State.

In summer 2002, government-employed receptionists and security staff in Bristol were told to stop calling members of the public 'dear' or 'love', and to address them as 'sir' or 'madam' instead.

In the meantime, traffic authorities in Beijing suspended a programme allowing car owners to have personalized number plates. Too many complaints had been launched about plates that were crude or politically incorrect.

At a meeting of the Euro-Atlantic Partnership Council (EAPC) on 22 November 2002 in Prague, the organizers chose French as the official language of the protocol. The unwanted Ukrainian President Leonid Kuchma could thus be kept apart from the leaders of the United Kingdom and the United States. The alphabetical seating order in French put Kuchma several seats away from the Prime Minister of 'Royaume-Uni' and the President of 'Etats-Unis'.

In February 2003, the State Duma in Moscow passed a law on Russian as the state language. It prohibits the use of foreign words or expressions that have Russian-language equivalents in public documents or in civil, criminal or administrative court proceedings.

On 21 November 2008 the Council of the European Union passed a European strategy for multilingualism that invites its member states and the Commission to

1. Promote multilingualism with a view to strengthening social cohesion, intercultural dialogue;
2. Strengthen lifelong language learning;
3. Better promote multilingualism as a factor in the European economy's competitiveness and people's mobility and employability;
4. Promote the linguistic diversity and intercultural dialogue by stepping up assistance for translation, in order to encourage the circulation of works and the dissemination of ideas and knowledge in Europe and across the world.[3]

These examples illustrate that political choices of language are variously motivated and take various forms. Diverse though they are, they are based on a common supposition: it is possible by means of political decisions to determine the language(s) that are used for certain purposes and how they are used. In many cases, an explicit language policy is adopted because of the coexistence of several languages in one polity and the necessity of regulating their functions and mutual relationships.

The definitions of 'language policy' are various, as are the theoretical approaches adopted for the analysis of political interventions into collective patterns of language use. Cooper (1989) is interested in the social effects of language policies and language planning, asking 'who plans what for whom and how?' Pool (1990) favours a political science approach, arguing that language regimes and political regimes constrain each other and that, accordingly, information about one kind of regime can be used to predict the characteristics of the other kind. Utility and other economic factors as the driving force underlying language policies are explored from different points of view by Grzega (2011), Rubinstein (2000), Grin (1996) and Coulmas (1992b), while Djité (2008) puts language policy in the context of empowerment and development. And Ager's (2001) analysis of language policy is centred upon the concept of motivation in terms of motives, attitudes and goals. Following this approach, the term 'language policy' is here used in the sense of explicitly stated motives for and goals of government action on language as opposed to customary laissez-faire practice. The underlying principle of modern language policy took shape in the nineteenth century when in France and Germany the idea of a nation defined by its territory and its (dominant) language gained currency (Spolsky 2012b: 4). While, in accordance with this principle, language policies are commonly formulated at the national level, local governments (Backhaus 2012) and supranational organizations such as UNESCO (2011) also pursue and enact language policies.

Language regimes and deliberate change

The goal of a language policy is to perpetuate, establish or undo a language regime. Some examples of language regimes are the European Charter for Regional and Minority languages,[4] China's recognition of fifty-five minority languages (Sun and Coulmas 1992; Mackerras 1994), Switzerland's territorialization of its official languages (Lüdi et al. 1997), Ireland's designation of Irish as its national and first official language (O'Riagáin 1997), Quebec's 1977 Charter of the French Language, which stipulates that all laws must be printed, published, adopted and approved in both French and English (Endleman 1995), and Singapore's trilingual education policy that, in addition to English and Chinese instruction for all citizens and permanent residents, provides for Mother Tongue learning (Chua 2011). Language planning is needed whenever a language regime is to be changed or a spontaneously occurring change is deemed undesirable. It is concerned with implementing language policy goals. Specific language-planning measures fall into two categories illustrated by the two articles of the East Timorese constitution quoted above: status planning and corpus planning corresponding, respectively, to macro- and micro-sociolinguistics. While Article 1 declares Tetum and Portuguese official languages thus determining their status, Article 2, which calls for Tetum and other languages to be developed, is concerned with not the status but the state of languages, their corpus. For a language policy to be effective, it needs status planning and corpus planning since both are interrelated. Tetum will not be able to serve the functions of an official language unless it is developed. A third category, acquisition planning, is sometimes considered separately in addition to the other two (e.g. Cooper 1989: 33).

Language planning involves making informed choices about language that counter quasi-natural, market-driven developments that are expected to take place in the absence of any intervention, or that have taken place, with or without intervention, and which the language policy is intended to halt or reverse. Tollefson (1991: 14) disputes that there are free and rational choices in language, pointing out that these are limited by the historical conditions of the society a person is born into. However, as we have seen, choice does not have to be rational or free to qualify as choice. Like any other regime, a language regime is the result of rival interests and reflects inequalities in social strength and power. It is in many cases supported by habit and inertia. Different groups, therefore, have different choices. Language regimes are a means of social control, and the ability to make language-related choices on the policy level and on that of language planning is distributed quite unevenly. Yet what distinguishes politically motivated language planning from unguided language development is deliberate choice.

Projections of the future

This makes language planning a subfield of sociolinguistics, albeit a special one. An obvious and important difference between choice in language planning and other sociolinguistic choices is that choices at the utterance level are intended to lead to changes in the sociolinguistic situation and/or the language regime. Thus language-planning choices are undertaken in the expectation that they will affect future developments in predictable ways. This requires a conditional model of language change of the form $X \rightarrow Y$, if you do X the outcome will be Y. A simple model of language planning includes the following elements:

- an initial sociolinguistic situation SLS_1 including speakers, languages and their functions;
- goals, summarized as a projected situation SLS_2;
- a set of measures suitable to transform SLS_1 into SLS_2;
- an authority to determine, and institutions to implement these measures;
- the actual implementation;
- monitoring the effectiveness of the measures over time;
- comparison of SLS_1 with SLS_2 and the actual outcome;
- modification of measures if grave disparities between actual outcome and SLS_2 are found.

In official and semi-official domains where language choice can be determined by explicit regulations, it is possible to proceed along these lines. For schools, courts of law, municipal and national assemblies, churches, local administrations and international organizations, it can be decided that they function in language(s) A (B, C, etc.) and not in others. Regulating speech behaviour in private domains is not so easy; for even in totalitarian states, it is impossible to control all aspects of people's speech. The effects of officially prescribed linguistic choices are hard to predict. A general model of sociolinguistic change that allows for reliable projections about future situations is not available yet.

The future is slippery territory in most scientific fields; with regard to language it is exceedingly problematic because of the multitude and complexity of the variables involved. Yet, projecting future patterns of language choice and language use is what language planning is all about. Under the best of circumstances, forecasts about particular, well-documented situations are possible, but generalizations are risky. In Chapter 5 above we have seen that describing the course of language change in retrospect, for example progress in language standardization, is a difficult undertaking. Charting out future developments is much more intricate since cause and effect are governed not by natural laws but by social processes involving active agents susceptible to various influences, such as new technologies, migration and political upheavals, which make forecasts about a society's demographic and linguistic structure notoriously difficult. What is more, data are often fragmentary and unreliable.

A seemingly simple question such as, 'how many people speak language A?' is more difficult than meets the eye because there is no uniform definition of what speaking language A means and because statistics may not be available. National census surveys do not necessarily contain language-related questions, and where such questions are included they do not necessarily yield information that is of use for sociolinguistic projections. 'First language', 'language of schooling', 'home language', 'usual language', 'maternal or paternal language' are rarely used as categories on census questionnaires. More commonly, respondents are labelled by language, that is, an unalterable one-person-one-language relation is assumed. Census data of this sort make it difficult if not impossible to assess the importance of widespread second languages and lingua francas and fail to grasp the extent of multilingualism as well as the fact that the dominant language of millions of people in many countries is not the language they first acquired and may continue to identify with.

What is more, the language ideologies originating in nineteenth-century Europe that connect if not identify languages, cultures and polities presuppose a homogeneity of these entities that does not reflect the reality in other parts of the world. Yet, the conception of languages as neatly delimited units has informed the descriptions of non-Western societies and their ways with words by Western missionaries and linguists on many occasions. New Guinea, because of its intricate linguistic diversity a great treasure trove and challenge for linguistic scholarship, presents an instructive example. Discussing the problem of language names, de Vries comments on what others have referred to as the 'Korowai language' as follows: 'Linguistic and cultural homogeneity and the idea of bound discrete entities called "Kombai language" or "Kombai culture" is the very opposite of the linguistic and cultural realities of New Guinea clan communities [. . .] where speakers' identities are not threatened by multilingualism, borrowing, mixing and adjusting linguistic and cultural practices to cross-language partners in communication' (de Vries 2012: 14).

The problems of language names and the identity of languages are not limited to speech communities outside the Western world. Prior to World War II, Luxembourgish was known as *Luxemburger Deutsch*, a German dialect, but linguistic separatism mirroring political events led to claims for independent language status (Kramer 1994). This is by no means a unique event. Early in the twentieth century, the respected French linguist Antoine Meillet identified five Slavic languages 'which cannot be confounded: Russian, Polish, Czech, Serbo-Croatian and Bulgarian' (Meillet 1918: 49). Less than a century later, the *International Encyclopedia of Linguistics*, second edition (2003), lists as many as seventeen Slavic languages, among them Serbo-Croatian, which Serbian and Croatian nationalists prefer to regard as two languages (Bugarski 2001).[5] Could Meillet have predicted such a proliferation of languages and/or change of classification and labelling? The point to note is not that Meillet's scholarship is out of date, but that changing language classifications render all statements about long-term developments in language demographics highly doubtful. Comparative statistical calculation is impossible if the number of speakers *n* refers to two different territorial populations at two points in time. This problem is an outgrowth of the basic fact addressed in this book, that language is a matter of choice. The ensuing difficulties are omnipresent in language planning; not only that, they are inseparable from the very idea of language planning which assumes that languages are not born but made.

The diversity of postcolonial societies (Vertovec 2006) has led to an increased awareness of the difficulties involved in gathering meaningful language statistics. For instance, the UK Office for National Statistics adopted two new questions on language for its 2011 census. 'The first of the new language questions collected information on main language. The second question collected information on English proficiency, but only for those whose main language is not English (or Welsh/English in Wales)' (Office for National Statistics 2008). The new questions were introduced in order to help public service agencies better assess the language support facilities they need to provide.

Because of the preeminence of the nation-state as the principal form of political organization since the nineteenth century and the identification of state and language that came with it, language policies in advanced countries were until recently premised on the notion of a national language and, in developing countries, associated with nation building, while linguistic pluralism was widely perceived as an obstacle to cohesion and advancement. Recently these precepts and attitudes have begun to give way to greater recognition of the positive aspects of multilingualism, notably in Europe. However, notwithstanding the fact that sociolinguistic arrangements are always in flux, language regimes tend to be entrenched and conservative.

Planning language status

The status of a language is a construct sanctioned by law or tradition. It can be an important factor in deciding the power structures of communication in a community. Although recourse to legal measures is just one of several strategies of language status allocation (Laporte 1994), the fact that the majority of the countries of the world, as listed in Table 11.1, have language-related provisions in their constitutions is indicative of the general importance attached to the matter.[6] It also testifies to the fact that most countries are linguistically heterogeneous and rely on legal provisions to manage internal diversity. (See Table 11.2 for a list of countries without language-related constitutional provisions.)

Statuses commonly distinguished are *national language*, *official language*, *working language*, *regional language* and *minority language*. These are not exclusive categories since various combinations are possible. National

Table 11.1 *Alphabetical list of countries with constitutional provisions related to language*

Afghanistan	Cambodia	Fiji	Mexico
Albania	Cameroon	Finland	Micronesia (Federated
Algeria	Canada	France	States of)
Andorra	Cape Verde	Gabon	Moldova
Antigua and Barbuda	Central African Republic	Georgia	Monaco
Argentina	China	Germany	Mongolia
Armenia	Colombia	Greece	Morocco
Austria	Comoros	Grenada	Mozambique
Azerbaijan	Congo (Republic of the)	Guatemala	Namibia
Bahamas	Congo (Democratic	Guinea	Nauru
Bahrain	Republic of)	Guyana	Nepal
Bangladesh	Costa Rica		New Zealand
Barbados	Croatia	Haiti	Nicaragua
Belarus	Cuba	Honduras	Niger
Belgium	Cyprus	Hungary	Nigeria
Belize	Djibouti	India	Norway
Benin	Dominica	Indonesia	
Bolivia		Iran	Oman
Bosnia and Herzegovina	East Timor	Iraq	
Botswana	Ecuador	Ireland	Pakistan
Brazil	Egypt	Italy	Palau
Brunei Darussalam	El Salvador	Ivory Coast	Panama
Bulgaria	Equatorial Guinea		Papua New Guinea
Burkina Faso	Eritrea	Jamaica	Paraguay
Burundi	Estonia	Jordan	Peru
	Ethiopia		Philippines
		Kazakhstan	
		Kenya	
		Kirbati	
		Korea (PDRK)	
		Kuwait	
		Kyrgyzstan	
		Laos	
		Latvia	
		Lebanon	
		Liberia	
		Libya, Arab Jamahiriya	
		Liechtenstein	
		Lithuania	
		Luxembourg	
		Macedonia (Former	
		Yugoslav Republic of)	
		Madagascar	
		Malawi	
		Malaysia	
		Maldives	
		Mali	
		Malta	
		Marshall Islands	
		Mauritania	
		Mauritius	

Poland	Saint Vincent and the Grenadines	Somalia	Tajikistan	United Arab Emirates
Portugal	Samoa	South Africa	Thailand	Uzbekistan
Qatar	Saudi Arabia	Spain	Togo	Vanuatu
Romania	Senegal	Sri Lanka	Tunisia	Venezuela
Russian Federation	Seychelles	Sudan	Turkey	Viet Nam
Rwanda	Singapore	Suriname	Turkmenistan	Yemen
Saint Kitts and Nevis	Slovakia	Sweden	Tuvalu	Yugoslavia
Saint Lucia	Slovenia	Switzerland	Uganda	Zambia
	Solomon Islands	Syrian Arab Republic	Ukraine	Zimbabwe

Source: www.unesco.org/most/ln2nat.htm#

Table 11.2 *Alphabetical list of countries without constitutional provisions related to linguistic rights*

Angola	Dominican Republic	Myanmar	Trinidad and Tobago
Australia	Guinea Bissau	Netherlands	United Kingdom
Bhutan	Iceland	San Marino	United States of America
Chile	Israel	Sierra Leone	Uruguay
Czech Republic	Japan	Swaziland	
Denmark	Korea (Republic of)	Tonga	

Source: www.unesco.org/most/ln2nat.htm#

language and official language can be identical; the national language or an official language can be a minority language; and a polity can have more than one national and/or official language. For instance, Switzerland, in Article 116 of its constitution, designates German, French, Italian and Rhaeto-Romance as national languages and German, French and Italian as official languages. The status of national language often carries symbolic import, whereas that of official language has many practical implications.

Acceptability

Status decisions can have profound effects on people's lives. For example, official multilingualism in Switzerland is coupled with the principle of territoriality, which means that most of the twenty-three cantons are officially monolingual. As a consequence, the language of schooling is decided on the cantonal level and cannot be chosen individually. This continues to be a contentious issue because linguistic boundaries do not in all cases correspond with intercantonal boundaries.[7] Similarly, Dutch-speaking Belgians who want to send their children to a school where French is the medium of instruction can do so only if they move from Flanders to Walloon, the French territory of Belgium. Thus, status allocations are subject to specific institutional arrangements.[8]

If institutional arrangements are unacceptable to sizeable groups of individuals or ethnolinguistic minorities, discontent may lead to social strife. Virtually all European countries have a history of discriminating against linguistic minorities (Coulmas 1991), and especially so since the nineteenth century when languages were transformed from properties of their users into national possessions imbued with 'national mentalities' and other aspects of cultural and spiritual essence. These ideological notions legitimized the 'one state – one language' model which gained ground as the bureaucratic state became charged with providing ever more services. Postcolonial nation building has led to similar status allocations in many Third World countries where it was felt that a proper state needs a national language, enjoying privileges over other languages spoken in the land. In several cases language policies predicated on this idea led to failure.

The 'Sinhala only' policy, by means of which English was replaced in 1956 by Sinhala as the only official language in newly independent Sri Lanka, is a case in point. This status decision disadvantaged the Tamil-speaking minority and was a major reason for the civil war that subsequently plagued the country for decades. It was only in 1987 that Tamil was granted co-official status alongside Sinhala and English.

In Pakistan, the decision to favour Urdu over Bengali ignited a battle for the status of Bengali, the language of 98 per cent of the then East Pakistanis, and eventually led to the secession in 1971 of East Pakistan and the coming into existence of a new state, Bangladesh (Musa 1996).

Turkey, whose government in the 1920s embarked on a modernization policy modelled on the French nation-state, long denied the Kurdish language official recognition. Discriminatory policies were partly repealed only in recent years as the Turkish government intensified its lobbying efforts to be considered for accession to the European Union. As a result of a long struggle by minority activists and because of the implausibility of granting status to 'small' national languages such as Irish and Luxembourgish while denying it to 'big' minority languages such as Catalan (Coulmas 1991), the EU has embraced a policy of non-discrimination (*Council of Europe* 1995; Varennes 1996).

A side effect of status allocation is that in many multilingual countries there are groups of speakers whose first or dominant language has no recognized status. Singapore allocates official status to Mandarin, Malay, Tamil and English. Other Chinese languages such as Hokkien, Teochew, Cantonese and Hakka have no status, although they are widely used native languages of Singapore. In the event, this status allocation does not defy the aspirations of these groups for their languages, the ethnic Chinese having a long tradition of identifying with one (written) Chinese language which is generally considered the language of officialdom and schooling. In the 1980s, Singapore's government started an ambitious language-planning project, the 'Speak Mandarin' campaign, designed to replace the Chinese 'dialects' with Mandarin. As can be inferred from Table 11.3, the campaign was highly effective, providing an example of how status allocation

Table 11.3 *Language most frequently spoken at home for Primary One Chinese pupils (%), quoted from Kwan-Terry (2000: 98)*

Year	Dialect	Mandarin	English	Others
1980	64.4	25.9	9.3	0.3
1984	26.9	58.7	13.9	0.4
1989	7.2	69.1	23.3	0.4

combined with supportive educational policies can bring about significant changes in a community's linguistic practice within a short time.

The question of status recognition is often controversial, especially where this instrument is used for purposes of social engineering in the face of political opposition. The status denial of Catalan in Francoist Spain (Vallverdú 1984); the banning of Korean from the official domain by the Japanese colonial administration in the 1930s (Rhee 1992); and the attempt by the Soviet state in the 1970s to reduce the status of Estonian in the Estonian Soviet Socialist Republic (Laitin 1996) are all examples of failed language policies that led to backlashes and continuing problems in interethnic and international relations and which were eventually overturned by new governments. In the three speech communities in question, language loyalty proved to be too strong to subjugate by discriminatory status planning rooted in assimilationist policies. In many other cases status problems are even more difficult to resolve, and relatively uncontroversial status allocation sometimes does not bring about the desired result. The recognition of Irish as the national and first official language in the constitution of the Republic of Ireland is an example. In the event, after the foundation of the Irish Free State in 1922, the Irish language was given legislative and ideological support, and the educational system introduced many requirements designed to promote it. Yet, Irish could not be established on a par with English in all spheres of public life in Ireland. The economic disincentives and the demands on individual effort proved to be too great.

To sociolinguists, it seems a foregone conclusion that language loyalty has a special importance. Language is said to be the most obvious 'vehicle of belongingness' (Tessarolo 1990: 28), 'the clearest indicator of ethnic difference' (Wardhaugh 1987: 55), capable of 'summing up all the other elements that define ethnicity' (Bright 1991: 12). However, this does not mean that on the individual level a sense of loyalty to a language is translated into a change of behaviour, nor does it on the national level solve the problem of how states should manage ethnically and linguistically diverse populations. How shall calls for autonomy be answered? One example must suffice to illustrate the complexity of the problem.

After a long period of suppression, Catalan gained official status in Catalonia. While the 1979 Statute of Autonomy of Catalonia called for both Castilian Spanish, the official language of all of Spain, and Catalan to be promoted within Catalonia, this was a victory for Catalan. Having re-emerged from the repressive language regime of the Franco government, the future of Catalan seemed bright in democratic Spain. However, no sooner was the outside pressure by the central government lifted than trouble arose from within. South of Catalonia, in Valencia, which some linguists consider part of the Catalan-speaking area, a language movement clamouring for the recognition of 'Valencian' came into existence, effectively undermining the position of Catalan in the Spanish state. Strubel i Trueta (1994) sees in the claim for language status for Valencian, which he considers a variety of Catalan, a misguided and tragic attempt at secession because it weakens the case of Catalan. A compromise between Catalan loyalists and Valencian supporters seems out of reach. If variety delimitation and language choice become political issues, conflict is a permanent threat.

Status upgrading and downgrading are political decisions which are assumed, and in many cases can be proven, to have repercussions on the development of the languages concerned as well as the sociolinguistic situations of which they are a part. As for all planning on the collective level, acceptance is crucial. Axelrod (1984: 24) has noted about public choice in general that, 'to be effective, a government cannot enforce any standard it chooses but must elicit compliance from a majority of the governed. To do this requires setting the rules so that most of the governed find it profitable to obey most of the time.' Language status decisions are doomed to failure unless they heed this general principle.

However, matters are even more complicated because acceptance of a status decision does not automatically produce a language practice in compliance with that decision. The policy of Arabization in Algeria, Morocco and Tunisia is a case in point. In all three countries, as in all other major Arab countries, Arabic enjoys official status, in some that of national language. To most Arabs, pledging allegiance to Arabic is a matter of national, and often religious, pride, but that doesn't imply an uncompromising commitment to use Arabic in all communication domains. The educated elites have been quite unwilling to renounce French, the sole official language of the three countries during the colonial period. Especially in Tunisia and Morocco, the colonial language legacy lingers on, causing a gap between the goals of Arabization and the actual inability to dislodge French which continues to occupy an important position in education and administration and is symbolic of access to modernity (Sirles 1999; Salhi 2002).

Many teachers say that if only they could, they would gladly teach in Arabic, but having been trained in French themselves and lacking up-to-date textbooks in Arabic, they find it difficult to do so. This explanation highlights two important general points. First, language planning is about speakers as much as it is about languages, and secondly, there is a vicious circle relating status planning with corpus planning. Implementing a decision that gives a language the status of school language is futile if the language lacks the functional registers and its speakers are, therefore, unable or unwilling to use it in this capacity. And if the language is not used for schooling, corpus-planning measures to develop these functional registers will be unsuccessful. Status planning and corpus planning, the social and linguistic aspects of language, are bound together and must be pursued in close coordination.

Planning corpus

The first quote at the beginning of this chapter illustrates the inter-relations of the two major aspects of language planning. If you want to assign a language the status of official language and use it for purposes of state, you need to be sure about what this language is and that it is up to the job. An important branch of corpus planning is concerned with measures designed to make sure the language to which they are applied can fulfil the functional requirements associated with its status. Every aspect of language that is open to individual choice can be made the object of corpus planning: phonology, lexicon, grammar and spelling. The general goal of corpus planning is to define a language by codification thereby differentiating it from other languages or varieties. Augmenting the lexicon with technical terms to increase the language's expressive power and cleansing it by banning lexical items – e.g. chairman – for political reasons from public discourse are both corpus-planning measures designed to influence speakers' choices.[9] As evidenced by many more or less successful attempts at banning words considered obscene, of foreign origin or politically incorrect, there is no clear-cut line between lexical planning and Newspeak-generating censorship.

Corpus planning highlights traits languages have by virtue of being constructed entities. Stressing the social aspects of corpus planning, Cooper (1989: 155) has pointed out that it is used 'by elites and counterelites as a tool for the acquisition and maintenance of power'. This is very much true of corpus planning for Arabic where counterelites have pushed the case of Arabization and find it hard to garner the support of the French-educated elites.

Much corpus-planning work has been done for Arabic, especially with regard to the codification of modern Standard Arabic and specialized terminologies of science and technology. Technical terminologies have been developed for various fields by language academies in Amman, Baghdad, Cairo, Damascus and Rabat, but disseminating them has proven difficult. Qualified linguists who can do the work are few and the processing of their terminology proposals by the educational authorities is slow, making it difficult to keep pace with rapid scientific and technological change (Elkhafaifi 2002). Specialized terminologies are crucial for any language expected to cover the full range of functions in modern life. Lexical limitations are not a principal obstacle to corpus planning for Arabic. Being a highly cultivated language with a rich literary tradition, Arabic is in a better position than most languages to adapt to modern life. The major weakness is inconsistency resulting from inter-Arab rivalry and lack of cooperation between the various language-planning institutions in Arab countries. Therefore, although Classical Arabic is a highly codified language, it has proven difficult to achieve standardization of the modern language. The lexical resources of Arabic have been developed variously in different dialects, posing a threat to the universality of the language. Some examples are given in Table 11.4.

Table 11.4 *Lexical diversity of Arabic (from Fassi Fehri 2002)*

English	Egyptian	Iraqi	Palestinian	Syrian	Algerian	Moroccan
exchange	taagir	baddal	tbaadal	daakaš	dayš	bəddəl
innovation	bidɛ	—	—	bəde	təxawridje	bədɛa
programme	Berograam	barnaamij	menhaaj	broogroom	beyaan	bərnaməj
scheme	—	jadwal	barnaamej	xətta	—	bərnaməj
wire (telegram)	išaara tiligrafiya	barqiyya	barqiyye	tallagraaf	—	bərqiya
cement	ismant	simint	šimento	'əsmant	bugli	bərslana
paralyze	—	šall	—	šall	xədel	bəttəl
infinite	ma luuš	ma-'il-nihaaya	biduun haddd	maa-lo nhaaye	bi-gayr	bla hədd

Terminology planning is a huge task under the best of circumstances. This task is undertaken by lexicographers working for language academies and national standard organizations. It requires sophisticated know-how, an institutional framework and considerable funds that only rich countries can afford.[10] The general point that economic disadvantage constrains linguistic choices comes to bear here.

Arguably, terminology adaptation is possible for all languages, but this is a theoretical possibility only. Most speech communities lack the resources. Hence extralinguistic factors have a lasting impact on the development of languages, as recent technological innovations demonstrate. The prevalence of electronic communication in science and technology makes the standardization and perpetual adaptation of terminologies more important than ever. Terminology databases comprise millions of terms, and rapidly developing fields require thousands of new ones every year. These needs are met in a few languages only, and as a result just a tiny fraction of the languages of the world are adjusted to science, technology, modern education, government and commerce.[11] If these communication needs pose problems for Arabic – one of the six official languages of the United Nations with one of the biggest speech communities of the world and one of the longest traditions of scholarship – how much greater must be the difficulties of lesser languages. Tetum is a case in point. In spite of the fact that it has official status and is singled out by a state as a language to be developed, it is unlikely ever to be used to express the realities of nanotechnology or genetic engineering. Tetum shares this fate with thousands of languages.

Inequality

Nowhere is the inequality of languages more visible than in the field of terminology, but there are many other aspects of language that make for deep-reaching disparities. These can be grouped under four categories: status, corpus, actual use and attitudes.

Status: recognition, national, international;
             status allocation: official, national, minority;
             legal protection;
             financial support.

Corpus: mode: oral and written, only oral, only written (classical language);
             codification, standardization;
             actual expressive power, functional range.

Actual use: domains: media, school, government, church, home;
             number of speakers;
             number of second-language speakers.

Attitudes: instrumental;
             emotional;
             prestige.

Judging languages against these criteria reveals the unequal communicative potential and hence the disparate range of choices they offer their speakers. Only some languages function as effective means of acquiring up-to-date knowledge and getting access to modern life in general. Since functional domain differentiation and division of labour between languages is a common feature of multilingual societies, this is not by and of itself a problem. However, the increasing interconnectedness of science and technology and market forces that is characteristic of our times has turned access into a crucial determinant of life chances and individual as well as collective welfare. As a result, languages with limited potential are abandoned by their speakers for lack of utility. For instance, many of Nigeria's minority languages are unlikely to be handed down to the next generation. Igboanusi and Peter (2004) blame this on 'the attitudes of the native speakers, particularly the youth, who prefer to speak to one another in either English or Hausa'. Since this is not an isolated case but representative of a global trend which seems bound to severely and irrevocably reduce the diversity of human languages, movements calling for the protection of endangered languages have come into existence. In their wake, reversing language shift (RLS)[12] has become a major preoccupation of language planning.

Planning for survival

According to some predictions (Robins and Uhlenbeck 1991), half the world's languages will not survive the twenty-first century, a development that is seen by many as a threat to humanity's cultural and epistemic heritage (Harrison 2007). If this development is to be countered, two questions must be answered. (1) Why does language shift occur, and (2) how can it be halted or reversed? There has been considerable progress with respect to the first question. As the social functions and opportunities to use a small language diminish, it loses the support of its users. Parents see better chances for their children if they receive schooling in a more widely spoken language and children fail to develop an interest in a language they consider obsolete and unsuitable for modern life. Shift to a larger language is the likely outcome. The second question, however, allows for case-by-case answers at best, due largely to the general difficulties concerning predictions about sociolinguistic developments pointed out above. Part of these difficulties stem from the fact that suitable measures to halt or reverse language shift crucially depend on 'a prior value consensus among those who advocate, formulate, implement and evaluate it' (Fishman 1991: 82).

Notwithstanding these difficulties and because language activists feel an acute sense of urgency that it will be too late if nothing is done, Fishman (1991, 2001) has proposed a conceptual framework designed to serve both the analysis of language decline and as an agenda for RLS planning. It is based on what he calls a Graded Intergenerational Dislocation Scale (Fishman 1991: 87). Domains of use and number of speakers are the main dimensions of the scale. At its lowest point, a severely reduced language has lost all or almost all speakers and disappeared from all communication domains. At the top of the scale, a full-blown language is used in the domains of education, work and government, as well as in the mass media. The crucial stage at which the fate of a language is decided is stage 6, at which intergenerational continuity in a home/family/neighbourhood/community is the basis of language transmission. Since 'the lion's share of the world's languages are at this very stage and they continue to survive' (Fishman 1991: 92), it is on this stage that language maintenance efforts must focus.

GIDS: Fishman's Graded Intergenerational Dislocation Scale

1. Education, work sphere, mass media and governmental operations at higher and nationwide levels;
2. Local/regional mass media and governmental services;
3. The local/regional work sphere, among the language's native speakers as well as non-native ones;
4a. Schools in lieu of compulsory education and substantially under the language's curricular and staffing control;
4b. Public schools for children, offering some instruction via the language, but substantially under another language's curricular and staffing control;
5. Schools for literacy acquisition in the language, for the old and the young, but not in lieu of compulsory education;
6. Intergenerational and demographically concerned home-family-neighbourhood activities;
7. Cultural interaction primarily involving the community-based older generation;
8. Reconstruction and adult acquisition as a second language.

(Fishman (1991: 395)

Languages decline or spread by domains more than by numbers of speakers. This is one of the lessons to be learnt from numerous case studies of language shift around the world: Basque and Catalan in Spain, French in Quebec, Irish, Frisian, Breton, Navajo and other Native American languages, aboriginal languages in Australia, Ainu and Ryukyuan in Japan, Maori in New Zealand, among many others. The recommissioning of Hebrew for communication in everyday life, the defence of French in Quebec and the restoration of Welsh in Wales are often presented as success stories. To some extent they certainly are, but in each case difficult problems remain unresolved. The decision to teach French to all English speakers in Canada met with little enthusiasm and so far has not turned the whole of Canada into a bilingual country. Hebrew attained its status as Israel's national language at the expense of Yiddish and against the resistance of its speakers. And Welsh has few friends in English-dominant southern Wales. If a general lesson can be drawn from these and many other cases, it is that in language-contact situations speakers of the stronger language cannot be motivated without compulsion to learn the weaker language in order to shore up its status.

It must also be noted that the show cases of successful language planning are all about literary languages with a long tradition and a sizeable speech community residing in wealthy countries. Rescue operations for small unwritten languages spoken in poor countries are a different matter (Harbert et al. 2009). Realistically, the prospects for these languages are bleak. Short of allowing or forcing their speakers to live a life in isolation, there is little that can guarantee the future existence of these languages, because in language-contact situations languages are indexed to social evaluations and groups opt for a language that promises access to resources deemed necessary to survival or advancement.

Western bias

Language planning as it has evolved so far typically assumes a notion of 'language' which best corresponds to European standard languages, one clearly distinguished from another. The fact that this state of affairs is itself a result of a long history of planned choices is sometimes overlooked. Mühlhäusler's remark, quoted at the beginning of this chapter, is not in jest, nor is Wright's remark exaggerated. The differences between the regional varieties of Medieval Latin were real. They came about as a result of speakers' choices in phonology, lexicon and grammar that were different on both sides of the Alps and in western and eastern parts of the language area. But the recognition of these differences as defining criteria of distinct languages that were different from Latin and from each other was the work of scholars who served their masters. A by-product of Europe's long history of language cultivation is a conception of the universe of languages where each language is an entity set off from other such entities. It is against this backdrop that current disputes such as that between the supporters of Catalan and Valencian must be seen. There is no room for language arrangements with overlapping, vague and unstable language identities where the language/dialect issue is unresolved because it is irrelevant. The appropriation by the European nation-states of individual languages and their elevation to the status of national languages has made such a situation unacceptable, both for governments and citizens who identify with the 'nation's language'. In other parts of the world, such as Africa (Djité 1990; Brenzinger 2007), India (Gupta, Abbi and Aggarwal 1995) and the Pacific (Mühlhäusler 1996), fluctuating linguistic identities and affiliations are a reality. It is, therefore, not surprising that language-planning theory has met with some scepticism as to its suitability for language situations outside the Western world. Singh's (1995: 43) is a representative voice:

> As a critique of language development theories emanating from the West, the sociologists of language from the third world … have pointed out that the theory of Language Planning as handed down to the developing nations has never been neutral in the first place. The theory was heavily loaded towards the West from where we could select our development models (as well as the grammatical ones).

Similarly, the descriptive differentiation of African languages has been shown to be based on preconceptions of the integrity of languages and a language/dialect relationship that are rooted in nineteenth-century European linguistics.

> The Europeans who described Senegalese languages in the nineteenth century saw their differentiation as reflecting differences in mentality, history, and social organization among their speakers. Working from an ideology that linked language with national and racial essence, European linguists represented the particular characteristics of Senegalese languages as emblematic of these supposed essential differences.   (Irvine and Gal 2000: 58)

The notion that language planning is predicated on Western scholarship and Western conceptions of language is hardly far-fetched, and it pertains not least to the various language-conservation initiatives that have sprung up over the past two decades which, as often as not, focus on languages as entities rather than speakers and their communication requirements. Languages, from this point of view, are seen as of and by themselves valuable, linguistic diversity as something worth preserving. It is mainly Western and Western-trained researchers who, on the basis of this view, decide what non-Westerners ought to be doing with their languages. The possibility that a small language may be a liability for its speakers is rarely admitted into the discussion. Ladefoged has put it clearly and simply: 'It is paternalistic of linguists to assume that they know what is best for the community' (1992: 810).

Conclusion

Language-planning agencies and language movements, no matter of what ideological inclination, operate under the assumption that language behaviour can be manipulated deliberately and that in this way languages themselves can be changed. Status planning is concerned with managing multilingualism by determining macro-choices as to the functions languages play in a community. Corpus planning aims at regulating micro-choices of lexical items, grammatical constructions and varieties of pronunciation. The overall goals of both kinds of planning are set by a language policy. Curricular language education based on codified grammars and dictionaries amounts to the most common and consequential means of controlling language choice which tends to be discussed in terms of language planning only when first institutionalized, or when established practices come under pressure to reform. Noticeable examples are spelling reforms, which will be discussed in the next chapter. Success of language planning is mixed, which is an indication not of the fact that the forces of natural evolution prevail over deliberate choice, but that the interaction of the many linguistic and social factors involved is not yet fully understood.

Questions for discussion

(1)   Find examples of national languages that are minority languages and consider reasons why a minority language may be allocated the status of national language.

(2)   Language activists have been lobbying for an amendment of the American constitution that would make English the official language of the United States. What would be the positive and detrimental consequences of such a status change?

(3)   In East Timor, Indonesian is more widely spoken than Portuguese. Yet Portuguese rather than Indonesian was chosen as one of the official languages of the country. Why, and was it a prudent choice?

(4)   The French government has enacted a number of laws designed to stem the tide of English loanwords in the French language. Is it (a) possible and (b) reasonable to restrict speakers' choices in such a way?

(5)   'Western researchers remain the judges of what behaviours undertaken by non-westerners will be considered "authentic" . . . There is more than a little neo-colonialism involved when westerners advise citizens of the developing world not to learn international languages so that western researchers have richer data to work with.' Discuss the problem of endangered languages, taking this argument by Douglas A. Kibbee (2003) into consideration.

Notes

1. Nebrija was the author of the first grammar of Spanish. This passage is quoted from Sánchez and Dueñas (2002: 282).
2. Domínguez and López's (1995) directory of language-planning organizations comprises public and private organizations of local, regional, national and/or international coverage devoted to language planning.
3. http://eur-lex.europa.eu/LexUriServ/LexUriServ.do?uri=OJ:C:2008:320:0001:01:EN: HTML
4. See http://conventions.coe.int/Treaty/EN/Treaties/Html/148.htm for the full text of the European Charter for Regional and Minority Languages.
5. The problem of proliferating languages is not limited to how to draw distinctions within a group of related speech forms. To confound matters, it has been suggested that Yiddish, generally classified as a Germanic language, is a Slavic language, too (Wexler 1991).
6. Gauthier, Leclerc and Maurais (1993) is a compilation of constitutional provisions relating to language.
7. Three cantons are bilingual, French and German, and one is trilingual, German, Romance and Italian.
8. For a detailed discussion of the principle of territoriality, see Laponce (1987).
9. Puristic and anti-sexist language cleansing are obvious examples. For a review of language cleansing in American English, see Ravitch (2003).
10. Under the guidance of the Office de la langue francaise (www.oqlf.gouv.qc.ca), Quebec has successfully pursued a frenchification programme including terminology work designed to favour the choice of French over English technical terms. For details see Daoust (1991).
11. Cf., for instance, the United Nations multilingual terminology databases: www.unlanguage.org/Careers/Terminologists/UNTerm/default.aspx
12. This term has been introduced by Fishman (1991) and is now widely used in scholarly and political discussions about declining languages.

Useful online resources

Most Clearing House, a UNESCO website about linguistic rights: www.unesco.org/most/ln2nat.htm#With

Communication Policy, Government of Canada: www.tbs-sct.gc.ca/pubs_pol/sipubs/comm/siglist-eng.asp

UNESCO Atlas of the World's Languages in Danger: www.unesco.org/culture/languages-atlas/

Laval University website on language planning worldwide, prepared and maintained by Jacques Leclerc: www.tlfq.ulaval.ca/axl/index.html

Council of Europe, Language Policy Division: www.coe.int/t/dg4/Linguistic/

UK National Statistics, 'Language': www.statistics.gov.uk/hub/people-places/people/language

Further reading

Ager, Dennis. 2001. *Motivation in Language Planning and Language Policy*. Clevedon: Multilingual Matters.
Cooper, Robert L. 1989. *Language Planning and Social Change*. Cambridge University Press.

Coulmas, Florian. 1991. European integration and the idea of a national language. In F. Coulmas (ed.), *A Language Policy for the European Community*. Berlin and New York: Mouton de Gruyter, 1–43.

Fishman, Joshua A. (ed.) 2001. *Can Threatened Languages Be Saved?* Clevedon: Multilingual Matters.

Mühlhäusler, Peter. 1996. *Linguistic Ecology: Language Change and Linguistic Imperialism in the Pacific Region*. London: Routledge.

Spolsky, Bernard (ed.) 2012a. *The Cambridge Handbook of Language Policy*. Cambridge University Press.

12 Select letters: a major divide

Put writing in your heart that you may protect yourself from hard labour of any kind.

Egyptian scribe of the New Kingdom[1]

In the Eskimo language Inuktitut, as it has come to be written in newspapers, relative clauses are actually developing from the ground up, having not existed at all in the language as it was spoken by hunter-gatherers.

McWhorter (2003: 247)

Within the global structure of power differentials, languages have a hierarchy.

Prah (2001: 127)

Outline of the chapter

This chapter deals with the sociolinguistic meaning of writing as a communication mode that introduces distinction and inequality among both speakers and languages. The oral–written divide has a social dimension in that the gap between ordinary speech and written language is greater for people coming from a socioeconomically disadvantaged background than for their better-off peers. And languages gain through writing prestige, communicative reach and the paraphernalia of power. Typically countries and speech communities have a default writing system representing past choices; however, in many cases the questions of which languages are to be used in writing and how they ought to be written are not settled and are sometimes a matter of controversy. The criteria for selecting a language and variety, a writing system and script, and determining spelling conventions are discussed, and it is shown that, in each case, both instrumental and symbolic considerations come to bear; for, thanks to its visibility, writing serves emblematic functions as an object of attitudes relating to language.

Key terms: written and unwritten language, literacy, writing system, spelling, writing community

Writing and language

Writing marks a deep divide. In early sociolinguistic work this was very obvious. Basil Bernstein's (1971) distinction between the 'restricted code' of working-class speakers and the 'elaborated code' of the middle classes mirrored that between spoken vernacular and written language. In largely literate societies, access to written language and the degree of written language skills remain strong indicators of social class, those with no or limited literacy ranging at the bottom of the social hierarchy.

Functional domains of language use are also divided along the oral/literate split, both unwritten languages and illiterate speakers being excluded from the domains of higher communication, such as education, government, and science and technology.

Gender and age, the other social dimensions that have formed the core of sociolinguistic research, likewise correlate with literacy (Stromquist 1999). In Third World countries where illiteracy continues to be a problem, such as India, illiteracy is highest among rural women,[2] as used to be the case in Europe prior to universal education. And as for age, a cardinal function of school education is to extend the pupils' oral language skills by introducing them to the written mode which is the indispensable entrance ticket to adult society. What is true of language users also holds for languages: writing amplifies the expressive power and creates a variety of linguistic expressions never used in casual speech.

Schooling has yet another effect. Although most pupils enter school as competent speakers of their first language, they spend the largest amount of time during their school career studying that language. What they study is what this language ought to be like, what it consists of, how it works. They learn to write. Grammar came into existence in ancient Greece as 'the art of letters of the alphabet' (*technē grammatikē*). Although nowadays our understanding of grammar is different, it carries its history with it. Both students of grammar and sociolinguists emphasize the primacy of speech; however, rarely acknowledged though it is, their tools are derived from thinking about written language. It has been argued, therefore, that the major concepts of linguistic analysis – 'sentence', 'word', 'phoneme', 'literal/lexical meaning' – are epiphenomena of writing (Linell 2005; Coulmas 2003). In literate societies most people think of words as visible things that can be looked up in the dictionary, rather than ephemeral sound waves. The concepts that were won from *looking* at language are deeply ingrained in our consciousness, shaping the way we think and evaluate language.

Lower levels of literacy and numeracy are associated with socio-economic deprivation.

One in six adults do not have the literacy skills expected of an 11 year old and half do not have these levels of functional numeracy.

Disadvantage is concentrated among those whose capabilities are at or below entry level 2. This is well below the working definition of literacy and numeracy officially used by Skills for Life, of level 2.

Country Background Report: Adult Basic Skills and Formative Assessment Practices in England, OECD 2005, www.oecd.org/dataoecd/38/4/40015467.pdf

In the global context, written and unwritten languages fall on two sides of a watershed in terms of expressive power, prestige, cultural capital and institutional protection. Writing, far from being a mere mapping of speech giving it visible form, transforms speech and works as a scaffold propping up the construction work in progress and leading the builders to proceed in certain ways rather than others. High-prestige languages are invariably written, and classical languages are by definition so. Writing affords a language discernibility, respect and, in many ways, its very existence. Marfany (2010) has rehabilitated the concept of 'patois' (see p. 27 above), arguing that sociolinguists who reject this notion on the grounds that the purported contrast between language and patois is artificial being based on an arbitrary prestige grading that lacks proper linguistic correlates are missing the point. Patois speakers' own assessment of their speech should not be ignored, for they are 'lucidly aware of the things they can and, even more so, they cannot do with it. And very particularly of one which is out of the question: ... it is not written' (Marfany 2010: 9). While it may be true that, as a matter of what is technically possible, any variety can be reduced to writing, it is a historical fact that some are and others are not and that, from a sociological point of view, this is a very significant difference. When a patois does get written, 'as it occasionally does, it is within a limited set of circumstances, in what amounts in effect to a transcription of oral utterances' (Marfany 2010: 9). Writing is not transcription of oral utterances, but using language in the visible mode that has distinctly different properties and structural implications from the oral mode (Coulmas 2013). In a society's communication repertoire, written language and speech fulfil different functions that sociolinguistics must account for. This includes the use of different writing systems.

More obviously than language, writing is an artefact, both in the generic sense and as particular, historically evolved systems. All writing systems are the product of a process of selection, many acts of choice having gone into their making. The selection process is highly involved, being influenced by social, political, scientific, religious and practical considerations. If proof were needed that rational choice theory, which assumes the maximization of utility as the defining feature of rationality, is ill-suited to explain human behaviour, the study of orthography selection provides plenty of evidence. In its crudest and most orthodox form, rational choice theory would predict that after six thousand years of literacy humanity should have settled on a common writing system applicable with appropriate modifications to all languages. The real world looks different. *Ethnologue*, the most comprehensive index of the world's languages, does not present information about the written status of each language. And while there are no reliable statistics on the number of communities that use their languages in writing, or on the number of extant writing systems that are used for what purposes, we do know that hundreds of writing systems continue to be employed. Investigating an orthography project for the Hmong language by immigrants in Australia, Eira (1998) has developed a model for understanding the motivations which drive the orthography selection process. Her analysis examines the discourses in which decision making is framed. Scientific, political and religious discourses are in the foreground of her model, but technological, historical and pedagogical imperatives also impinge on the process. She demonstrates that, because of the wide range of motivations and demands arising from differing sources of authority, decisions in this field must be analysed within a sociological context. A single yardstick such as linguistic or technological optimality does not suffice to answer the question: 'How shall we write our language (if we want to write it)?'[3]

Choice of language

Historically, only a fraction of the languages of the world have been written. Great empires have always been multilingual, and they have always been selective with regard to the language(s) sanctioned for writing. The earliest instances of official recognition of multilingualism by public display go back thousands of years. Monumental inscriptions in the Achaemenid empire of the sixth century BCE were in Akkadian, Elamite and Old Persian, and the famous Rosetta stone, inscribed in 196 BCE, testifies to official Greek/ Egyptian bilingualism in Ptolemaic Egypt. Writing always meant distinction, and consequently language groups since antiquity have vied to attain written status for their languages. A written language used for government, law, schooling and cult is at the same time an instrument and symbol of dominance. The linguistic arrangement of large empires invariably consisted of one written language, with a few ancillary ones perhaps, and a large number of vernaculars. Aramaic, Latin and Chinese were imperial languages of long-distance communication in antiquity, a function these languages could never have fulfilled without writing. Inequality between languages was taken for granted. In Medieval Europe, 'true' languages, notably Latin, Greek and Hebrew, were distinguished from 'vulgar' languages which, with an illuminating expression, were also called 'linguae illiteratae'. As Blanche-Benveniste (1994: 61) explains, this expression reflected the common notion that the languages so called, being too amorphous, could not be written down. Writers, grammarians and other scholars who did write them down have therefore been called 'language makers' (Harris 1980). That writing makes a language, as opposed to a dialect or patois, is a notion that linguists find hard to accept, but many ordinary people consider it a matter of course.

Visible status

In Europe, the preeminence of Latin was broken only when its functions could be taken over by vernacular languages written down, which subsequently were made imperial languages in their own right, notably

Figure 12.1 *Sign in the Latin and Gurmukhī scripts on the Southall (ਸਾਊਥਹਾਲ) train station in London. (Creative Commons 2.5 Generic)*

Portuguese, Spanish, French, English and Dutch. Even in the postcolonial world, these languages have remained the major medium of written communication in many parts of the world, although their status has been challenged. Urbanization since the early nineteenth century has greatly increased public display of written material. In multilingual cities this led to competition for space and in many cases to regulations concerning the visible presence of languages. There is no more obvious way for a group to assert its existence than by putting up billboards. In combination with commercial and political interests, the ethnolinguistic identity issue has turned written-language cityscapes into a stage for playing out competition and conflict arising out of language contact. When in 2001 the First Great Western railway company erected a sign at the Southall train station in London in Latin and Gurmukhī letters (Figure 12.1), a language row quickly erupted. The Gurmukhī script is commonly used for Punjabi which thus, in the opinion of other ethnic groups, was given too much prominence. As the sign also provoked the ire of white supremacists, the train operator removed it, informing customers that 'it would be impossible to provide station signage for every language' and hoped 'to reach a solution that meets the needs of local people'.

By contrast, in recent years many train operators in metropolitan Tokyo, a much less multilingual and multiethnic city than London, introduced multilingual station signs such as the one of Denenchofu, in Japanese, Chinese, Korean and Latin letters (Figure 12.2), without provoking any complaints. Why multilingual signs are contentious in some environments but not in others is a question that can be answered only if the sociodemographics and community relations on the ground are taken into consideration. In any event, signage with multilingual contents is in many ways indicative of sociolinguistic situations, and the process resulting in the selection of languages and scripts for public display can be analysed accordingly.

Chinese in abbreviated characters

Japanese in Hiragana

Korean in Hageul

Japanese romanized

Japanese in Chinese characters

Figure 12.2 *Sign in Japanese, Chinese, Korean and Latin scripts on the Denenchofu train station in Tokyo (photograph F.C.)*

The sociolinguistic dynamics of written language display has been systematically investigated for a number of cities such as Jerusalem (Spolsky and Cooper 1991), Montreal (Conseil de la langue française 2000), Brussels (Wenzel 1996) and Tokyo (Backhaus 2007). However, multilingualism in the written mode is still a new and relatively unexplored area of sociolinguistics, although the issue of deliberate language choice is more evident here and often more contentious than in other domains of language use.

The visibility of a language is strongly indicative of its status and, therefore, subject to political decision. The proscription of Chinese characters in public display by the Indonesian authorities in the 1960s was a blow to the Chinese and reinforced interethnic tension. Since the break-up of Yugoslavia in 1991, Cyrillic letters have become stigmatized in Croatia (Magner 2001). In India, people have died for the Devanagari script of Hindi or the Perso-Arabic script of Urdu (King 2001). The Turkish government passed a law in 2002 enabling the use of Kurdish on the air, but it steadfastly refused to augment the official Turkish alphabet with the letters Q, W and X. In 2010, Turkish sociologist İsmail Beşikçi was accused of spreading propaganda for the outlawed Kurdistan Workers Party (PKK) many of whose activists are based in the Qandil Mountains in northern Iraq. Evidence presented against him included his writing of the word 'Qandil' with Kurdish <Q> rather than proper Turkish <K>. The defence lawyer pointed out that New York appears in the Turkish press as 'New York' rather than 'Nev York', although <w> is not part of the Turkish alphabet either. However, 'Nev York' is not any ethnic group's preferred spelling. Barring a minority language from public view is a common component of repressive language regimes; even a couple of letters can be a bone of contention. It is worth pointing out that where no minority is explicitly targeted by a repressive policy, the preference given to one writing system over others usually goes unnoticed or is considered a matter of practical necessity, although it is nonetheless part of a language regime.

In the world today, most countries have a default writing system.[4] This is because the organization of modern societies depends on written language for administering government and law, implementing formal education, and managing trade and business. The default writing system is that which is taught at school and in which legal codes are drafted. In many countries it enjoys explicit legal protection, as, for instance, the Latin alphabet in many European countries and in the Americas. Preferential treatment of the default writing system is more common than negative discrimination of other systems which, however, as the proscription of Kurdish Q, W and X illustrates, is not unheard of. In cases where disagreements about writing coincide with ethnic conflicts, the political nature of writing systems as part of a nation's language regime comes to the fore. In many countries where no such conflicts are topical, it is less conspicuous, but in official documents choice of letters is invariably restricted. For instance, when checking into a hotel, I cannot register my family name as Κουλμάσης, as it is written in Greek, let alone ク ル マ ス, in Japanese, assuming that for some reason or other I would prefer that because of my Greek descent or present country of residence. This may seem a far-fetched example; however, José's deplorable fate testifies to the same point. In the State of California he is forced to part with the accent mark on his name in all official documents. In the form of laws, regulation and conventions, governments decide what letters it is permitted to use.

On the other hand, giving a language public exposure can be an important element of an inclusive community policy. The publication of multilingual documents by Tokyo city wards amounts to the recognition of minority groups (Figure 12.3). In the event, the inclusion of Korean serves symbolic rather than practical needs; for ethnic Koreans in Japan are bilingual, but have long felt discriminated against by unaccommodating government policies. In publications of the kind illustrated in Figure 12.3, the issuing authority uses the languages of certain groups of residents without allotting them official status. At the next step up the ladder of status and prestige, the government addresses its citizens in several languages, all of which it considers its own. The most conspicuous place to display official language status is on stamps and on bank notes (Figure 12.4).

Obviously, only written languages can be acknowledged in such a way, and the currency that circulates in society is a powerful symbolic means of under-lining the difference between 'real' languages recognized as such by the government and vernaculars. Swiss bank notes have four legends in German, Rhaeto-Romance, French and Italian: 'Schweizerische Nationalbank, Banca

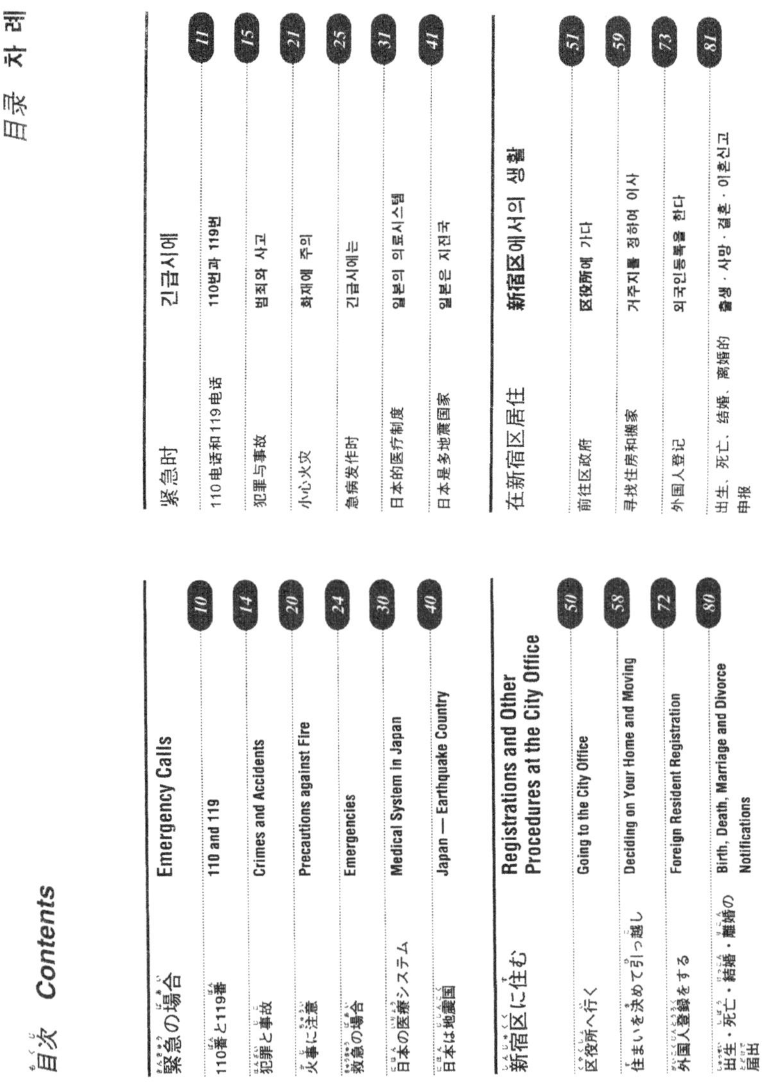

目次 Contents

緊急の場合	Emergency Calls	
110番と119番	110 and 119	10
犯罪と事故	Crimes and Accidents	14
火事に注意	Precautions against Fire	20
救急の場合	Emergencies	24
日本の医療システム	Medical System in Japan	30
日本は地震国	Japan — Earthquake Country	40
新宿区に住む	Registrations and Other Procedures at the City Office	
区役所へ行く	Going to the City Office	50
住まいを決めて引っ越し	Deciding on Your Home and Moving	58
外国人登録をする	Foreign Resident Registration	72
出生・死亡・結婚・離婚の届出	Birth, Death, Marriage and Divorce Notifications	80

目录 차례

紧急时	긴급시에	
110电话和119电话	110번과 119번	11
犯罪与事故	범죄와 사고	15
小心火灾	화재에 주의	21
急病发作时	긴급시에는	25
日本的医疗制度	일본의 의료시스템	31
日本是多地震国家	일본은 지진국	41
在新宿区居住	新宿区에서의 생활	
前往区政府	区役所에 가다	51
寻找住房和搬家	거주지를 정하여 이사	59
外国人登记	외국인등록을 한다	73
出生、死亡、结婚、离婚的申报	출생・사망・결혼・이혼신고	81

Figure 12.3 *Table of contents of an official guide to the public services of Shinjuku Ward, Tokyo, published by the Ward Office. The languages are, from left to right, Japanese (with reading aid in smaller print above Chinese characters), English, Chinese and Korean.*

Naziunala Svizra, Banque Nationale Suisse, and Banca Nazionale Svizzera'. Indian Rupees are even more copiously adorned (Figure 12.4). Most literary languages of India have their own script, making sure that their speakers' claim for recognition cannot be overlooked. Attempts by the Government of India (1966) to implement a common script for India have come to naught.

With the advance of literacy, the difference between written and unwritten languages became more conspicuous and more relevant for a greater number

Figure 12.4 *The language panel of an Indian 1,000 rupee note*

of people; for to become literate implied the need for speakers of unwritten languages to acquire a second language. Although this had been quite normal in societies with restricted literacy, the ideas of equality, democracy and universal schooling, and the proliferation of the politics of identity have lent credence to the notion that having to acquire literacy in a second language is an undue disadvantage.[5] What is more, as long as there is the visible difference between written and unwritten languages, the politically correct assertion of the equality of all languages is implausible to anyone but linguists, and the demand that no one be discriminated against on the basis of language remains unfeasible. As a consequence, many unwritten languages have been reduced to writing in modern times.

How many written languages?

How many written languages are there, then? Once again, a precise answer is elusive. One would expect written languages to be easier to count than unwritten ones, precisely because writing distinguishes them one from another. However, the general problem of counting languages is only slightly shifted because it is not clear what should count as a written language. Just by virtue of the fact that a PhD student constructs a suitable alphabet for it or a missionary translates a gospel into it – Mark is popular because it is the shortest – a vernacular does not become a written language.

The most extensive survey ever of the written languages of the world was undertaken by the Centre International de Recherche sur le Bilinguisme at Laval University (Kloss and McConnell 1978–9). It describes in great detail the methodological difficulties of determining what counts as a written language and to what extent a language is actually used in writing. For illustration, one example must suffice:

> Limitations became particularly evident where our questionnaires asked whether publications of a certain type were either: 1) *frequent*, 2) *occasional* or 3) *lacking*. How were our informants to decide what was frequent and what occasional? In some cases, we gave them a hint by pointing out that we considered 1–3 magazines or books as *occasional*, and four or more as *frequent* for tribal languages. However, three periodicals may mean a lot in the case of a speech community numbering hardly 10,000 persons while six periodicals or other publications would hardly be impressive in the case of a speech community of more than five million speakers.   (Kloss 1978: 34)

The degree of use of a language for literacy functions is an important variable which has a bearing both on its social status and on structure and language change. The written languages that are actually employed for all literacy functions are a select group. The Universal Declaration of Human Rights of 1948 is available in some 384 translations from Abkhaz to Zulu (by June 2012).[6] This is a sizeable number. However, upon closer inspection, the list includes classical languages such as Latin and Sanskrit; double listings (Hebrew/Ivrit, Japanese/Nihongo); competing varieties of languages (twelve varieties of Quechua, three varieties of Hmong); languages rarely if ever used in writing, such as Friulian, Haiti Creole, Occitan Auvergnat, Sardinian; languages whose names and slightly non-standard spellings amount to a political statement by language activists, e.g. Walloon and Bosnian (in Cyrillic and Latin) as distinct from Serbian and Croatian; and languages of which the Declaration of Human Rights is, and will likely remain, the only written trace, such as Huitoto Murui spoken by a couple of thousand speakers in Colombia and Peru, and Pipil, a Uto-Aztecan language which counted twenty speakers in 1987.

Making a major document available in a small language is often a matter of great symbolic importance, but it is not enough to make it a viable written language. Even people who take pride in their first language do not choose their language(s) of written communication for symbolic reasons alone. For conferring status on a language and marking its presence in the modern world are only two minor functions of writing. A language that has been used in writing over an extended period of time, building up a body of literature and exercising a lasting influence on the spoken language, is an enormous asset, an accumulation of cultural capital. Since acquiring literacy is an investment, communities and individuals calculate the costs and benefits of the available choices. Symbolic values enter into the calculation, but they are not decisive.

The story of Afrikaans in the twentieth century is an instructive example. Writing it down around the end of the nineteenth century brought linguistic independence to what was then a substandard variety of Dutch. Since Afrikaans was widely used as a lingua franca and the language of an economically powerful group, it was accepted as a written language and gained status rapidly, notwithstanding the co-presence of English. However, of late, tarnished by the Apartheid regime in South Africa, it lost again what

---

Universal Declaration of Human Rights, Articles 1 and 2, in Bichelamar

Atikol 1

Evri man mo woman i bon fri mo ikwol long respek mo ol raet. Oli gat risen mo tingting mo oli mas tritim wanwan long olgeta olsem ol brata mo sista.

Atikol 2

Evriwan i gat raet long evri raet mo fridom we i stap long Deklereisen ia, wetaot eni kaen difrens, olsem long reis, kala blong skin, seks, langwis, rilijen, politikol o narafala kaen tingting, we i kamaot long saed blong neisen o sosol, propeti, taem we man i bon long hem o emi narafala sosol saed olsem.

   Andap long hemia, bambae wan man o woman i no save mekem eni difrens long level blong politik, eria we wok hem i kavremap o intenasonol level blong kaontri o teritori blong narafala man o woman ia, nomata we hemi indipenden, tras, non-self-gavening o anda eni narafala arenjmen blong soverenti.

www.ohchr.org/EN/UDHR/Pages/Language.aspx?LangID=bcy

---

it had gained. The 1996 constitution of the Republic of South Africa (Act 108) confers official status on eleven languages: Sepedi, Sesotho, Setswana, siSwati, Tshivenda, Xitsonga, Afrikaans, English, isiNdebele, isiXhosa and Zulu. The objective of this provision is that 'all South Africans should be able to operate in any spoken or written official language(s) of their choice appropriate for a range of social and public contexts' (Alexander n.d., 117). Being given this freedom of choice, South Africans have turned away from Afrikaans, at least in writing, and have shown little inclination to use African languages instead. Their overwhelming choice, particularly as the language of schooling, is English (Louw 2004), which promises a greater return on investment than any of the other official languages. This is also true of other parts of Africa where European languages have for centuries served as principal literary languages. Although many attempts were made to provide education in African languages and enable local populations to read Christian scriptures in their own languages, 'the graphization of many … African languages did not turn them into media of learning and literacy' (Pasch 2008: 99).

Individuals and communities choose the languages they want to use for written communication. Their choices are restricted by political preferences, established school curricula and tradition, factors which enter into a calculation of instrumental and symbolic values. Accessibility, utility and prestige are important variables which interact with written status. For a language to be used in writing is a major determinant of its utility, but notice that utility has both a social and a linguistic side. The point is not just that if a language is used more in writing by a growing number of users its utility will also increase, but that a language that has been used extensively in writing over a long period of time is a more useful instrument than one that has not.

The written mode affords the language user more numerous and more differentiated choices than the spoken mode, but it takes time for these choices to make themselves felt in the language. There is little doubt that, as McWhorter's remark at the head of this chapter suggests, writing has an influence on language. However, the strength and kind of this influence vary with the degree of use, length of time and literacy rate of the speech community. As we have seen in Chapter 8, in speech communities with limited literacy, the influence of writing on language leads to diglossia, whereas universal or widespread literacy allows it to affect the 'common language'. In either case it is a lengthy process which is impossible to replicate in quick motion.

A full-blown written language is a major tool of communication and the acquisition of knowledge. Its possession is an undeniable advantage which must be taken into account by any attempt to explain how and why individuals and communities choose their written language(s), because the choices they make are not between equal items. This is why, within the current configuration of functional domain differentials of the world's languages, it is hard for hitherto unwritten languages to join the ranks of written languages. Yet, it is precisely because of the actual and perceived differences that distinguish written from unwritten languages that speech communities strive for written status for their languages.

Choice of variety

When the speakers of an unwritten language decide to give it a written form, the first and most problematic choice to make is that of which variety to write, for even within the context of unwritten languages there is a prestige gradient of dialects. Ferguson (1983) describes the rise of Faeroese to written status. The Faeroe Islands in the North Atlantic had been under Danish control for centuries, and Danish, a sister-language of Faeroese, used to be the islanders' written language. Eventually the idea that Faeroese, too, could be made into a 'real' language gained ground in the community. Someone made a start by translating the gospel of Matthew into Faeroese. That, according to Ferguson, was a mistake. It was a mistake not because Matthew is longer than Mark, but because the translator had chosen Southern Faeroese which most people considered 'the language of "those backward people down in the southern part" [which] could not possibly be used for anything serious' (Ferguson 1983: 30). The mistake was later corrected when someone else picked a more central dialect which people accepted more willingly as the reference variety of a supradialectal norm, allowing it to take over most of the functions of Danish.

A similar success story is reported of Shona, one of the main languages of Zimbabwe. Until the 1930s, it existed as a group of dialects that were hardly

Table 12.1 *Shona alphabets, 1932 and 1967*

1932: a, b, ɓ, b, c, e, ɗ, f, g, h, i, j, k, m, n, ny, ŋ, o, p, r, s, ʃ, ʂ, t, u, v, w, x, y, z, ʒ, ⱬ,
1967: a, b, bh, ch, d, dh, e, f, g, h, i, j, k, m, mh, n, nh, ny, n', o, p, r, s, sh, sv, t, u, v, vh, w,
       y, z, zh,

if ever used in writing, and if so by missionaries who used makeshift spelling conventions corresponding to their own languages. These dialects were Kerekore in the north, Zezuru in the centre, Karanga in the south, Manyinka in the east, Ndau near the Mozambique border and Kalanga in the west. To call them 'dialects of Shona' is misleading because at the time they were what are sometimes called 'roofless dialects', that is, dialects without a commonly accepted norm as a reference point. Shona was made that reference point by 'language makers', notably Clement Martyn Doke who seems to have first used the name 'Shona' in his 1931 'Report on the Unification of the Shona Dialects'. Once again, the choice of variety for the written norm was decisive. 'Doke chose a remarkable path. He opted for a dialect which was widely used in what was to become the political and economic centre of the country, that is, the Zezuru dialect of the capital Harare rather than the Karanga dialect of the former centre of power in feudal times' (Brauner 1994: 175). A standard dictionary and a unified orthography were designed for the written norm which was then given the name 'Shona'.

At the core of the standardization process stood a unified spelling system, consisting first of thirty-two letters of the Africa Script developed by the International African Institute which, however, because of the unavailability of a number of special letters on a regular typewriter keyboard was later replaced by a system that makes do with standard roman letters using digraphs for language-specific phonemes, such as implosives (Table 12.1).

Shona and Faeroese acquired language status as a result of being given a written form, thus living up to the expectations entertained by language enthusiasts who devoted their efforts to the project. Faeroe Islanders and speakers of Shona dialects were happy to see that there was a speech form they could identify with which was not a substandard vernacular but had all the trimmings of a regular language. This cannot be taken for granted. Rather, variable choice for writing has several unpredictable aspects of which the acceptability to the community of the selected variety is just one.

The community may not want to use its speech form in writing at all. The Swiss, for example, are overwhelmingly supportive of *Schriftdeutsch*/Swiss German diglossia instead of language split by making the latter take over the functions of writing from the former. A recent episode in the history of African American Vernacular English can be interpreted similarly. In 1996, the Oakland school board passed a resolution to recognize Black English under the name of 'Ebonics' as the primary language of African American students in that California district.[7] Although this was not intended by its initiators, the resolution was widely understood as a proposal to teach Ebonics rather than English and elevate it to the status of a written language. The vast majority of African Americans rejected this as a means of cementing the ghetto walls that isolate a segment of the black community from mainstream society. Many commentators scorned Ebonics as 'the language of illiteracy', and even enthusiastic admirers of the black vernacular argued against its elevation to language status. In the event, the strong racial and social index of the variety made its formal separation from English by means of a written norm of its own tantamount to racial segregation and thus unacceptable.

Literacy is seen as a force of empowerment, but vernacular literacy is two-edged. Under normal circumstances the allocation of the functions of speech and writing to different languages and varieties is in equilibrium. Elevating a vernacular to written status upsets this equilibrium in ways that are hard to predict. Language activists have advocated vernacular literacy as a means of protecting endangered languages. However, as Barton (1994: 207) points out,

> The act of creating a written form changes a language; usually it is intimately connected with standardizing the language and this act can destroy much variety. Inevitably in writing a language down, some aspects get highlighted, and others are ignored or suppressed. So that missionary organizations, for instance, which have been at the forefront of writing down languages at the same time may be 'christianizing' the vocabulary and ignoring other meanings in the culture. Their roles in saving languages may not involve saving the cultures.

Choosing a variety for elevation to written-language status is a goal that must be balanced against other goals and considered in the context of the overall configuration of functional domain allocations in the community concerned.

Choice of writing system and script

The next items to be considered are the writing system and the script of the written language. Since the most visible subsystem of a language is at issue here, the choices involved are fraught with symbolic meaning. Many cases of adopting a writing system and script for vernacular languages and of the replacement of existing systems by others are documented in the literature. The reasons stated for one or the other typically draw on scientific, social, political, religious and technological considerations. For orthographic adjustment in any society is related to social transformations, and since the envisaged changes touch what in public perception is the heart of the language, a debate of their linguistic merits is indispensable. There are writing systems and spelling conventions that are better than others, to be sure, but the criteria for evaluating them are not at all transparent and, what is more, evidence that quality differences in this regard really matter is at best inconclusive. It has not been possible, for instance, to correlate literacy rates with writing systems or spelling systems. (Japan with a rather complex writing system has relatively high literacy, whereas the United States has a relatively high illiteracy rate, although supposedly simple alphabetic systems are used throughout. In Taiwan where traditional, i.e. complex, Chinese characters are used, literacy is higher than in China which uses simplified characters.) In the end, literacy rates depend less on the nature of the writing system than on social variables such as the quality, accessibility and effectiveness of the educational system.

Supported as they are by literate elites, established writing conventions tend to be conservative, which is in itself a significant factor in any reform process. The choices one's parents and teachers have made tend to be accepted as the best solution by those who have mastered the extant system, seeing in it a marker of authenticity and status. When the Korean alphabet was first promulgated in 1446, it was unacceptable to the literati, although it was clearly superior as a writing system for Korean and much easier than the Chinese script (King 1998). On the other hand, it is not coincidental that changes in the written language are brought about in the context of social upheavals. The great French spelling reform of 1762 gained general accept-ance in the context of the French Revolution (Certeau, Julia and Revel 1975). Turkey replaced the Arabic script with the Latin as part of a sweeping reform programme designed to reorient the country towards the West and propel it into modernity (Lewis 1984). The Bolshevik Revolution saw in its wake the creation of numerous new writing systems for unwritten languages and the Russification with Cyrillic letters of others (Smith 1998). Both Latin and Cyrillic were tentatively introduced in Mongolia, purportedly to pro-mote mass literacy to which the traditional Mongolian script was said to be an impediment. In the late 1980s along with democratization, attempts were made to reintroduce Mongolian as the official script of the country (Grivelet 1999). After the People's Republic of China was founded in 1949, the new leaders made writing reform one of their earliest priorities (Chen 1996a). And after the disintegration of the Soviet Union, several of the follower republics adopted a de-Russification policy, shifting from Cyrillic to Arabic or Latin script (Landau and Kellner-Heinkele 2001; Clement 2008).

In all of these cases, to which many others could be added, reforms were accompanied by fierce debates. Invariably, both advocates and opponents invoke linguistic, psycholinguistic, cultural and social reasons to make their case. Writing systems and scripts are said to be more systematic, simpler, quicker to learn and easier to read, more elegant, truer to 'the spirit of the language', more economical and more suitable for global electronic com-munication. They are defended for representing a traditional image of the language people can identify with or, conversely, recommended for embodying progress and a departure from outdated ways.

Choice of spelling conventions

Another part of the question, 'how shall we write our language?', concerns the spelling system. A language's orthography is a system of rules, however complex, that maps onto structural levels of that language, and since languages change, the need is sometimes felt to change the spelling rules, too. In the event, the script remains in place and the effects on the outer appearance of the language are, therefore, only minor. Yet, spelling reforms rarely pass without passionate debates which are much more interesting for the fact that they occur than for what they are about. The German spelling reform, at long last agreed upon by Austria, Germany and Switzerland in 1996, just a few years after the absorption of East Germany by West Germany, well illustrates the point. The reform that was phased in, starting in 1998, concerns five areas of the spelling system: sound/letter correspondence, capitalization, compounds, punctuation, and hyphenation and word division at the end of a line. Some unsystematic rules were scrapped and some spellings were made more regular. For example, in the old system, a hyphen could not be inserted between <s> and <t> even if the juncture coincided with a syllable boundary, as in *Kis-ten* 'boxes'. This rule had no linguistic rationale having grown out of the printers' practice to typeset <st> as a ligature. The new rules make no exception for <st>, permitting word division in consonant clusters at syllable boundaries. Another change makes the spelling of <ß> more regular. Following the new rules it is used for [s] only after long vowels and diphthongs. Thus, new *Fluss* 'river' (with a short vowel) rather than old *Fluß*.

After the reform, written German is not very different from what it was before. For example, of the 1,417 words elementary school pupils learn to spell from first to fourth form, 32 are affected by the new rules. Of these, 28 involve a change from <ß> to <ss>, a spelling that has long been the norm in Switzerland which uses no 'curly s' at all. The remaining four concern instances of capitalization and word separation, e.g. *zu viel* 'too much' spelt as two words rather than one. Hardly a traumatic transformation.

However, the uproar the reform provoked suggests that it spelt nothing less than the demise of the German language. Twelve German district courts ruled on it, inconclusively, before the whole exercise was referred to the Constitutional Court, Germany's highest court. Of course, the court did not have to deliberate whether *Fluss* violates the German constitution. The more interesting issue it had to address was this: who has the right to choose? Who should have the authority to determine the norm? Can a spelling reform be enacted by ministerial decree or does it require parliamentary approval or even a plebiscite? Opponents of the reform held that spelling was too important a matter to be left to bureaucrats and misguided linguists. The Constitutional Court did not follow their arguments and allowed the reform to pass. However, it did not dismiss the case as petty or declare itself incompetent.

For years newspapers were swamped with articles arguing for and against the reform; numerous conferences, academic and intergovernmental, were convened; dozens of books were published.[8] Virtually no one who took part in the debate said that it was a tempest in a teapot. The fact that there were competent linguists on both sides indicates not so much that objective criteria for the goodness of an alphabetic orthography are elusive as that even professionals are unable to confine their deliberations to these criteria. Selecting the right letters is such an intricate issue because in a literate society it concerns everyone. The willingness to entrust orthography choice to a group of experts varies from one writing community to another. What is more, a writing tradition, however awkward, is a factor to be reckoned with. In the absence of obvious ideological (political, religious) motives, it is hard to promote a choice that leaves the trodden path. Notice that the only reform of English spelling deserving of that name was realized by American nationalist Noah Webster who opined, and succeeded in convincing others, that differentiating American from British spelling was a valid goal in itself: 'As an independent nation, our honor requires us to have a system of our own, in language as well as government' (Webster [1789] 1992: 34). Discussing the diffusion of Webster's innovations, Weinstein (1983: 75) concludes with an observation of general validity:

> Linguistic choices can affect frontiers in these ways only during key moments in the history of the rise of ethnic and national groupings. At these times, as at the beginning of American independence, disorder is great: group identities, purposes, values, and the existing political, religious, and economic institutions are seriously questioned or severely damaged.

Language activists have hailed the Internet for providing opportunities to promote and develop unwritten languages. A large number of fonts have been made available, and online display makes minor languages look respectable at a stroke and little cost. However, people choose to use a written language not just because they appreciate its symbolic value as a marker of identity, but also for practical reasons. What Pasch observes for Sango, the national language of the Central African Republic, is true of many others. The marginal role of Sango as a means of written communication on the Internet reflects its use in print publications. Books and Web pages in Sango are produced almost exclusively by religious organizations ... and international political organizations (Pasch 2008: 100).

People who seek information and read for contents rather than for symbolic satisfaction will turn to other languages that more readily meet their demands in this regard. This is a hurdle faced by all languages that are latecomers to literacy which is getting ever more difficult to overcome as the lead of modern languages used in writing for science, scholarship, technology, commerce, politics and law keeps growing. It remains to be seen whether the Internet will significantly change the imbalance between the few written languages and the many unwritten ones.

Conclusion

Writing is an artefact, and every written norm is the result of many deliberate acts of choice. The multiplicity of past and present writing systems, scripts and orthographies is testimony to

– the power of the trodden path;
– the tendency to identify writing and language;
– the appropriation of language for political, cultural and religious purposes;
– and the desire to use written language as a marker of identity.

Every extant written language with its proper orthography and script is a compromise between the various demands consequent upon these functions. Because every projected change potentially upsets the compromise, writing reform proposals always meet with opposition, no matter how well motivated they may be in terms of linguistic systematicity and elegance. The force of normative decisions is apparent here, as is the fact that no single yardstick can explain linguistic choices in the realm of written language. Being tied to literacy practices, these choices are contingent on a complex interplay of social, cultural, linguistic, technological and political factors which combine to endow a written language with both symbolic value and utility-value. It not just gives expression to, but is part of its society's power structure. Proposals to change extant patterns of language use, be it by promoting vernacular literacy or advocating reform of an established system, therefore tend to elicit reactions of great intensity, bringing to the fore that people have strong feelings about their language which under normal circumstances remain invisible. Linguistic choices on the written-language level are more obvious and open to reflection than other linguistic choices, but for all that, they affect a community's patterns of language use in various ways which are sometimes hard to predict.

Questions for discussion

(1)   What does it take for an unwritten language to be turned into a written language, and how good are the chances for the number of written languages of the world to increase?

(2)   What are the pros and cons of vernacular literacy in industrial societies?

(3)   Can the promotion of vernacular literacy encourage minority language speakers to maintain their own language rather than shift to metropolitan languages?

(4)   Who should be the master of a written language and determine its form?

(5)   What are some of the likely consequences of internet communication for unwritten languages?

Notes

1. Quoted from Goody and Watt (1968: 37).
2. According to the COL Literacy Project in India, literacy rates after the 2001 census were estimated at 75 per cent for men and 54 per cent for women (http://censusindia.gov.in/2011-prov-results/data-files/mp/07Literacy.pdf). However, as per Population Census of India 2011, the literacy rate has gone up to 74.04 per cent in 2011 from 65.38 per cent in 2001. For a ranking of Indian States for literacy rates, see www.indiaonlinepages.com/population/literacy-rate-in-india.html.
3. The superiority of a phonemic over all other scripts is often presumed unquestioningly, but Boone (1994), Battestinii (1997), Harris (2000) and Coulmas (2003), among others, argue against an evaluation scale to assess the quality of writing systems which puts phonemic writing at the top.
4. India, which recognizes in its constitution twenty-two languages, most with their own writing systems, is exceptional. As many as fifty of the numerous languages of India were found to have a written form and were used in it (Padmanabha et al. 1989).
5. Ever since UNESCO in its 1953 statement formulated the principle that people acquire literacy best in their mother tongue, this principle has been axiomatic, although it was clearly quite naïve at the time. The vast majority of languages were unwritten and consequently the notion of mother tongue had to be greatly stretched in literacy programmes throughout the world.
6. www.ohchr.org/EN/UDHR/Pages/Introduction.aspx
7. For the full text of the Oakland school board's resolution and an extensive discussion of it, see Rickford and Rickford (2000: 166f–9).
8. For an overview of the debate, see Eroms and Munske (1997).

Useful online resources

The World Literacy Foundation's website: www.worldliteracyfoundation.org/

Literacy rates of the world are listed and mapped at: http://world.bymap.org/LiteracyRates.html

A blog for teachers, parents and students interested in literacy: www.theliteracyblog.com/

The Culturomics projects offers access to a large corpus of written text consisting of 5.2 million books written in seven languages. The site is a research tool that allows study of frequency timelines of words and phrases. Intended for the quantitative study of human culture, it also holds potential for linguistic research: www.culturomics.org/

Further reading

Barton, David. [1994] 2007. *Literacy: An Introduction to the Ecology of Written Language*. 2nd edn. Oxford: Blackwell.
Coulmas, Florian. 2013. *Writing and Society*. Cambridge University Press.
Harris, Roy. 2000. *Rethinking Writing*. London: Athlone Press.
Martin-Jones, Marilyn and Kathryn Jones (eds.) 2000. *Multilingual Literacies: Reading and Writing Different Worlds*. Amsterdam and Philadelphia: John Benjamins.
Olson, David R. and Nancy Torrance (eds.) 2001. *The Making of Literate Societies*. Oxford: Blackwell.
Sebba, Mark. 2007. *Spelling and Society*. Cambridge University Press.

13 The language of choice

English is destined to be in the next and succeeding centuries more generally the language of the world than Latin was in the last or French is in the present age.

John Adams (1780)

Our most dangerous foe is the foreign-language press.

Theodore Roosevelt (1917)

Adewale is known to me as an editor for the Heinemann African Writers series, Africa correspondent for *Index on Censorship* and a fellow Nigerian Englishman (though *his* English is Scots and mine Irish). A difference that fascinates: he was brought up in Lagos, I'm from London.

Gabriel Gbadamosi (1999: 187)

Outline of the chapter

In the preceding chapters, we have examined choices concerning linguistic units, styles, discourse patterns and sociolinguistic arrangements. This chapter turns to language choice in a global setting, examining the role of English in the world today. It recapitulates some of the conditions that made English an international language and discusses arguments that welcome and criticize this development. From a sociolinguistic point of view, global language dispersion calls for a unified explanation. Two theoretical models are introduced, one borrowing the concept of biodiversity and its reduction from biology, the other conceiving of the world's languages as a market place by way of referring to economics. Both approaches seek to explain how the spread of English affects other languages. The many ways in which English itself is influenced by coming into contact with other languages and being used in many different cultural settings are dealt with in the last section of the chapter.

Key terms: language spread, global English, language contact, pluricentric language, standard

Global English

English has captured the world. When John Adams, second president of the United States, penned the above quoted words in 'A Letter to the President of Congress' while on a diplomatic mission to Europe, many would have brushed them aside as megalomania, but his prediction has been borne out more thoroughly than even he himself is likely to have expected. When we turn on the news to find out what is happening in Afghanistan, inhabitants of Kabul and Kandahar tell us about it on banners and posters in English, and not just because those who wield the biggest guns in their country wouldn't listen to anything else. The same holds true of Baghdad, Beijing, Damascus, Manila, Sarajevo, São Paolo, Jerusalem, even Paris. From Bangkok to Budapest, from Caracas to Casablanca, from Rotterdam to Rio, English is the language of choice if people want to reach out. In a world of instantaneous communication, English is the language that allows news to cross linguistic and national boundaries, a powerful testimony that we live in *one* world. We can share valuable information more easily and know about each other more readily than ever before, which, however, is not to say that everything said and written in English is worth knowing. Rather, thanks to the global reach of English in combination with that of modern communications technology, protecting ourselves against useless information has become a pressing need for many. And this is not the only reason why the ascent of English to world language status is perceived as a mixed blessing. Some have hailed English as the first democratic universal language that enables effective international communication, facilitates the mobilization of transnational civil society, is conducive to business and provides access to the richest accumulation of knowledge ever in any language. Others have denounced the diffusion of English around the globe as a residue of colonialism and the spearhead of US imperialism that erodes personal and collective identities, alienates people from their cultural roots, obliterates linguistic diversity and paves the way for the Americanization of the world. What unites them all is that they speak English. The CEOs of the IMF and the World Bank express themselves in English as a matter of course, and the complaints of globalization critics on the other side of the fence would die away unheard unless they were voiced in English, too. It is the same language that is praised and demonized.

The enormous spread of English has developed its own self-reinforcing dynamics. This is noticeable not least in sociolinguistics. Other languages are just as good and, as sociolinguists never tire of declaring, as interesting and as worthy of study as English. But it is a fact that more sociolinguists live on English than on all other languages combined. There are more sociolinguistic studies about English than any other language, and this is not just because there are so many speakers of English, but also because of their great diversity. Having been indigenized to more places and cultures and adapted to a wider range of contexts than any other language, English encompasses local, social and functional variation on a greater scale than has been observed at any time in the linguistic history of the world. Unlike other language names, *English* has a plural. 'World Englishes' has become an established field of study with its own journals and conferences.

The Global Spread of English

Praise	*Condemnation*
Facilitates international communication;	Affords native speakers undue advantage;
Offers access to the greatest accumulation of knowledge ever;	Obliterates traditional knowledge;
Saves time, energy and expenses for translation;	Threatens linguistic diversity;
Is neutral and thus suitable to bridge ethnolinguistic divisions in multilingual countries;	Sustains inequality in post colonial countries and widens the discrepancy between social classes;
Is non-elitist and enables people from all social classes to benefit from globalization;	Corrupts proper English;
Helps the rest to catch up with the West.	Promotes Americanization.

Sociolinguistics, it was pointed out in Chapter 2, is rooted in Western society in the same sense and for similar reasons that imperialism is rooted in the West, and the spread of English is a contributing factor. English teachers followed the empire, and so do sociolinguists. Like it or not, even Western critics of this trend, short of falling silent, cannot but reinforce it, by virtue of the English language. One of the most widely quoted books about the political background and consequences of the worldwide expansion of English, Robert Phillipson's 1992 *Linguistic Imperialism*, which decries language spread as a morally questionable occurrence, is, needless to say, in English. Had it been published in Albanian or Chinese, for that matter, it would hardly have made the grade of any citation index, for it is truer today than it ever has been that the language barrier is forbidding. What economist John Kenneth Galbraith dryly remarked about the unknown Swedish predecessors of John Maynard Keynes' famous aggregate demand theory also applies to sociolinguistic theory or pretty much any theory in the social sciences: 'Great economic ideas were not expected to come from small countries' (Galbraith 1989: 225).

The worldwide diffusion of English holds opportunities and challenges for sociolinguistics. Empirical studies about English outside the Western world have made it clear that models of social inequality derived from Western industrial societies are not always suitable to explain how linguistic variation and functional domain allocations relate to social structure. As Cheshire (1991: 4) points out, exploring English in different cultural contexts brings to the fore 'the importance of assessing the relative cultural salience of different social categories in the communities whose speech is being investigated'. The themes of sociolinguistics played out in a context where English is one or the only language involved are too numerous to be discussed in this book. However, some of them must be touched upon, if only because the present discussion of why people choose to speak as they do would be very incomplete without even a brief look at the specific question of why they choose to speak English.

Limits to growth?

The British Empire carried English to many parts of the world, and when it crumbled, US business, military and pop culture continued the job. Although English has never been promoted by a central academy or language-planning agency, its spectacular spread has been helped along by deliberate efforts of various sorts sponsored by governments, special interest groups, the mass media, economic agents and, last but not least, Christian churches, often at the expense of other languages. In the United States, although the original thirteen colonies were all multilingual, from early on the anglophones were in the majority. They promoted English aggressively, turning the United States into an English-dominant country which at times was moderately tolerant towards other languages and at other times openly hostile, as witnessed, for example, by Theodore Roosevelt's remark quoted at the beginning of this chapter. A tug of war between these two attitudes continues to this day,[1] although the advocates of linguistic pluralism have usually been in the weaker position. There are considerable differences between states, but bilingualism was never preferred by the powers that be, the general tendency being strongly assimilationist, favouring English monolingualism. The overall willingness to accommodate minority languages has been limited, and wave after wave of immigrants submitted to adjusting to the majority. They chose to speak and learn English in their own interest, for, while command of English did not guarantee social advance, the failure to learn it almost invariably worked as an impediment.

Demographics in the United States and, to a lesser extent, Canada, Australia and New Zealand was the main growth factor of the L1 community of English outside Britain and Ireland, whereas the community of L2 and EFL (English as a foreign language) speakers grew in the British and American colonies in Africa, Asia, Oceania, the Caribbean and South America. Estimates by the British Council put the number of English L1 speakers at 375 million; it is an additional language in bi/multilingual contexts for 450 million speakers, and EFL speakers number at least 750 million. The categories are fluid, estimates of the total number of speakers reaching 1.5 billion.

> **Countries where English enjoys official status**
>
> Antigua and Barbuda, Australia, The Bahamas, Bangladesh, Barbados, Belize, Botswana, Brunei, Cameroon, Canada, Dominica, Ethiopia, Eritrea, Fiji, The Gambia, Ghana, Grenada, Guyana, Hong Kong (People's Republic of China), India, Ireland, Jamaica, Kenya, Kiribati, Lesotho, Liberia, Malawi, Maldives, Malta, Marshall Islands, Mauritius, Micronesia, Namibia, Nauru, New Zealand, Nigeria, Pakistan, Palau, Papua New Guinea, Philippines, Rwanda, Saint Kitts and Nevis, Saint Lucia, Saint Vincent and the Grenadines, Samoa, Seychelles, Sierra Leone, Singapore, Solomon Islands, Somalia, South Africa, Sri Lanka, Swaziland, Tanzania, Tonga, Trinidad and Tobago, Tuvalu, Uganda, United Kingdom, United States, Vanuatu, Zambia, Zimbabwe.

Political frame conditions have a significant bearing on the status of English and thus on individual speakers' choices. Many colonies retained it as an official language after independence, notwithstanding the fact that intellectuals in the liberation struggle often commented on the adverse effects of the language of their masters. Mohandas Gandhi, for example, as early as 1937 remarked: 'If English had not ousted the languages of the people, the provincial languages would have been wonderfully rich today' (Gandhi 1965: 44). He even called for 'banishing English as a cultural usurper as we successfully banished the political rule of the English usurper' (1965: 116). But he continued to address himself to his supporters and to all Indians in English, and near the end of his life, when independence was imminent, he remarked resignedly: 'The British Empire will go because it has been and still is bad; but the empire of the English language cannot go' (1965: 131). The reasons most commonly mentioned for keeping English in the former colonies refer to status rather than to corpus. Ethnic detachment is presented as a great advantage of English; it is seen as a 'neutral link language' (Kachru 1986: 8f.) as opposed to the indigenous languages of linguistically highly fragmented countries (Lowand Hashim 2012). Notice, however, that Gandhi's above quoted remark implies an interaction between status and corpus: 'The provincial languages' did not develop because English enjoyed superior status and served higher functions of communication. During the British Raj this was imposed from above, but after independence English retained its preeminence.

Lack of an obvious majority language and fear of provoking ethnic strife and community unrest by singling out indigenous languages for national or official status have been strong motivations for retaining English in post-colonial states. However, this is just one scenario in which English was, and continues to be, the preferred choice. The forces motivating people to choose English over other languages are multiple, working on different levels – political, economic and cultural. A crucial factor is the strength of English as a second language. In countries such as Pakistan, Kenya, Singapore, South Africa and Jamaica, the growing middle classes cultivate English as an indispensable means of their children's social advance, increasingly using it in the family domain. At the same time, English has become the first foreign language practically everywhere outside L1 English countries, having replaced other languages in the classroom, such as Russian, for example, in Eastern Europe after the break-up of the Soviet Union.

There is still potential for further growth. In China, for example, which opened up to the world only recently, English is no longer the language of capitalist depravity, but a symbol of progress. A 2003 survey of city-dwellers in Beijing, Shanghai and Guangzhou found that the vast majority of respondents of all age groups agreed that fluency in English was a key to success, with the under-35 group being particularly united at 80 per cent (see Figure 13.1).[2] Most of them do not hold this key yet, knowing only a smattering of the language, but the notion that English will help them to get on in the world has been implanted in their minds. Meanwhile English language training in Chinese schools grows steadily and Chinese students go abroad to study by the hundreds of thousands, mainly to anglophone countries (Chang 2006). The 2008 Olympics in Beijing triggered a nation-wide epidemic of 'English fever' as China prepared to welcome the world. *Crazy English*, an instruction method involving total physical response verging on a cult, allegedly attracted millions of students (Osnos 2008).

As in other subfields of sociolinguistics, it is hard to make predictions, but, for the present, people around the world show no sign of losing their

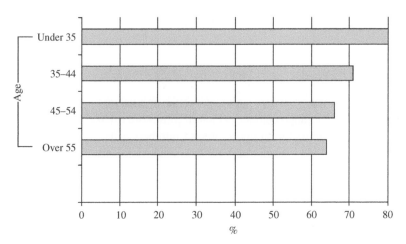

Figure 13.1 *Chinese city-dwellers see English as 'the key to success' (adapted from* Far Eastern Economic Review, *27 November 2003)*

appetite for English. The Chinese situation shows that it would be wrong to suggest that the dominant position of English is only the result of its being forced down the throat of subjugated populations who have no choice. 'The fact remains that popular demand for English is growing in most postcolonial societies' (Powell 2002: 268), and in the rest of the world it is the unchallenged foreign language. Yet, how the dominant position that English has attained should be explained is still a contentious issue. While Wright (2004: 134) argues that the spread of English is driven by demand, Phillipson (2012: 199) insists that 'choice of language is not a matter of "neutrality" or "convenience" but of top-down control'.

Today English is the language with the greatest vehicular load. Where this will lead and how it will impinge on the linguistic map of the world are major topics for future sociolinguistic research. They should be framed in terms of why speakers choose English rather than what makes a reified English grow. For it is because of speakers' choices, for better or for worse, that in the twenty-first century English is

- the dominant language of the world's greatest military power;
- allocated (co-)official status in a third of the world's countries;
- spoken by the very rich and the very poor;
- used across a wide range of cultures and nationalities;
- employed for every conceivable literary genre;
- the basis of the world's biggest language industry;
- the most common second language;
- more widely taught as a foreign language than any other;
- the most valuable linguistic component of human capital;
- the foremost language of international scholarship;
- the language most connected with others by means of bilingual dictionaries;
- involved in more language-contact situations than any other language.

Contact issues

Except for the rare situation where colonists settle uninhabited lands, language spread implies language contact, which in turn more often than not implies conflict. It is impossible to quote precise numbers of the languages spoken in North America when the first European colonists arrived, but it must have been several hundred. Many of them have since been wiped out by disease, demographic decimation, proselytism and enforced language shift. Fewer than 150 remain today, two-thirds of which have fewer than 1,000 speakers (Zepeda and Hill 1991). The Aboriginal languages of Australia and Oceania (Dixon 1991), parts of Africa (Brenzinger 1998) and Southeast Asia (Matisoff 1991) have met with a similar fate. To be sure, English was not the only colonial language transplanted from Europe to other parts of the world, but its spread has been involved in the replacement of more indigenous languages than others. English has, therefore, been branded as a 'killer language', an expression popular among those who look at languages as living organisms rather than instruments with a certain utility. 'Tool' and 'organism' are two metaphors which belong to two explanatory models of language spread, one grounded in economics, the other in biology.

In keeping with the biological metaphor, language spread has been called 'linguistic genocide' defined as 'the systematic replacement of an indigenous language with the language of an outside, dominant group, resulting in a permanent language shift and the death of the indigenous language . . . The Hawaiian language is an example of linguistic genocide' (Day 1985: 164f.). Many linguists feel that they have a special obligation to call attention to the problem of endangered languages and that it is both necessary and justified to use terms such as 'death', 'extinction' and even 'murder'. For example, Nettle and Romaine (2002: 6) argue that such metaphors are useful 'because languages are intimately connected with humans, our cultures and our environment'. More than that, the notion of a language ecology has been developed beyond the metaphorical in that parallels and correlations between biodiversity and linguistic diversity have been investigated (e.g. Gorenflo et al. 2012). There is evidence that both forms of diversity are threatened by economic and technological developments that are summarily referred to as globalization to which the spread of English is concomitant. Apart from that it must be acknowledged that the search for a model that can explain the dynamics of language spread and language shift continues.

The economic model conceptualizes the totality of the world's languages as a market place. The focus is on the variable practical utility of languages and on the fact that in a contact situation yield on the investment in a language is asymmetrical because of the existence of a dominant language (Breton and Mieszkowski 1977). Over the past 400 years of expansion the contact situations in which English is dominant have steadily increased as a result of accumulating investments by its L1, L2 and EFL speakers. Investment in this sense is quantifiable in terms of time, money and effort expended for acquiring language skills, plus investments in language technology such as dictionaries, grammars, databanks, automatic translation programmes, etc. In all categories English has secured a higher rate of investment and return on investment than other languages (Coulmas 1992b). Its command, moreover, offers a premium in the labour market which in turn makes it more attractive to learn. In this regard English trumps even its nearest competitors. Bilingual Montreal is a case in point. Grenier and Nadeau (2011) found that in Montreal, for English mother-tongue speakers, using French at work does not pay, while there is a high payoff to using English at work for French mother-tongue speakers. Applying world system theory, de Swaan (2001) points out that languages learnt in addition to the mother tongue will almost always be of greater utility, having a wider range and being more suitable for international communication. By multiplying the proportion of the population who use a language by the proportion of multilingual speakers who use it, de Swaan calculates the Q-value of each language which is indicative of its attractiveness as a foreign language. Such a calculation reveals the real strength of English. Chinese has a bigger community of native speakers, and Spanish and Arabic may surpass it in the near future, but on account of its number of L2 and FL speakers English is today and will for the foreseeable future be unrivalled as a lingua franca.

The biological model proposed by Abrams and Strogatz (2003) conceptualizes languages as groups competing with each other for members in a given territory. This model assumes that the attractiveness of a language increases with the number of speakers and its perceived status, an assumption which is compatible with the economic model. It further assumes, for simplicity's sake, that the members of two groups, X and Y, interact with each other, that they are all monolingual and that, therefore, learning each other's language means conversion. In the model, the probability of an individual converting from Y to X is given as $P_{yx}(x, s)$, where x is the fraction of the population speaking X, and $0 \leq S \leq 1$ is a measure of X's relative status. $y = 1-x$ is the complementary fraction of the population speaking Y at time t. On the basis of these assumptions, the minimal model of language shift presented by Abrams and Strogatz is

$$(1) \qquad dx/dt = yP_{yx}(x, s) - xP_{xy}(x, s)$$

The equation (1) has three fixed points, only the extremes x = 0 and x = 1 being stable. It therefore predicts that X and Y cannot coexist in permanent equilibrium.

Both this model and the economic model predict that except in isolated or fully protected environments where no interaction between the two groups of speakers takes place, two languages will not coexist stably. One will eventually drive the other to extinction, as speakers make the investment with the highest yield and conversion goes predominantly in one direction. Abrams and Strogatz have applied their equation to a number of cases such as Scottish Gaelic in Sutherland, Scotland, using what historical data are available; see Figure 13.2. The curve depicts a steady decline of speakers.

What happened to Scottish Gaelic is what happened in countless other cases over the past 400 years. Will this trend continue? Is it possible to extrapolate from the past to the future? What are the prospects for the continuing spread of English? Will it one day be the only language left on the planet? That would be a premature conclusion because modelling takes place under laboratory conditions on a high level of abstraction. There are

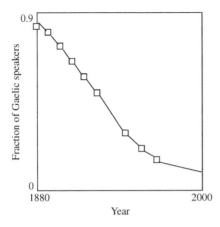

Figure 13.2 *The decline of Scottish Gaelic (after Abrams and Strogatz 2003)*

many imponderable factors that impinge on any language-contact situation and hence in even larger measure on the development of the linguistic map of the world. If this development were a natural process, language planning, language education and all other interventions in the ways individuals and societies handle their languages would be futile. Perhaps this is so. However, contrary to the predictions of the free-market model and the biological group conversion model, bilingual and multilingual societies with a great deal of interaction across language boundaries and the ensuing sociolinguistic patterns described in the previous chapters do exist, many as the result of deliberate policies. This suggests that choice is possible, including the choice of bilingualism, domain specific or otherwise. Possibly, what we are witnessing is the emergence of a global bilingualism, English being moulded to fulfil the functions of long-distance communication around the globe. The 'global village' may be a hackneyed metaphor; however, the fact is that environments and markets have only recently emerged as global concerns of humanity as a whole. Those who promote globalization of markets, knowledge creation, science and technology, resources management, etc. and those who oppose it in the name of resisting environmental degradation, providing information about climate change and protecting the world from the downside of raw capitalism want to communicate with each other and, therefore, speak English. For most of them the question of whether the resultant spread of English causes or only co-occurs with the demise of other languages is of little interest.

It will be a challenge for the sociolinguistics of global English to determine the conditions under which the benefits of an international language can be maximized, while minimizing the adverse effects on other languages. Future research will have to investigate the factors that counter or slow down the forces of language decimation, that is, the forces motivating people to make choices that defy utility and quasi-natural evolution. The asymmetry of language contact is conspicuous and, as we have seen, the chief reason for the dynamics that leads to language shift. However, language contact does not only affect the weaker member of the contact situation, but the stronger one as well. English has proved to be very susceptible to the influence of other languages with which it has come into contact. This raises the question of what the globalization of English is doing to English itself.

The standard question

In the course of the nineteenth century, the idea of a native language became interpreted in Europe as a national language which was not only a nation's pride but also its prerogative. This view is still strong among those who feel the need to defend their language against decay. The French are often mentioned in this connection as the paradigm case. However, linguistic nationalism is so powerful an ideology that it permeates even the discourse about the most powerful language of the world. In a speech to the Royal Society of St George, conservative British law maker Enoch Powell made the point:

> Others may speak and read English – more or less – but it is our language not theirs. It was made in England by the English and it remains our distinctive property, however widely it is learnt or used.[3]

According to this view those who speak and read English – more or less – outside Britain have no business meddling with the language. The view from sociolinguistics is different. A side effect of the internationalization of English has been to expose the historical contingency of the identity and identification of language and nation. The colonial dislocation was profound. As early as 1982, Charles Ferguson remarked: 'The predominant view, that English is a European language, is steadily being eroded and seems likely to disappear.' Since American nationalists broke away from metropolitan British English, American English has evolved from 'a colonial substandard to a prestige language' (Kahane 1982). No longer is British English the peerless model for EFL learners. In many parts of the world, it competes with American English, the ELT industry having joined the US army as a major vehicle to 'see the world'.

English is today 'a pluricentric language'. This felicitous term was coined by Michael Clyne (1992) to characterize languages such as Spanish with multiple centres in Castile and Latin America (Thompson 1992), Portuguese with its Iberian, Brazilian and African varieties (Hagège 1992), and Mandarin Chinese as it is spoken and written in mainland China, Taiwan and Singapore varieties (Chen 1996b). Unlike roofless *dialects* which have no central reference norm, pluricentric *languages* have several. English has many regional varieties, some of which have evolved into national norms that differ notably from standard British English. Standard American English is codified in dictionaries,[4] and Canada and Australia, too, have underlined their quest for linguistic separatism by publishing national dictionaries. Australia became independent much later than the USA, in 1901, and, therefore, British standard RP continues to serve as a reference point for the pronunciation of educated Australians. The situation is compounded, however, in that Australian English since World War II has increasingly come under the influence of American English.

The weakening of the British norm in the former colonies finds expression in the destigmatization of local varieties which has been going on for some time. Local pronunciations and other features of English usage resulting from language contact and creative adaptation have steadily moved up the prestige gradient from peripheral jargon to local standard, gaining acceptance in norm setting and enforcing institutions, notably schools. Discussing English language teaching in Nigeria, Bamgbose (1982: 99, 105) asks:

> Whose usage is to be accepted? I hasten to suggest that it should not be that of the purist (who does not believe in a Nigerian English anyway) nor that of the foreign educated elite ... The natural and spontaneous usage of the locally educated Nigerian user of English is a more reliable guide to the identification of typical Nigerian usage.

Indian English has long shed the image of a deficient variety, or rather, set of varieties, whose relative deficiencies are measured in terms of their distance from standard British English. It has been acculturated and hence emerged as a self-contained system with its own sets of rules which make it difficult to classify locally current forms as mistakes (Verma 1982). There is a certain tension between Indian English and standard British English in India giving rise to new patterns of addressee-specific code-switching. Sailaja's (2009) distinction between Standard Indian English Pronunciation and other non-standard varieties of English pronunciation in India is indicative of the progressing formation of an Indian norm. While clearly distinct from RP, it does not depart from it too radically, a matter of some importance for the English language industry because India continues to be one of its biggest markets (Graddol 2010).

In the West Indies, English is part of a Creole continuum where, on one hand, the connection with the metropolitan standard is sought by the educated elite, while, on the other hand, local forms have gained increasing acceptance by members of that same elite leading to a situation where 'standard and non-standard items are not necessarily always in contrast' and 'where the distinction between the two is often vague' (Roberts 1988: 182).

Literature has greatly contributed to the multiplication of standards, as 'the empire writes back' (Ashcroft, Griffiths and Tiffin 2002). Some of the most acclaimed modern writers in the English language are not native speakers or speakers of indigenized varieties of English. English accounts for almost one-third of all Nobel Prizes in Literature awarded so far, but the laureates hail from eight different countries (UK, USA, Ireland, South Africa, Australia, Nigeria, Santa Lucia, and Trinidad and Tobago). Writers from the periphery are enriching the language in various ways that depart from British and American usage through 'abrogation' and 'appropriation', two mechanisms defined as follows:

> Abrogation is the refusal of the categories of the imperial culture, its aesthetic, its illusory standard of normative or 'correct' usage, and its assumption of a traditional and fixed meaning 'inscribed' in the words.

> Appropriation is the process by which the language is made to 'bear the burden' of one's own cultural experience ... Language is adopted as a tool and utilised to express widely differing cultural experiences.
>
> (Ashcroft, Griffiths and Tiffin 2002: 38f.)

To many African, Asian and Caribbean writers English, rather than being their inescapable patrimony, is the language of choice. The hero of R. K. Narayan's autobiographical novel *The English Teacher* explains:

> I always fancied that I was born for a poetic career and some day I hoped to take the world by storm with the publication. Some of the pieces were written in English and some in Tamil. (I hadn't made up my mind as to which language was to be enriched with my contributions to its literature, but the language was unimportant. The chief thing seemed to be the actual effort.)
>
> (Narayan 1990: 45)

An effort it takes in any event, but those who have come to English as an additional language calculate the costs and benefits of language choice, perhaps, extra carefully, and on the whole they find that English promises the highest reward.

The English language publishing industry, concentrated as it is in Britain and the USA, still fulfils powerful regulating functions, but since indigenized forms have been widely accepted in the press and in the networks of countries where English is used as an additional language, local models of English have become respectable and in many cases favoured over the British and American standards. At present it is unclear whether claims for additional national standards, for example in India and Nigeria, will proliferate, and opinions are divided as to whether this is desirable. While turning an imperial language into a local language is generally welcomed, there is also concern that further concessions to local norms will diminish the value of English for international communication. The title of Ostler's 2010 book, *The Last Lingua Franca: English until the Return of Babel*, suggests that the expansion of English may have peaked already and that English will experience the same fate as other dominant languages in the past. Whether his hunch is right that English is on its way out only time and rigorous empirical study will show.

What can be said with certainty is that the issue of the standards of pluricentric English is still in flux. The diversity of coexisting and, in certain parts of the world, competing norms makes it unlikely that a single standard will emerge in the foreseeable future; for it is hard to predict how the British and North American standards will be affected by the internationalization of English. Global English comes back through the rear entrance, putting the fear of death into L1 dogmatists. Not least because the USA, Britain and Australia are English-speaking countries, they continue to attract immigrants from all over the world who bring their varieties of English as well as many other languages with them and thus change the linguistic makeup of these countries. Some 300 languages were counted in London alone (Baker and Eversley 2000). Their speakers all have an interest in keeping English together to secure intercommunicability, but at the same time they are no longer willing to look at English as a gift they received by those who made it. It is theirs, and they claim the right actively to take part in shaping its future, because it is the language of their choice.

Conclusion

The ascent of English to world language status is one of the most conspicuous and intriguing sociolinguistic phenomena. Over the past half-century or so, ever more people in many countries have chosen English as a means of communication and in the process turned it into the first global language. At the same time, a great many other languages have been driven to extinction or come under pressure. We cannot fail to observe that this has greatly changed the linguistic map of the world, although our understanding of how the first phenomenon – the globalization of English – relates to the second – the decline of local languages – is still only fragmentary. If choice is what drives both of these processes, and the arguments supporting this tenet are strong, difficult questions remain. One such question is to what extent people really choose the sociolinguistic makeup of their society. Considering the extreme case of a language that ceases to be spoken, we may ask how often people willingly and deliberately abandon their language. Probably very rarely. Yet, it is individual choices that combine to produce a situation where a language is no longer viable, although no one intended or anticipated this outcome. People make many choices, and the enlightened individualistic point of view that dominates our world today forces us to argue that they are accountable for their choices; in other words, if English booms it does so because speakers of other languages choose to use it; and if a language vanishes it does so because its speakers choose to let it decline. This scenario is open to two serious counterarguments. One is that people do not always appreciate the consequences of their doings because they lack complete information. This is a well-known problem in public choice theory. How individual choices combine to form collective trends and what effects they produce are not always predictable. The other argument is that while the meaning of the word 'choice' suggests a potentially free decision, language-contact situations are always imbalanced and may be so skewed that the resulting language shift must be characterized as choice under duress. If there is hardly anyone who shares your language, is it then your free choice to shift to another for going about your everyday dealings? If you want to succeed in business and science in many parts of the world, you had better speak and publish in English, for opting for a less widely used language instead will seriously curtail your opportunities. These two cases are very different; however, it is hard to overlook a common tendency from small to big which concurs with many other tendencies in the wake of the globalization of capitalism.

The dominant position of English is a result of many choices by governments, educational authorities, companies, media and individuals who all contribute to a self-reinforcing dynamics of language spread. It is nonetheless difficult to demonstrate that the current situation is the result of intentional efforts and to ascertain cause and effect.

Languages are entities of a very special kind. Some argue they should not be conceptualized as objects because such reification obscures the fact that languages are faculties that reside in individual speakers' minds. This is undoubtedly so, but at the same time they only exist because they reside in many speakers' minds in sufficiently similar form to serve as a means of communication. Thus, they have a supra-individual existence, being socially controlled, and cannot usefully be owned. They depend on a public that creates and recreates them in constant flux. A public is constitutive of a language, and vice versa. In the course of modernization and the spread of participatory government, the public steadily expanded, to the nation-state with its national language first and subsequently to international organizations. In our day and age, the global public that creates its language for global communication needs has become a reality. This view does not deny or ignore the existence of strong interested forces promoting the spread of English in various ways with nothing but their own gain in mind. This, however, is true of every aspect of globalization. As we have seen in this chapter, global English is welcomed by some as harbinger of international understanding and decried by others who oppose the disappropriation of their patrimony and others again who see in it a threat to linguistic and cultural diversity. These opinions underscore the importance of a theme repeatedly touched upon on the pages of this book: language has both utility and emotional value. The sociolinguist's task is to study how both impinge on speakers' choices that lead to the spread of some and the decline of others.

Questions for discussion

(1)   What are the advantages and weaknesses of the biological and economic metaphors for explaining the expansion of English?

(2)   Is English one language or many?

(3)   Some have portrayed the spread of English as a natural process resulting from free choice, while others see in it a violent incursion into unprotected territories. Can the difference be resolved?

(4)   If economic factors are involved in the spread of English, does English give Britain and other English-speaking countries special economic advantages?

(5)   Writers from very diverse cultural backgrounds have chosen English as their medium of literary expression. What are the implications for Whorfianism (linguistic relativism/determinism)?

Notes

1. See, for example, the 'English Only' debate as documented in Crawford (1992) and González and Melis (2000).
2. The survey was conducted in August–September 2003 by Synevate Ltd. *Far Eastern Economic Review*, 27 November 2003.
3. *The Independent*, 23 August 1988.
4. The large reference grammar by Quirk et al. (1985) includes a section on national standards of English where aspects of pronunciation, vocabulary, usage, as well as some grammatical distinctions are discussed with reference to British and American English, Scotland, Ireland, Canada, South Africa, Australia and New Zealand.

Useful online resources

Helen Fallon's research guide on comparing world Englishes is available online: http://onlinelibrary.wiley.com/doi/10.1111/j.0883-2919.2004.00354.x/pdf

The London-Lund corpus of spoken English: www.helsinki.fi/varieng/CoRD/corpora/LLC/index.html

The Santa Barbara Corpus of Spoken American English: www.linguistics.ucsb.edu/research/sbcorpus.html

The Wellington Corpus of Spoken New Zealand English: http://icame.uib.no/wsc/index.htm

English in India on the British Library's website 'Sounds Familiar?': www.bl.uk/learning/langlit/sounds/case-studies/minority-ethnic/asian/

The International Dialects of English Archive (IDEA), University of Kansas includes MP3 audio files of scripted and spontaneous speech representing dialects of English worldwide as well as non-native accents: www.ku.edu/~idea/

English corpora is a website that offers a list of historical and current English language corpora: www.corpora4learning.net/resources/corpora.html#other

UsingEnglish.com offers a large collection of ESL resources and tools for students, teachers and researchers of English as a Second Language: www.usingenglish.com/

The International Association of World Englishes website offers information about conferences and its official journal *World Englishes*: www.iaweworks.org/

Further reading

Cheshire, Jenny. 1991. Introduction: sociolinguistics and English around the world. In Jenny Cheshire (ed.), *English around the World: Sociolinguistic Perspectives*. Cambridge University Press, 1–12.

Crystal, David. [1997] 2003. *English as a Global Language*. 2nd edn. Cambridge University Press.

Hayhoe, M. and S. Parker (eds.) 1994. *Who Owns English?* Buckingham and Philadelphia: Oxford University Press.

McCallen, Brian. 1989. *English: A World Commodity. The International Market for Training in English as a Foreign Language.* Special report, no. 1166. London: The Economic Intelligence Unit Ltd.

Mesthrie, Rajed and Rakesh Bhatt. 2008. *World Englishes: The Study of New Linguistic Varieties*. Cambridge University Press.

Widin, Jacqueline. 2010. *Illegitimate Practices: Global English Language Education*. Bristol: Multilingual Matters.

14 Research ethics

Science sans conscience n'est que ruine de l'ame.[1]

François Rabelais, *Pantagruel* (1532)

The research aims of any study should both benefit society and minimise social harm. www.respectproject.org/ethics/guidelines.php

Outline of the chapter

This chapter introduces the salient issues relating to research ethics in sociolinguistics. It addresses obligations on the part of the researcher towards research participants and discusses the question of legitimacy of data, the importance of anonymity and under what circumstances informed consent should be sought. The dilemma that arises out of the legitimate quest for knowledge and the equally legitimate concerns to protect privacy and personality rights is also expounded.

Key terms: Legitimate data, anonymity, informed consent, moral responsibility

Introduction

I once shared an office at a research institute in Tokyo with a postdoctoral fellow who was interested in giving directions, that is, in the speech event of giving and receiving directions and following the directions received. This is an everyday situation we have all experienced many times; but how to get any quantitative data from which more general patterns can be derived than chance observations reveal? My colleague had a practical solution. He paid a taxi driver a small amount of money to allow him to place a tape recorder in his car. Since taxi customers often give directions, he was able in the course of a couple of weeks to gather a fine corpus of the data he needed. I was astonished when he happily told me about his ingenious ploy, although, I have to admit, until that time I had never given much thought to the matter of the ethics of fieldwork myself. At the time, in the 1980s, few people had; in biomedical and health research, yes, but not in the social sciences. My American colleague was surely no exception. In the event, however, it seemed obvious to me that recording people's conversations surreptitiously was problematic, to say the least. It was like wiretapping, I told my colleague, who was nonplussed. 'Why would they care?! Not even I know their identity,' he said. However, whether or not the participants in our research 'care' is not the only issue to be kept in mind when it comes to securing proper ethical conduct in research.

Sociolinguistics is a largely data-driven field of scholarship that depends on observing the speech behaviour of individuals and groups of speakers. The process of gathering empirical data, in one way or another, establishes a relationship between researchers and speakers. This may or may not be a relationship of direct contact, but however that may be, researchers have a moral obligation to make sure that the rights of those they study are protected and that their wellbeing is not negatively affected by the research. They also have a responsibility to society at large to disseminate their findings and make data available for examination and potential replication of results.

As sociolinguists we are committed to the advancement of knowledge about social life and the role of language in it; and we should be aware that our work can have consequences for society. Often the consequences and applications of scientific findings are hard to anticipate. Nevertheless, we should recognize the fact that scientific research implies responsibilities to society and accept the obligation to reflect on the dangers of compromising research ethics before engaging in fieldwork or other empirical studies. While most sociolinguistic investigations, as opposed, for example, to drug testing, can be classified as being of minimal risk of harm to research participants, field researchers should always attend to the risk of potential harm that may ensue from the participants' involvement in the research setting or from the dissemination of results.

In the electronic media environment, it is easier to share data with colleagues and more difficult to prevent abuse than in former times when empirical social research was based on handwritten field notes that would normally never leave the researcher's office. For this reason and because of science's vital function in modern society, ethical concerns about social investigations have gained in importance and must be taken into account from the very beginning of planning a research project. The British Government Office for Science (2007) promotes the three Rs of ethics for scientists – Rigour, Respect, Responsibility – intended for 'anyone whose work uses scientific methods, including social, natural, medical and veterinary sciences, engineering and mathematics'. It is essential to be cognizant of general ethical norms that guide investigators in all fields of knowledge, notably honesty, openness, fairness, social responsibility and impartial curiosity. They are of no less importance in sociolinguistics, but there are also more specific tenets to observe.

Gathering data

Data collection is not always easy. A general difficulty of empirical research, known as the 'observer's paradox', is well known: we can never be sure that the data remain undistorted by the data-gathering process. There are many speech situations where the presence of an observer or a recording device would almost certainly alter the participants' speech behaviour, not to mention the fact that most people would object to being taped or even refuse to speak in the presence of a third party. Think of medical interviews, confessions to a priest, lawyer–client conversations, job interviews and business negotiations, for example. Yet, a clear understanding of the dynamics and patterns of such speech events could be of interest in many ways. Secret recording, especially when we have reason to think that 'people don't care' is, therefore, tempting, and some linguists have argued that in the interest of knowledge it is inevitable and permissible. The ethics of covert research are controversial (Allen 1997), but while there may be well-reasoned exceptions, as a general principle it is unacceptable to obtain data by covert means. Needless to say, social researchers are accountable to the law, including, in Britain, the Data Protection Act of 1998 (amended 2003) and similar laws in other countries. The Data Protection Act stipulates eight general principles and many specific regulations concerning the collection, storage and transfer of personal data.[2]

Many universities and research institutes have an ethics committee whose approval is required for any research project involving human participants/ informants. In order to obtain approval, the outline of the project must explain the nature of the data that are sought and state how informants are selected and how they are to be informed about the purpose of the project and their participation in it. In sociolinguistics, many research questions cannot be answered by questioning informants directly, for instance by asking them how they usually pronounce a given word – 'Do you say [kjat'] or [kæt]?' – whether they hold negative attitudes towards a dialect, or engage in a certain speech behaviour, such as code-switching – 'Do you mix languages?' Norms of correctness, prejudices and tacit and/or conscious ideas about the admissibility of such prejudices are likely to influence the answer and thus invalidate the investigation. In order to solicit information that otherwise would be difficult or impossible to obtain, research instruments such as the matched guise technique (Lambert et al. 1960) have therefore been designed with the deliberate purpose of circumventing conscious introspection. Matched guise studies have been used to study attitudes towards languages or language varieties that coexist in a community. Subjects are made to listen to recorded text passages in each of the varieties – the guises – and then asked to evaluate the speakers' character traits. They do not know that among the recordings are some made by bilingual speakers in both languages or varieties; the recordings are identical in every other way. By comparing the evaluations of the bilingual speakers' two recordings, the researcher can tell whether some traits are associated more with one variety/language than with the other, for everything else that might influence the respondents' evaluations is equal. In such a setting, the subjects are deceived, or, if that is too harsh a word, not informed about the true purpose of their participation in the research. For a long time, deception of this kind has not been regarded as unethical. Matched guise experiments continue to be carried out in studies about language ideologies and language attitudes, among others. However, in recent years subjects are often informed about the true nature of the experiment after the fact, in order to meet ethical requirements.

Collecting speech samples for documentation purposes does not usually involve deception. In the event, it is sufficient to let research participants know that their speech behaviour will be recorded and analysed. In the event, sociolinguists often try to minimize the disturbance of their research by using small recording devices, or by engaging community members to carry out recordings and interviews. This is considered ethically sound by most researchers doing empirical research. However, if very personal or confidential information may be involved, the investigator has to carefully weigh the options and solicit an ethics committee's opinion.

Whatever the decision, one problem remains. Recruiting informants is always difficult as it entails establishing an asymmetrical relationship between researcher and researched. No matter whether the researcher assumes the role of visitor, observer or friend, the underlying motivation of getting involved with the community that a sociolinguist intends to study is unfamiliar to most members of that community and may not be easy to understand. Lay conceptions and theories of language and speech behaviour differ significantly from scientific ones, and it is not just impractical, but may be counterproductive, to instruct research participants about these differences. The nature of the relationship, therefore, is usually one of subject and object and thus requires tact and delicacy.

Like other social research, sociolinguistic work involves community engagement of different levels of intensity. In recent years, a research methodology called Participatory Action Research (PAR) has evolved, which requires, as an ethical precondition, research projects about groups of people to produce knowledge that is useful to these groups. Rather than detached observation, PAR promotes a research partnership between researcher and community where the community does not just supply data, but partakes actively in determining the research agenda. Research topics are to be selected with the express purpose of bringing about change where change is beneficial to the community. For instance, research about illiteracy should not just improve our general understanding about the extent and the social causes of illiteracy, etc., but should also contribute to improving the situation of the community and empowering its members (Mordock and Krasny 2001). Likewise, research about language-related academic problems experienced by immigrant children should help children partaking in the study. PAR methodology is not equally applicable to all sociolinguistic research, but its critical impetus fosters useful reflection on the motivation for and implications of our work. Collecting language data in a community may affect individual speakers and the wider community in various ways that the researcher should consider beforehand, taking into account the wishes and objections that the community or some of its members may have.

Protecting the rights of research participants

The research participants should be provided with information about the general nature of the investigation and the purpose for which it will be used – an article for a scholarly journal, a needs assessment of linguistic services provided by public agencies, recommendations to educational authorities, etc. They should also be informed of the researcher's identity and institutional affiliation. Prospective participants should be given the opportunity to familiarize themselves with all aspects of the research and be alerted to potential repercussions to themselves and members of their community. To the extent possible, researchers should provide information about intended and potential uses of the data to be collected and where they will be housed.

Informants must be told that their participation is voluntary and that they can decline or withdraw at any time without giving any reasons. This is particularly important where access to informants is gained through intermediaries or institutions such as schools, universities and hospitals. In many cases it may be necessary to secure the research participants' explicit consent. In questionnaire research, respondents manifest their consent by filling in the questionnaire. Therefore no consent forms need to be handed out together with the questionnaire, but the questionnaire should contain information about the purpose of the research and make it clear that cooperation is voluntary. By administering a questionnaire in a classroom the voluntary character of completing it may be compromised. Even if the teacher keeps in the background, the institutional setting is likely to make students think that their cooperation is expected. In order to neutralize this tendency, the researcher, while appealing to the students' recognition of the desirability of their cooperation, should make a point of emphasizing that participation is discretionary. It should also be borne in mind that research in institutional settings such as schools, day-care centres, churches, etc. requires the study to be approved by the institution in question.

In sociolinguistic research involving interviews and/or recordings it is necessary to obtain the research participants' *informed consent*. Having researchers and subjects sign informed consent contracts has been common practice in biomedical and psychiatric research for a long time; it has been less customary in sociolinguistics but is receiving more attention of late, as sociolinguistic research has started to address groups of speakers who may not be able to assess potential risks or adequately protect themselves, such as illegal immigrants and other speakers with limited competence in the dominant language. Work with speakers suffering from communication and/or cognitive disorders, such as dementia and other medical conditions, obviously requires special attention. In the wake of population ageing in developed countries, care communication (Backhaus 2011), sometimes called 'gerontolinguistics', has emerged as a new field of study where ethical issues are highly relevant.

Ideally, researchers should give informants enough time to decide whether to grant or withhold consent and should obtain informed consent in writing. The necessary preparations are laborious and time-consuming. What is more, having to sign a form is prone to make potential research participants suspicious of the research. Some researchers therefore video-record participants' oral consent, which is an acceptable alternative if given in the researcher's presence. Documentation of informed consent should be archived separately from the data obtained. Research participants should be given a copy of the consent form they signed or a copy of the video recording.

In order to obtain informed consent, the capacity to make decisions and understand information about the research presented to the subjects must be established, and for video and audio recordings the consent of all the people who take part in the recording session needs to be obtained. Extra precautions are necessary for research involving minors, people under guardianship and marginalized groups. In institutional settings well thought-out research designs may turn out to be impractical because too many people whose informed consent needs to be obtained are eventually involved. It may be difficult to exclude from a recording session people who are not the focus of the study who have not consented or even been asked, as, for example, when residents of a retirement home unexpectedly join a conversation which is being recorded with the consent of the other participants, or when an informal get-together in a restaurant, being recorded with the agreement of participants, inadvertently includes a waiter taking orders for food or drink. Difficult decisions about necessary cuts or even the elimination of collected data may arise as a result. In case of doubt, personal rights, including those of accidental research participants, override research goals.

A set of sensitive ethical issues pertains to culture. In the age of super-diverse societies (Vertovec 2006), sociolinguistic research often deals with cultural differences, that is, differences within the population under investigation as well as differences between researchers from mainstream (Western) culture and research participants from minority or marginalized groups. In the big cities of developed countries, massive migration movements have brought about a mix of ethnic diversity and social stratification that continues to develop in more complex ways than ever before. Innovative language varieties and linguistic practices come into existence, constituting a new field of sociolinguistic research that is fascinating and challenging in equal measure.

Obeying the law of the country where the research is carried out is a matter of course; but it is only a necessary, not a sufficient condition for ensuring ethical soundness. Working in a culturally diverse environment requires special sensitivity and the researchers' awareness that their own belief systems, behavioural norms and views of interpersonal relationships may not be congruent with those of their research participants. Cultural norms are very powerful, but often go unnoticed, even though they are shaping our perceptions and behaviour. It takes an effort to recognize our own immersion in cultural norms and not just that of others. When engaging in work with participants of different cultural backgrounds, it is particularly important to make sure that our blindness to our cultural norms does not impede our research. Specifically, informed consent is a notion that is deeply grounded in Western concepts of privacy, individual autonomy and personal responsibility that inform the entire legal systems of Western societies. However, obtaining informed consent is not just about satisfying legal and behavioural norms, but also about treating research participants in ways that meet their expectations, which may not coincide in every detail with the researcher's assumptions. For instance, whereas from the researcher's point of view an informant's signed consent form establishes the contractual basis of the relationship between the two, the informant, in spite of having signed the form, may still expect to be asked for his or her consent repeatedly in the course of the research.

In addition to face-to-face interviews and community observation where the members of the community are personally known to the researcher, sociolinguists also make use of recordings of speech behaviour in public. It is advisable to check data obtained in this way carefully for any information that may inadvertently have negative repercussions for individuals or groups of people. This also holds for language material collected in the sphere of online communication – another sociolinguistic research domain of growing interest (Forey and Lockwood 2012). Opinions differ on the extent to which online communication venues such as chat rooms and discussion forums are in the public domain. Cavazos and Morin (1996) have argued that all texts posted through online networks are published works and as such protected by copyright law. On the other hand, texts submitted to online discussion groups may in some cases be considered private. For research about such venues, it is particularly important to solicit advice about copyright questions; for as a result of rapid advances in communications technology and the development of online communication, the dividing line between public and private is shifting, forcing a reconsideration of many copyright issues. For example, the UK Digital Economy Act 2010 came under review as soon as it was passed, because of uncertainties relating to copyright infringement provisions, including 'orphan works', that is, copyrighted works for which a copyright owner cannot be found. Copyright laws and their application to the Internet are still in flux. It will take some time before they are adapted to the new media environment. In the meantime careful attention should be paid to the question of intellectual property rights of any data obtained from online resources for research. Ess and the Association of Internet Researchers (2002) and NOLO (2010) offer overviews of ethical decision making and Internet research.

Processing and storing data

The most important principle for processing and storing data gathered in empirical research is guaranteeing confidentiality and the anonymity of the research participants. As a general rule data should be completely anonymized in such a way that the participant's identity cannot be reconstructed. There is rarely any reason to record the informant's name, but it may be desirable, especially in long-term studies that include repeated interviews with the same speakers, to be able to identify individuals in a corpus of recordings. In these circumstances it is advisable to assign speakers a code or a fictitious name and to store the coded recordings separately from the metadata. For most studies it is not necessary to store any personal information other than the usual social data such as age, sex, ethnicity, social background, etc. that do not reveal an individual speaker's identity.

Questionnaires do not usually contain the respondents' names. There is accordingly little risk of breaching confidentiality and anonymity. Notice, however, that special conditions hold for online surveys. There is a real possibility that respondents can be traced via their computer's IP address or their e-mail address(es), which the researcher may request for some technical reason. Data security and respondents' anonymity are more difficult to guarantee than for postal or telephone surveys. The researcher should inform respondents about these risks while at the same time assuring them that any information they provide will be considered confidential and will not be disclosed to others.

Sociolinguistic data are of various kinds and processed in various ways. Researchers should in any event try to preserve their original data for future reference and examination; for processing raw data for analysis and presentation implies various transformations and abstractions that it may turn out to be important to retrace. At the same time, the form in which recorded speech data are stored has different implications for securing anonymity.

Non-specialists cannot usually identify individual speakers on the basis of transcripts, but audio recordings and moving pictures are more likely to reveal a speaker's identity. Research participants should therefore be informed whether their speech samples will be stored by the researcher for analytical purposes only or archived for public or restricted access and, if so, whether only a transcript will be stored or also audio and video data. Their wishes regarding storage, distribution, access and display, publicly or for scientific purposes, of the samples they provide should be respected, and they should know that they can request their speech samples to be removed from the archive (which, however, may turn out to be difficult when recordings are stored anonymously). The question of whether recorded speech data – for example lengthy narratives – are subject to intellectual property rights should be considered. Sociolinguistic recordings do not have a big commercial potential, but copyright questions concerning archived data can get complicated. In any project that includes data collection for storage and distribution, it is advisable to get information about what copyright provisions may exist.

For data that are made available for other sociolinguists to study, information about time and methods of data collection and other relevant details of the fieldwork should be supplied without compromising confidentiality and anonymity. It is important to describe transcription and coding methodologies, and where data are derived from radio or TV the dates of the original broadcasts must be stated.

Returning favours

Should informants be paid? Sociolinguists may derive professional recognition and, admittedly seldom, material profit from the research they have carried out in a community. It stands to reason, therefore, to ask whether there is any return to the community or individual informants. In questionnaire research it is not uncommon to send out or drop off the questionnaire together with a token of recognition, such as a pen or a book voucher. The motivation for doing this, however, is not a perceived moral obligation to compensate the respondents for their time and effort, but to increase the response rate, based on the experience that people who accept a gift are more likely to comply with a request.

It is one of the fundamental assumptions of the European Enlightenment and the modern society it helped to shape that scientific inquiry is for the betterment of humanity and that scientists work for the common good. Everyone should contribute to this grand endeavour, be it by submitting to a psychological test, having one's genome sequenced and analysed, keeping a log of everyday activities, or providing speech samples. Yet, it is no secret that this is too rosy a picture. There is plenty of research dedicated to destructive purposes, personal enrichment and other designs that are hard to associate with the common good. What is more, not everyone may agree about what constitutes the common good. We should, therefore, not consider it a matter of course that others ought to support our research. Rather, sociolinguists should decide on a case-by-case basis whether some kind of remuneration for the research participants' collaboration is appropriate.

Much depends on the research design. In some studies it is possible to correct or at least lessen the imbalance between researcher and researched by employing the latter as paid language consultants instead of using them as data suppliers. Detailed grammatical descriptions and ethnolinguistic portrayals may necessitate many time-consuming interviews with or lengthy visits to the community. For research of this sort, informants should be offered compensation. In other studies that require a random collection of speech samples, it may be impractical or prohibitively expensive to remunerate the informants. In the end, the researcher can only appeal for participant help. For example, for his sound atlas of Irish English, Hickey (2004) made 1,500 short recordings of nearly 1,200 informants, who were asked in an anonymous context, often on the street, to read a small set of sentences to be tape-recorded, a task that on average took less than two minutes. Between these two extremes – weeks of intrusion and a few minutes of casual discourse – are many gradations of cooperation that may call for some kind of gratuity that the researcher should consider (Wolfram 1997).

Dissemination of research results

The final step towards concluding a research project in an ethically acceptable manner is the publication of findings. It may, perhaps, make you want to bemoan the sorry state of humanity that people can make a living by developing plagiarism detection software, but it is a fact that in the age of copy-and-paste and ubiquitous information availability, it is easier than it ever has been to borrow a convincing example here and a cogent phrase there. Therefore it is not superfluous to call to mind that scientific publications are expected to meet the most rigorous ethical standards. This is perhaps the most fundamental ethical principle of scientific work.

Researchers must not engage in plagiarism or fabricate and falsify data, results and consent forms. In both oral presentations and published articles, data, illustrations and text from other sources must be correctly attributed to their originators. Contributions by collaborators, students and research participants should be duly acknowledged. Research participants should be informed about published results where possible, and researchers should not put their names on work they have not done.

Conclusion

This chapter has touched on only the most important of the manifold ethical questions facing today's sociolinguists. The implicit norms and explicit regulations governing the conduct of research in this as in other fields continue to evolve amid intricate debates about conflicting priorities. The relative importance of freedom of information, on one hand, and intellectual property protection, on the other, is a general concern, but of particular importance in academia. Similarly, the pursuit of knowledge through effective research and the need to minimize potential harm to research participants are vital concerns that we do not always know how to reconcile with each other. Against this background it is important to be aware of the dangers of compromising research ethics before engaging in fieldwork and other empirical studies and to reflect on how to conduct and disseminate scientific investigations in an ethical manner.

Questions for discussion

(1)   If speech samples consist of trivial discourse only, why should research participants nonetheless be assured of confidentiality?

(2)   Are there any conditions under which covert data collection is admissible? Think of examples and discuss the pros and cons.

(3)   TeenSpeak is an online discussion forum. Observing discussions on the site can greatly facilitate data collection. Discuss any ethical problems that a researcher who registers on the site for this purpose may face.

(4)   A sociolinguist inherits a cell phone from his daughter, who believes she needs a new one. The data she left on the old phone include hundreds of instant messages like 'Me too, but I've g2g now.' that form a serendipitous corpus. Can he use it for his study?

Notes

1. Science without conscience is but the ruin of the soul.
2. See The Data Protection Act 1998 (amended 2003): www.legislation.gov.uk/ukpga/1998/29/contents

Useful online resources on research ethics

Applied Ethics Resources on: www.ethicsweb.ca/resources/research/index.html

The British Government Office for Science's 2007 universal ethical code for scientists, *Rigour, Respect, Responsibility*: www.berr.gov.uk/files/file41318.pdf

British Association for Applied Linguistics. Recommendations on Good Practice. www.baal.org.uk/dox/goodpractice_full.pdf

Linguistic Society of America, Ethics Statement 2009: www.lsadc.org/info/pdf_files/Ethics_Statement.pdf

Further reading

Allen, Charlotte. 1997. Spies like us: when sociologists deceive their subjects. *Lingua Franca* 7: 31–9.

Dwyer, Arienne. 2006. Ethics and practicalities of cooperative fieldwork and analysis. In Jost Gippert, Nikolaus P. Himmelmann, Ulrike Mosel (eds.), *Essentials of Language Documentation*. Berlin and New York: Mouton de Gruyter, 31–66.

Ess, Charles and Association of Internet Researchers. 2002. Ethical decision-making and Internet research. http://aoir.org/reports/ethics.pdf

Holton, Gary. 2005. Ethical practices in language documentation and archiving languages. www.language-archives.org/events/olac05/olac-lsa05-holton.pdf

Glossary of terms

accommodation   The usually unconscious tendency of people to make adjustments in their speech under the influence of the speech of those they are talking to.

age-grading   Linguistic variation that correlates with a particular phase in life (e.g. adolescence) and is repeated in successive generations, as opposed to language change.

apparent time   as opposed to real time. In apparent-time studies, the age difference between coexisting generations is interpreted as period of time. Variation in the speech of members of different generations is thus taken as evidence of language change.

audience design   The keying of one's utterance to suit those who are being addressed.

baby-talk   (1) A simplified speech form used by adults to young children. (2) The speech of young children characterized by limitations on choices due to incomplete language acquisition.

bilingual   An individual who controls two languages.

Black English   The English spoken by African Americans in the United States, also known as 'African American Vernacular English' (AAVE) and sometimes called 'Ebonics'.

caste   A system of social stratification associated with occupation and place of residence which in contradistinction to social class is hereditary and allows for no social mobility.

class   *see* social class

code   A system of signs used for sending messages. In sociolinguistics, a system of linguistic signs, used by some scholars to mean a socially distinct variety.

code-switching   The systematic choice by one speaker of elements of two or more languages, dialects, or varieties during a single conversation.

corpus   A collection of linguistic data. In language planning, the totality of linguistic subsystems, including pronunciation, grammar, vocabulary and spelling.

corpus planning   Regulatory measures designed to influence structural aspects of a language such as the lexicon, grammar, writing system and spelling rules.

creole   A pidgin that has acquired native speakers.

dialect   A language variety in which pronunciation, grammar and vocabulary are indicative of the regional background of the speakers.

diglossia   A situation where two distinct varieties of one language coexist throughout a speech community, each being allotted a range of different functions with little overlap.

domain   A typical social situation of language use, such as home, school, workplace, church and market.

Ebonics   *see* Black English.

endangered language   A language no longer passed on by its speakers to the next generation.

ethnolinguistic vitality   An aggregate of sociocultural factors that determine a group's ability to function as a distinct collective entity by maintaining its language.

foreigner talk   A simplified speech form used to address foreigners who are (thought to be) unable to understand regular speech.

formality   A variable factor of politeness.

gender   The social as distinct from the biological differences between the sexes.

home language   The language most commonly used in the family.

hypercorrect   The overgeneralization of a grammatical rule beyond the norm of a target variety which the speakers perceive as a marker of the social class they want to belong to.

idiolect   A variety characteristic of an individual speaker.

jargon   Expressions used by a group of specialists, which are not generally understood by the speech community at large.

language attitude   The feelings and ideas people have about their own language and other languages.

language contact   A situation where, because of geographic proximity or migration, bilingual speakers bring two or more languages into contact with each other.

language loss   The gradual decline in use of a language by individuals and a speech community, resulting in its disappearance from the repertoire of that community.

language loyalty   The degree to which speakers in situations of potential language shift hold on to their language.

language maintenance   A situation where, in spite of strong incentives to shift to another language, people continue to use their native language.

language planning   Any systematic, theory-informed design to solve the communication problems of a society by influencing speakers' choices concerning languages and varieties (status planning) as well as structural features of language such as pronunciation, grammar, vocabulary and terminology (corpus planning).

language shift   The process by which a community increases the use of one language at the expense of another.

marked   Unusual and deviating from a norm or common expectation.

multilingualism   A situation where several languages are used side by side within one society.

networks   Groups of people who because of shared residence, work or interest regularly communicate with each other.

norm   An (officially) recommended form of a language which defines correct usage.

pidgin   A speech form created by speakers in a language-contact situation who share no common language. It has no native speakers and is characterized by instability.

pluricentric language   A language with more than one standard variety.

politeness   A dimension of linguistic choice and social behaviour which includes such notions as courtesy, formality, rapport, deference, respect and distance.

prestige variety   A speech form associated with high social standing.

received pronunciation (RP)   An accent of British English which is not marked for a geographic region but for a relatively high level of education and relatively high social class.

register   A speech form considered appropriate to a situation. Speech situations vary with respect to several factors, such as formality, the medium of communication, e.g. speech or writing, and the subject matter of the discourse.

repertoire   The totality of speech forms of an individual or speech community.

social class   A system of social stratification defined in terms of occupation, income, education. The study of class distinctions in speech in Western societies has been the point of departure of sociolinguistics. No universally accepted definition of 'class' is available.

speech community   A group of people who share the same language and/or the same knowledge about the distribution and differential use of a set of languages and varieties.

standard   A prestige variety of language, providing a written institutionalized norm as a reference form for such purposes as language teaching and the media.

status planning   Regulatory measures designed to determine when and for what functions a language is used in a society.

style   Any situationally distinct choice of language made by individuals and social groups.

terms of address   Kinship terms, names, titles and second-person pronouns used to address other speakers and to express social relationships. A T/V differentiation in second-person pronouns is common in several European languages, where the singular T form (from French *tu*) marks closeness and familiarity, and the plural V form (from French *vous*) marks distance and politeness.

urban dialect   The language variety of a city. The study of urban dialects takes into consideration not just regional variation, but other factors that differentiate urban populations and their speech forms, such as social class and ethnicity.

variable   A cluster of linguistic features, such as sounds or grammatical forms, which speakers choose according to circumstances.

variation   Systematic changes of pronunciation, grammar and vocabulary brought about by speakers' choices.

variety   Any language or dialect that can be identified by its speakers and speakers of other varieties.

vernacular   The indigenous variety of a community, as distinct from its standard or prestige variety.

vitality   *see* ethnolinguistic vitality.

References

Abbi, Anvita. 2006. *Endangered Languages of the Andaman Islands. LINCOM Studies in Asian Linguistics*, **64**. Munich: Lincom Europa.

Abbi, Anvita, Bidisha Som and Alok Das. 2007. Where have all the speakers gone? A sociolinguistic study of the Great Andamanese. *Indian Linguistics* **68**: 325–48.

Abrams, Daniel M. and Steven H. Strogatz. 2003. Modelling the dynamics of language death. *Nature* **24**: 900.

Adams, J. N. 2003. *Bilingualism and the Latin Language*. Cambridge University Press.

Adank, Patti, Peter Hagoort and Harold Bekkering. 2010. Imitation improves language comprehension. *Psychological Science* **21**: 1903–9.

Ager, Dennis. 1996. *'Francophonie' in the 1990s: Problems and Opportunities*. Clevedon: Multilingual Matters.

 2001. *Motivation in Language Planning and Language Policy*. Clevedon: Multilingual Matters.

Alexander, Neville. n.d. Linguistic rights, language planning and democracy in post-Apartheid South Africa. In Steven J. Baker (ed.), *Language Policy: Lessons from Global Models*. Monterey Institute of International Studies, 116–29.

Alexiou, Margaret. 1982. Diglossia in Greece. In W. Haas (ed.), *Standard Languages: Spoken and Written*. Manchester University Press, 156–93.

Allard, Rodrigue and Réal Landry. 1992. Ethnolinguistic vitality beliefs and language maintenance and loss. In W. Fase, K. Jaespaert and S. Kroon (eds.), *Maintenance and Loss of Minority Languages*. Amsterdam: John Benjamins, 171–95.

Allen, Charlotte. 1997. Spies like us: when sociologists deceive their subjects. *Lingua Franca* **7**: 31–9.

Alsagoff, Lubna. 2010. English in Singapore: culture, capital and identity in linguistic variation. *World Englishes* **29**: 336–48.

Altehenger-Smith, Sherida. 1987. Language choice in multilingual societies: a Singapore case study. In Karlfried Knapp, Werner Enninger and Annelie Knapp-Potthoff (eds.), *Analyzing Intercultural Communication*. Berlin and New York: Mouton de Gruyter, 75–94.

Ammon, Ulrich (ed.) 1979. *Dialect and Standard in Highly Industrialized Societies*. Special issue, *International Journal of the Sociology of Language* 21.

 2002. *The Dominance of English as a Language of Science: Effects on other Languages and Language Communities*. Berlin: Walter de Gruyter.

Amonoo, Reginald F. 1994. La situation linguistique au Ghana et les problèmes de standardisation. In Georges Lüdi (ed.), *Sprachstandardisierung–Standardisation des langues–Standardizzazione delle lingue – Standardization of languages*. Freiburg: Universitätsverlag, 23–32.

Andersen, Elaine Slossberg. 1992. *Speaking with Style: The Sociolinguistic Skills of Children*. London and New York: Routledge.

Androutsopoulos, Jannis. 2006. Introduction: sociolinguistics and computer-mediated communication. *Journal of Sociolinguistics* **10**(4): 419–38.

Annamalai, E. 1989. The language factor in code mixing. *International Journal of the Sociology of Language* **75**: 47–54.

Appel, Rene and Pieter Muysken. 1987. *Language Contact and Bilingualism*. London: Edward Arnold.

Appiah, A. K. and H. L. Gates (eds.) 1995. *Identities*. University of Chicago Press.

Arends, Jacques, Pieter Muysken and Norval Smith (eds.) 1994. *Pidgins and Creoles: An Introduction*. Amsterdam: John Benjamins.

Ashcroft, Bill, Gareth Griffiths and Helen Tiffin. 2002. *The Empire Writes Back: Theory and Practice in Post-Colonial Literature*. London: Routledge.

Auer, Peter. 1984. *Bilingual Conversation*. Amsterdam: John Benjamins.

(ed.) 1998. *Code-Switching in Conversation: Language, Interaction and Identity*. London and New York: Routledge.

Auer, Peter and F. Hinskens. 1996. The convergence and divergence of dialects in Europe: new and not so new developments in an old area. *Sociolinguistica* **10**: 1–30.

Axelrod, Robert. 1984. *The Evolution of Cooperation*. New York: Basic Books.

Backhaus, Peter. 2002. Sprachwandel in Japan: Pronominale Selbstreferenz bei männlichen Sprechern. Unpublished MA thesis, Heinrich Heine Universität, Düsseldorf.

2007. *Linguistic Landscapes: A Comparative Study of Urban Multilingualism in Tokyo*. Clevedon: Multilingual Matters.

(ed.) 2011. *Communication in Elderly Care: Cross-Cultural Perspectives*. London, New York: Continuum.

2012. Language policy at the municipal level. In B. Spolsky (ed.), *The Cambridge Handbook of Language Policy*. Cambridge: Cambridge University Press, 226–242.

Backhaus, Peter and Florian Coulmas (eds.) 2009. *Social Aging and Language, International Journal of the Sociology of Language*, no. 200 (November).

Bailey, Guy. 2002. Real and apparent time. In J. K. Chambers, Peter Trudgill and Natalie Schilling-Estes (eds.), *The Handbook of Language Variation and Change*. Oxford: Blackwell, 312–32.

Bailey, Guy, Tom Wikle, Jan Tillery and Lori Sand. 1991. The apparent time construct. *Language Variation and Change* **3**: 241–64.

Baker, Philip and John Eversley (eds.) 2000. *Multilingual Capital*. London: Battelbridge.

Baltes, M. and H. Wahl. 1996. Patterns of communication in old age: the dependent-support and independence-ignore script. *Health Communications* **8**: 217–31.

Bamgbose, Ayo. 1982. Standard Nigerian English: issues of identification. In Braj B. Kachru (ed.), *The Other Tongue: English across Cultures*. Oxford: Pergamon Press, 99–111.

Bargiela-Chiappini, Francesca and Dániel Z. Kádár (eds.) 2010. *Politeness across Cultures*. Basingstoke: Pelgrave Macmillan.

Baron, Dennis E. 1982. *Grammar and Good Taste*. New Haven and London: Yale University Press.

Barton, David. 1994. *Literacy: An Introduction to the Ecology of Written Language*. Oxford: Blackwell.

Battestini, Simon. 1997. *Ecriture et texte: contribution africaine*. Quebec: Les Presses de l'Universitè Laval.

Bayraktaroğlu, Arin and Maria Sifianou (eds.) 2001. *Linguistic Politeness across Boundaries: The Case of Greek and Turkish*. Amsterdam: John Benjamins.

Becker, U. 1989. Class theory: still the axis of critical social scientific analysis? In Eric O. Wright (ed.), *The Debate on Classes*. London: Verso, 127–56.

Beebe, Leslie M. and Howard Giles. 1984. Speech-accommodation theories: a discussion in terms of second language acquisition. *International Journal of the Sociology of Language* **46**: 5–32.

Bentahila, Abdelâli and Eirlys E. Davies. 1998. Codeswitching: an unequal partnership? In Rodolfo Jacobson (ed.), *Codeswitching Worldwide*. Berlin and New York: Mouton de Gruyter, 25–49.

Berk-Seligson, Susan. 1986. Linguistic constraints on intrasentential code-switching: a study of Spanish/Hebrew bilingualism. *Language in Society* **15**: 313–48.

Bernstein, Basil. 1971. *Class, Codes and Control: Theoretical Studies towards a Sociology of Language*. London: Routledge and Paul.

Beykont, Zeynep F. 2010. 'We should keep what makes us different': youth reflections on Turkish maintenance in Australia. *International Journal of the Sociology of Language* **206**: 93–107.

Bickerton, Derek. 1981. *Roots of Language*. Ann Arbor: Karoma.

Birch, Barbara M. 1995. Quaker Plain Speech: a policy of linguistic divergence. *International Journal of the Sociology of Language* **116**: 39–59.

Blanche-Benveniste, Claire. 1994. The construct of oral and written language. In Ludo Verhoeven (ed.), *Functional Literacy: Theoretical Issues and Educational Implications*. Amsterdam and Philadelphia: John Benjamins, 61–74.

Blau, Joshua. 1977. The beginnings of Arabic diglossia: a study of the origins of Neoarabic. *Afroasiatic Linguistics* **4**: 175–202.

Blom, Jan-Petter and John J. Gumperz. 1972. Social meaning in linguistic structures: code-switching in Norway. In John J. Gumperz and Dell Hymes (eds.), *Directions in Sociolinguistics*. New York: Holt, Rinehart and Winston, 407–34.

Bloomfield, Leonard. 1933. *Language*. New York: Holt, Rinehart and Winston.

Boberg, Charles. 2004. Real and apparent time in language change: late adoption of changes in Montreal English. *American Speech* **79**(4): 250–69.

Bokamba, Eyamba. 1988. Code-mixing, language variation and linguistic theory: evidence from Bantu languages. *Lingua* **76**: 21–62.

Bonfiglio, Thomas P. 2002. *Race and the Rise of Standard American*. Berlin and New York: Mouton de Gruyter.

Boone, Elisabeth. 1994. Introduction: writing and recorded knowledge. In E. Broone and W. Mignolo (eds.), *Writing without Words*. Durham, NC: Duke University Press, 3–26.

Botha, Rudolf P. 2010. What are windows on language evolution? In Rudolph P. Botha and H. de Swart (eds.), *Language Evolution: The View from Restricted Linguistic Systems*. LOT Ocasional Series 10, Utrecht, 2009, pp. 1–20. http://lotos.library.uu.nl/publish/articles/000279/bookpart.pdf.

Brauner, Siegmund. 1994. Zur Herausbildung und Entwicklung des Schona als moderne nationale Literatursprache Simbabwes. In I. Fodor and C. Hagège (eds.), *Language Reform: History and Future*. Hamburg: Buske, vol. III, 163–85.

Brenzinger, Matthias. 1992. Patterns of language shift in East Africa. In Robert Herbert (ed.), *Language and Society in Africa*. Cape Town: Witwatersrand University Press, 287–303.

  1996. Language contact and language displacement. In F. Coulmas (ed.), *The Handbook of Sociolinguistics*. Oxford: Blackwell, 273–84.

  1998. Various ways of dying and different kinds of death: scholarly approaches to language endangerment on the African continent. In Kazuto Matsumura (ed.), *Studies in Endangered Languages*. Tokyo: Hituzi, 85–100.

  2007. Language endangerment in southern and eastern Africa. In M. Brenzinger (ed.), *Language Diversity Endangered*. Berlin: Walter de Gruyter, 179–204.

Breton, Albert and Peter Mieszkowski. 1977. The economics of bilingualism. In Wallace E. Oates (ed.), *The Political Economy of Fiscal Federalism*. Toronto and Lexington, MA: Lexington Books, 261–73.

Breton, Roland J.-L. 1991. *Geolinguistics: Language Dynamics and Ethnolinguistic Geography*. Trans. and expanded by Harold F. Schiffman. Ottawa and Paris: University of Ottawa Press.

Bright, William. 1990. *Language Variation in South Asia*. New York: Oxford University Press.

  1991. Small linguistic societies from a global perspective. *IT and Mass Media for Small Linguistic Societies*. Special issue, *EMI: Educational Media International* **29**(1): 11–18.

Britto, Francis. 1986. *Diglossia: A Study of the Theory with Application to Tamil*. Washington, DC: Georgetown University Press.

Brown, Penelope and Steven Levinson. 1987. *Politeness: Some Universals in Language Usage*. Cambridge University Press.

Browning, Robert. 1969. *Medieval and Modern Greek*. London: Hutchinson University Library.

Brouwer, Dédé and Roeland van Hout. 1992. Gender-related variation in Amsterdam vernacular. *International Journal of the Sociology of Language* **94**: 99–122.

Bucholtz, Mary. (ed.) 2004. *Language and Woman's Place: Text and Commentaries*. New York: Oxford University Press.

Bugarski, Ranko. 2001. Language, nationalism and war in Yugoslavia. *International Journal of the Sociology of Language* **151**: 69–87.

Burstein, J. 1989. Politeness strategies and gender expectations. *CUNY Forum: Papers in Linguistics* **14**: 31–7.

Cameron, Deborah (ed.) 1990. *The Feminist Critique of Language: A Reader*. London and New York: Routledge.

1992. 'Not gender difference but the difference gender makes': explanation in research on sex and language. *International Journal of the Sociology of Language* **94**: 13–26.

2006. *On Language and Sexual Politics*. London: Routledge.

Casagrande, Joseph B. 1948. Comanche baby language. *International Journal of American Linguistics* **14**: 11–14.

Cavazos, Edward and Gavino Morin. 1996. *Cyberspace and the Law: Your Rights and Duties in the On-line World*. Cambridge, MA: MIT Press.

Cedergren, Henrietta. 1973. The interplay of social and linguistic factors in Panama. PhD dissertation, Cornell University.

Certeau, Michel, Dominique Julia and Jacques Revel. 1975. *Une politique de la langue: La Révolution Française et les patois*. Paris: Gallimard.

Cerulo, K. 1997. Identity construction: new issues, new directions. *Annual Review of Sociology* **23**: 385–409.

Chalmers, David J. 1996. *The Conscious Mind: In Search of a Fundamental Theory*. Oxford University Press.

Chambers, Jack K. 1995. *Sociolinguistic Theory*. Oxford: Blackwell.

Chambers, Jack K., Peter Trudgill and Natalie Schilling-Estes (eds.) 2002. *The Handbook of Language Variation and Change*. Oxford: Blackwell.

Chang, Junyue. 2006. Globalization and English in Chinese higher education. *World Englishes* **25**: 513–25.

Chatterjee, Suhas. 1986. Diglossia in Bengali. In Bh. Krishnamurti (ed.), *South Asian Languages: Structure, Convergence and Diglossia*. Delhi: Motilal Banarsidass, 294–311.

Chen, Ping. 1996a. Toward a phonographic writing system of Chinese: a case study in writing reform. *International Journal of the Sociology of Language* **122**: 1–46.

1996b. Modern written Chinese, dialects and regional identity. *Language Problems and Language Planning* **20**: 223–43.

Cheshire, Jenny. 1991. Introduction: sociolinguistics and English around the world. In Jenny Cheshire (ed.), *English around the World: Sociolinguistic Perspectives*. Cambridge University Press, 1–12.

2002. Sex and gender in variationist research. In Jack K. Chambers, Peter Trudgill and Natalie Schilling-Estes (eds.), *The Handbook of Language Variation and Change*. Oxford: Blackwell, 423–43.

Cheshire, Jenny, Paul Kerswill, Susan Fox, and Evind Torgersen. 2011. Contact, the feature pool and the speech community: the emergence of Multicultural London English. *Journal of Sociolinguistics* **15**(2): 151–96.

Chomsky, Noam. 2000. *New Horizons in the Study of Language and Mind*. Cambridge University Press.

Christiansen, Morton, Nick Chater and Florencia Reali. 2009. The biological and cultural foundations of language. *Communicative and Integrative Biology* **2**(3) 221–2. www. ncbi.nlm.nih.gov/pmc/articles/PMC2717525/.

Chua, Siew Kheng Catherine. 2011. Singapore's language policy and its globalized concept of Bi(tri)lingualism. *Language Planning* **11**(4), 413–29.

Clark, Terty N. and Seymour M. Lipset. 2001. *The Breakdown of Class Politics: A Debate on Post-industrial Stratification*. Baltimore: Johns Hopkins University Press.

Clayton, Thomas. 2002. Language choice in a nation under transition: the struggle between English and French in Cambodia. *Language Policy* **1**(1): 3–25.

Clement, Victoria. 2008. Emblems of independence: script choice in post-Soviet Turkmenistan. *International Journal of the Sociology of Language* **192**: 171–85.

Clyne, Michael. 1991. *Community Languages: The Australian Experience*. Cambridge University Press.

(ed.) 1992. *Pluricentric Languages*. Berlin and New York: Mouton de Gruyter.

Coggle, Paul. 1993. *Do You Speak Estuary?* London: Bloomsbury.

Conseil de la langue française. 2000. *La langue de l'affichage à Montréal de 1997 à 1999.* Québec: Conseil de la langue française.

Cooper, Robert L. 1984. The avoidance of androcentric generics. *International Journal of the Sociology of Language* **50**: 5–20.

1989. *Language Planning and Social Change.* Cambridge University Press.

Coulmas, Florian (ed.) 1981a. *Conversational Routine: Explorations in Standardized Communication Situations and Prepatterned Speech.* The Hague: Mouton.

(ed.) 1981b. *A Festschrift for Native Speaker.* The Hague: Mouton.

1986. Reported speech: some general issues. In F. Coulmas (ed.), *Direct and Indirect Speech.* Berlin and New York: De Gruyter, 1–28.

1987. What writing can do to language: some preliminary remarks. In Simon Battestini (ed.), *Developments in Linguistics and Semiotics, Language Teaching and Learning Communication across Cultures: Georgetown University Roundtable on Languages and Linguistics 1986.* Washington, DC: Georgetown University Press, 107–29.

1989. Language adaptation in Meiji Japan. In F. Coulmas (ed.), *Language Adaptation.* Cambridge University Press, 1–25.

1991. European integration and the idea of a national language. In F. Coulmas (ed.), *A Language Policy for the European Community.* Berlin and New York: Mouton de Gruyter, 1–43.

1992a. Linguistic etiquette in Japanese society. In Richard J. Watts, Sachiko Ide and Konrad Ehlich (eds.), *Politeness in Language: Studies in its History, Theory and Practice.* Berlin and New York: Mouton de Gruyter, 299–323.

1992b. *Language and Economy.* Oxford: Blackwell.

1999. The Far East. In Joshua A. Fishman (ed.), *Handbook of Language and Ethnic Identity.* New York and Oxford: Oxford University Press, 399–413.

2002. Comment [to Hudson 2002]. *International Journal of the Sociology of Language* **157**: 59–62.

2003. *Writing Systems: An Introduction to their Linguistic Analysis.* Cambridge University Press.

2010. The ethics of language choice in immigration. *Policy Innovations.* www.policy innovations.org/ideas/commentary/data/000162.

2013. *Writing and Society.* Cambridge University Press.

Council of Europe. 1995. *Framework Convention for the Protection of National Minorities.* http://conventions.coe.int/Treaty/en/Treaties/html/157.htm

Coupland, Nikolas. 2004. Age in social and sociolinguistic theory. In Jon F. Nussbaum and Justine Coupland (eds.), *Handbook of Communication and Aging Research.* Mahwah, NJ: Erlbaum, 69–90.

2010. Accommodation theory. In Jürgen Jaspers, Jan-Ola Östman and Jef Verschueren (eds.), *Society and Language Use.* Amsterdam: John Benjamins, 21–7.

Coupland, Nikolas, Justine Coupland and Howard Giles. 1991. *Language, Society and the Elderly: Discourse, Identity and Ageing.* Oxford: Blackwell.

Cravens, Thomas D. and Luciano Giannelli. 1995. Relative salience of gender and class in a situation of competing norms. *Language Variation and Change* **7**: 261–85.

Crawford, James (ed.) 1992. *Language Loyalties: A Source Book on the Official English Controversy.* Chicago and London: University of Chicago Press.

Croft, William. 2000. *Explaining Language Change: An Evolutionary Approach.* London: Longman.

Crowston, Kevin and Ericka Kammerer. 2010. Communicative style and gender differences in computer-mediated communications. http://crowston.syr.edu/content/communicative-style-and-gender-differences-computer-mediated-communications-o.

Crystal, David. [1997]2003. *English as a Global Language.* Cambridge University Press.

2000. *Language Death.* Cambridge University Press.

Cukor-Avila, Patricia. (1995). The Evolution of AAVE in a Rural Texas Community: An Ethnolinguistic Study. PhD dissertation. Ann Arbor: University of Michigan.

Dailey-O'Cain, Jennifer and Grit Liebscher. 2011. Language attitudes, migrant identities and space. *International Journal of the Sociology of Language* **212**: 91–133.

Daoust, Denise. 1991. Terminological change within a language planning framework. In David F. Marshall (ed.), *Language Planning: Focusschrift in Honor of Joshua A. Fishman on the Occasion of his 65th Birthday*. Amsterdam and Philadelphia: John Benjamins, 281–309.

Davies, Alan. 1991. *The Native Speaker in Applied Linguistics*. Edinburgh University Press.

Day, Richard R. 1985. The ultimate inequality: linguistic genocide. In Nessa Wolfson and Joan Manes (eds.), *Language of Inequality*. Berlin, New York and Amsterdam: Mouton Publishers, 163–81.

De Bot, Kees and Robert W. Schrauf (eds.) 2009. *Language Development over the Lifespan*. Abingdon, Oxon: Routledge.

De Vries, Lourens. 2012. Speaking of clans: language in Awyu-Ndumut communities of Indonesian West Papua. *International Journal of the Sociology of Language* **214**: 5–26.

DeFrancis, John. 1984. *The Chinese Language: Fact and Fantasy*. Honolulu: University of Hawaii Press.

DePaulo, Bella M. and Lerita M. Coleman. 1981. Evidence for the specialness of the 'baby talk' register. *Language and Speech* **24**: 223–31.

Deshpande, Madhav. 1979. *Sociolinguistic Attitudes in India*. Ann Arbor: Karoma Publishers.

Devine, Fiona. 1996. *Social Class in Britain and America*. Edinburgh University Press.

Devine, Monica. 1991. *Baby Talk: The Art of Communicating with Infants and Toddlers*. New York: Plenum Press.

Dhir, Krishna S. and Theresa Savage. 2002. The value of a working language. *International Journal of the Sociology of Language* **158**: 1–35.

Dilke, Charles Wentworth. 1868/9. *Greater Britain: A Record of Travel in English-Speaking Countries*. London: Macmillan.

Dixon, R. M. W. 1991. The endangered languages of Australia, Indonesia and Oceania. In R. H. Robins and E. M. Uhlenbeck (eds.), *Endangered Languages*. London and New York: Berg, 229–55.

Djité, Paulin G. 1990. The place of African languages in the revival of the Francophonie movement. *International Journal of the Sociology of Language* **86**: 87–102.

  2008. *The Sociolinguistics of Development in Africa*. Clevedon: Multilingual Matters.

Dobson, J. E. 1956. Early modern standard English. *Transactions of the Philological Society* **1955**: 25–54.

DoE 1995. *1991 Deprivation Index: A Review of Approaches and a Matrix of Results*. London: HMSO.

Domínguez, Francesc and Núria López. 1995. *Language International World Directory of Sociolinguistic and Language Planning Organizations*. Amsterdam and Philadelphia: John Benjamins.

Dorian, Nancy C. 1982. Language loss and maintenance in language contact situations. In R. D. Lambert and B. F. Freed (eds.), *The Loss of Language Skills*. Rowley, MA: Newbury House Publishers, 44–59.

  (ed.) 1989. *Investigating Obsolescence: Studies in Language Contraction and Death*. Cambridge University Press.

  2009. Age and speaker skills in receding languages: how far do community evaluations and linguists' evaluations agree? *International Journal of the Sociology of Language* **200**: 11–25.

Downes, William. 1984. *Language and Society*. London: Fontana.

Du Plessis, Theo. 1990. *The Liberation of Afrikaans*. ABLA Papers no. 14. Brussels: Research Centre on Multilingualism.

Dwyer, Arienne. 2006. Ethics and practicalities of cooperative fieldwork and analysis. In Jost Gippert, Nikolaus P. Himmelmann, Ulrike Mosel (eds.), *Essentials of Language Documentation*. Berlin and New York: Mouton de Gruyter, 31–66.

Eckert, Penelope. 1989. The whole women: sex and gender differences in variation. *Language Variation and Change* **1**: 245–68.

  (ed.) 1991. *New Ways of Analyzing Sound Change*. San Diego: Academic Press.

Eckert, Penelope and Sally McConnell-Ginet. 2002. *Language and Gender*. Cambridge University Press.

Edgell, Stephen. 1993. *Class*. London: Routledge.

Edwards, John. 1985. *Language, Society and Identity.* Oxford: Basil Blackwell.

1994. *Multilingualism.* London: Routledge.

2012. *Multilingualism: Understanding Linguistic Diversity.* London: Continuum.

Edwards, W. (ed.) 1992. *Utility Theories: Measurements and Applications.* Dordrecht: Kluwer Academic.

Eelen, Gino. 2001. *A Critique of Politeness Theories.* Manchester: St Jerome Publishing.

Ehlich, Konrad. 1992. On the historicity of politeness. In Richard J. Watts, Sachiko Ide and Konrad Ehlich (eds.), *Politeness in Language: Studies in its History, Theory and Practice.* Berlin and New York: Mouton de Gruyter, 71–107.

Eideneier, Hans. 2000. *Zur mittelalterlichen Vorgeschichte der neugriechischen Diglossie.* Hamburg: Sonderforschungsbereich Mehrsprachigkeit.

Eira, Christina. 1998. Authority and discourse: towards a model for orthography selection. *Written Language and Literacy* **1**(2):171–224.

Elkhafaifi, Hussein M. 2002. Arabic language planning in the age of globalization. *Language Problems and Language Planning* **26**(3): 253–69.

Endleman, Shalom. 1995. The politics of language: the impact of language legislation on French- and English-language citizens of Quebec. *International Journal of the Sociology of Language* **116**: 81–98.

Ennaji, Moha. 2005. *Multilingualism, Cultural Identity, and Education in Morocco.* New York: Springer.

Eroms, Hans-Werner and Horst Haider Munske (eds.) 1997. *Die Rechtschreibreform: Pro und Kontra.* Berlin: Erich Schmidt Verlag.

Ess, Charles and Association of Internet Researchers. 2002. Ethical decision-making and internet research. http://aoir.org/reports/ethics.pdf.

Ethnologue. 16th edn. 2009. www.ethnologue.com/.

European Commission. 2006. *Europeans and their Languages.* Special Eurobarometer 243. http://ec.europa.eu/public_opinion/archives/ebs/ebs_243_en.pdf.

Extra, Guus. 2010. Mapping linguistic diversity in multicultural contexts: demolinguistics perspectives. In J. A. Fishman and O. Garcia (eds.), *Handbook of Language and Ethnic Identity.* 2nd edn. New York: Oxford University Press, 107–22.

Extra, Guus and Durk Gorter (eds.) 2001. *The Other Languages of Europe.* Clevedon: Multilingual Matters.

Extra, Guus and Kutlay Yagmur. 2004. *Urban Multilingualism in Europe: Immigrant Minority Languages at Home and School.* Clevedon: Multilingual Matters.

Faas, Daniel. 2010. *Negotiating Political Identities: Multiethnic Schools and Youth in Europe.* Farnham, Surrey: Ashgate.

Fabricius, Anne H. 2000. T-glottaling between stigma and prestige: a sociolinguistic study of modern RP. PhD dissertation, Copenhagen Business School.

Fairclough, Norman. 1989. *Language and Power.* New York: Longman.

Fasold, Ralph. 1984. *The Sociolinguistics of Society.* Oxford: Blackwell.

1990. *The Sociolinguistics of Language.* Oxford: Blackwell.

Fassi Fehri, Abdelkader. 2002. The multidialectal Arabic lexicon. *Recherches Linguistiques, Linguistic Research.* Rabat: Publications de l'Institut d'Etudes et de Recherches sur Arabisation.

Ferguson, Charles A. 1959. Diglossia. *Word* **15**: 325–40.

1964. Baby talk in six languages. *American Anthropologist* **66**: 103–14.

1977. Baby talk as simplified register. In Catherine E. Snow and Charles A. Ferguson (eds.), *Talking to Children: Language Input and Acquisition.* Cambridge University Press, 209–35.

1982. Foreword. In Braj B. Kachru (ed.), *The Other Tongue: English across Cultures.* Oxford: Pergamon Press, vii–xi.

1983. Language planning and language change. In Juan Cobarrubias and Joshua A. Fishman (eds.), *Progress in Language Planning.* Berlin, New York and Amsterdam: Mouton, 29–40.

Fernández, Mauro. 1995. Los orígenes del término diglossia: historia de una historia mal contada. *Historiographia Linguistica* **22**: 163–95.

Finlayson, Rosalie and Sarah Slabbert. 1997. 'I'll meet you halfway with language': code-switching within a South African urban context. In Martin Pütz (ed.), *Language Choices:*

Conditions, Constraints and Consequences. Amsterdam and Philadelphia: John Benjamins, 381–421.

Fischer, John L. 1958. Social influences on the choice of a linguistic variant. *Word* **14**: 47–56.

Fishman, Joshua A. 1964. Language maintenance and language shift as fields of inquiry. *Linguistics* **9**: 32–70.

1965. Who speaks what language to whom and when? *La Linguistique* **2**: 67–88.

(ed.) 1966. *Language Loyalty in the United States*. The Hague: Mouton.

1967. Bilingualism with and without diglossia; diglossia with and without bilingualism. *Journal of Social Issues* **23**: 29–38.

1972. *The Sociology of Language: An Interdisciplinary Social Science Approach to Language in Society*. Rowley, MA: Newbury House.

1980. Bilingualism and biculturism as individual and as societal phenomena. *Journal of Multilingual and Multicultural Development* **1**: 3–15.

1989. *Language and Ethnicity in Minority Sociolinguistic Perspective*. Clevedon: Multilingual Matters.

1991. *Reversing Language Shift: Theoretical and Empirical Foundations of Assistance to Threatened Languages*. Clevedon: Multilingual Matters.

(ed.) 2001. *Can Threatened Languages Be Saved?* Clevedon: Multilingual Matters.

2002. Comment [to Hudson 2002]. *International Journal of the Sociology of Language* **157**: 93–100.

2010. Sociolinguistics: language and ethnic identity in context. In J. A. Fishman and O. García (eds.), *Handbook of Language and Ethnic Identity*. 2nd edn. Oxford and New York: Oxford University Press, xxiii–xxxv.

Fishman, Joshua A., Andrew W. Conrad and Alma Rubal-Lopez (eds.) 1996. *Post-Imperial English: Status Change in Former British and American Colonies, 1940–1990*. Berlin and New York: Mouton de Gruyter.

Fletcher, Paul and Brian MacWhinney. 1995. *The Handbook of Child Language*. Oxford: Blackwell.

Fodor, Istvan. 1983. Quelques conclusions: comment les 'Esqimaux' développent-ils leurs parlers en langues littéraires? In I. Fodor and C. Hagège (eds.), *Language Reform: History and Future*. Hamburg: Buske, vol. **III**, 455–81.

Forey, Gail and Jane Lockwood (eds.) 2012. *Globalization, Communication and the Workplace: Talking across the World*. London: Continuum.

Frangoudaki, Anna. 1997. The metalinguistic prophecy on the decline of the Greek language: its social function as the expression of a crisis in Greek national identity. *International Journal of the Sociology of Language* **126**: 63–82.

2002. Comment [to Hudson 2002]. *International Journal of the Sociology of Language* **157**: 101–7.

Fraser, Bruce. 1990. Perspectives on politeness. *Journal of Pragmatics* **14**: 219–36.

Fukuzawa, Y. 1966. *The Autobiography of Yukichi Fukuzawa*. Rev. trans. Eichii Kiyooka. New York: Colombia University Press.

Gal, Susan. 1979. *Language Shift*. New York: Academic Press.

Galbraith, John Kenneth. 1989. *A History of Economics*. Harmondsworth: Penguin.

Gandhi, Mohandas K. 1965. *Our Language Problem*. Edited by Anand T. Hingorani. Bombay: Bharatiya Vidya Bhavan.

Gardner-Chloros, Penelope. 1991. *Language Selection and Switching in Strasbourg*. Oxford University Press.

2009. *Code-switching*. Cambridge University Press.

Gauthier, François, Jacques Leclerc and Jacques Maurais. 1993. *Langues et constitutions: recueil des clauses linguistiques des constitutions du monde*. Québec: Office de la langue française.

Gbadamosi, Gabriel. 1999. The road to Brixton Market: a post-colonial travelogue. In Steve Clark (ed.), *Travel Writing and Empire*. London and New York: Zed Books, 185–94.

GEN: Global English Newsletter. www.engcool.com/GEN/weblog.php.

Gibbon, Margaret. 1999. *Feminist Perspectives on Language*. London: Longman.

Giles, Howard, Richard Bourhis and D. M. Taylor. 1977. Towards a theory of language in ethnic group relations. In Howard Giles (ed.), *Language, Ethnicity and Intergroup Relations*. London: Academic Press, 307–48.

Givón, Talmy. 1986. Prototypes: between Plato and Wittgenstein. In Colette Craig (ed.), *Noun Classes and Categorization*. Amsterdam: Benjamins, 77–102.

Goldthorpe, John H. and Gordon Marshall. 1992. The promising future of class analysis: a response to recent critiques. *Sociology* **26** (3): 381–400.

González, Roseann Dueñas and Idikó Melis (eds.) 2000. *Language Ideologies: Critical Perspectives on the Official English Movement*. Mahwah, NJ: Lawrence Erlbaum.

Goody, Jack and Ian Watt. 1968. Introduction. In Jack Goody (ed.), *Literacy in Traditional Societies*. Cambridge University Press, 1–68.

Gordon, Edmund W., and Doxey A. Wilkerson. 1966. *Compensatory Education for the Disadvantaged*. New York: College Entrance Examination Board.

Gordon, Elizabeth. 1997. Sex, speech and stereotypes: why women's speech is closer to the standard. *Language in Society* **26**: 47–63.

Gorenflo, L. J., Suzanne Romaine, Russell A. Mittermeier and Kristen Walker-Painemilla. 2012. Co-occurrence of linguistic and biological diversity in biodiversity hotspots and high biodiversity wilderness areas. *Proceedings of the National Academy of Sciences of the United States*, May 7. www.pnas.org/content/early/2012/05/03/1117511109.full.pdf +html.

Gould, Stephen Jay. 2000. *Wonderful Life: The Burgess Shale and the Nature of History*. New York: Vintage.

Government of India. 1966. *A Common National Script for Indian Languages*. New Delhi.

Graddol, David. 1997. *The Future of English?* London: British Council.

   2010. *English next India*. London: The British Council. www.britishcouncil.org/learning-english-next-india-2010-book.htm.

Greenberg, Joseph (ed.) 1963. *Universals of Language*. Cambridge, MA: MIT Press.

Gregory, Gerry. 2011. Teaching and learning about language change (part one). *Changing English: Studies in Culture & Education* **18**(1): 3–15.

Grenier, Gilles and Serge Nadeau. 2011. English as the lingua franca and the economic value of other languages: the case of the language of work of immigrants and non-immigrants in the Montreal Labour Market. Working Paper #1107E, Department of Economics, University of Ottawa. www.socialsciences.uottawa.ca/eco/eng/documents/1107E_000.pdf.

Grenoble, Leonora A. and Lindsay J. Whaley (eds.) 1998. *Endangered Languages: Current Issues and Future Prospects*. Cambridge University Press.

Grice, Paul. 1975. Logic and conversation. In P. Cole and J. L. Morgan (eds.), *Syntax and Semantics*, vol. **III**: *Speech Acts*. New York: Academic Press, 41–58.

Grillo, Ralph. D. 1989. *Dominant Languages: Language and Hierarchy in Britain and France*. Cambridge University Press.

Grin, François (ed.) 1996. Economic approaches to language and language planning: an introduction. *International Journal of the Sociology of Language* **121**: 1–16.

   2001. English as economic value: facts and fallacies. *World Englishes* **20**: 65–78.

Grivelet, Stéphane. 1999. *La digraphie: changements et coexistences d'écritures*. Doctoral thesis, Université Montpellier III – Paul Valéry.

Grosjean, François. 1985. The bilingual as a competent but specific speaker-hearer. *Journal of Multilingual and Multicultural Development* **6**: 467–77.

   2010. *Bilingual: Life and Reality*. Cambridge, MA: Harvard University Press.

Grzega, Joachim. 2011. On the correlation between socioeconomics and policies of languages in official contexts. *International Journal of the Sociology of Language* **212**: 23–41.

Guerini, Federica. 2006. *Language Alternation Strategies in Multilingual Settings: A Case Study – Ghanian immigrants in Northern Italy*. Bern: Peter Lang.

Gumperz, John J. 1967. Language and communication. In Bertram M. Gross (ed.), *The Annals of the American Academy of Political and Social Sciences* **373**: 219–31.

   1982. *Discourse Strategies*. Cambridge University Press.

Gunaratne, Shelton A. 2003. Proto-Indo-European expansion, rise of English, and the international language order: a humanocentric analysis. *International Journal of the Sociology of Language* **164**: 1–32.

Günthner, Susanne. 1996. Male-female speaking practices across cultures. In Marlis Hellinger and Ulrich Ammon (eds.), *Contrastive Sociolinguistics*. Berlin and New York: DeGruyter, 447–74.

Gupta, R. S., Anvita Abbi and Kailash S. Aggarwal (eds.) 1995. *Language and the State: Perspectives on the Eighth Schedule*. New Delhi: Creative Books.

Haaland, Gunnar. 1969. Economic determinants in ethnic processes. In Fredrik Barth (ed.), *Ethnic Groups and Boundaries: The Social Organization of Culture Difference*. Oslo: Universitetsforlaget, 58–74.

Haas, Walter. 2002. Comment [to Hudson 2002]. *International Journal of the Sociology of Language* **157**: 109–15.

Hagège, Claude. 1992. *Le souffle de la langue*. Paris: Odile Jacob.

Hale, Ken. 1997. Cultural politics of identity in Latin America. *Annual Review of Anthropology* **26**: 567–90.

Hall, Kira and Mary Bucholtz. 1995. *Gender Articulated*. New York: Routledge.

Hamilton, Heidi E. 1994. *Conversations with an Alzheimer's Patient: An Interactional Sociolinguistic Study*. Cambridge University Press.

Hansen, Anita B. 2001. Lexical diffusion as a factor of phonetic change: the case of Modern French nasal vowels. *Language Variation and Change* **13**: 209–52.

Harbert Wayne, with help from Sally McConnell-Ginet, Amanda Miller, and John Whitman (eds.) 2009. *Language and Poverty*. Bristol: Multilingual Matters.

Harris, John. 1991. Ireland. In Jenny Cheshire (ed.), *English around the World: Sociolinguistic Perspectives*. Cambridge University Press, 37–50.

Harris, M. B. 1992. When courtesy fails: gender roles and polite behaviors. *Journal of Applied Social Psychology* **22**: 1399–416.

Harris, Roy. 1980. *The Language Makers*. Ithaca, NY: Cornell University Press.

   2000. *Rethinking Writing*. London: Athlone Press.

Harrison, K. D. 2007. *When Languages Die: The Extinction of the World's Languages and the Erosion of Human Knowledge*. Oxford University Press.

Harwood, Jake, Howard Giles and Richard Y. Bourhis. 1994. The genesis of vitality theory: historical patterns and discoursal dimensions. *International Journal of the Sociology of Language* **108**: 167–206.

Hashimoto, Kenji. 2003. *Class Structure in Contemporary Japan*. Melbourne: Trans Pacific Press.

Haspelmath, Martin and Uri Tadmor (eds.) 2009. *Loanwords in the World's Languages: A Comparative Handbook*. Berlin and New York: Mouton de Gruyter.

Haugh, Michael. 2005. The importance of 'place' in Japanese politeness: implications for cross-cultural and intercultural analyses. *Intercultural Pragmatics* **2**(1): 41–68.

Haust, Delia and Norbert Dittmar. 1998. Taxonomic or functional models in the description of codeswitching? Evidence from Mandinka and Wolof in African contact situations. In Rodolfo Jacobson (ed.), *Codeswitching Worldwide*, vol. **I**. Berlin and New York: Mouton de Gruyter, 79–90.

Hayhoe, M. and S. Parker (eds.) 1994. *Who Owns English?* Buckingham and Philadelphia: Oxford University Press.

Head, B. F. 1978. Respect degrees in pronominal reference. In J. H. Greenberg (ed.), *Universals of Human Language*, vol. **III**: *Word Structure*. Stanford University Press.

Heine, Bernd and Tania Kuteva. 2008. Constraints on contact-induced linguistic change. *Journal of Language Contact*, **2**: 57–89.

Heinrich, Patrick. 2002. *Die Rezeption westlicher Linguistik im modernen Japan bis Ende der Showa-Zeit*. Munich: Iudicium.

Held, Gudrun. 1992. Politeness in linguistic research. In Richard J. Watts, Sachiko Ide and Konrad Ehlich (eds.), *Politeness in Language: Studies in its History, Theory and Practice*. Berlin and New York: Mouton de Gruyter, 131–53.

Heller, Monica. 1992. The politics of code-switching and language choice. *Journal of Multilingual and Multicultural Development* **13**: 123–42.

   1995. Language choice, social institutions, and symbolic domination. *Language in Society* **24**: 373–405.

Hellinger, Marlies and Hadumond Bußmann (eds.) 2001/2. *Gender across Languages*, vols. I–III. Amsterdam and Philadelphia: John Benjamins.

Herbert, Robert K. 2001. Talking in Johannesburg: the negotiation of identity in conversation. In Rodolfo Jacobson (ed.), *Codeswitching Worldwide*, vol. **II**. Berlin and New York: Mouton de Gruyter, 223–49.

Hermann, M. E. 1929. Lautveränderungen in der Individualsprache einer Mundart. *Nachrichten der Gesellschaft der Wissenschaften zu Göttingen, Philosophisch-historische Klasse* **11**: 195–214.

Herring, Susan C. 2003. Gender and power in on-line communication. In Janet Holmes and Miriam Meyerhoff (eds.), *Handbook of Language and Gender*. Oxford: Blackwell, 202–8.

Hibiya, Junko. 1988. *A Quantitative Study of Tokyo Japanese*. Philadelphia: University of Pennsylvania Press.

Hickey, Raymond. 2004. *A Sound Atlas of Irish English*. Berlin and New York: Mouton de Gruyter.

Hill, Jane H. 1993. Structure and practice in language shift. In Kenneth Hyltenstam and Åke Viberg (eds.), *Progression and Regression in Language*. Cambridge University Press, 75–93.

Holmes, Janet. 1992. *An Introduction to Sociolinguistics*. London: Longman.

    1995. *Women, Men and Politeness*. London: Longman.

Holmes, Janet and Miriam Meyerhoff (eds.) 2003. *Handbook of Language and Gender*. Oxford: Blackwell.

Holton, David. 2002. Modern Greek: towards a standard language of a new diglossia? In Mari C. Jones and Edith Esch (eds.), *Language Change: The Interplay of Internal, External and Extra-linguistic Factors*. Berlin and New York: Mouton de Gruyter, 169–79.

Holton, Gary. 2005. Ethical practices in language documentation and archiving languages. www.language-archives.org/events/olac05/olac-lsa05-holton.pdf.

Honey, John. 1989. *Does Accent Matter?* London and Boston: Faber.

Hudson, Alan. 2002. Outline of a theory of diglossia. *International Journal of the Sociology of Language* **157**: 1–48.

Hull, Geoffrey. 1994. Maltese, from Arabic dialect to European language. In I. Fodor and C. Hagège (eds.), *Language Reform: History and Future*. Hamburg: Buske, vol. **VI**, 331–46.

Hurford, James R. 1991. The evolution of the critical period for language acquisition. *Cognition* **40**: 159–201.

Hwang, Juck-Ryoon. 1990. 'Deference' versus 'politeness' in Korean speech. *International Journal of the Sociology of Language* **82**: 41–55.

Hyltenstam, Kenneth and Åke Viberg (eds.) 1993. *Progression and Regression in Language*. Cambridge University Press.

Hymes, Dell. 1974. *Foundations in Sociolinguistics: An Ethnographic Approach*. Philadelphia, PA: University of Pennsylvania Press.

    1980. *Language in Education: Ethnolinguistic Essays*. Washington, DC: Center of Applied Linguistics.

Ide, Sachiko and Megumi Yoshida. 1999. Sociolinguistics: honorifics and gender differences. In Natsuko Tsujimura (ed.), *The Handbook of Japanese Linguistics*. Oxford: Blackwell, 444–80.

Igboanusi, Herbert and Lothar Peter. 2004. Oppressing the oppressed: threats of Hausa and English on Nigeria's minority languages. *International Journal of the Sociology of Language* **170**: 131–40.

Ige, Busayo. 2010. Identity and language choice: 'We equals I'. *Journal of Pragmatics* **42**(11), 3047–54.

Imada, Takatoshi. 1991. Modernity and its deconstruction: metamorphosis of civilization. *International Review of Sociology New Series*, **3**: 197–211.

Inoue, Fumio. 1994. *Hōgengaku no shin chihei* [New Horizons in Dialectology]. Tokyo: Meiji Shoin.

    1997. S-shaped curves of language standardization. *Issues and Methods in Dialectology* **8**: 79–93.

Inoue, Miyako. 1994. Gender and linguistic modernization: a historical account of the birth of Japanese women's language. In Mary Bucholtz, A. C. Liang, Laurel A. Sutton and

Caitlin Hines. (eds.), *Cultural Performances: Proceedings of the Third Berkeley Women and Language Conference*. Berkeley: Women and Language Group, 322–33.

Internet World Stats 2010. www.internetworldstats.com/stats7.htm.

Irvine, Judith T. and Susan Gal. 2000. Language ideology and linguistic differentiation. In Paul V. Kroskrity (ed.), *Regimes of Language. Ideologies, Polities, and Identities*. Santa Fe: School of American Research Press, 35–83.

Jacobs, Greg. 1996. Lesbian and gay male language use: a critical review of the literature. *American Speech* **71**: 49–71.

Jacobson, Rodolfo. 1977. The social implications of intra-sentential code-switching. In Jon Amastae and Lucía Elías-Olivares (eds.), *Spanish in the United States: Sociolinguistic Aspects*. Cambridge University Press, 182–208.

1996. In search of the deeper message: codeswitching rationales of Mexican-Americans and Malaysians. In Marlis Hellinger and Ulrich Ammon (eds.), *Contrastive Sociolinguistics*. Berlin and New York: Mouton de Gruyter, 77–102.

1998a. Conveying a broader message through bilingual discourse: an attempt at contrastive codeswitching research. In Rodolfo Jacobson (ed.), *Codeswitching Worldwide*. Berlin and New York: Mouton de Gruyter, 51–76.

(ed.) 1998b. *Codeswitching Worldwide*. Berlin and New York: Mouton de Gruyter.

2001a. Language alternation: the third kind of codeswitching mechanism. In Rodolfo Jacobson (ed.), *Codeswitching Worldwide*, vol. **II**. Berlin and New York: Mouton de Gruyter, 59–72.

(ed.) 2001b. *Codeswitching Worldwide*, vol. **II**. Berlin and New York: Mouton de Gruyter.

Ji, Shaojun. 2000. Face and polite behaviours in Chinese culture. *Journal of Pragmatics* **32** (7): 1059–62.

Johns, Lindsay. 2009. We live in London, so speak proper English. *London Evening Standard*, 27 August. www.thisislondon.co.uk/news/we-live-in-london-so-speak-proper-english-6734771.html.

Johnstone, Barbara. 2010. Language and geographical space. In Peter Auer and Jürgen Erich Schmidt (eds.), *Language and Space: Theories and Methods*. Berlin and New York: Mouton de Gruyter,

Kachru, Braj B. 1986. *The Alchemy of English: The Spread, Functions and Models for Non-Native Englishes*. Oxford: Pergamon Press.

Kádár, Dániel Z. and Sara Mills. 2011. *Politeness in East Asia*. Cambridge University Press.

Kahane, Henry. 1982. American English: from a colonial substandard to a prestige language. In Braj B. Kachru (ed.), *The Other Tongue: English across Cultures*. Oxford: Pergamon Press, 229–36.

Kahneman, Daniel, P. Slovic and A. Tversky (eds.) 1982. *Judgment under Uncertainty: Heuristics and Biases*. Cambridge University Press.

Kakavá, Christina. 1997. Sociolinguistics and modern Greek: past, current, and future directions. *International Journal of the Sociology of Language* **126**: 5–32.

Kamusella, Tomasz. 2012. The global regime of language recognition. *International Journal of the Sociology of Language*, **218**: 59–86.

Kamwangamalu, Nkonko M. 2003. Globalization of English, and language maintenance and shift in South Africa. *International Journal of the Sociology of Language* **164**: 65–81.

Kaplan, Robert B. and Richard B. Baldauf. 1997. *Language Planning: from Practice to Theory*. Clevedon: Multilingual Matters.

Karpf, Anne. 2006. *The Human Voice*. London: Bloomsbury.

Kasper, Gabriele. 1996. Linguistic etiquette. In F. Coulmas (ed.), *The Handbook of Sociolinguistics*. Oxford: Blackwell, 373–85.

Keller, R. E. 1982. Diglossia in German-speaking Switzerland. In W. Haas (ed.), *Standard Languages: Spoken and Written*. Manchester University Press, 70–93.

Kemper, S. 1994. 'Elderspeak': speech accommodation to older adults. *Aging and Cognition* **1**: 17–28.

Kerswill, Paul. 2007. Socio-economic class. In C. Llamas and P. Stockwell (eds.), *The Routledge Companion to Sociolinguistics*. London: Routledge, 51–61.

Kerswill, Paul and Peter Trudgill. 2005. The birth of new dialects. In Peter Auer, Frans Hinskens and Paul Kerswill (eds.), *Dialect Change: Convergence and Divergence in European Languages*. Cambridge University Press, 196–220.

Khubchandani, Lachman M. 1983. *Plural Languages, Plural Cultures: Communication, Identity and Socio-Political Change in Contemporary India*. Honolulu: East-West Center.

Kibbee, Douglas A. 2003. Language policy and linguistic theory. In Jacques Maurais and Michael A. Morris (eds.), *Languages in a Globalizing World*. Cambridge University Press, 47–57.

King, Robert D. 2001. The poisonous potency of script: Hindi and Urdu. *International Journal of the Sociology of Language* **150**: 43–59.

King, Ross, 1998. Nationalism and language reform in Korea: the Questione della Lingua in precolonial Korea. In Hyung Il Pai and Timothy R. Tangherlini (eds.), *Nationalism and the Construction of Korean Identity*. Berkeley: Center for Korean Studies, Institute of East Asian Studies, University of California, Berkeley, 33–72.

Kloss, Heinz. 1978. Introduction. In Heinz Kloss and Grant D. McConnell, *The Written Languages of the World: A Survey of the Degree and Modes of Use*, vol. **I**, 19–79.

Kloss, Heinz and Grant D. McConnell. 1978–1989. *The Written Languages of the World: A Survey of the Degree and Modes of Use*, vols. **I–III**.

Kramer, Johannes. 1994. Lëtzeburgesch – eine Nationalsprache ohne Norm. In István Fodor and Claude Hagège (eds.), *Language Reform: History and Future*. Hamburg: Buske, vol. **VI**, 391–405.

Krauss, Michael. 1992. The world's languages in crisis. *Language* **68**: 4–10.

Krishnamurti, Bh. (ed.) 1986. *South Asian Languages: Structure, Convergence and Diglossia*. Delhi: Motilal Banarsidass.

Kristiansen, Tore, and Nikolas Coupland (eds.) 2011. *Standard Languages and Language Standards in a Changing Europe*. Oslo: Novus Press.

Kroskrity, Paul. 2004. Language ideology. In Alessandro Duranti (ed.), *Companion to Linguistic Anthropology*. Oxford: Blackwell, 496–517.

Krumbacher, K. 1902. *Das Problem der neugriechischen Schriftsprache*. Munich: Königlich-Bayrische Akademie der Wissenschaften.

Kummer, Manfred. 1992. Politeness in Thai. In Richard J. Watts, Sachiko Ide and Konrad Ehlich (eds.), *Politeness in Language: Studies in its History, Theory and Practice*. Berlin and New York: Mouton de Gruyter, 325–36.

Kwan-Terry, Anna. 2000. Language shift, mother tongue, and identity in Singapore. *International Journal of the Sociology of Language* **143**: 85–106.

Labov, William. 1963. The social motivation of sound change. *Word* **19**: 273–309.

    1966. *The Social Stratification of English in New York City*. Washington, DC: Center for Applied Linguistics.

    1981. What can be inferred about change in progress from synchronic descriptions? *Variation Omnibus* (NWAVE VIII), 177–200.

    1990. The intersection of sex and social class in the course of linguistic change. *Language Variation and Change* **2**: 205–54.

    1994. *Principles of Linguistic Change*, vol. I: *Internal Factors*. Oxford: Blackwell.

Labrie, Normand. 1993. *La construction linguistique de la Communauté européenne*. Paris: Champion.

Ladefoged, Peter. 1992. Another view of endangered languages. *Language* **68**(4): 809–11.

Laitin, David D. 1993. Migration and language shift in urban India. *International Journal of the Sociology of Language* **103**: 57–72.

    1996. Language planning in the former Soviet Union: the case of Estonia. *International Journal of the Sociology of Language* **118**: 43–61.

Lakoff, George and Mark Johnson. 1985. *Metaphors We Live By*. University of Chicago Press.

Lakoff, Robin T. 1975. *Language and Woman's Place*. New York: Harper & Row.

Lambert, W. E., R. C. Hodgson, R. C. Gardner, and S. Fillenbaum. (1960) Evaluational reactions to spoken language. *Journal of Abnormal and Social Psychology* **60**(1): 44–51.

Landau, Jacob M. and Barbara Kellner-Heinkele. 2001. *Politics of Language in the Ex-Soviet Muslim States; Azerbayjan, Uzbekistan, Kazakhstan, Kyrgyzstan, Turkmenistan and Tajikistan*. London: Hurst and Co.

Landry, Rodrigue and Réal Allard (eds.) 1994. *Ethnolinguistic vitality.* Topic issue, *International Journal of the Sociology of Language,* no. **108** (March).

Lanza, Elisabeth and Bente Ailin Svendsen. 2007. Tell me who your friends are and I *might* be able to tell you what language(s) you speak: social network analysis, multilingualism, and identity. *International Journal of Bilingualism* **11**: 275–300.

Laponce, Jean A. 1987. *Languages and their Territories.* University of Toronto Press.

Laporte, Pierre-Etienne. 1994. Les mots-clés du discours politique en aménagement linguistique au Québec et au Canada. In Claude Truchot (ed.), *Le Plurilinguisme européen.* Paris: Champion, 97–114.

Lauring, Jakob. 2008. Rethinking Social Identity Theory in international encounters: Language use as a negotiated object for identity making. *International Journal of Cross Cultural Management* **8**(3): 343–61.

Leech, N. Geoffrey. 1983. *Principles of Pragmatics.* London and New York: Longman.

Lenneberg, Eric H. 1967. *Biological Foundations of Language.* New York: Wiley.

Le Page, Robert. 1986. Acts of identity. *English Today* **8**: 21–4.

Le Page, R. B. and Andrée Tabouret-Keller. 1985. *Acts of Identity: Creole-Based Approaches to Language and Ethnicity.* Cambridge: Cambridge University Press.

Lévi-Strauss, Claude. 1949. *Les structures élémentaires de la parenté.* Paris: Presses Universitaires de France.

Lewis, G. L. 1984. Atatürk's language reform as an aspect of modernization in the Republic of Turkey. In Jacob M. Landau (ed.), *Atatürk and the Modernization of Turkey.* Boulder, CO: Westview Press, 195–213.

Li, David C. S. 2003. Between English and Esperanto: what does it take to be a world language? *International Journal of the Sociology of Language* **164**: 33–63.

Li Wei. 1994. *Three Generations, Two Languages, One Family.* Clevedon: Multilingual Matters.

1996. Network analysis. In Hans Goebel, Peter H. Nelde, Zdenek Stary and Wolfgang Wölck (eds.), *Contact Linguistics: An International Handbook of Contemporary Research.* Berlin and New York: Walter de Gruyter, 805–11.

1998. The 'why' and 'how' questions in the analysis of conversational code-switching. In Peter Auer (ed.), *Code-Switching in Conversation: Language, Interaction and Identity.* London and New York: Routledge, 156–76.

Li Wei, Jean-Marc Dewaele and Alex Housen (eds.) 2002. *Opportunities and Challenges of Bilingualism.* Berlin and New York: Mouton de Gruyter.

Linell, Per. 2005. *The Written Language Bias in Linguistics.* Abingdon, Oxon: Routledge.

Lippi-Green, Rosina. 1997. *English with an Accent: Language, Ideology, and Discrimination in the United States.* London: Routledge.

Livia, Anna and Kira Hall (eds.) 1997. *Queerly Phrased: Language, Gender and Sexuality.* Oxford University Press.

Louw, P. Eric. 2004. Political power, national identity and language: the case of Afrikaans. *International Journal of the Sociology of Language* **170**: 43–58.

Low Ee-Ling and Azirah Hashim. 2012. *English in Southeast Asia: Features, Policies and Language in Use.* Amsterdam: John Benjamins.

Lüdi, Georges. 1986. Forms and functions of bilingual speech in pluricultural migrant communities in Switzerland. In Joshua A. Fishman, Andrée Tabouret-Keller, Michael Clyne, Bhadriraju Krishnamurti and Mohammed Abdulaziz (eds.), *The Fergusonian Impact: In Honor of Charles A. Ferguson,* vol. **II**: *Sociolinguistics and the Sociology of Language.* Berlin and New York: Mouton de Gruyter, 217–36.

1987. Les marques transcodiques: regards nouveaux sur le bilinguisme. In G. Lüdi (ed.), *Devenir bilingue-parler bilingue.* Tübingen: Max Niemeyer, 1–21.

2010. Images concurrentielles de l'anglais dans des entreprises multinationals de la region bâloise. In Dominique Huck and Thiresia Choremi (eds.), *Parole(s) et langue(s), espaces et temps: Mélanges offerts à Arlette Bothorel-Witz.* Université de Strasbourg, 307–16.

Lüdi, Georges and Bernard Py. 2009. To be or not to be…a plurilingual speaker. *International Journal of Multilingualism* **6**(2): 154–67.

Lüdi, Georges, Iwar Werlen, Rita Franceschini, Francesco-Antonini, Sandro Bianconi et al. (eds.) 1997. *Die Sprachenlandschaft der Schweiz.* Bern: Office fédérale de la statistique.

Mackerras, Colin. 1994. *China's Minorities: Integration and Modernization in the Twentieth Century*. Hong Kong: Oxford University Press.

Mackey, William F. 1989. Determining the status and function of languages in multinational societies. In Ulrich Ammon (ed.), *Status and Function of Languages and Language Varieties*. Berlin and New York: Walter de Gruyter, 3–20.

2003. Forecasting the fate of languages. In Jacques Maurais and Michael A. Morris (eds.), *Languages in a Globalizing World*. Cambridge University Press, 64–81.

Magner, Thomas F. 2001. Digraphia in the territories of the Croats and Serbs. *International Journal of the Sociology of Language* 150: 11–26.

Maher, John C. and Y. Kawanishi. 1995. Maintaining culture and language: Koreans in Osaka. In J. C. Maher and G. Macdonald (eds.), *Diversity in Japanese Culture and Language*. London: Kegan Paul International, 160–77.

Major, Roy C. 2010. *Foreign Accent. The Ontogeny and Phylogeny of Second Language Phonology*. Mahwah, NJ: Lawrence Erlbaum.

Marçais, William. 1930. La diglossie arabe. *L'enseignement public*, **97**: 401–9; **105**: 20–39, 120–33.

Marfany, Joan-Lluís. 2010. Sociolinguistics and some of its concepts: a historian's view. *International Journal of the Sociology of Language* **206**, 1–20.

Marshall, David F. 1986. The question of an official language: language rights and the English Language Amendment. *International Journal of the Sociology of Language* **60**: 7–75.

Martin-Jones, Marilyn and Kathryn Jones (eds.) 2000. *Multilingual Literacies: Reading and Writing Different Worlds*. Amsterdam and Philadelphia: John Benjamins.

Matthews, Stephen and Virginia Yip. 2011. Contact-induced grammaticalization: evidence from bilingual acquisition. In J. Clancy Clements and Shelome Gooden (eds.), *Language Change in Contact Languages: Grammatical and Prosodic Considerations*. Amsterdam and Philadelphia: John Benjamins, 107–35.

Matisoff, James A. 1991. Endangered languages of mainland Southeast Asia. In R. H. Robins and E. M. Uhlenbeck (eds.), *Endangered Languages*. London and New York: Berg, 189–228.

McCallen, Brian. 1989. *English: a world commodity. The International Market for Training in English as a Foreign Language*. Special report, no. 1166. London: The Economic Intelligence Unit Ltd.

McWhorter, John. 2003. *The Power of Babel: A Natural History of Language*. London: Arrow Books.

Meeuwis, Michael and Jan Blommaert. 1998. A monolectal view of code-switching: layered code-switching among Zairians in Belgium. In Peter Auer (ed.), *Code-Switching in Conversation: Language, Interaction and Identity*. London and New York: Routledge, 76–98.

Mehrotra, R. R. 1995. How to be polite in Indian English. *International Journal of the Sociology of Language* **116**: 99–110.

Meillet, Antoine. 1918. *Les langues dans l'Europe nouvelle*. Paris: Payot.

Mendoza-Deton, Norma. 2002. Language and identity. In J. K. Chambers, Peter Trudgill and Natalie Schilling-Estes (eds.), *The Handbook of Language Variation and Change*. Oxford: Blackwell, 475–99.

Menn, Lise and Jean Berko Gleason. 1986. Babytalk as a stereotype and register: adult reports of children's speech patterns. In Joshua A. Fishman et al. (eds.), *The Fergusonian Impact: In Honor of Charles A. Ferguson*, vol. I: *From Phonology to Society: The Fergusonian Impact*. Berlin and New York: Mouton de Gruyter, 111–25.

Mesthrie, Rajend and Rakesh Bhatt. 2008. *World Englishes: The Study of New Linguistic Varieties*. Cambridge University Press.

Mills, Sara. 2003. *Gender and Politeness*. London: Cambridge University Press.

Milroy, James. 1980. *Language and Social Networks*. Oxford: Basil Blackwell.

1992. *Linguistic Variation and Change*. Oxford: Blackwell.

Milroy, Lesley and James Milroy. 1992. Social networks and social class: toward an integrated sociolinguistic model. *Language in Society* **21**: 1–26.

1997. Varieties and variation. In F. Coulmas (ed.), *The Handbook of Sociolinguistics*. Oxford: Blackwell, 47–64.

Milroy, Lesley and Pieter Muysken (eds.) 1995. *One Speaker, Two Languages*. Cambridge University Press.

Moelino, Anton M. 1994. Standardization and modernization in Indonesian language planning. In Georges Lüdi (ed.), *Sprachstandardisierung–Standardisation des langues–Standardizzazione delle lingue–Standardization of Languages*. Freiburg: Universitätsverlag, 117–30.

Møller, Janus and Pia Quist. 2003. Research on youth language in Denmark. *International Journal of the Sociology of Language* **159**: 45–55.

Mordock, K., and M. Krasny. 2001. Participatory action research: a theoretical and practical framework for EE. *Journal of Environmental Education* **32**: 15–20.

Motschenbacher, Heiko. 2011. Taking Queer Linguistics further: sociolinguistics and critical heteronormativity research. *International Journal of the Sociology of Language* **212**: 149–79.

Mühlhäusler, Peter. 1994. Language planning and small languages: the case of the Pacific area. In Georges Lüdi (ed.), *Sprachstandardisierung–Standardisation des langues–Standardizzione delle lingue–Standardization of Languages*. Freiburg: Universitätsverlag, 131–60.

1996. *Linguistic Ecology: Language Change and Linguistic Imperialism in the Pacific Region*. London: Routledge.

Mühlhäusler, Peter and Rom Harré. 1990. *Pronouns and People: The Linguistic Construction of Social and Personal Identity*. Oxford: Basil Blackwell.

Müller-Thurau, Claus-Peter. 1985. *Lexikon der Jugendsprache*. Düsseldorf and Vienna: Cornelsen.

Musa, Monsur. 1996. Politics of language planning in Pakistan and the birth of a new state. *International Journal of the Sociology of Language* **118**: 63–80.

Muysken, Pieter. 2000. *Bilingual Speech: A Typology of Code-Mixing*. Cambridge University Press.

Myers-Scotton, Carol. 1993a. *Social Motivations for Codeswitching: Evidence from Africa*. Oxford: Clarendon Press.

1993b. *Duelling Languages: Grammatical Structure in Codeswitching*. Oxford: Clarendon Press.

1997. Code-switching. In F. Coulmas (ed.), *The Handbook of Sociolinguistics*. Oxford: Blackwell, 217–37.

(ed.) 1998. *Codes and Consequences: Choosing Linguistic Varieties*. New York and Oxford: Oxford University Press.

Nakano Jun. 1993. *Nihonjin no nakigoe* [Japanese Crying Voices]. Tokyo: NTT Shuppan.

Narasimhan, R. 1998. *Language Behaviour: Acquisition and Evolutionary History*. New Delhi and London: Sage Publications.

Narayan, R. K. [1945]1990. *The English Teacher*. London: Mandarin.

Navarro, V. 1990. Race or class versus race and class: mortality differentials in the United States. *Lancet* **2**: 139–71.

Nelde, Peter H., Hans Goebl, Zdenek Stary and Wolfgang Wölck (eds.) 1995. *Contact Linguistics: An Interdisciplinary Handbook of Contemporary Research*. Berlin and New York: Walter de Gruyter.

Nelde, Peter H., Miquel Strubell and Glyn Williams. 1996. *The Production and Reproduction of the Minority Language Groups in the European Union*. Luxembourg: Office for Official Publications of the European Communities.

Nettle, Daniel and Suzanne Romaine. 2002. *Vanishing Voices: The Extinction of the World's Languages*. Oxford and New York: Oxford University Press.

Ngom, Fallou. 2002. Linguistic borrowing as evidence of the social history of the Senegalese speech community. *International Journal of the Sociology of Language* **158**: 37–51.

Ngũgĩ Wa Thiong'o. 1981. *Decolonising the Mind: The Politics of Language in African Literature*. London: Heinemann.

Nichols, Patricia. 1983. Linguistic options and choices for black women in the rural South. In B. Thorne, C. Kramarae and N. Henley (eds.), *Language, Gender and Society*. Cambridge, MA: Newbury House, 54–68.

NOLO. 2010. The 'fair use' rule: When use of copyrighted material is acceptable. www.nolo.com/legal-encyclopedia/article-30100.html.

Nomoto, Kikuo. 1975. How much has been standardized over the past twenty years? In Fred C. C. Peng (ed.), *Language in Japanese Society*. Tokyo University Press.

Nortier, Jacomine. 1989. *Dutch and Moroccan Arabic in Contact: Code-Switching among Moroccans in the Netherlands*. Utrecht: Foris.

Nussbaum, Jon F. and Justine Coupland (eds.) 2004. *Handbook of Communication and Aging Research*. Mahwah, NJ: Lawrence Erlbaum.

Office for National Statistics. 2008. Proposed language questions for the 2011 Census. www. ons.gov.uk/ons/guide-method/census/2011/the-2011-census/2011-census-questionnaire-content/proposed-language-questions—cwestiynau-arfaethedig-am-iaith/index.html.

Ogierman, Eva. 2009. *On Apologizing in Negative and Positive Face Cultures*. Amsterdam: John Benjamins.

Ohara, Y. 1997. Shakaionseigaku no kanten kara mita nihonjin no koe no ko-tei [High and low pitch of the voice of Japanese from the point of view of sociophonetics]. In Ide Sachiko (ed.), *Josei no sekai* [The World of Women]. Tokyo: Meiji Shoin, 42–58.

Okamoto, Shigeko and Janet S. Shibamoto Smith (eds.) 2004. *Japanese Language, Gender, and Ideology: Cultural Models and Real People*. New York: Oxford University Press.

Oksaar, Els. 1997. Pragmatic and semiotic agreement, behavioreme-switching and communicative awareness: on concepts in the analysis of bilingual behavior. In Stig Eliasson and Ernst Håkon Jahr (eds.), *Language and its Ecology: Essays in Memory of Einar Haugen*. Berlin and New York: Mouton de Gruyter, 287–300.

Olson, Darik C. 2004. *Lone Nouns in Spanish/English Mixed Discourse: Code-Switches or Borrowings? A Variationist Analysis*. University of Washington.

Olson, David R. and Nancy Torrance (eds.) 2001. *The Making of Literate Societies*. Oxford: Blackwell.

Ó Muirithe, D. (ed.) 1977. *The English Language in Ireland*. Dublin: The Mercier Press.

Ó Neill, Edward T., Brian F. Lavoie and Rick Bennett. 2003. Trends in the evolution of the public Web: 1998–2002. *D-Lib Magazine*, 9.4. www.dlib.org/dlib/april03/lavoie/04lavoie.html.

Ó Riagáin, Pádraig. 1997. *Language Policy and Social Reproduction*. Oxford and New York: Oxford University Press.

Orton, Harold, Wilfred J. Halliday and Michael V. Barry (eds.) 1962–71. *Survey of English Dialects: Basic Materials*. 4 vols. Leeds: E. J. Arnold & Son.

Osmond, John (ed.). 2008. *Creating a Bilingual Wales*. Cardiff: Institute of Welsh Affairs.

Osnos, Evan. 2008. Crazy English. The national scramble to learn a new language before the Olympics. *The New Yorker*, 28 April, www.newyorker.com/reporting/2008/04/28/080428fa_fact_osnos?

Ostler, Nicholas. 2010. *The Last Lingua Franca: English until the Return of Babel*. London: Penguin.

Ó Tuathaigh, Gearóid. 2005. Language, ideology and national identity. In Joseph N. Cleary and Claire Connolly (eds.), *The Cambridge Companion to Modern Irish Culture*. Cambridge University Press, 42–58.

Padmanabha, P., B. P. Mahapatra, V. S. Verma and G. D. McConnell. 1989. *The Written Languages of the World: A Survey of the Degree and Modes of Use (2. INDIA, Book 1, Constitutional Languages, Book 2, Non-Constitutional Languages)*. Jointly published by the International Centre for Research on Bilingualism and Office of the Registrar General, India, Laval University Press, Quebec.

Pan, Yuling. 2000. *Politeness in Chinese Face-to-Face Interaction*. Stamford: Ablex.

Pan, Yuling and Dániel Z. Kádár. 2011. *Politeness in Historical and Contemporary Chinese*. London and New York: Continuum.

Pandharipande, Rajeshwari V. 1998. Is genetic connection relevant in code-switching? Evidence from South Asian languages. In Rodolfo Jacobson (ed.), *Codeswitching Worldwide*, vol. I. Berlin and New York: Mouton de Gruyter, 201–20.

Pasch, Helma. 2008. Competing scripts: the introduction of the Roman alphabet in Africa. *International Journal of the Sociology of Language* **191**: 65–109.

Pattanayak, D. P. 1985. Diversity in communication and languages; predicament of a multilingual nation state: India, a case study. In Nessa Wolfson and Joan Manes (eds.), *Language of Inequality*. Berlin: Walter de Gruyter, 399–407.

Paunonen, Heikki. 1996. Language change in apparent time and in real time: possessive constructions in Helsinki colloquial Finnish. In Mats Thelander, Lennart Elmevik and Britt-Louise Gunnarsson (eds.), *Samspel & Variation: sprakliga studier tillägnade Bengt Nordberg pa 60-arsdagen*. Uppsala Universitet, Institut för Nordiska Sprak **3**.2: 375–86.

Pecchioni, Loretta L., Kevin B. Wright and Jon F. Nussbaum. 2005. *Life-span Communication*. Mahwah, NJ: Lawrence Erlbaum.

Pedersen, Inge Lise. 2003. Traditional dialects of Danish and the de-dialectalization 1900–2000. *International Journal of the Sociology of Language* **159**: 9–28.

Pederson, Lee, Susan Leas McDaniel, Guy Bailey and Marvin Bassett. 1986. *Linguistic Atlas of the Gulf States*, vol. I: *Handbook*. Athens, GA: University of Georgia Press.

Pennycook, Alistair. 1994. *The Cultural Politics of English as an International Language*. London: Longman.

Pfaff, Carol W. 1990. Turkish in contact with German: language maintenance and loss among immigrant children in Berlin (West). *International Journal of the Sociology of Language* **90**: 97–130.

Phillipson, Robert. 1992. *Linguistic Imperialism*. Oxford University Press.
    2012. Book review: Nicholas Ostler: *The Last Lingua Franca. Language Policy* **11**: 197–200.

Philological Society. 1978. *The Neogrammarians*. Oxford: Blackwell.

Picard, Dominique. 1998. *Politesse, savoir-vivre et relations sociales*. Paris: Presses Universitaires de France.

Pimienta, Daniel, Daniel Prado and Álvaro Blanco. 2009. *Twelve Years of Measuring Linguistic Diversity in the Internet: Balance and Perspectives*. Paris: UNESCO.

Pinker, Steven. 1994. *The Language Instinct*. New York: HarperPerennial.

Pizziconi, Barbara. 2003. Re-examining politeness, face and the Japanese language. *Journal of Pragmatics* **35**: 1471–1506.

Pool, Jonathan. 1990. Language regimes and political regimes. In Brian Weinstein (ed.), *Language Policy and Political Development*. Norwood, NJ: Ablex, 241–61.

Poplack, Shana. 1982. Bilingualism and vernacular. In Beverly Hartford, Albert Valdman and Charles R. Foster (eds.), *Issues in International Bilingual Education: The Role of the Vernacular*. New York: Plenum, 1–23.
    (ed.) 2000. *The English History of African American English*. Oxford: Blackwell.

Popper, Karl R. and John C. Eccles. 1977. *The Self and its Brain: An Argument for Interactionism*. Berlin and London: Springer International.

Powell, Richard. 2002. Language planning and the British Empire: comparing Pakistan, Malaysia and Kenya. *Current Issues in Language Planning* **3**: 205–79.

Prabhakaran, Varija. 1998. Multilingualism and language shift in South Africa: the case of Telugu, an Indian language. *Multilingua* **17**: 297–319.

Prah, Kwesi K. 2001. Language, literacy, the production and reproduction of knowledge, and the challenge of African development. In David D. Olson and Nancy Torrance (eds.), *The Making of Literate Societies*. Oxford: Blackwell, 123–41.

Pranjković, Ivo. 2001. The Croatian standard language and the Serbian standard language. *International Journal of the Sociology of Language* **147**: 31–50.

Prince, Ellen F. 1987. Sarah Gorby, Yiddish folksinger: a case study of dialect shift. *International Journal of the Sociology of Language* **67**: 83–116.

Quirk, Randolph, Sidney Greenbaum, Geoffrey Leech and Jan Svartik. 1985. *A Comprehensive Grammar of the English Language*. London: Longman.

Rampton, Ben. 1995. *Crossing: Language and Ethnicity among Adolescents*. London: Longman.

Ravitch, Dianne. 2003. *The Language Police*. New York: Knopf.

Renfrew, Colin. 1987. *Archaeology and Language: The Puzzle of Indo-European Origins*. London: Penguin Books.

Rhee, M. J. 1992. Language planning in Korea under the Japanese colonial administration, 1910–1945. *Language, Culture and Curriculum* **5**(2): 87–97.

Rickford, John R. 1986. The need for new approaches to social class analysis in socio-linguistics. *Language and Communication* **6**(3): 215–21.

Rickford, John R. and Russel J. Rickford. 2000. *Spoken Soul: The History of Black English*. New York: Wiley.

Rintell, Ellen. 1981. Sociolinguistic variation and pragmatic ability: a look at learners. *International Journal of the Sociology of Language* **27**: 11–34.

Roberts, Peter A. 1988. *West Indians and their Language.* Cambridge University Press.

Robins, Robert H. and Eugenius M. Uhlenbeck (eds.) 1991. *Endangered Languages.* Oxford: Berg.

Romaine, Suzanne. 1984. *The Language of Children and Adolescents.* Oxford: Basil Blackwell.

1999. *Communicating Gender.* Hillsdale, NJ: Lawrence Erlbaum.

Rubin, Joan. 1985. The special relation of Guarani and Spanish in Paraguay. In Nessa Wolfson and Joan Manes (eds.), *Language of Inequality.* Berlin: Walter de Gruyter, 111–20.

Rubinstein, Arial. 2000. *Economics and Language.* Cambridge University Press.

Rudby, Rani. 2005. Remaking Singapore for the new age: official ideology and the realities of practice in language-in-education. In Angel M. Y. Lin and Peter W. Martin (eds.), *Decolonisation, Globalisation: Language-in-Education Policy and Practice.* Clevedon: Multilingual Matters, 55–74.

Ryan, Ellen Bouchard. 1979. Why do low-prestige language varieties persist? In H. Giles and R. N. St Clair (eds.), *Language and Social Psychology.* Oxford: Blackwell, 145–58.

Sadiqi, Fatima. 2003. *Women, Gender and Language in Morocco.* Leiden and Boston: Brill.

Safran, William. 1999. Nationalism. In J. A. Fishman (ed.), *Handbook of Language and Ethnic Identity.* New York and Oxford: Oxford University Press, 77–93.

Sailaja, Pingali. 2009. *Indian English.* Edinburgh University Press.

Salhi, Kamal. 2002. Critical imperatives of the French language in the Francophone world: colonial legacy – postcolonial policy. *Current Issues in Language Planning* **3**: 317–45.

Sanada, Shinji. 1987. *Hyōjungo no seiritsu jijō* [The circumstances of language standardization]. Tokyo: PHP.

Sánchez, Aquilino and María Dueñas. 2002. Language planning in the Spanish-speaking world. *Current Issues in Language Planning* **3**(3): 280–305.

Sandelin, B. and N. Sarafoglou. 2004. Language and scientific publication statistics. *Language Problems and Language Planning* **28**: 1–10.

Sankoff, David and Shana Poplack. 1981. A formal grammar of code-switching. *Papers in Linguistics* **14**(2): 3–46.

Sankoff, Gillian. 2004. Cross-sectional and longitudinal studies in Sociolinguistics. In Ulrich Ammon, Norbert Dittmar and Klaus Mattheier (eds.), *Sociolinguistics, Soziolinguistik: An International Handbook of the Science of Language and Society.* 2nd edn. Berlin and New York: Walter de Gruyter, 1003–13.

Saussure, Ferdinand de. 1959. *Course in General Linguistics.* New York: Fontana/Collins.

Schieffelin, Bambi B. and Elinor Ochs. 1986. *Language Socialization across Cultures.* Cambridge University Press.

Schiffman, Harold. 1996. *Linguistic Culture and Language Policy.* London and New York: Routledge.

Schiffrin, Deborah. 1996. Narrative as self-portrait: sociolinguistic constructions of identity. *Language in Society* **25**: 167–203.

Schlobinski, Peter. 1995. Jugendsprachen: speech styles of youth subcultures. In Patrick Stevenson (ed.), *The German Language and the Real World: Sociolinguistic, Cultural, and Pragmatic Perspectives on Contemporary German.* Oxford: Clarendon Press, 315–37.

Searle, John. 1984. *Minds, Brains and Science.* Cambridge, MA: Harvard University Press.

Sebba, Mark. 2007. *Spelling and Society.* Cambridge University Press.

Shaw, Susan, Ailsa Haxell and Terry Weblemoe. 2012. *Communication across the Lifespan.* Oxford University Press.

Siegel, Jeff. 2008. *The Emergence of Pidgin and Creole Languages.* Oxford University Press.

Siegel, Lee. 1999. *Love in a Dead Language.* University of Chicago Press.

Silva-Corvalán, Carmen. 1983. Code-shifting patterns in Chicano Spanish. In Lucía Elías-Olivares (ed.), *Spanish in the U.S. Setting.* Arlington, VA: National Clearinghouse for Bilingualism, 71–87.

Silverstein, Michael. 1984. Language and the culture of gender: at the intersection of structures, usages and ideology. In E. Mertz and P. Parmentier (eds.), *Signs in Society*. London and New York: Academic Press, 219–59.

Simpson, Andrew. 2007. *Language and National Identity in Asia*. Oxford University Press.

Singh, Rajendra (ed.). 1998. *The Native Speaker: Multilingual Perspectives*. New Delhi and London: Sage Publications.

Singh, Udaya Narayan. 1995. Comments. In R. S. Gupta, Anvita Abbi and Kailash S. Aggarwal (eds.), *Language and the State: Perspectives on the Eighth Schedule*. New Delhi: Creative Books, 42–8.

Sirles, Craig A. 1999. Politics and Arabization: the evolution of postindependence North Africa. *International Journal of the Sociology of Language* **137**: 115–29.

Smakman, Dick. 2012. Towards an international definition of the standard language. *International Journal of the Sociology of Language*, **218** (November): 25–58.

Smith, Michael G. 1998. *Language and Power in the Creation of the USSR, 1917–1953*. Berlin and New York: Mouton de Gruyter.

Smith-Hefner, Nancy J. 1988. Women and politeness: the Javanese example. *Language in Society* **17**: 535–54.

Smyth, Ron, Greg Jacobs and Henry Rogers. 2003. Male voices and perceived sexual orientation: an experimental and theoretical approach. *Language in Society* **32**: 329–50.

Snow, Don. 2010. Hong Kong and modern diglossia. *International Journal of the Sociology of Language* **206**: 155–179.

Solèr, Clau. 1991. *Romanisch im Schams*. Zurich: Phonogrammarchiv der Universität Zürich.

Song Zhengchun. 1992. Multilingual families of the Tuvinian people in Xinjiang (Mongolia). *International Journal of the Sociology of Language* **97**: 23–35.

Sotiropoulos, Dimitri. 1992. The standardization of modern Greek. *Sociolinguistica: Internationales Jahrbuch für Europäische Soziolinguistik* **6**: 163–83.

Spender, Dale. 1985. *Man Made Language*. 2nd edn. London: Routledge & Kegan Paul.

Spolsky, Bernard (ed.) 2012a. *The Cambridge Handbook of Language Policy*. Cambridge University Press.

2012b. What is language policy? In B. Spolsky (ed.), *The Cambridge Handbook of Language Policy*. Cambridge University Press, 3–15.

Spolsky Bernard and Robert L. Cooper. 1991. *The Languages of Jerusalem*. Oxford: Clarendon Press.

Srivastava, R. N. 1984. Linguistic minorities and national languages. In F. Coulmas (ed.), *Linguistic Minorities and Literacy*. Berlin, New York and Amsterdam: Mouton Publishers, 99–114.

Steinberg, Danny D., Hiroshi Nagata and David P. Aline. 2001. *Psycholinguistics: Language, Mind and World*. 2nd edn. London: Longman.

Stokoe, Elizabeth. H. 2005. Analysing gender and language. *Journal of Sociolinguistics* **9**: 118–33.

Strevens, Peter. 1985. Standards and the standard language. *English Today* **1**(2): 5–8.

Stromquist, Nelly P. 1999. Gender and literacy development. In Daniel A. Wagner, Richard L. Venezky and Brian V. Street (eds.), *Literacy: An International Handbook*. Boulder, CO: Westview Press, 271–6.

Strubell i Trueta, Miquel. 1994. Catalan in Valencia: the story of an attempted secession. In Georges Lüdi (ed.), *Sprachstandardisierung–Standardisation des langues–Standardizzione delle lingue–Standardization of Languages*. Freiburg: Universitätsverlag, 229–54.

Stubbs, Michael. 1997. Language and the mediation of experience: linguistic representation and cognitive orientation. In F. Coulmas (ed.), *The Handbook of Sociolinguistics*. Oxford: Blackwell, 358–73.

Subbarao, K. V., R. K. Agnihotri and A. Mukerjee. 1991. Syntactic strategies and politeness phenomena. *International Journal of the Sociology of Language* **92**: 35–53.

Sugimoto, Yoshio. 1997. *Japanese Society*. Cambridge University Press.

Sun Hongkai and Florian Coulmas (eds.) 1992. *News from China: Minority Languages in Perspective*. Special issue, *International Journal of the Sociology of Language* 97.

Swaan, A. de. 2001. *Words of the World: The Global Language System*. Cambridge: Polity Press.

Swan, Toril. 1992. Women's language in Sweden. *International Journal of the Sociology of Language* **94**: 173–84.

Tabouret-Keller, Andrée. 1996. Language and identity. In F. Coulmas (ed.), *The Handbook of Sociolinguistics*. Oxford: Blackwell, 315–26.

Tagliamonte, Sali. 2002. Comparative sociolinguistics. In J. K. Chambers, Peter Trudgill and Natalie Schilling-Estes (eds.), *The Handbook of Language Variation and Change*. Oxford: Blackwell, 729–63.

Takahara, Kumiko. 1991. Female speech patterns in Japanese. *International Journal of the Sociology of Language* **92**: 61–85.

Tannen, Deborah. 1991. *You Just Don't Understand: Women and Men in Conversation*. London: Virago.

Terkourafi, Marina. 2012. Politeness and pragmatics. In Katarzyna Jaszczolt and Keith Allan (eds.), *The Cambridge Handbook of Pragmatics*. Cambridge University Press, 617–37.

Tessarolo, M. 1990. *Minoranze linguistiche e imagine della lingua: una ricera sulla realá italiana*. Milan: Franco Angeli.

Thibault, Pierrette. 1991. La langue en mouvement: simplification, régularisation, restructuration. *LINX (Linguistique – Paris X, Nanterre)* **25**: 79–92.

Thibault, Pierrette and Diane Vincent. 1990. *Un corpus de français parlé*. Montréal: Recherches Sociolinguistiques 1.

Thomas, George. 1991. *Linguistic Purism*. London and New York: Longman.

Thompson, Robert W. 1992. Spanish as a pluricentric language. In M. Clyne (ed.), *Pluricentric Languages*. Berlin: Mouton de Gruyter, 45–70.

Thorne, Barrie and Nancy Henley (eds.) 1975. *Language and Sex: Difference and Dominance*. Rowley, MA: Newbury House.

Tillery, Jan, and Guy Bailey. 2003. Approaches to real time in dialectology and sociolinguistics. *World Englishes* **22**: 351–65.

Togeby, Ole. 1992. Is there a separate women's language? *International Journal of the Sociology of Language* **94**: 63–73.

Tollefson, James W. 1991. *Planning Language, Planning Inequality*. London and New York: Longman.

Tóth, Gergely. 2007. *Linguistic Interference and First Language Attrition*. New York: Peter Lang.

Trautmann, Thomas R. 2001. The whole history of kinship terminology: before Morgan, Morgan, and after Morgan. *Anthropological Theory* **1**(2): 268–87.

Treffers-Daller, Jeanine. 1994. *Mixing Two Languages: French–Dutch Contact in a Comparative Perspective*. Berlin and New York: Mouton de Gruyter.

Truchot, Claude. 2003. The linguistic influence of the European Union. In Jacques Maurais and Michael A. Morris (eds.), *Languages in a Globalizing World*. Cambridge University Press, 99–110.

Trudgill, Peter. 1984. *Sociolinguistics*. 2nd edn. London: Penguin Books.

1986. *Dialects in Contact*. Oxford: Blackwell.

1988. Norwich revisited: recent linguistic changes in an English urban dialect. *English World Wide* **9**: 33–49.

1994. *Dialects*. London: Routledge.

2001. *Sociolinguistic Variation and Change*. Edinburgh University Press.

Uchida, Aki. 1992. When 'difference' is 'dominance': a critique of the 'antipower-based' cultural approach to sex differences. *Language in Society* **21**: 547–68.

UNESCO. 2011. Language policies. www.unesco.org/new/en/communication-and-information/access-to-knowledge/linguistic-diversity-and-multilingualism-on-internet/language-policies/.

Vallverdú, Francesc. 1984. A sociolinguistic history of Catalan. *International Journal of the Sociology of Language* **47**: 13–28.

van Bezooijen, Reneé. 1995. Sociocultural aspects of pitch differences between Japanese and Dutch women. *Language and Speech* **38**: 253–65.

Van Hoorde, Johan. 1998. Let Dutch die? Over the Taalunie's dead body. *InfoNT* 2 (Conférence des Services de Traduction des Etats Européens, The Hague), 6–10.

Varennes, Fernand de. 1996. *Language, Minorities and Human Rights*. London: Martinus Nijhoff.

Verdoodt, Albert. 1989. *Western Europe* (vol. III of H. Kloss and G. D. McConnell (eds.), *The Written Languages of the World: A Survey of the Degree and Modes of Use*). Quebec: Laval University Press.

Verma, Shivendra K. 1982. Swadeshi English: form and function. In J. Pride (ed.), *New Englishes*. Rowley, MA: Newbury House, 174–87.

Vertovec, Steven. 2006. *The Emergence of Super-Diversity in Britain*. Working Paper no. 25, Centre on Migration, Policy and Society, Oxford University. www.compas.ox.ac.uk/fileadmin/files/Publications/working_papers/WP_2006/WP0625_Vertovec.pdf.

Wang, Hahn-Sok. 1990. Toward a description of the organization of Korean speech levels. *International Journal of the Sociology of Language* **82**: 25–39.

Wardhaugh, Ronald. 1987. *Languages in Competition*. Oxford: Blackwell.

Watts, Richard J. 2003. *Politeness*. New York: Cambridge University Press.

Watts, Richard J., Sachiko Ide and Konrad Ehlich (eds.) 1992. *Politeness in Language: Studies in its History, Theory and Practice*. Berlin and New York: Mouton de Gruyter.

Weber, Max. 1968. *Economy and Society*. New York: Bedminster.

Webster, Noah. [1789] 1992. Dissertation on the English language: with notes, historical and critical. Excerpts in James Crawford (ed.), *Language Loyalties: A Source Book on the Official English Controversy*. Chicago and London: University of Chicago Press, 33–6.

Wegner, Daniel. 2002. *The Illusion of Conscious Will*. Cambridge, MA: Harvard University Press.

Weinreich, Uriel. 1953. *Languages in Contact*. New York: Columbia University Press.

Weinstein, Brian. 1983. *The Civic Tongue. Political Consequences of Language Choices*. New York and London: Longman.

Wenzel, Veronika. 1996. Reclame en tweetaligheid in Brussel. In *Brusselse thema's* **3**, Brussels: Vrije universiteit, 45–74.

Wexler, Paul. 1991. Yiddish – the fifteenth Slavic language: a study of partial language shift from Judeo-Sorbian to German. *International Journal of the Sociology of Language* **91**: 9–150.

Widdicombe, Sue and Robin Wooffitt. 1995. *The Language of Youth Subculture*. Brighton: Harvester.

Widin, Jacqueline. 2010. *Illegitimate Practices. Global English Language Education*. Bristol: Multilingual Matters.

Williams, Colin. 1999. The Celtic World. In J. A. Fishman (ed.), *Handbook of Language and Ethnic Identity*. New York and Oxford: Oxford University Press, 267–85.

Williams, Glyn. 1987. Bilingualism, class dialect, and social reproduction. *International Journal of the Sociology of Language* **66**: 85–98.

Wodak, Ruth. 2006. Mediation between discourse and society: assessing cognitive approaches in CDA. *Discourse Studies* **8**: 179–90.

Wolfram, Walt. 1991. *Dialects and American English*. New York: Prentice Hall.

　　1997. Dialect in society. In F. Coulmas (ed.), *The Handbook of Sociolinguistics*. Oxford: Blackwell, 107–26.

Woods, Nicola. 1997. The formation and development of New Zealand English: interaction of gender-related variation and linguistic change. *Journal of Sociolinguistics* **1**: 95–126.

Wright, Eric O. 1989. *Class Counts: Comparative Studies in Class Analysis*. Cambridge University Press.

Wright, Eric. O. and L. Perrone. 1977. Marxist class categories and income inequality. *American Sociological Review* **42**: 32–55.

Wright, Roger. 1991. *Latin and the Romance Languages in the Early Middle Ages*. London: Routledge.

Wright, Sue. 2004. *Language Policy and Language Planning*. Basingstoke: Palgrave Macmillan.

Wunderlich, Dieter. 1980. *Arbeitsbuch Semantik*. Königstein: Athenäum.

Wurm, Stephen A. 1994. Graphisation and standardisation of languages. In Georges Lüdi (ed.), *Sprachstandardisierung, Standardisation des langues–Standardizzazione delle lingue–Standardization of Languages*. Freiburg: Universitätsverlag, 255–72.

Yağmur, Kutlay. 2004. Language maintenance patterns of Turkish immigrant communities in Australia and Western Europe: the impact of majority attitudes on ethnolinguistic vitality perceptions. *International Journal of the Sociology of Language* **165**: 121–42.

Youssef, Valerie. 1993. Children's linguistic choices: audience design and societal norms. *Language in Society* **22**: 257–74.

Youssi, Abderrahim. 1995. The Moroccan triglossia: facts and implications. *International Journal of the Sociology of Language* **112**: 29–43.

Zepeda, Ofelia and Jane H. Hill. 1991. The condition of Native American languages in the United States. In R. H. Robins and E. M. Uhlenbeck (eds.), *Endangered Languages.* London and New York: Berg, 135–55.

Zimin, Susan. 1981. Sex and politeness: factors in first- and second-language use. *International Journal of the Sociology of Language* **27**: 35–58.

Index